THE DONNELLYS

JOHN LITTLE

THE DONNELLYS

VOLUME I

POWDER KEG, 1840–1880

Purchase the print edition and receive the eBook free. For details, go to ecwpress.com/eBook.

This book is also available as a Global Certified Accessible™ (GCA) ebook. ECW Press's ebooks are screen reader friendly and are built to meet the needs of those who are unable to read standard print due to blindness, low vision, dyslexia, or a physical disability.

Published by ECW Press
665 Gerrard Street East
Toronto, Ontario, Canada M4M 1Y2
416-694-3348 / info@ecwpress.com

Cover design: David A. Gee
Map designs: Rhys Davies

LIBRARY AND ARCHIVES CANADA CATALOGUING IN PUBLICATION

Title: The Donnellys / John Little.

Names: Little, John R., 1960- author.

Description: Contents: v. 1. Powder keg, 1840–1880.

Identifiers: Canadiana (print) 20210191104 | Canadiana (ebook) 20210191120

ISBN 978-1-77041-629-1 (v. 1 ; softcover)
ISBN 978-1-77305-845-0 (v. 1 ; ePub)
ISBN 978-1-77305-846-7 (v. 1 ; PDF)
ISBN 978-1-77305-847-4 (v. 1 ; Kindle)

Subjects: LCSH: Donnelly family. | LCSH: Murder—Ontario—Lucan. | LCSH: Criminals—Ontario—Lucan.

Classification: LCC HV6810.L8 L58 2021 | DDC 364.152/3092271325—dc23

This book is funded in part by the Government of Canada. *Ce livre est financé en partie par le gouvernement du Canada.* We acknowledge the support of the Canada Council for the Arts. *Nous remercions le Conseil des arts du Canada de son soutien.* We acknowledge the support of the Ontario Arts Council (OAC), an agency of the Government of Ontario, which last year funded 1,965 individual artists and 1,152 organizations in 197 communities across Ontario for a total of $51.9 million. We also acknowledge the support of the Government of Ontario through Ontario Creates.

PRINTED AND BOUND IN CANADA   PRINTING: MARQUIS   5   4   3   2   1

Cover image by permission of Ray Fazakas, author *The Donnelly Album* and *In Search of the Donnellys.*

MIX
Paper from responsible sources
FSC   FSC® C103567
www.fsc.org

"Shake my boy, we don't have to go out in
every rainstorm to wash the blood off *our* hands."
— BOB DONNELLY

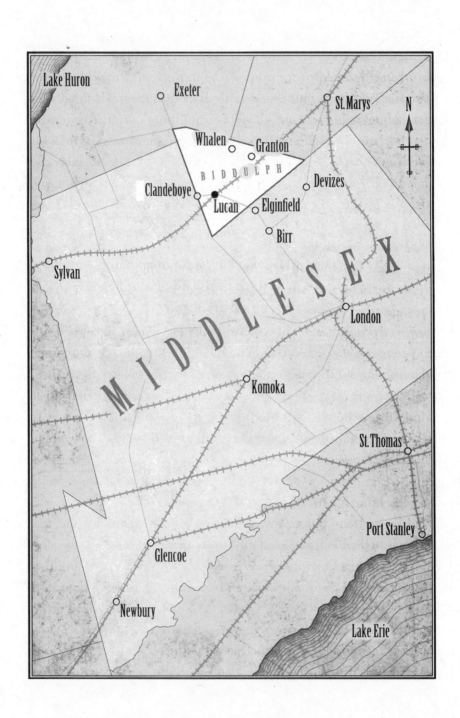

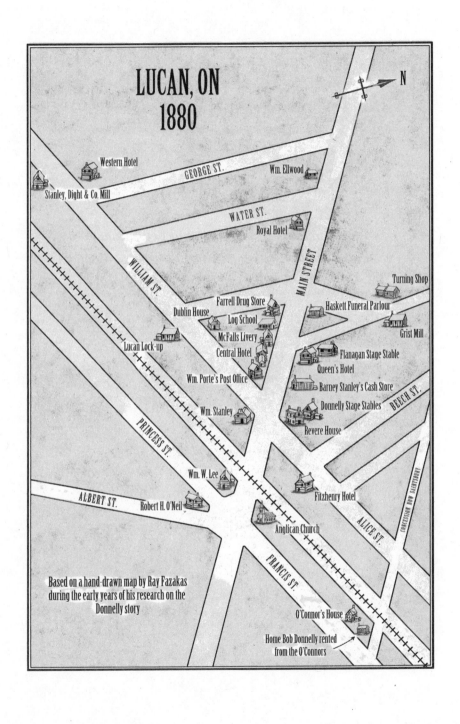

LUCAN, ON 1880

N

Western Hotel

GEORGE ST.

Wm. Ellwood

Stanley, Dight & Co. Mill

WATER ST.

Royal Hotel

MAIN STREET

Turning Shop

WILLIAM ST.

Farrell Drug Store

Haskett Funeral Parlour

Dublin House

Log School

Grist Mill

McFalls Livery

Lucan Lock-up

Central Hotel

Flanagan Stage Stable

Queen's Hotel

Wm. Porte's Post Office

Barney Stanley's Cash Store

PRINCESS ST.

Wm. Stanley

Donnelly Stage Stables

BEECH ST.

Revere House

Wm. W. Lee

CONCESSION ROW SIDEROAD

ALBERT ST.

Fitzhenry Hotel

Robert H. O'Neil

Anglican Church

ALICE ST.

FRANCIS ST.

Based on a hand-drawn map by Ray Fazakas during the early years of his research on the Donnelly story

O'Connor's House

Home Bob Donnelly rented from the O'Connors

To the tireless efforts of Ray and Bev Fazakas,
who not only researched this story
but lived it for many decades.

TABLE OF CONTENTS

PREFACE

The Donnelly family headstone, indicating the family members
who were murdered on February 4, 1880. (Photo by author)

It's eleven o'clock on Saturday, November 8, 2014. My youngest son, Ben, and his South Muskoka Bears Minor Midget hockey team have just finished their first game of a tournament in St. Marys, Ontario. They won their game and Ben scored a nice goal, so I'm happy. But the team's next game isn't until two o'clock that afternoon, so we're going to be doing a lot of sitting around until an hour or so before the next game. Ben, understandably, wants to hang out with his friends on the team during this interval, which means he's going to park himself at the arena. Consequently, I now find myself alone with three hours on my hands to fill. It occurs to me that I'm not that far from the Roman Line, maybe a thirty-minute drive. I've always wanted to go there, as somewhere on that stretch of roadway sits the property upon which the Donnelly story played out. The infamous Donnelly children were raised on that lot of land and four members of the family were murdered there on a cold February night in 1880.

Despite being taught nothing of this bit of southern Ontario history in school, when I first learned about the Donnellys, their story gripped me like few stories have (before or since). Indeed, some thirty years previously, during my second year of university, a roommate had invited me to spend a weekend at his parents' home in Mitchell, Ontario. During the course of meeting his parents, we sat down at the family table to eat. Some small talk was exchanged and then I posed a question that I thought would be a good icebreaker: "How far away is Lucan?" His father, a lawyer in town, answered, "Oh, about half an hour. Not far. Are you interested in going to Lucan?" "Definitely!" I replied enthusiastically. "Why?" he asked. "I understand that's where the Donnellys were killed," I replied. Although my statement was wrong (i.e., the Donnellys were killed within their farmhouse on the Roman Line in Biddulph — not Lucan, which is about four and a half miles southwest from where they lived), my enthusiasm was obvious. But then a look fell over the father's face that immediately let me know I would not be going to Lucan. "We don't talk about that *here*," he said. And the table fell quiet until someone introduced a subject that was evidently far less contentious. I never forgot that, and the father's attitude only served to further fan the flames of my nascent curiosity.

So now, thirty years later, I find myself driving along Breen Drive, a country road in Biddulph Township, looking to intersect the infamous Roman Line concession road. Just my luck, it starts to rain. As the windshield wipers engage to sweep the water from my windshield, I keep looking left and right like I'm going to recognize something; perhaps a big neon arrow with the words "Donnelly home here!" will present itself. A stop sign looms up ahead, which causes me to slow down and then come to a complete stop. I must be lost. I hit the button to roll down the passenger side window of the truck to see if I can read the road sign that sits on my side of the small intersection. And there it is — the "Roman Line." I throw the truck in park and step out. This is the road that author Thomas P. Kelley, in his book *The Black Donnellys*, had said horses were afraid to run along at night after the murders had occurred. An old wives' tale to be certain, but such tales have grown into legends that, rightly or wrongly, have become accepted as facts. There is a deep history to this road and I am overtaken by the urge to stand right smack in the middle of it and take in the view. The weather has made it darker than it ought to be for a fall afternoon, but given the road's connection to violence and murder, it seems eerily appropriate. I return to the truck, turn right and now find myself driving along the Roman Line. I've called ahead to the man who presently owns the old Donnelly property, Robert Salts. He's a retired schoolteacher who used to give tours on his plot of land; he lives in a house that was constructed on the property by three of the surviving Donnelly brothers back in 1881. The house has been added to over the years but the original building still remains. He had told me that he would be happy to sign a copy of his book about the property (*You're Never Alone*) for me, but he isn't feeling up to conducting any more tours. This is fine by me. I'm excited just to see the land.

I pull up to the front of Lot 18, and immediately am taken by the fact that it was here, in this exact spot, that a group of twenty (some would claim forty) men came at 12:30 a.m. in the early morning hours of February 4, 1880, with the sole intent of murdering the Donnelly family. It's admittedly creepy, and the house looks creepy too. The dark sky and rain are simply augmenting the uncomfortableness of the experience. I leave the truck and knock on the door of the house and Salts invites me in. He's a nice person; so is his wife. After some small talk he presents me with a copy of his book and I hand him some cash. I get the feeling that he'd rather I leave. I'm sure he's given the Donnelly talk thousands of times before and, since he's recently closed his property to tours, he's probably done with it. I'm fine with that, as I really just wanted to experience the place where it all went down. I ask if I can take a few photos from the driveway and roadway, to which he graciously consents. I snap away with my iPhone, photographing the exterior of the house and the original Donnelly barn that was built by the brothers of the family sometime in the 1880s and lifted onto a cement base by Bob Donnelly shortly after he acquired the property in 1905. I snap images of the fieldstones that are placed at distinct corners in the lawn beside the present house, said to mark the foundation of where the original Donnelly farmhouse stood. The area just in front of it is where Tom Donnelly, the youngest son, was beaten to death. In the corner of the property are the ruins of what once was the Donnelly schoolhouse — a place where the local children came to learn how to read and write. Across the road is nothing, although the Donnellys' neighbours used to have homes on the east side of the road. Nothing stands there anymore. The rain picks up, but that's okay. I've seen enough. Ben's game starts in an hour. I get back in my truck and turn it toward St. Marys.

I decide to take a different route on my way back to the arena and find myself passing St. Patrick's Church. This is cause to stop the truck again. St. Patrick's played host to the Donnelly family — and those who killed them. They all attended church services here. Moreover, all but three of the Donnellys are buried in the church cemetery. It's worth braving the rain once more to pay my respects. St. Patrick's is a beautiful church with a huge wooden door that all the major players in the drama walked through at one time or another. Every member of the Donnelly family, and all of their friends and all of their enemies, came here to attend services, for confession, to attend family weddings and funerals. Father John Connolly, another major player in the story, once lived in the small stone rectory out back and when he ventured inside for his sermons he occasionally spoke out against the Donnelly family. After a while, I locate the headstone for the murdered family members. It's standard in size, at least compared to its predecessor, which was an eleven-foot monument that stood over the grave like a sentinel for seventy-some years, until it was replaced by this more modest offering in the mid-1960s, when the administrators of the church had grown tired of having endless streams of people tramping through their property and holding drinking vigils next to it. In any event, it's time to go.

On the way back, my memories of what had piqued my interest in the Donnelly story return. I see my friend's father sternly telling me that the Donnellys were a subject that wasn't talked about in this area. Twenty years before that, my sister Jane had read a passage to me from Kelley's book while at our dining room table in Agincourt, in which Johannah Donnelly, the matriarch of the family, walloped one of her sons in the back of the head with a cast-iron frying pan, laying him out cold on the farmhouse floor. And then there were the internet videos and the books on the subject I've read over the years, books by Kelley, Orlo Miller and Ray Fazakas, with each providing a different perspective on the story. Such reading simply instilled a desire in me to dig deeper into the story, to find out who the Donnellys were as people, and to wonder how a sworn society could come into existence for the sole purpose of their destruction. From that day in 2014 until 2021 I have immersed myself in researching the Donnelly story in an attempt to answer these questions and to try get to know and understand the Donnellys. A two-volume book series on the Donnelly story is the result.

I must confess that authors have a bad habit when writing on historical subjects of taking sides or of advancing opinions that are thinly disguised as facts. This has been particularly evident in the Donnelly literature. I have fought that tendency in my writing and, at times when I have succumbed to the temptation, I have forewarned the reader so my opinion on the matter is not mistaken for fact. Whenever possible, I have attempted to let the actual persons in the drama speak for themselves, as it is their story after all. They were there when it transpired, I wasn't. And now, seven years later, having researched the story as thoroughly as I could, I believe I have found the answers to my initial questions, and gotten to understand the Donnelly family — as well as their enemies — a little better as well.

The reader should further be forewarned that while we like clear-cut heroes and villains in our dramas, sometimes these roles oscillate. Very few people are pure evil, and none of them are saints. And so it is with the Donnellys, and their enemies. Theirs is a human story, nothing more and nothing less. Like a saga from Norse mythology, there is nothing redeemable about the tale. It is a story about tough times and the tough people who lived in those times. It's a story about pride perhaps most of all — pride of family and pride of self, versus the threat that such pride poses to those outside of one's own group. There is no evidence that the murder of the Donnelly family was the culmination of a feud that was transported from the Emerald Isle (as Orlo Miller believed); it didn't need to be. It was a local problem that was dealt with locally, the particulars of which caused it to be discussed nationally, and then internationally. It's a story about ostensibly good, hard-working people who ended up doing bad things, primarily out of the fear of a monster of their own making. The shocking thing about the murders is that they could easily happen again, with another group of good people — if the environment in which they live is allowed to develop in the same way it did around the Donnelly family. It points out the powder keg that lies dormant within human beings that requires but a few strikes of stone against flint to produce the single spark that will set it off.

— JOHN LITTLE,

BRACEBRIDGE, ONTARIO, 2021

PROLOGUE

The London Asylum for the Insane.
(Ivey Family London Room, London Public Library)

B ob Donnelly had not slept at all during the night. It hadn't
been the moaning and inhuman howling that echoed intermit-
tently through the corridors that had kept him awake; there was
danger afoot. Somebody was planning to kill him. There was a plot
being hatched at that very moment to cut off his head and burn his
body until there was nothing left but charred bones. At least, that's
what Bob Donnelly sincerely believed as he paced within his room
at the London Asylum for the Insane in the early morning hours of
June 24, 1908.[1]

Unlike most of the patients committed in this institution, however,
his delusion had its basis in fact. Indeed, had he experienced these

same thoughts twenty-eight years earlier, they wouldn't have been delusions at all. He had, after all, ended up serving two years in prison as a result of people lying under oath to have him sent away. And then there had been the successful plot that resulted in the brutal murder of his family and the destruction of the family home. The last time he had seen his parents — or, what had once been his parents — he was looking at a small assortment of scorched bones that had been placed within a small wooden box. There had been no skulls among the remains — those had already been stolen by the very community that had murdered them.

When the sun rose above the surrounding fields several hours later, an asylum attendant (of whom we know little, save for his surname "Reid") walked from his dormitory on the grounds of the institution and began his morning inspection of the patients' rooms within the various wards of several buildings on the compound. The London Asylum for the Insane housed patients who suffered from various conditions, ranging from those who were merely depressed or anxious to the seriously delusional, the homicidal, the suicidal and even those who had been considered to be too open in the expression of their sexuality for the tastes of Victorian Ontario. Those beyond remedy or who were otherwise unable to care for themselves were kept in a locked ward within the "North Building." Others who were almost self-sufficient lived within one of three "cottages," which were simply three adjoined buildings, each three storeys high, that housed a total of 180 patients. The main building of the asylum had its own wards and private rooms, as did the infirmary or reception hospital.[2]

In time, Attendant Reid arrived at the infirmary building and eventually worked his way through its three floors to the door of Patient Number 5924, the room of Bob Donnelly. Reid opened the door and stepped inside but was surprised to discover that the patient was not in his bed. What happened next surprised him even more. Bob Donnelly launched an eleven-pound spittoon at the attendant,[3] which hit Reid with such force in the shoulder that he thought his arm had been broken.[4] The terrified attendant quickly bolted from the room, slammed the door behind him and locked it shut. Wincing as he held his throbbing shoulder, he ran along the corridor and down the stairs to the medical superintendent's office.

After having his shoulder examined and discovering to his relief that his arm wasn't fractured, Reid, along with a Dr. Forster and a phalanx of attendants, returned to Bob Donnelly's room. Donnelly seemed even more disturbed, but he must have calmed down at some point (perhaps his hours of agitation and sleeplessness having finally caught up with him), as Dr. Forster was able to convince him to go back to bed without further incident.[5] As a result of what had transpired earlier, however, Bob Donnelly was flagged as a potential problem for which more serious measures might be required in the event that he should become violent again.

His family and friends had all agreed that Bob Donnelly's personality was not what it used to be. The change had begun six months previously, in December, when he'd started to withdraw from social contact. He seemed depressed but, over time, that depression in turn gave way to episodes of anxiety and finally paranoia. His wife, Annie, and his nephew, James, had noticed this change in behaviour and grew increasingly concerned for the man for whom they cared so deeply. Bob Donnelly had noticed the change as well, and it scared him. What scared him most was that he seemed no longer able to control his emotional state. It was as if a huge wave had picked him up and was carrying him in a direction he didn't wish to go, but he was powerless to stop it.

He had first been admitted to the asylum for a brief stay back in April. It was agreed by all that his getting out of Lucan and into a facility that sat upon three hundred acres of land in the country — and was populated by doctors of various specialties — might be good for him. His family refused to consider that he was suffering from some form of mental illness, and instead believed he was in the grip of something perhaps environmental. Consequently, they weren't sending him to a facility for "lunatics" and "idiots," but rather a sanitarium — a place where he could go and convalesce for a few weeks. His stay during this time had not resulted in any real change in his condition, but it hadn't gotten worse either. The doctors thought his stay had done him good. They were wrong.

Not long after his release, his depression returned with a vengeance; he attempted to kill himself on two occasions. Admittedly, the attempts were poor, but they suggested that whatever his problem was, it hadn't gone away but had gotten worse. And when, during a fit of delusion, he had threatened his wife physically, Annie and James decided that a longer stay in the asylum might be a necessity. His condition having now reached a crisis point, Bob, together with his wife and nephew, had gone to see Dr. James Sutton, a local doctor who practised out of Clandeboye and Lucan, for an official assessment, which was a requisite for long-term admittance to the London Asylum for the Insane. Sutton's assessment was as follows:

> APPEARANCE: Melancholy — dull — and ill.
> CONDUCT: Pays little attention. Does not care to converse and inattentive.
> CONVERSATION: Only answers questions when asked and is not talkative.[6]

Needing certificates from two medical doctors in order for Bob Donnelly to meet the qualifications for a protracted stay in the asylum, they next took him to be assessed by Dr. Thomas Hossack, a man who had known Bob Donnelly and his family for decades. He evaluated his old friend thusly:

APPEARANCE: Usually friendly and cheerful, now
sullen. Tries to'hide away. Suspicious of everybody.
Very nervous.
CONDUCT: Wants to remain continually in bed,
slovenly in his habits.
CONVERSATION: Refuses to talk, only in
monosyllables.[7]

Both physicians further noted in their assessment certificates that
Donnelly's wife and nephew had confided in them about his attempts
to take his life. Sutton wrote that Donnelly "has lost interest in
everything, has made several ineffectual attempts to destroy himself.
Fancies everything about him is going to ruin. Told me by his nephew,
James Donnelly, who has been looking after him since he has been
going wrong."[8] Hossack wrote, "Attempted to destroy himself by
pushing rags down his throat, also attempted to get poison. Told
[to me] by his wife and nephew — James Donnelly — who lives
with him."[9]

Of the two medical assessments, Dr. Sutton's was by far the
more thorough and fascinating, as it included a list of fifty-six questions that were posed to and answered by Bob Donnelly, such as:

Has the patient exhibited any marked mental
peculiarity, recently or in early life?
Brutal worry since the tragedy.

What has been the patient's habits as regards sleep,
when considered well? Has there been any recent
insomnia?
A good sleeper until his recent trouble.

What has been the patient's habits as to the use of: (a)
alcoholic stimulants, (b) narcotic drugs, opium, etc.?

Very temperate so far as to alcoholic stimulants —
never used drugs.

*What appears to have been the exciting cause or
causes of the present attack? Was there, in addition
to changes in general health, any mental or moral
shock, any loss, great grief or disappointment, any
overwork or overstrain?*
The tragedy was the first shock which seems to have
troubled him more or less continually since.

*What were the first mental symptoms observed —
depression or excitement?*
Depression.

*Any loss of memory, defects in judgement,
confusion, or self-accusation?*
Loss of memory, defects in judgement, confusion, no
[self-accusation].

*Have the mental changes been progressive and
regular, or have they suddenly varied; the patient at
times seeming much better or the contrary?*
Progressing regularly.

*What are the changes which have taken place in
patient's mental and physical symptoms since the
commencement of the attack?*
Delusive fancies. Voice much changed. Walking
unsteady. No fainting, nor loss of consciousness, no
convulsions, no paralysis, nor impairment of any set
of muscles.

*Has the patient shown any appreciation of the
changes in his mental condition?*
Yes.

*Has suicide or violence to others been threatened or
attempted?*
Suicide. Has attempted violence to his wife.

*Other facts bearing on the case, in the patient's past
or present history?*
Sometimes very excitable.[10]

It's clear from Dr. Sutton's notes that Donnelly's reaction to the
tragedy had been a "brutal worry" that had "troubled him more
or less continually ever since." The tragedy referred to was, of
course, the murder of his family, which had occurred in the early
morning hours of February 4, 1880 — some twenty-eight years
earlier. Despite his always having been a tough, hard-working man,
Bob Donnelly was the taciturn one of the family. His parents had
raised him to never display emotions that could be perceived as
soft, particularly in the company of the Donnelly family's many
enemies. This would be showing them your weak spot and, thus,
inviting them to strike at it. Indeed, at the wake of his parents, two
brothers and niece, Bob Donnelly had been overcome by emotion,
whereupon his older brother William had pulled him aside until he
calmed down. But William had been dead now for eleven years and,
ever since his passing, Bob Donnelly's suppressed grief and rage at
the "tragedy" had slowly started bubbling toward the surface of
his emotions until he was no longer able to control them. It was
concluded by the doctors that Bob Donnelly would be a danger,
both to himself and to others, if he remained on the outside. The
London Asylum for the Insane seemed a practical choice, as it was

only sixteen and a quarter miles south of Lucan, making it the closest asylum to where his family lived (the Hamilton Asylum was ninety-five miles away, the Toronto Asylum 120 and Kingston 273 — all to the east). Its proximity to Lucan made Donnelly's relatives comfortable, knowing that he was only a few hours' travel away by wagon or (in the winter) sleigh, meaning that they could still see him from time to time. It was for the best.

The asylum patients' accommodation, food and treatment was, for the most part, paid for by the government of Ontario. But those patients or their families who could afford to pay to have a family member institutionalized were charged between $1.50 and $2.75 a week for a private room. Bob Donnelly had money, and so he fell into the latter category.[11] He had been the most successful financially of all the Donnelly brothers — covering the cost of his stay was not an issue. And so, at the stroke of midnight on June 15,[12] a mere nine days prior to his attack on Attendant Reid, Bob Donnelly was admitted to the asylum's infirmary building,[13] which would be his home for the next six months. He was an older man now, having turned fifty-five[14] in October. He no longer knew his actual date of birth with any degree of precision (nor those of any of his family members), as all the family records had perished along with his parents' home when it had gone up in flames in 1880.[15] His hair had thinned quite a bit, he was starting to go bald on the top of his head, and there were flecks of grey in his moustache and beard.[16] His ward admission record noted that he had "sores on back of neck, top of head, backs of hands, shins and feet. Also scars from old sores."[17] The clothing he had packed for his stay was modest: one hat, one overcoat, one coat, one vest, one pair of pants, one pair of shoes, two pairs of socks, one nightshirt, two coloured shirts, two undershirts, two pairs of underwear, one tie, one pair of suspenders, five handkerchiefs and a small handbag within which these items had been packed.[18] The clothes, the attendants said, were "clean and fairly good." Donnelly himself was said to appear "clean" but "not very well nourished."[19] In his pockets, he was carrying one pair of buttons for the cuffs of his shirts, and two collar buttons.[20] The Donnelly brothers had always prided themselves on wearing respectable clothing.

While the main building of the asylum had opened in 1870, the infirmary where Bob Donnelly would be staying wouldn't be completed until 1903. It had initially been used as the medical examination building on the compound, but by 1908 its function had changed to that of reception hospital, where new patients could be admitted, examined and housed in either dormitories or individual rooms within the building. The infirmary was an imposing structure: three storeys high, plus a basement area. It was constructed with yellow bricks on its exterior, and its three floors were interconnected by wooden stairways with railings. It had its own sunroom and dining area, and a surgical suite on its top level. In short, the infirmary was considered to be the perfect building for patients who would be staying short-term within the institution, which could be anywhere from two months to two years.

The infirmary was only one of the buildings on the compound. The main building was very much a structure of its time: Gothic Revival in style, with steep-angled gabled roofs, lancet windows and yellow bricks, and set squarely within some three hundred acres that lay just on the fringe of the London city limits. Other buildings on the grounds included a chapel, a mortuary, a few workshops, a barn and a bakery.[21] The attendants and medical superintendent lived on the property, making them always available for any emergencies that should crop up.

The asylum's superintendent was Dr. William John Robinson, a well-decorated physician (winning the University Gold Medal and the Star Gold medal in his final year of studying medicine at the Toronto School of Medicine), who had practised privately in Arthur, prior to moving to Guelph, where he would become the health officer for that city. He then moved on to London, where he would become the superintendent of the Ontario Hospital of London, as well as the head of psychiatry in their Department of Medicine. In 1908, Robinson had taken over as the medical superintendent of the Asylum for the Insane from Dr. George McCallum, who, in turn, had taken over the position in 1902 from Dr. Richard Maurice Bucke. In retrospect, if not at the time, Bucke had had some dangerously bizarre and gruesome ideas regarding the treatment of certain mental disorders, particularly among the female patients at the asylum. Believing there to be a direct connection between "displaced" or "damaged" reproductive organs and insanity, he oversaw over 106 surgeries performed on women patients from 1895 to 1898. There was, of course, no link ever discovered between the uterus and insanity, and Bucke's superintendentship marked the darkest point in the history of the London Asylum for the Insane. It was not a coincidence that, after his departure from the asylum, the number of gynecological surgeries diminished substantially.

And while Dr. Bucke and his gruesome treatments had been gone from the hospital for eight years by the time of Bob Donnelly's arrival, the doctor's belief that the body and its internal organs had a direct link to the state of one's mental health was one that would endure. If one's emotional health was off-kilter, the solution, it was believed, lay in treating the body. At the London Asylum, this treatment typically consisted of "hydrotherapy." Water, because it could be heated or cooled, could impact patients in different ways: warm water was believed to help cure insomnia; cold water was said to be a tonic for manic-depressive behaviour. Baths were thus frequently administered to patients — lasting over a period of hours to several days. If baths didn't take, then water would be applied via spraying the patient continuously over a period of time, or by "packs": soaking towels in either very cold (48 degrees Fahrenheit to 70 degrees Fahrenheit) or warm water (92 degrees Fahrenheit to 97 degrees Fahrenheit) and wrapping them around the patient. Often the patient who displayed "excitement and increased motor activity" would be wrapped in the cold wet blankets and straps would be fastened around them for immobilization (and to prevent the patient from removing the towels). The patient would then be left this way for hours at a time in the belief that this therapy slowed blood flow to the brain and would thus help to elicit compliance. You did not want to draw attention to yourself in the London Asylum for the Insane.

As Bob Donnelly had been removed from his home several days before he had been taken to the asylum, Annie and James were both understandably worried about him. On June 15, James wrote a letter to the institution inquiring about visiting his uncle:

> Dear Doc,
>
> Just a line asking you to let me know at your first opportunity how Uncle Robert is getting along and how he takes it. Aunt is very anxious and uneasy about him.
>
> You will kindly let me know also if you think it will do him any harm in calling on him and oblige.
>
> Yours Sincerely,
> James Donnelly[22]

Dr. Robinson replied from London on June 18:

> Dear Sir,
>
> In reply to your letter of June 15th I beg to state that Mr. Donnelly's condition is little changed since his admission. He is quite fretful and despondent, yet I would prefer that the friends do not visit him for a while yet while he is in this despondent mood.

Yours truly,
W.J. Robinson,
Medical Superintendent[23]

Despite what concerns had been expressed in the medical superintendent's letter, it hadn't really looked as though Bob Donnelly was going to pose any problem for the institution. His symptoms were still present, but manageable. He was by no means a model patient, but it was sincerely supposed by the asylum's doctors and staff that Donnelly's next several months in the institution might well work wonders. Or so it was believed — until the restlessness and anxiety set in and continued to build until the incident of June 24. And it wasn't over yet.

Somewhere around three o'clock in the afternoon of June 27 the paranoia returned. Bob Donnelly once again detected the presence of evil around him and became convinced that somebody was going to try to kill him. Initially, he was convinced that fire would be the assassin's weapon of choice, and that he would be burned. Later, he was certain that the plan was to seal him in a coffin, which would then be placed in the cellar of the asylum.[24] Once word got out about his latest delusions, the attendants showed up, en masse, and attempted to physically restrain him. Donnelly fought back, struggling and shouting.[25] Finally, the attendants overpowered him and sedated him with hyoscine,[26] which was used at the asylum to induce sleep in excitable individuals and insomniacs. The drug did its job quickly; Donnelly's resistance weakened long enough for the attendants to drag him to the hydrotherapy room, where they then wrapped him tightly in a cold pack.[27] He was left completely immobilized and shivering, wrapped like a mummy from feet to neck within the cold towels and secured by restraining straps. He yelled for help repeatedly to no avail. He then yelled out in frustration and agony; his teeth chattered and his body shook almost to the point of convulsing. One of the attendants had seen enough, writing in his report:

> It seemed inhuman to hold him in the pack against
> his terrible resistance and he was taken out; his heart
> was throbbing. He was dressed and was to be taken
> out in the airing court at the N.B. [the North Building,
> where the genetically incurable were housed] but he
> became quiet on the way and sat and watched the
> Cricket game. He was restless that night till 2 a.m.
> and said he wanted some toast carried up to his wife.
> He was given a bath and then slept 4 hours.[28]

The day after this entry was filed, the same nameless attendant wrote: "His condition has been much relieved ever since."[29] This evidently would remain the case, as there exists nothing in Bob Donnelly's psychiatric asylum files to indicate that he suffered from any more delusions that summer, nor that he required any additional hydrotherapy.

In mid-September, after repeated written requests from James Donnelly to allow his uncle to come home for a brief visit, Dr. Robinson finally acquiesced. Bob Donnelly would be allowed to return home on probation for a period of two months. James was to keep oversight of his uncle, and also send to Dr. Robinson a fortnightly account of his condition (both mental and physical).[30] And so, on September 19, 1908, Bob Donnelly went home. And, on September 28, 1908, Bob Donnelly went AWOL. The *London Free Press* reported the story:

> LUCAN, September 28 — Robert Donnelly, one of
> the surviving members of the Donnelly family of
> Biddulph, who has been unwell for the past year,
> and now returned from the asylum at London ten

days ago somewhat improved, disappeared from his home in this village at 3 o'clock Monday morning, and since then no trace of him has been found, although search parties were out twenty minutes after he had gone.

Mr. Donnelly is aged 55 years, but in appearance has grown much older during the past few months. His face bears a ten-days' growth of beard and a scar on the left cheek. He was scantily attired, having hurriedly dressed himself under the pretense of stepping outside for a few minutes. At the time he was being closely watched, and was seen to scale the picket fence at the rear of the lot. A moment later his nephew was in pursuit, but the morning was intensely dark, and no trace of him could be found. He wore only a pair of trousers, an undershirt, a pair of house slippers without socks, and a light-coloured fedora hat. It is thought he may be heading for Glencoe, his former home.[31]

That Bob Donnelly was now on the loose was obviously of concern to a great many people — friends and foes alike. He was a Donnelly, after all, and that name still meant something in and around London, Ontario. But how had it come to this — a once proud and feared man, still dangerous to be certain, but now deeply delusional and running somewhere about the township of Biddulph in a fedora and slippers? To better understand what led to Bob Donnelly's rather erratic behaviour at such a late stage in his life, it will first be necessary to travel back in time to the morning of the "tragedy" — February 4, 1880. For that was the day Bob Donnelly's world changed, and an entire nation lost its moral innocence upon the world stage.

CHAPTER ONE

THE MORNING AFTER

London, Upper Canada West, watercolour, circa 1850, by Richard Airey.
(McIntosh Collection, Purchase, Library Collections)

T he city of London sits almost exactly 120 miles between Detroit, Michigan, and Toronto, Ontario. Some locals call it the "Forest City," because it required a considerable clearing of forest when it was founded back in 1826. It had once been pegged to be the capital of Upper Canada, but the War of 1812 had made this proposition untenable, particularly after the United States had invaded Hungerford Hill (now Reservoir Hill), in southwest London. The Province of Canada fought back, with its British soldiery invading the District of Columbia and setting fire to the Capitol, the Treasury and the White House, among other buildings. It remains an impressive wartime accomplishment, marking the only time since the American

Revolutionary War that a foreign power has ever captured and occupied the capital of the United States. Prior to this very momentary claim to fame, the region that became London had been populated by First Nations peoples — the Odawa, Neutral and Ojibwe — until the Beaver Wars in 1654, when the Iroquois rose up and drove all competing bands from the area. And then the Europeans arrived and finished off what the Iroquois had started, driving out the Iroquois and all remaining native bands from the territory. Apart from the Pleistocene glaciers, the silt and the clay, a fair bit of human blood gave shape and substance to the land that would become London.

The stamp of its British namesake still imprints the city: it has a Thames River, a Covent Garden Market, a Blackfriars Bridge, a Victoria Park, an Oxford Street and a Piccadilly Street, just to remind Canadians that they weren't always a nation unto themselves. The English influence accelerated civilization in the region, such that by the nineteenth century, London was about as cosmopolitan a city as Upper Canada could get. The spiritual needs of its approximate population of 18,000 were served by churches of all the major denominations; its financial requirements were looked after by the foremost banking institutions of the day; and apart from horse and wagon, entrance and egress to the city were serviced by two railway lines — the Great Western and Grand Trunk. There were two breweries — Labatt's and Carling — and refineries, insurance companies, foundries and tanneries.

The city further boasted two newspapers, the *London Advertiser* (a morning paper) and the *London Free Press* (an evening paper), to keep its populace informed of the daily goings-on within both London and its neighbouring townships. And until February 4, 1880, the biggest news story to hit London had been the fire of 1845, which destroyed one-fifth of the city, laying waste to 150 buildings (along with the town's only fire engine), and torching the better part of thirty acres of land. It was said to be the province's first "million-dollar fire."[1]

After February 4, however, another story would come to fill the columns of the London newspapers, and it would remain on their front pages for many months to come. It was a story of the massacre of a local family; a story so out of place for the Federation of Canada (the new country had been granted sovereignty of a sort thirteen years earlier, with the British North American Act of 1867), and so grisly in its details that it would soon be picked up by newspapers throughout the Federation, and by certain cities within the United States.

The story would be covered for the *London Free Press* by a twenty-one-year-old reporter named John Lambert Payne,[2] who, shortly after learning of the news the morning of February 4, had climbed aboard a stagecoach and headed north to visit the scene of the crime. The stage left London along the Proof Line Road, an icy, gravel thoroughfare that extended for the better part of eighteen miles. It could not have been a pleasant ride, as the destination lay three and a half hours away[3] and required travel over deeply rutted country roads. Periodically, both the stage and its occupants would shift and pitch violently as the wheels of the coach caught the odd furrow. In looking out through the windows the reporter would have seen nothing but snow-covered farmers' fields. And beyond these, nothing but flat lands that stretched on for miles and led nowhere.

His editor had told him that the murders had taken place within a farmhouse that sat somewhere along the Roman Line, a stretch of roadway also known as the "Chapel Line," as it led, ultimately, to St. Patrick's Church in the township of Biddulph. The Roman Line was a concession road (more technically, it was called "Concession Road Six"), one of many such roads in Upper Canada, the primary function of which was to provide access to already surveyed but yet undeveloped government land which had been made available to new settlers for the purpose of farming. Concession Road Six had acquired the epithet "Roman Line" in deference to the fact that a large number of Irish Roman Catholic families that had immigrated to Ontario had opted to settle along either side of it. The road itself extended a little over eight and a half miles and somewhere along that stretch was the farmhouse in which the murders had occurred. It would be Payne's task to find out where.

There were three tollgates set up along the Proof Line Road, each spaced exactly five miles apart, that required all traffic to stop briefly in order to pay the levies.[4] The first two stops that morning had been momentary, hardly requiring the stagecoach driver to slow down at all. However, by the time the stage had reached the final gate there was a lineup of sleighs, cutters and wagons waiting to pass through. Around the booth a small group had congregated, and as Payne's stage drew closer, the reporter could pick up on snippets of conversation he heard coming from outside the coach. Someone from within the assembly turned to another and asked, "Have you heard about that awful affair at the Donnellys'?" Before the person could answer, another voice from the crowd piped up that "They were smashed to pieces and burned! And we have just heard that another of the brothers was called out of his house, over beyond, and shot dead!"[5] Word about the murders was clearly now a matter of common knowledge among the local population. Within minutes, the stage was clear of the tollgate and rattling its way north through Ryan's Corners, and then gradually easing west until it reached the base of the Roman Line. To Payne's surprise, an inordinate number of horse-drawn conveyances were on the road now, all apparently heading in the same direction that he was. Each wagon and carriage appeared to the reporter to be "crowded to its fullest capacity."[6]

The stagecoach passed by St. Patrick's Church, which was (and remains) a parish that had been tending to the spiritual needs of Biddulph Township since the 1850s, and then continued on its way north along the Roman Line. Into view came small and simple farmhouses, most being single-level, constructed of hand-hewn timbers, and all, it seemed, with green-painted doors.[7] The occupants within these dwellings could be seen staring out of their windows at the small caravan of wagons and sleighs that passed by. It had been thirty minutes since the stage had left the final tollgate when it finally came to a stop in front of Lot 18 on the west side of the Roman Line, the location where the murders had taken place. Looking out from the stagecoach, Payne noted that a multitude of people were milling about the property. He stepped from the conveyance and watched as it slowly pulled away. The people on the property stood together in muted awe before the ghastly spectacle that lay before their eyes — the smouldering remains of what had once been the Donnelly family home. The reporter walked closer and observed the still-smoking outline of the floor of the farmhouse — it formed a perfect square. Less than one hundred yards to the west of the home stood the deceased family's stables, granary and barn, all of which looked to have been untouched by the blaze. It appeared as if time had stood still for this section of the property.

The fence that lined this plot of land was also in excellent condition, and the fields of the property revealed themselves to have been well worked over a period of many decades. There was not a stump to be seen. Even the farm animals — pigs, horses and cattle — were still in their pens and stalls. Some were seen meandering about the property as if nothing out of the ordinary had occurred. The horses, for example, could be seen pulling at straw from a large stack that stood near the granary,[8] clearly oblivious to the tragedy that had befallen the owners of the property only hours earlier. This juxtaposition of life and death was surreal; pastoral splendour and, twenty yards east of it, the grisliest horror scene that one could imagine. As Payne would later recall:

> Every vestige of the old log house was destroyed,
> and the smoke which was emitted, rose rather from
> the baked ground than any inflammable material

which remained. The first object to excite attention was in the ruins of the old-fashioned kitchen stove in the northwest corner of the smoking plot, and a black mass lying beside it.[9]

The reporter advanced closer to the ruins, where he quickly discovered that the "black mass" he had observed from afar was, in fact, the charred remains of not one, but two human beings — human beings that had been burned so severely that they were now "black, unrecognizable and ghastly."[10] In assessing the scene, Payne surmised that

> [t]hey had evidently been piled together against the log wall, but beyond the ash-coloured skulls and the upper trunk, no outline of a single body could be drawn from the charred mass. The arms and legs were gone, but one or two ribs remained, and with the exception of a single lung, there were but few traces of flesh. On the surface of the upper body lay a warped pocket knife which showed that this remnant of a human form once contained the soul of James Donnelly, father of the family, and owner of the property. The skull of the other corpse was broken in pieces and some of its fragments scattered three feet away; yet a sufficient portion remained intact to be distinguishable. Ten feet further south, on the border of the cellar, but within the area covered by the little kitchen, lay another corpse burned to even a smaller crisp than the ones just referred to. The skull was broken, but the fracture did not indicate whether it had been done by a falling beam or some instrument in the hands of the murderers. A few rags of tweed showed this to

be the remains of Thomas Donnelly, a son of the
murdered father. Within a few feet of where the
front door stood, and on the surface of a smoking
pile of potatoes, lay another sickening remnant of
humanity. This body could not be reached without
the aid of a ladder, but from the upper ground it
could be seen that the fire had left the trunk more
complete than in any of the other three cases. The
extremities, however, could not be traced, and
the skull appeared as though it had been buried
in the ground for years, and through that agency
had been thoroughly bleached and dried.[11]

It should be noted at this point that while the reporter's testimony was truthful, Payne had been mistaken in one detail that
he could not possibly have known and that wouldn't be disclosed
until the trials that would eventually follow: the corpse with the
"few rags of tweed" had in fact been that of Johannah Donnelly,
the fifty-six-year-old matriarch of the Donnelly clan. The corpse
of Thomas Donnelly (who at twenty-five years of age was the
youngest son of James and Johannah) was the one Payne had spied
lying on its back on the potato pile in the root cellar. But this aside,
and upon further survey of the wreckage, Payne would go on to
note even more pitiful and peculiar artefacts: next to the charred
body of James Donnelly was the head of an axe, as well as metal
buttons from a jacket that the Donnelly family patriarch had been
wearing at the time that he was killed. And next to these, a pair of
spectacles, and a small amount of money — a quarter, a dime and
a penny. In the most easterly portion of what would have been the
kitchen, next to the skull of Mrs. Donnelly, was the grotesque sight
of ringlets from a portion of her still-preserved hair, which had been
held in shape by the ash that had surrounded it. Beneath the body
that lay upon its back in the vegetable cellar could be seen the blade

of a spade — the iron strap that had once secured it to a wooden handle was visible, although its wooden handle had perished in the flames. Discernable on the top of this corpse were more metal buttons, as well as the buckles from a pair of suspenders. These metal objects had been seared into the corpse once its clothing had caught on fire. A pocket watch on a chain was also visible next to the body.[12]

The only evidence of what had once been the outer walls of the home were shards of broken glass from the several windows in the establishment that had blown out during the conflagration, along with some screws and nails that had been in the support beams and trusses. In among the debris were other artefacts: a tin dish and the spout of a shattered china teapot were observed poking out from among the ashes.[13] Within what had been one of the bedrooms were the scorched remains of a rifle, a shotgun and three revolvers, the stocks and handles having burned away. The family had clearly perceived that a threat upon their lives had been imminent, but had been surprised by the attack, as the guns were nowhere near the bodies. Several axe heads were noted lying within the ruins, as well as a pick and a hammer — objects that typically would not have been brought into the home by its owners. And finally, the reporter's eyes came to rest upon a metal latch — still in the unlocked position — that had once served to secure the Donnelly's front door.[14]

Then Payne noticed an object that intrigued him. Next to one of the charred corpses, and within what had been the little kitchen area, he saw a small, shiny lump of metal and glass. He walked over and picked it up — it was still warm to the touch. Turning the object over in his hand, it dawned on him that what he was now looking at was all that remained of Mrs. Donnelly's eyeglasses.[15] For reasons known only to himself he then placed the object in his pocket and continued his trek through the ruins. Perhaps one of the spectators had taken notice of Payne's petty pilfering, as soon other items began to disappear. The head of a shovel that had earlier been observed lying beneath the skull of James Donnelly[16] — perhaps one of the murder weapons employed on that fateful night (as the Donnellys had no need for a shovel in their kitchen) — would vanish at some point during the next twenty-four hours.[17] A neighbour would also observe another neighbour lifting Tom Donnelly's gold watch and chain from his carbonized body.[18] And the thefts became more macabre — some of the skulls and teeth of the victims would soon be spirited away.[19] And such ghoulish thefts weren't limited to just the human interlopers, as one of the most shocking acts occurred when a neighbouring dog arrived on the scene, having lately picked up on the scent of burning flesh, and within minutes was seen tugging on the remains of an exposed lung from one of the victims. Eventually working it free, the animal ran off from the ruins with the charred organ hanging from its mouth. The dog would later be tracked down and shot by someone.[20]

While Payne's perambulation of the property had revealed the extreme carnage that had befallen the late Donnelly family, it also revealed something else — a rather large number of footprints, clearly visible in the snow, that, as far as he could ascertain, had not been made by any of the looky-loos who had assembled there that morning. But surely this was a problem for the local constables to puzzle over once they arrived on the scene, not a junior reporter working on his first big story. As he reached what had been the front of the Donnelly home, Payne observed that the snow in this area was melted for a good twenty feet or so; a consequence of the intense heat from the fire.[21] Once again he saw numerous sets of footprints bordering the area — and then his eyes caught sight of something else entirely: it looked to be a small pool of blood. It was hard to discern the quantity of it at first glance, as someone had placed boards across it, obviously in an attempt to conceal it from public view. He bent down and lifted the boards to look beneath and discovered that they had in fact been concealing a *very* large pool of blood.[22] Replacing the boards, the reporter turned and continued to walk about the property. As he did so he picked up on a strange attitude that seemed to be shared by members of the crowd. He would later write that "[t]hose above the ruins spoke in whispers, and no one even wanted the names of the probable perpetrators, although hundreds visited the scene during the day. The affair was spoken of as a mystery."[23]

Payne eventually made his way across the road and noticed even more footprints heading north along the roadway.[24] Also across the road stood a large farmhouse. Spying a man walking in front of the home, the young reporter approached him to ask a few questions. The man, John Whalen, was thirty-four years old, and, like most of the people who lived on the Roman Line, a farmer by profession. He shared with the reporter what he knew of the fire at his neighbour's home:

> About two o'clock this morning I was awakened by my little one crying and, on rising, I noticed a bright red light streaming in through the window. I said to the old woman, "There is a fire!" And on running to the door I saw it was Donnelly's place. The fire was breaking out by the windows, and yet I saw no one about, and could hear no other sounds than the crackling of the fire. After waiting for nearly half an hour, during which time I dressed, I went over to Donnelly's and found the back kitchen burned down, but the front portion of the house was still blazing. There were no neighbours about, and it was four hours afterwards when the fire had burned out, that the bodies were found. I saw the marks of blood at the front door, but did not know whether the Donnellys had been killing pigs or how it came there. I went over to my father's house [his father

and mother, Patrick and Ann Whalen, lived about forty yards away alongside the same road] and found a small boy there, who was frightened almost to death. He came to my father's house about two o'clock in the morning. After waking the inmates up, he told them the Donnellys' place was on fire. After being in the house for some time, he said he guessed some of them were killed, as there had been a great fight, and the bodies of the old man Donnelly, the old woman, Tom and Bridget Donnelly had been left in the house. We saw by the bodies the boy was right. I have lived a neighbour to James Donnelly for a great many years but, with the exception of one little quarrel, have always been on the best terms with the whole family. I believe, however, that the people hereabouts were afraid of them.[25]

The people, it seemed, were currently afraid of a lot of things. Years later, Payne would write, "I can recall the excitement and fear which gripped the whole countryside. Nor have I forgotten the glowering looks that were cast upon me as I sought information along the Roman Line."[26]

Nevertheless, the news he had been given about the boy was certainly intriguing, as it revealed that there had been an eyewitness to the murders. Moreover, at this point, what the boy had seen was known only to a handful of people. Indeed, the police would not hear of it for another several hours, but by then the whole country would know about the crime. Payne wrapped up his interview with John Whalen and returned to the Donnelly property. On the northwest corner of the lot he took notice of a modest building that evidently was a schoolhouse. Indeed, it was referred to locally as the "Donnelly School," as the land upon which it sat had been donated by the Donnelly parents to the Township of Biddulph in

1861.[27] There were no classes today, however, as the teachers and children who had arrived at the school earlier this morning had been shocked by the fact that the neighbouring Donnelly house had burned down during the night. Naturally curious, the schoolchildren had climbed the short fence that served to separate the late family's farm from the schoolhouse and meandered through the property to get a look at the carnage. With more people coming to the property every hour, Payne decided to take his leave. He still had another murder scene to visit that morning.

John Donnelly, the thirty-three-year-old son of the old couple who had met their end in the horrific fire on the Roman Line, had been visiting his brother, William, at the latter's home. There he had been shot. By whom, or for what reason, wasn't known presently. Payne, however, was determined to find out what he could about the matter — after all, that John's murder coincided with the massacre of his family couldn't have been an accident — and so he next travelled to an intersection of two concession roads that was referred to locally as "Whalen's Corners." This destination three miles to the northeast required travel by sleigh over bumpy, stump-covered sideroads. The ride took the better part of forty-five minutes, but he soon found himself standing before the home of William Donnelly, the second-oldest child of James and Johannah. According to Payne,

> On the 8th and 9th concessions of the same township,
> in a clump of houses which imparts to that portion of
> the road the appearance of a little village, is situated
> the residence of William Donnelly, eldest [surviving]
> son of the murdered James. The house is a frame
> one, and was once a neat little white-painted Gothic
> building, but the storms of a dozen years have worn
> off the paint, and left it pretty much in the condition

of other buildings in that neighbourhood. Within
ten feet on either side are buildings, and neighbours
are near and numerous. There are four entrances to
the building, which seems to have been added to at
different times, and externally presents an uneven
appearance. It is what would be considered in any
locality a comfortable and perhaps a cozy dwelling.[28]

The reporter soon heard the sound of voices coming from behind
the house. Walking in the direction of the voices he noticed that
a group of men were gathered in a small laneway at the rear of
the building. As he approached, he overheard them discussing the
shooting that had taken place. At the right side of the house was a
side door that led into what looked to be a large kitchen. A portion
of the roof projected out and over the entranceway, offering some
present protection from the elements. As the door was already
open, he ventured up the steps and was about to enter when he
abruptly stopped himself in his tracks. Smeared on the floor before
him was a large trail of blood, which led from the doorway through
the kitchen and into what looked to be a side bedroom.

With cautious steps so as to avoid the bloody trail, Payne
tracked the pathway of the smeared blood into a bedroom where,
stretched out on the floor before him, lay the body of the deceased.
It was a gruesome sight:

> Lying on his back and partially covered with a
> quilt, his face and familiar curly hair were easily
> distinguished. A rough working shirt and an
> undergarment was turned back, exposing to view a
> breast punctured by twenty-six dark blood-clotted
> holes. His face was marked with blood, and on the
> floor was a large pool of the same crimson fluid.[29]

Clasped tightly within the victim's lifeless hands was what was left of a blessed candle,[30] which had been placed there shortly before the deceased had drawn his last breath.[31] Presently a woman entered the room: Nora Donnelly, the wife of William Donnelly and the sister-in-law of the deceased. She appeared somewhat taken aback by the sight of a complete stranger in her home. With apologies for the intrusion, Payne introduced himself. The woman seemed somewhat relieved to learn that he was simply a reporter from London. When he inquired if she could tell him anything about what had happened to cause the death of her brother-in-law, Nora had explained that his death had been a case of mistaken identity. As Payne would later report:

> Although his [John's] home was with the old people
> [James and Johannah Donnelly], he had been away
> for several days, and had dropped in at his brother's
> house after nightfall. Presumably, the object of the
> lynchers was to kill William, the most hated member
> of the family, and John's presence in his brother's
> home was unknown to them. When the sleeping
> household was aroused, John went to the door,
> while his sister-in-law held a lamp. As he opened the
> door a charge of buckshot caught him in the breast
> and he fell dead.[32]

Payne asked the grieving woman if her husband was at home. She shook her head no — William had ridden his horse to the house of a friend, and then was going to report the murder to the local authorities. Not wanting to disturb Mrs. Donnelly any more than he already had, but still needing something more tangible for his story, Payne asked a direct question — had she seen any of the men who had committed the murder? Payne later wrote, "She seemed afraid to talk. She said, however, that Bill had seen some of them."[33]

Given what he had already witnessed, along with the fact of William's absence, Payne knew that there wasn't much more to be gleaned for his story from this location. Besides, he had already seen enough that morning to file his first dispatch with the newspaper. But to do this he would have to get himself back to London. Upon leaving the house, he again noted an inordinate number of footprints surrounding the property.[34]

As Payne made his way toward London, members of the local constabulary were starting to investigate the crime scenes. Back on the Roman Line, County Constable George Walter Clay was looking to conduct a few interviews of his own. And while there was a general attitude of both shock and empathy for the murdered family among most of the people in the community, Constable Clay learned that there were also those within several of the neighbouring farmhouses who were of a far less sympathetic disposition toward the Donnellys. According to Clay,

> Going from house to house, I came across a young woman of the name of Farrell. She stated that she was glad [they were killed], for the Donnellys had killed her father some years ago. And now she laughed that they would not do anymore harm as they are out of the way. [Farther] down the Roman Line, a young man whose name I found out to be Carroll, came up to me and wanted to know who I was. I did not inform him, but said I was a stranger from Toronto. Then he spoke up and said, "You damned strangers had better look out, or you will get a few bullet holes in your hearts . . ."[35]

The constable could not have picked two more significant people to converse with regarding the Donnelly tragedy, as the young man who had made the threatening comments might well have been

James Carroll, a man who would soon be arrested under suspicion of having been the ringleader of the Donnelly murders, while the death of the young woman's father, Patrick Farrell, almost twenty-three years previously, was believed by most to have been the event that set the wheels of the Donnelly family's destruction into motion.

CHAPTER TWO

THE THINGS WE DO FOR LAND

The Roman Line (Biddulph Township, Middlesex County).
(Photo by author)

I n order to see the full picture of what led up to the massacre of the Donnelly family, it is important to know that it was very much the product of a different time and place. Rural Ontario in the nineteenth century was a rugged environment that bred in its inhabitants a peculiar toughness and ability to endure hardships — hardships that came at them on a daily basis and with a fury. Nature threatened them with unpredictable weather, unmerciful winters, unyielding soil and wild animals. Neighbours could also pose a danger, not only from diseases such as typhus (that often arrived attached to the new immigrants), but also from the more predatory types among them who looked to exploit any perceived weakness, and who were almost reflexively hostile and violent to both people and mores that differed from their own. Consequently, one's survival depended upon caution and the cultivation of a strong and well-callused disposition.

And while most residents of the community were churchgoing folks, that held only for Sundays. The remaining six days of the week required an unwillingness to "turn the other cheek" in matters both in and outside the home. If you had been wronged or suffered an impertinence, you were expected to handle the matter on your own, or through your family, or members of your group. Appealing to outside agencies such as the police (or what passed for police in those days in these rural areas) or the courts to intervene was viewed as an unnecessary step, particularly when a far more direct solution lay within the power of one's own hands. For example, in June 1879, two farmers in Biddulph had a dispute. Patrick "Grouchy" Ryder believed that two sons of a fellow community member, Patrick Whalen, had trespassed in an abandoned barn that Ryder owned on the Seventh Concession. Rather than taking the matter before the local magistrates, the two farmers decided to have their sons fight it out. On June 20, twenty-one-year-old James Ryder and thirty-three-year-old John Whalen met at a designated spot on the Roman Line and fought it out in front of a crowd of some fifty of their neighbours for a period of thirty straight minutes. Eventually John Whalen called out that he'd had enough, at which point the crowd dispersed back to their respective farms.[1] The matter had effectively been settled as per the mores of the community. This was simply how things were handled — and one either chose to make one's peace with that fact or left the region on account of it.

Those who were willing to accept these terms for survival came from all walks of life. The village of Wilberforce, for example, had been settled by former African-American slaves who'd been recently liberated from Cincinnati, Ohio. They had left the United States and arrived into an environment of forest and swamps, and yet, through their industriousness and foresight, created a colony with three schools, three sawmills and a grist mill. Soon more residents began arriving from the American cities of New York, Boston, Rochester, Albany and Baltimore. By 1835, the eight-hundred-acre area[2] boasted a population of between one hundred and fifty and two hundred families.[3]

These settlers cleared the land, made roads and built farms. So successful was the colony that, in time, there was talk of a railway coming through the Wilberforce region, which made the property values of the inhabitants soar in the eyes of speculators. With the potential of escalating property values came envy from their neighbours, the Irish Protestants, who begrudged the freemen not only their superior land, but also their timing, as the Americans had been the first to arrive in the region, and therefore had first opportunity to claim the prime pieces of real estate. Soon a concerted effort was made to drive the African-Americans from the region. Barns and homes were burned,[4] and families threatened and assaulted.[5] After a while, the constant exposure to such hostilities, along with the superior opportunities for earning money that beckoned from nearby Canadian and American cities, saw the Wilberforce black population diminish into virtual non-existence.

At the same time the African-American population was withdrawing from the region, the Irish Roman Catholic population was arriving, and this, too, posed a threat to the Irish Protestants who knew, first-hand, what the problems had been between these two factions back in their native Ireland. And both groups, it seemed, were quite prepared to continue these problems on the soil of their new homeland. And so, the troubles continued, and they were troubles for which the weak of spirit had no stomach. It was natural law and survival of the fittest (and most ruthless) that held sway, and so it would remain until civilization — which is merely social restraint mutually agreed upon for group survival — could find anchorage. However, in 1846, civilization had not yet taken root in the rural communities, and the various factions within those communities manufactured (and held to) their own rules of conduct in order to ensure the survival and protection of their respective groups. But in all cases, the potential upsides — freedom, the rights to the fruits of one's own labour (however modest) and a chance at a future — were weighed in the balance against the adversity to be encountered and were found by most to be well worth the price to be paid in sweat, tears and blood.

This was the "new world" that waited to greet James and Johannah Donnelly and their first-born son, James Jr. (along with tens of thousands of other Irish immigrants), when they stepped off their ship from the Emerald Isle and onto the shores of Grosse Isle, one of the principal landing points for immigrants from Ireland, in the province of Quebec. To reach Grosse Isle was something of an accomplishment in itself, as thousands of would-be immigrants from Ireland perished during the voyage (by some estimates as many as one out of every five would die en route to Canada). Still more expired during the quarantine period that followed their arrival.[6] Truly, so high was the death rate among the new arrivals that their vessels of transportation were commonly referred to as "coffin ships." By June 1847 it was reported that forty of these ships, packed with 14,000 Irish immigrants, were lined up for two miles along the St. Lawrence River, waiting to dock with their sickly passengers.[7]

While a good number of these new arrivals opted to remain in Quebec, others ventured east to the Maritime provinces of Nova Scotia, Prince Edward Island, New Brunswick (the point of landing there being Partridge Island) and Newfoundland. The bulk of the Irish immigrants, however, chose to travel a further five hundred or so miles west to the province of Ontario, in what was then called Upper Canada.[8] The 2,730-mile ocean voyage lasted some three months,[9] which provided the ambitious settlers plenty of time to envision what their new future could be. No matter what hardships lay before them, these people felt ready for the task that awaited them on these far shores. They looked ahead with hope, a commodity that was non-existent in the life that they had left behind, for they had been promised land that, with sufficient sweat equity, they might one day own for themselves. This held high appeal. In Ireland, the Roman Catholics were second-class citizens — they could work the land of their Protestant masters who, in turn, bent their collective knees to their British superiors, but even they were not entitled to own property. In Canada, it was said, it was every man for himself with no institutionalized class structure based upon religious or political affiliation. It was a clean slate. At least, that was how the dream was sold to them. It was certainly the dream that was embraced by James and Johannah Donnelly.

James Donnelly was said to have arrived in Ontario in 1842,[10] perhaps with his wife and son, although some researchers have speculated that James arrived first, and at least a year would pass before Johannah and James Jr. would be reunited with him in the new land.[11] James Donnelly was twenty-six years old;[12] Johannah was nineteen;[13] their son, James Jr. (Jim), was not yet a year old. Never afraid of hard work, James Donnelly didn't take long to find employment in London.[14] He worked in that city for several years until he felt fully acclimated to his new surroundings. And then, sometime between 1847 and 1848, James, together with his family, which by now had grown to include two more sons in the persons of William and John, made the move to Biddulph Township.

Biddulph Township is situated in the northern region of the county of Middlesex, lying approximately sixteen miles to the north of London. In James Donnelly's time it consisted of almost 39,300 acres, not including the village of Lucan (which would remain a separate entity until it eventually amalgamated with Biddulph in 1999, forming Lucan Biddulph), and formed a part of what became known as the "Huron Tract," which was a very large parcel of land that extended from the county of Waterloo to the shores of Lake

Huron to the west, and New Hamburg to the east. This land was owned by the Canada Company, which had purchased some 2.5 million acres from the Upper Canada Government in 1826, at a cost of $295,000. The company had been created for the express purpose of colonization.[15]

One of the directors of this company was John Biddulph, from whom the township secured its name. It was within Biddulph that James Donnelly discovered one hundred acres of decent land that was unoccupied, and that he believed would be the perfect spot upon which to build his family farm. Not yet being able to afford the purchase price, Donnelly discovered the name of the man who held its lease, John Grace, and, presumably, approached him with an arrangement whereby he would lease the plot from him.[16] If so, it was done with the understanding that if James Donnelly cleared the property of its heavy forestation and made the soil cultivatable, not only would his lease payments be reduced (owing to the improvements he had made) but also that he might, one day, be in a position to purchase the property outright.

As it stood, the land in and around Biddulph required a tremendous amount of work in order to make it both farmable and livable. Here were hardwood trees — oak, ash, cherry, maple — which served no real purpose in terms of commerce (unlike the softwoods — cedar, pine and spruce — which always found a ready market owing to their utility in construction). And these hardwoods had to be removed from the land at great labour and often for too little return. But this was only one area that required a family's time, muscle and sweat: because much of the available property in the region was set within or near swampland, the trees within such sections often would become so heavily grown over that no wind could penetrate the area, which made the land all but useless unless additional (and considerable) labour was expended to denude the landscape of their presence. Such areas posed additional problems apart from their non-arability — left abandoned, they invariably became a haven for wildlife that were inclined to steal onto farmers' properties in the night and plunder livestock or destroy any structures that might contain food.

And then there was the need to locate water, to dig wells, to pull and burn stumps, and to square timbers for use in homes, granaries, barns and stables. In addition, new landowners had to craft shingles from the wood, create roofs, construct rails for the creation of fences, locate and transport field stones for wells and for the foundations of houses, and the county had to excavate ditches and drainage systems and bring roadways into existence in order to allow would-be farmers access to their properties. Such work was dangerous, particularly to those who knew only the well-worked gardens and fields of Ireland.

For some, the harsh lifestyle required to transform a wilderness into farmland simply didn't take, and depression descended as they watched their dreams of prosperity diminish. In certain cases, the situation became bad enough to lead to suicide.[17] Others died in the effort of doing what was necessary in the attempt to survive — some falling to their deaths from trees they had climbed in an effort to affix ropes at barn-raising bees,[18] others crushed to death by felled trees.[19] One man perished as a result of a vital artery in the leg being severed from a misplaced axe swing while chopping wood.[20] Other settlers met their fate being crushed to death by ox carts,[21] and still others were simply found dead in the surrounding fields.[22] Children were particularly at risk, not yet being of age to recognize potential danger. A fifteen-month-old toddler drowned as a result of falling into an uncovered well,[23] while a two-year-old was found dead of unknown causes in a field near his father's home.[24] These were just some of the pitfalls that awaited the settlers in this new land. Those who avoided them were lucky, if you could call it that, as the physical toil never ceased.

If one was fortunate enough to clear one's land of rocks and stumps and trees and to cultivate arable land, the real work began.

When the snow left, it was time to plant, and so into the tilled soil went potatoes, onions, carrots, turnips, peas and cabbages. Oats and hay also had to be cultivated in order to feed the livestock that would work the land. It was important to plant wheat, for it was one of the few crops that, after harvesting, could be bartered for items the farm could not produce — such as sugar, coffee, tea and items for the home. Weeds were an omnipresent threat and had to be pulled from the fields during the spring and summer months. By mid-summer, the hay needed to be cut, with some of it being bound and stored for the winter months, while barley and oats would be likewise cut and bound, with the sheaves stacked prior to being taken to granaries for threshing. The freshly harvested soil required manure to augment future planting, and straw was needed for the livestock. In the fall, all crops were planted afresh and, if a good harvest had been produced, any money brought in from the sale of such crops totalling over and above that which was required for farming equipment and household goods might be put toward purchasing the lease to one's property, which ultimately meant freedom.

Throughout each season, the cutting of firewood was a chore that needed to be tended to on a daily basis. According to Donnelly historian William Davison Butt,

> Each settler started with a shanty for his family and
> his ox, and his first part-acre of wheat and potatoes
> planted among the stumps of what few trees he had
> managed to cut. It would be years before a farm
> could be built in this manner from the forest.[25]

James and Johannah Donnelly took eagerly to agrarian life; they cleared a significant portion of their land and were soon cultivating crops — harvesting fifteen bushels of grain and thirty bushels of potatoes.[26] Like other farmers in their community, they also raised livestock — pigs, cows and sheep.[27]

Given that survival hinged on the fertility of the farm, neighbours often helped one another out at harvest time and in clearing land. This formed a bond of sorts between them, with outsiders to these bonds being eyed with a large measure of suspicion, if not outright contempt. When, for example, an American visitor made the mistake of stopping into a Biddulph tavern, one of the locals, James Hodgins, spit in his face and threw a beer at him. "I will not let the damned Yankees rule over us!" he exclaimed.[28] Consequently, factions formed quickly in the rural communities and the phrase "strength in numbers" was accepted not just as an adage, but as a practical means to expand and fortify a given group's chances of survival. The appearance of a rival group would awaken and bring to the surface more primal impulses of self-defence that, in different times or circumstances, might otherwise have remained dormant. Such tribalism came to the fore repeatedly in Biddulph Township, most readily in matters of religion and politics.

At this point in its history Canada was not yet a country. Rather, certain regions of what would become Canada were considered a "province" under the dominion of England. These regions were divided into two areas: Upper Canada, which consisted of what is now the province of Ontario, and Lower Canada, comprised of the southern portion of what is now Quebec, and the Labrador region of what is now Newfoundland. And as with all geography populated by humans, it didn't take long before political groups came into existence: the two primary political bodies of Upper Canada were the Liberal-Conservative (or Conservative) Party and the Reform (or Liberal) Party. In the Biddulph Township riding of Huron, the political split fell along religious lines, with the Irish Protestants generally voting Liberal-Conservative, and the Irish Roman Catholics aligning themselves with the Reform Movement. In the

1857 election for the Legislative Assembly for the Sixth Parliament of the Province of Canada, the Liberal-Conservatives were fronted by future Canadian prime minister John A. Macdonald, while the opposition was led by George Brown, the leader of the Reform Movement. In the Huron riding, the two parties were represented by William Cayley for the Liberal-Conservatives and John Holmes for the Reform.

On the night of December 24, 1857, after the polls for the election had closed, a successful Lucan businessman, Bernard Stanley, who was a Protestant supporter of Conservative William Cayley, gathered together a group of men of similar persuasion and, armed with clubs, they boarded a sleigh and set off toward a destination halfway between Lucan and London. They were heading for a tavern owned by Andrew O'Keefe that was known to be an institution frequented by many Roman Catholic Reform supporters in the area. And, given that their man Cayley had just lost the election, Stanley's men were in a foul mood and blamed their Catholic neighbours for his defeat. Upon arriving at O'Keefe's, they set upon one of his patrons, beating him senseless, and then proceeded to beat the bartender of the establishment when he came outside in an attempt stop the assault. Stanley and his mob continued on in their rage, smashing the windows of the tavern, tearing off its sidings, and then going inside and trashing its interior. When charges were eventually brought against Stanley and his gang, Stanley threatened the life of James Hodgins, the chief of the committing magistrates. The Assizes[29] were awash with charges and countercharges; however, eventually all involved in the assault and destruction were acquitted.[30] On another occasion, Robert McCormack, a local Roman Catholic, stopped off to have a drink at a Biddulph tavern and there got into an argument with a drunken Protestant. As he returned home that night on his sleigh, he was attacked and killed on the road by Thomas Harlton and some of his Protestant friends.[31] Once again charges were filed and, once again, those who committed the crime were acquitted.[32]

But the Catholic community was not beneath getting its hands bloody as well. Richard Brimmacombe, a Protestant who also had the misfortune of being an Englishman in a predominantly Irish community, had broken up a fight during a home-building bee that was held on his property in the fall of 1856. The fight took place between the man he had hired to frame his house and a Roman Catholic labourer by the name of William Casey. Casey was getting the worst of the fight when Brimmacombe and a neighbour pulled the two men apart. Perhaps in Casey's mind it was another case of an Englishman inserting himself into the affairs of an Irishman that set him off; perhaps it was the grog consumed that day. Whatever the reason, Casey turned his fury to the Englishman, threatening both him and the neighbour who'd broken up the fracas. Casey waited until February 1857 and, together with another Catholic friend, Patrick Ryder, ambushed Brimmacombe while the latter was walking alone on the Roman Line. Their attack fractured the Englishman's skull and Casey and Ryder then left him to die in a ditch on the side of the road.[33] As in the previous examples, by the time Casey and Ryder went to trial, the community closed ranks around its own and both men were acquitted.[34] Twenty-three years later, Casey would be elected magistrate in the same district.

Two things quickly became apparent to the settlers in Biddulph Township: first, if you ran afoul of someone along political or religious lines, then dire consequences would soon be heading your way from the community you had offended; second, you couldn't look to the law courts to dispense any justice in the matter. Besides, the Province of Canada was under British rule and British law, no different than it was back home in Ireland. And the settlers had (they hoped) left that taint of England behind them. In the new world they were not going to submit their autonomy to the British or to the law courts that served the British, as beseeching the British legal system to solve their problems was seen by many of the Irish as being just this side of treasonous. Indeed, in 1867, William Carleton penned a book entitled *Traits and Stories of the Irish Peasantry*, in which he related how an entire family, including babies and children, were murdered by an Irish mob in cold blood for the transgression of having appealed to British law to intervene in the matter of having a gun returned to the family that it had been stolen from.[35] According to author and Donnelly historian James C. Reaney, "In the eyes of their enemies, they had transgressed the *real* laws which Irish farmers should obey: the laws of the Irish-Catholic society, never the laws of the imperializing British society."[36]

These "real laws" were the laws of the clan of which you were a member. And if you happened to be dragooned into serving on a jury that stood in judgement on one of your own, it would be dangerous to even consider convicting the accused. This fact was also made known to the higher-ups politically when Robert Cooper, a judge of the Huron County Court, wrote to then–attorney general John A. Macdonald about the problems he faced in attempting to secure convictions in the Township of Biddulph:

> Goderich
> March 28, 1859
>
> My Dear Attorney
>   Pray excuse my troubling you in the enclosed
> criminal case, as we have no County Attorney.
> And even if we had, I should feel anxious to have
> your advice. You may perhaps remember a long
> report concerning certain murders and burnings
> in Biddulph, in these counties, in which cases it
> was extremely difficult to obtain evidence owing
> to the disposition of the witnesses to screen the

guilty parties. One case in particular, the murder of Brimmacombe, of which [Patrick] Ryder was accused, has given us much trouble and led to much expense, and Ryder is still at large.

The state of the neighbourhood is very bad owing to the fear each entertains of his neighbour, and the fights which occasionally take place. The J.P.s [Justices of the Peace] are not safe. I, for one, always go there in daylight. The Coroner is in real danger. Now we have got at the names of the witnesses, but if Ryder is arrested they will all bolt for fear of his violence should he be acquitted.

I have done my best in charges to the grand jury to persuade them against this old Irish system of shielding criminals, "won't be an informer" — and so forth. . . .

Hodgins, who laid the information, dare not do it publicly, so I have concealed his name from the other magistrates.

I am
yours faithfully,
R. Cooper[37]

And while Patrick Ryder had been able to successfully escape the long arm of the British law courts in Biddulph in 1859, by 1865 his enemies finally caught up with him. He was found on the railway tracks near Lucan — mutilated and headless.[38] Even Andrew O'Keefe, the Catholic tavern owner, was once again targeted for violence, this time from those within his own faction, when arsonists burned down his stables, killing ten of his horses.[39] But, again, that's how matters were typically handled in Biddulph Township. The only time the courts held appeal was if one could use them to one's benefit by having lawyers and judgements bleed out an adversary's finances in court costs and legal fees, as money was a commodity in short supply for most farmers in Biddulph Township.

In other words, all the settlers in Biddulph knew where they stood and, if one of their own got in trouble, it was pretty much a given that nobody from within the accused person's group would do anything to assist in his prosecution, even if the accused had clearly committed the crime. Such transgressions, for example in the case of the Roman-Catholic factions, could be handled in the street or in the confessional, not the courtroom. A conviction resulted in nothing but the diminishment of the group's number and, thus, that group's strength in the community. And if anyone within that group thought otherwise or opted to place the lofty concepts of "right" and "wrong" behaviour (particularly as defined by British lawmakers) above the more primal bonds of loyalty to God and clan, then that person also knew what sort of consequences would soon be heading his way.

By the mid-1850s times were reasonably good for many of the farmers in Biddulph, as the Crimean War had driven up the price of Canadian grain when the Eastern European supply of wheat was cut off to the British. Consequently, many settler families who farmed that particular crop (of which the Donnellys were one) were able to make money in sufficient quantity to afford expenditures, including the purchase of land. John Grace, as the man whose name was on the title of the property where the Donnellys lived, now recognized it had become a seller's market for real estate. The lot he had originally secured with a down payment of a mere thirteen shillings[40] (the equivalent of perhaps eight to ten dollars in present Canadian currency) was, by 1855 (particularly with the sweat equity that the Donnellys had put into the land), now worth considerably more.[41] And he had a willing buyer for it, one Michael Maher from London, Ontario.

Without consulting the Donnellys, Grace talked Maher into purchasing the southern fifty acres of the lot upon which the Donnelly family was living (Lot 18, Concession 6), and the deal was finalized on December 10, 1855.[42] Presumably, Grace believed that, given the prosperous times in which they were now living, he could convince James Donnelly to buy the northern fifty acres of the lot, which would allow for Grace to make a very tidy profit. Indeed, his selling price to Maher for the southern fifty acres was four pounds an acre, or two hundred pounds.[43] However, Grace's plans were brought to an abrupt halt when he learned that not only was his tenant not in any position financially to purchase the northern fifty acres at this point in time, but also that James Donnelly was furious that Grace had sold the southern fifty acres of the property — that he had spent so many years clearing and farming — right out from underneath him! From Donnelly's perspective, the lot had been nothing but forest when he had first leased it from Grace, but now it was very desirable farmland. If the lot was now worth more than it was, it was due to Donnelly's sweat equity and had nothing to do with John Grace, who had never been anything more than an absentee landlord. However, James Donnelly didn't hold title to the land — John Grace did. And, from his perspective, if James Donnelly didn't want to buy the remaining northern fifty acres, then Grace knew that Michael Maher would.

When word of Grace's intention to sell the northern fifty acres of Lot 18 to Maher reached James Donnelly, he came up with an idea that might be a win-win for both him and Grace. Donnelly had caught wind that a former adversary of his from back in Ireland, Patrick Farrell, had recently immigrated to Ontario, and was now looking for farming property on or near the Roman Line. Donnelly had recently laid claim to a vacant lot on the Seventh Concession road, and believed it would fit the bill perfectly in terms of what Farrell was looking for. Donnelly didn't own it, mind you, but Farrell didn't need to know that detail for the time being. If he could convince Farrell to purchase the lot, then Donnelly could swap his rights to that property with John Grace in exchange for the northern fifty acres of the lot on which Donnelly and his family were presently living. Grace could then sell the other lot to Farrell. The purchase price would be such that the cost of the new lot could easily be absorbed, and Grace would still come out of it with money in his pocket. It was a scheme by which Grace would be paid and James Donnelly — finally — could become a bona fide landowner.

Both Donnelly and Grace apparently agreed to the deal. The only problem was that the third party, Patrick Farrell, had somehow discovered that James Donnelly didn't own the rights to the property that he had offered to sell to him. Moreover, Farrell had spotted a more desirable lot directly across the road from the one that Donnelly was pitching to him. Since no paperwork had been signed, Farrell withdrew from the transaction with Donnelly and purchased the other property. James Donnelly was left with no means by which to barter with Grace for the land on which he was living.[44]

Donnelly was livid. Farrell's sudden change of mind had just put the kibosh on his dream of owning his land. It didn't take long before both men could no longer stand the sight of the other, with Donnelly believing Farrell to be a liar for pulling out of a deal that he had verbally (at one point) agreed to, and Farrell believing Donnelly to be a swindler. One day while drinking heavily at Andrew Keefe's pub, which was situated directly across the road from St. Patrick's Church, the men became embroiled in an argument. When their tempers reached a certain critical point, Donnelly left the bar and returned moments later with a rifle. The patrons of the tavern, including Farrell, all scurried for cover as James Donnelly fired off a shot at his adversary.[45] Fortunately, as a result of either poor marksmanship or deliberateness on Donnelly's part, the shot missed its mark. But it understandably resulted in a warrant being issued for James Donnelly's arrest. When the matter was eventually brought to court, Donnelly was bound over to keep the peace between him and Patrick Farrell for a period of one year.

But this sideshow did nothing to pacify Grace's desire to sell the northern fifty acres of his property. If anything, the violent reaction of his tenant had only proven to be a deterrent to prospective buyers. In addition, the winter of 1856 had been a brutal one for Canadian farmers. The upswing the local economy had enjoyed since the Crimean War started in 1853 had come crashing down to earth in February 1856, when the war had ended. Canadian grain prices plummeted, and farmers who'd held on to their crops speculating that the market might take an upturn in the near future ended up with nothing. Some committed suicide.[46] Suddenly real estate was not for everyone a valuable asset, but rather a costly liability, as mortgages, leases and taxes still required payment, and, with the market dropping, the money simply wasn't coming in like it used to.

Sensing a downturn in the value of his real estate holdings, Grace became highly motivated to sell the northern fifty acres of Lot 18 quickly — but he had no desire to confront James Donnelly directly on the matter. It thus appeared to the landlord that his most expedient route toward resolving the issue would be to take it to court and move to have Donnelly ejected from the property. With any luck, Donnelly would be pushed out in short order, and Grace could still get a decent return on the property before the market bottomed out. And, on May 26, 1856, Grace was delighted when the court ruled in his favour, awarding him the ejection notice he sought for his problematic tenant.[47]

James Donnelly didn't even bother to attend the hearing; a British law court trying to dispossess him of the land that he had worked so hard to clear? This was not even a remote possibility. Constables to enforce court orders were not plentiful in 1856, and, given the modest population in and around Biddulph Township, most of the constables knew James Donnelly and his temperament and, thus, were not particularly keen on making their job more dangerous than it needed to be. Moreover, by this point in time, the Donnelly family had expanded; James and Johannah now had seven sons: Jim, who was now fifteen; William, who was twelve; John, who was nine; Patrick, who was seven; Mike, who was six; Bob, who was three; and Tom, who was two. James Donnelly Sr. would be particularly hard to evict now that he had a large family to support, and his farmland was his sole means of doing so. There was no way that he was going to simply surrender his family's livelihood — to anybody — and so when he was finally delivered the ejection notice he simply ignored it.

Grace waited and watched as the real estate value in Biddulph Township continued to drop. By the time late summer arrived, he, together with Michael Maher, decided to take the matter back to court and sued to eject James Donnelly and his family in order to recover the northern fifty acres of Grace's property. Once again, the court ruled in the plaintiff's favour and awarded Maher an ejection notice to be delivered to Donnelly in August of that same year.[48] However, despite Maher having a bona fide court order for James Donnelly to vacate Lot 18, the problem remained of who was going to serve it to him. Maher, like Grace before him, did not wish to be involved in any attempt to physically remove James Donnelly from his home. And with the real estate market dropping in value with each passing month, it appeared to Grace that the wisest course might be simply to cut his losses and come to some sort of arrangement with the gritty Irishman. He ultimately decided he would sell the northern fifty acres to Donnelly and be done with it. In light of the considerable improvements to the land that the Donnelly family had made over the years, Grace sold James Donnelly the northern fifty acres of Lot 18 for a mere one pound per acre — fifty pounds in total. It was one quarter of what Maher had paid for the southern fifty acres only ten months previously.[49] The solution was bittersweet for Donnelly. He and his family had worked the entire one hundred acres for many years and, in his heart of hearts, he had envisioned that one day his family would own all of it. Instead, he would have to settle for half the acreage. To the positive, however, the purchase price was agreeable, and it could now be said that, after fourteen long years of toil in Canada, James Donnelly could count himself among those who owned their own property, which was something of a rarity in itself. This last thought took a bit of the sting out of the matter for him.

And while James Donnelly may have had mixed emotions about purchasing the northern fifty acres, there was only one emotion that emanated from Michael Maher: rage. Maher felt betrayed by Grace, as it was no secret that he'd coveted the entire one hundred-acre lot, not merely half of it. Moreover, he, too, had witnessed the property values in the area declining, which included the value of the southern fifty acres he had purchased from Grace. And when he learned that James Donnelly had acquired his fifty acres at a quarter of the price that he had paid, it was impossible for Maher not to feel as though he had been grossly taken advantage of in the matter. He vented his frustration to whoever was willing to listen to him, and one of the people in his circle who was willing to lend a sympathetic ear was Patrick Farrell.

While there was certainly no love lost between Farrell and Donnelly, in truth, there wasn't much love lost between Farrell and anybody, as he was said to have been a man of a naturally foul disposition.[50] And James Donnelly's proposed property switch and the shooting incident that followed certainly had not done anything to improve the farmer's temperament. Moreover, it had not been the first time Farrell had clashed with James Donnelly. Indeed, the two were known to have quarrelled on a prior occasion when they both were living in Ireland.[51] Their mutual dislike had simply accompanied both men overseas to their new home in Canada. Making matters worse by contrast was the fact that, during the boom years of the mid-1850s, James Donnelly had been reasonably successful in his farming whereas Patrick Farrell had not. In truth, Farrell was now having trouble making the mortgage payments on his recently acquired lot.[52] Like Donnelly, Patrick Farrell also had a family to provide for, with his wife Sarah and five children.[53] Unlike Donnelly, however, he found himself in no position to do it. With Donnelly still smarting at the loss of the southern half of his property, and Farrell's anger growing daily at his lot in life, a perfect storm was brewing. And it would soon reach its breaking point when the two men showed up to take part in a logging bee at a neighbour's farm on a sunny Thursday morning on June 25, 1857.

The day had started out peacefully enough; a total of eighteen men had arrived at the lot of two brothers, Cornelius and William Maloney, who lived just one concession road and slightly north from the Donnelly property. As per the custom, a grog boss was on site to ladle out booze to the working men in an effort to take the edge off their intensive labours that day. The men were broken up into three groups of six apiece, which allowed various sections of the land to be worked simultaneously. Perhaps with an eye toward warding off any unnecessary trouble before it started, Patrick Farrell and James Donnelly had been placed in different groups. The morning passed without incident.[54] However, according to testimony from others who were present at the bee, Donnelly was looking for a quarrel[55] and Farrell was known to be "quarrelsome when in liquor."[56] When alcohol was factored into the mix, there wasn't a chance of this day ending peacefully.

By early afternoon[57] the hostility that had been percolating in both men reached a boiling point and they confronted each other. Accusations about the aborted property deal[58] and counter-accusations of Donnelly using Farrell for target practice[59] were brought forth. Donnelly then issued a challenge to Farrell that they should settle the matter with their fists, which Farrell at first refused.[60] Donnelly persisted[61] — he was not going to let the matter drop. Farrell, who, according to some, was fond of wrestling, particularly after a few drinks,[62] eventually had consumed enough hooch that he felt up to the task, and the two men then stepped away from their respective groups to have it out in a nearby field.[63] As both Farrell and Donnelly had been drinking heavily, none of their blows was particularly crisp or impactful. Indeed, so uneventful was the scrap that the rest of the men working at the bee that day didn't deem it worth leaving their tasks to witness it.[64] Be that as it may, the brawl went on for a good twenty minutes.[65] During the course of the fight, the two pugilists were separated several times by Cornelius Lanagan[66] and the grog boss Thomas McLaughlin,[67] but no sooner were the men separated than they would rush back at each other. McLaughlin was told (or decided on his own) that neither man would be the recipient of any more liquid refreshment that day.[68] Finally, either from a blow or from drunken exhaustion, Farrell hit the ground.[69]

"I've had enough!" he said in between laboured breaths. "I will fight no more."[70]

James Donnelly stepped back and asked onlooker Michael Carroll for a chew of tobacco.[71] Putting it in his mouth, he eyed his adversary warily. Suddenly Farrell reached for a handspike[72] that was lying on the ground next to him.[73] His intent was obvious not only to Donnelly, but also to the men who by now had gathered around them. As Farrell rose to his feet brandishing the handspike, Cornelius Lanagan intercepted him and, in an effort to diffuse the situation, told Farrell to go home.[74] Farrell, however, was having none of such counsel.

"Keep away from me!" Farrell hissed, raising the wooden handspike threateningly at Lanagan, "or I'll hit *you*!"[75] Recognizing that words were not having the intended effect, and in an effort to stave off a potential homicide, Martin Mackey now moved to intercept the drunken farmer and, grabbing hold of Farrell's wrist, attempted to wrestle the handspike away from him. Farrell broke free briefly and then swung the handspike at Mackey, who deflected the blow.[76] Mackey was quickly joined by Lanagan and the pair moved to overpower Farrell. Together they attempted to pry the handspike free from Farrell's hands, which caused the farmer to lose his balance and fall to the ground.[77] Donnelly, who had been knocked aside by Mackey and Lanagan when they had rushed Farrell, now bristled with anger. If Farrell wanted to fight him with a cudgel, then a duel with clubs it would be. While Farrell was attempting to pick himself up from the ground, Donnelly picked up a handspike of his own, and, lifting it with both arms high in the air, brought it crashing down on the left side of Farrell's head.[78] The impact from the blow instantly fractured Farrell's skull,[79] causing him to fall to the ground where he landed on his right side and remained motionless.

"The man is killed!" shouted one of the men.[80] Michael Carroll rushed to the fallen man and, cradling his head in his arms, turned to the group and asked, "*Who* struck him?" The men, however, had been stunned into silence by what had just occurred. Carroll asked again, "*Who* struck him?"[81] John Toohey, a twenty-eight-year-old farmer from the Seventh Concession, looked at Carroll and then nodded toward James Donnelly. "Donnelly struck him,"[82] he said. James Donnelly, who was still full of adrenalin and alcohol, turned to the men.

"There's your friend for you now," he said, pointing at Farrell. "For five years I've wished to do that. My children will have satisfaction about this when I'm in my grave."[83]

The men looked at each other in disbelief. Did Donnelly actually say what they thought they had just heard — that he had *wished to do that*? To murder another man in cold blood? A farmer from within the group now found his voice: "Donnelly, you have murdered the man!"[84] There was a pause as James Donnelly surveyed the intent of the crowd that had by now gathered in the area and were surrounding the body of his fallen adversary.

The reality of the man's words, together with the fact that Farrell hadn't moved since he'd been struck, underscored the severity of what had just transpired. This sobered James Donnelly up considerably. Donnelly suddenly felt numb. All he knew for certain at this moment was that he had to get away from the area — and the body of Patrick Farrell. He left the field without saying another word, and headed toward his farmhouse. How would he explain this to Johannah? The well-being of his family depended upon the success of the farm, and the farm required work, which could not be accomplished if he was in jail — or hanged.

The men lifted Farrell's limp body and carried it inside Maloney's house.[85] Patrick Farrell was still unconscious. For the moment, however, the men could detect that he was breathing, but that was about all.[86] Cornelius Maloney looked around and spotted young Edward Orange Jr., a ten-year-old boy from the area,[87] and instructed the youth to run and tell Mrs. Farrell that he wanted to speak with her, and to have her come over to his farmhouse immediately. The youngster left the farm and ran as quickly as he could in an effort to track down Sarah Farrell. When he finally did catch up with her, she would later recall, "I asked what was the matter; if Patrick Farrell was hurt or killed. I asked him who done it and he said, 'Oh, who done it before.' From that expression I knew it was Donnelly he meant."[88]

Meanwhile, James Donnelly had made it back to his farmhouse and told his wife the tragic news. The pair stayed in their home that Thursday evening, no doubt praying and hoping against hope that Farrell would pull through. As Patrick Farrell's condition was dire, the farmers had decided to move his body back to the Farrells' farmhouse, which would have necessitated it to be transported by wagon along the Roman Line, and right past the Donnellys' home, which would not have escaped the attention of the family inside the cabin. The next day James Donnelly did not venture off his property;[89] he remained on pins and needles as he waited for any news about Farrell's condition. Later that day the news came — Patrick Farrell had died.[90]

A t some point later that afternoon, a physician was summoned to the Farrell home to conduct a postmortem on the body. This could not have been pleasant for anyone involved, as the heat of the summer had caused the body to decompose rapidly, to the point where the attending physician, Charles G. Moore, declared that it was "impossible to identify the deceased."[91] Dr. Moore's inspection of the skull revealed the extent of the damage that James Donnelly had inflicted:

> [I] found a contused wound of the scalp on the
> left side of the head, extending from a little above
> the left ear slanting forwards to nearly the top of the
> head. The cut was from three to four inches long.
> On examination of the skull, a fracture without any
> appreciable depression extended directly across the
> head, following at first the top part the transom or
> front parietal suture, and afterwards continuing
> downwards to the base of the skull, down through
> the frontal bone. Just over the orbits, the front part
> of the skull came away without any force being used.
> On the right side of the head, about opposite to
> the situation of the cut in the scalp, I found a large
> clot of effused blood, evidently from a ruptured
> branch of the right meningeal artery. It is my opinion
> that a blow on the left side of the head from some
> heavy weapon caused the fracture and the effusion of
> blood, and that the latter was the cause of the death
> of Farrell.[92]

The news of Farrell's death undoubtedly caused panic and grief in the Donnelly home. On Saturday morning, the day after the autopsy, James Donnelly felt compelled to venture over to visit one of his neighbours who had also been present at the logging bee, Michael Carroll. He displayed contrition, saying that he was sorry for what he had done.[93] Not that it mattered. The next day John Hyndman, the local coroner, empanelled a jury to investigate the matter. Testimony from witnesses such as Cornelius and William Maloney, Michael Carroll and Patrick Ryan, among others, along with that of Dr. Moore and Sarah Farrell, pointed the finger directly at James Donnelly as the guilty party who had caused the death of Patrick Farrell. A warrant was promptly issued for Donnelly's arrest. That night James Donnelly bid goodbye to his family, returned to Carroll's home to again indicate his regret in the matter[94] — and then disappeared.

For the next eleven months James Donnelly evaded the law.[95] Often his friends in the community and/or members of his group either took him in or warned him in advance as to when the county constables were about to arrive. On five different occasions the police went on extensive manhunts for him, once tracking him for thirty-three miles over a two-day period. Another time they travelled twenty-two miles, and on still another occasion they tracked him for ten miles. They even camped overnight in the woods next to the Donnelly farmhouse in the hope that they might apprehend him should he return. During the month of October, constables rode thirty-five miles throughout Biddulph and into the township of McGillivray looking for him, while in November, two men canvassed a distance of eighteen miles through the woods behind the Donnelly farm hoping to detect his whereabouts. In no instance did they get close to him; the neighbourhood was too determined to protect its own. In an effort to break through the dam of clan loyalty, a $400 reward was posted for the "apprehension and delivery" of James Donnelly to the local jail,[96] yet no one from within the township of Biddulph offered to come forward. John Holmes, the warden for Huron County, wrote to the provincial secretary about the problem the law was facing in its attempt to capture the fugitive:

> Provincial Secretary's Office
> 16 October 1857
>
> To his Excellency the administrator of the
> Government in Canada
> The Municipal Council of Huron and Bruce
> has instructed me to submit for your Excellency's
> consideration the following facts.
> In the month of June last a most brutal murder
> was committed in the Township of Biddulph. The
> murderer Donnelly has since eluded justice, although
> efforts have been made to arrest him, yet such is the
> state of society in his neighbourhood that as soon
> as the officers of Justice approach, he is [apprised]
> thereof and hitherto has escaped.
> The Municipal Council aforesaid offers reward
> for the apprehension of Donnelly, which will appear
> by the accompanying advertisement.
> It is hoped that your Excellency in Council will
> be pleased to offer an additional reward in order if
> possible that justice may be done.
>
> I have the honor to be
> Your Excellency's most obedient Servant,
> John Holmes
> Warden, Huron & Bruce [Counties][97]

Despite being on the lam, James Donnelly had evidently been able to return to his farm every so often when the coast was clear to help out with the chores. A rumour that persisted from this time suggests he even dressed in woman's clothing while working in the fields around his home,[98] so that anyone who saw him might mistake him for his wife. During the winter the Donnellys' eighth and last child was born. Her parents named her Jane, although she was more commonly called Jennie.

In May, James Donnelly's brother Patrick arrived from Tipperary, Ireland, and made a special trip to Biddulph to lend some aid to his fugitive brother's family.[99] A short time later, James and Patrick, together with family friend Constable Mitchell Haskett, decided that it was time for James to stop running from the law. After all, being charged with murder was no guarantee that one would be convicted of murder — at least not in Biddulph. Perhaps the judge would be willing to weigh in the balance the long-standing feud that had existed between the two men, or that alcohol had been consumed, or that both men had agreed to fight. Also, Farrell had been the first one to take up a handspike — in which case Donnelly doing likewise wasn't murder, but self-defence. This, together with the incentive of a $400 reward that, if he should be sent to jail, would most certainly be of some help to his family, swayed James Donnelly's thinking on the matter. The result being that on May 7, 1858, in the presence of Constable Haskett, he turned himself in to the Huron authorities. However, the authorities, sensing a collaboration of sorts had taken place between the prisoner and the arresting constable, reneged on the reward money.[100] James Donnelly's trial took place on May 14 with ten witnesses for the prosecution and two for the defence. Justice Sir John Beverly Robinson found James Donnelly guilty of murder and, to everyone's surprise, sentenced him to death; he was to be hanged on September 17, 1858.[101]

While a dazed James Donnelly was led back to jail, his wife Johannah immediately rushed to the office of local lawyer John Wilson. With his assistance, she had several petitions drawn up and circulated throughout the region. She was appealing to have her husband's life spared; a prison sentence was acceptable, but with eight children and only Johannah to raise them, capital punishment would destroy the family. Her petitions received signatures from people of significance from within (and without) Biddulph Township. Johannah was even said to have walked to Goderich from her home on the Roman Line, forty-six miles due north, while collecting signatures en route. Her goal was to bring these petitions directly to the Governor General of the province, Sir Edmund Head.[102] On July 26, Head put before the executive council of the province — consisting of Head, Georges Cartier, Inspector General William Cayley and future Canadian prime minister John A. Macdonald[103] — Johannah's petitions, in addition to the report of Chief Justice Robinson, which considered all the particulars of the case. Johannah's efforts succeeded: the council ruled to commute James Donnelly's sentence from death to imprisonment.[104] Donnelly's life had been spared. However, he was going to be away from home for a while — his sentence was seven years within Kingston Penitentiary.

Donnelly would remain in the Goderich jail until August 5, at which point a bailiff and the local sheriff accompanied him on the Buffalo and Lake Huron Railway line to the Kingston penitentiary.[105] There he would serve out his seven-year sentence.

James's brother, Patrick, continued to help out on the Donnelly farm for another month or so, but then decided it was time to move on to a life of his own, which turned out to be in Toledo, Ohio.[106] Johannah would be left to raise her eight children on her own.

CHAPTER THREE

GROWING UP DONNELLY

Johannah Donnelly as interpreted by a sketch artist after her death.
No photograph of her has survived. (Toronto *Globe*, Feb. 20, 1880)

H istory has not seen fit to remember Johannah Donnelly. No
photograph of her exists, nor have any items in which she
placed value survived. No letters. No diary. Nothing. It is as if any
and all trace of her ever having walked upon this earth was burned
out of existence along with her body in the early morning hours of
February 4, 1880.

To make matters worse, almost all of what has been passed
down to us regarding the materfamilias of the Donnelly family
has been contributed by the family, friends and sympathizers of
those who murdered her. Consequently, the image of Johannah
Donnelly they have left us is grotesque, that of a witch-like figure —

a huge and hideous homicidal creature who lusted after violence and bloodshed. Witness, for example, the following, written a mere twenty-four hours after she had been murdered: "There need be no sympathy for Mrs. Donnelly . . . she had a wicked soul. . . . she prayed on her knees that the souls of her sons might forever and ever frizzle in hell if they ever forgave an enemy, or failed to take vengeance."[1]

And, this, from a letter penned some eighty-three years later by a relative of one of her many enemies:

> A woman came down the street in her bare feet and
> an axe over her shoulder. She was tall, over six feet.
> Stopped at the corner, danced a sailor's hornpipe,
> swearing at the top of her voice in language lurid, to
> put it mildly, and she called on High Heaven and the
> Almighty to witness that she had seven sons, and she
> hoped every one of them would kill a man. Mother
> was terrified and called Harriet, who snorted, "Oh,
> that's Johannah Donnelly" and shut the shutters.[2]

However, if the reader is interested in digging a little more deeply into the matter, he or she will encounter contradictory testimony regarding the character of Johannah Donnelly:

> She was kind-hearted, and did lots of little acts of
> kindness . . .[3]

> One very wet morning a lady schoolteacher was
> passing the house of the Donnellys, when the old
> woman hailed her. "Good morning, Miss. Come in
> and dry yourself before going to school." "Thank
> you, Mrs. Donnelly, but I haven't time," responded
> the teacher. "Sure, your feet are all wet. Come in

till I get you a pair of dry stockings." The teacher, however, hurried on. Mrs. Donnelly then passed into the house, and calling one of the passing scholars [teachers] she gave her a pair of dry stockings to carry to the teacher. "Tell the teacher to change her feet," was the quaint, but good-natured, direction of the murdered woman.[4]

The above statements, taken together, paint a rather confusing portrait of the matriarch of the Donnelly family. It is, after all, hard to square the image of an old woman going out of her way to ensure that a local schoolteacher has dry stockings on a rainy day with that of an axe-wielding, swearing, homicidal maniac. Indeed, even some of those interviewed by the local press immediately after the tragedy seem confused on the matter, as the same man who went on record as saying of Mrs. Donnelly that "she was kind-hearted and did lots of little acts of kindness" added in his very next sentence, "but she had a wicked mind."[5]

In terms of her run-ins with the law, of all the Donnellys (with the exception of her daughter Jennie, who never faced a legal charge in her lifetime), she was almost angelic by comparison. Unlike her notorious sons, Johannah faced only three legal charges throughout her fifty-seven years of life: the first was an allegation that she was housing stolen goods (a charge that was never prosecuted);[6] the second being the disputed allegation that she had used coarse language in response to a man who had stuck a revolver in her face;[7] and the third was a completely trumped-up charge that was laid against both her and her husband for the burning of a neighbour's barn.[8] It should be noted that the latter two charges occurred during a period of time when a secret committee had been organized for the express purpose of running the Donnelly family out of Biddulph and had more or less taken control of the local constabulary. Moreover, the records testify to the fact that, rather than crying out for her sons to commit acts of bloodshed, she was, like most mothers, very concerned about her sons' actions, and had even confided to her priest that she would do what she could to try to bring her boys in line. But she also added, correctly, that her boys were not the only ones in the county who had been getting up to mischief, despite them being the only ones to be singled out. One would have expected a veritable shopping list of charges and convictions against a woman who was said to have danced around the neighbourhood with an axe in her hands while beseeching the Almighty to have her sons commit murder.

There is no denying that Johannah Donnelly had to have been a tough woman; the survival of her family depended on it, given the circumstances of her life. She made the three-thousand-mile voyage to Canada alone, save for the company of her recently born son, on a ship that was infested with dysentery and typhus. And again, with just her son for company, she made the five-hundred-mile trek from the shores of Quebec to the wilds of Ontario, where, as the only other adult in the family, she then helped her husband clear a wilderness in order to build a family home together, and assisted in cultivating the soil they would have to rely upon for their food. It was her labour, every bit as much as her husband's, that built whatever life they had in this new land.

It's safe to presume that she, like most immigrants before and since, wanted a good life for her family — or at least a better life than the one than she had left behind in Ireland. And that she valued her family and friends — in that order. On top of this, however, she had been set the towering task of having to raise and provide for eight children on her own, as a result of her spouse being sent to prison. Add into this mix that the Donnelly farm required not only daily upkeep during this period, but also money to be raised in order to pay the taxes and mortgages on the property (which, again, fell solely upon her shoulders) and it is no wonder that she acquired a reputation in some circles for having little time for small talk or social graces. She was said to have been a tall woman,[9] and not particularly attractive[10] — but these descriptions, again, came after her death from those who despised both her and the family that she raised, as well as authors who never looked into the facts of the Donnelly story very thoroughly.

Interestingly, while the enemies of the family seldom missed an opportunity to castigate the physical appearance of its matron, and the press seldom missed an opportunity to print it, history has shared no such bias with regard to the looks of the male members of her family:

> [James Donnelly had been] remarkably good looking in his younger days.[11]

> Chief McKinnon [who was no fan of the Donnelly family] describes the Donnellys as fine looking, muscular men, with an air of cool desperation that awes at first sight.[12]

> The boys grew up to be fine looking and most intelligent under the circumstances of their bringing up, and they had many friends.[13]

> None finer [looking] in Biddulph.[14]

> None finer [looking] in the province.[15]

> By 1873 the sons had all grown to manhood, and it was then admitted on all sides that a finer-looking family did not live in Biddulph. They were all well-built, muscular men, with curly hair and well-cut features.[16]

Everything they did, they did well. They danced
well and with a flair that was also present in their
running and boxing. They had breeding.[17]

While the boys' physical appearance and athletic ability were inherited from their parents, there is no question that their "breeding," such as it was, was directly attributable to their mother. Johannah was always the primary caregiver and voice of authority and direction within the household. One of the Donnelly boys, William, would inherit from his mother the additional attributes of an alert mind and a caustic wit, which served him as additional weapons to wield over his adversaries. William had need for such extra protection, as he had been born with a club foot, which limited his ability around the farm and left him an inviting target for mockery by the other boys within the township. Of all the Donnelly boys, William was the most intellectual — he was a voracious reader, fond of the writings of satirists and poets. As he grew into manhood he cultivated considerable skill in logic and debate and earned the reputation of being a formidable adversary in a courtroom, irrespective of the pedigree of the lawyers who lined up against him.

Johannah Donnelly had raised her children to be tough, proud and self-confident, and they would remain that way throughout the remainder of their lives. And it was these character attributes, in combination with a fierce sense of family loyalty and a ready willingness to fight, that quickly made the Donnelly sons a considerable force to be reckoned with. The boys' reputation for toughness was known throughout the community, and their fighting prowess served to discourage a good many bullies in the Roman Catholic community from mocking them for being the sons of a man who had broken the fifth of the Ten Commandments. According to a newspaper report from the time, "The neighbours taunted the boys about their father's disgrace, and hence ill feelings arose. The boys were goaded on by their mother to resent the insults then offered to the family, which they did in real earnest by not over-scrupulous means."[18]

While the Donnelly boys were successfully employing their fists in the service of their family's honour in and around the neighbourhood, the various factions that operated within their community were using far more severe methods in resolving their personal disputes. William Donnelly would later recollect one of the incidents that occurred within Biddulph Township while he and his siblings were growing up:

There lived on the Cedar Swamp line a man named Dunigan. He had a falling out with some of his neighbours about an oak tree that was stolen off his farm. Dunigan and his neighbours met at a bee where whiskey was plenty, and what occurred? Nine or ten men stripped poor Dunigan off, and then put red hot irons all over his body, roasting the flesh on his bones. They then put him behind what was called the back log of the fire-place, and afterwards took him out and threw him in a mud hole, one of the party striking him with a [maul] head for splitting rails[19] and making the remark: "What about the oak tree now, Dunigan?" They next went to cut off his ears, but were prevented by a woman who risked her life to save the man from any further torture. On the following day Father Crinnan (who is now Bishop of Hamilton) came to see Dunigan, and when the priest turned him in bed the flesh actually fell off his bones. The good priest, horrified at the sight, looked to heaven and said he was afraid the hand of God would fall on

Biddulph. The whole affair was hushed up for a few dollars.[20]

William further recalled that not that long prior to the above incident, an Englishman had the misfortune of building his house on a much-coveted lot that adjoined Biddulph and was owned by the Canada Company. A small mob, led by a local man, then cut down the trees on his property so that they fell onto the man's house, "smashing it to pieces." The terrified Englishman fled the area, after which the leader of the gang erected a shanty on his property and lived there for a number of years until the Canada Company later evicted him from it.[21]

And the crimes continued. In 1856, the Grand Trunk Railway line (GTR) advertised that it was looking for bids from local contractors to extend the railway through the Biddulph area. This required it to pass through portions of several local farms in the process. Two such farms belonged to a farmer, Dennis Toohey, and his oldest son, John. Both father and son decided between themselves that they were the ones who should be awarded the contract. And it was a lucrative deal for them to secure, to be certain, as the GTR was willing to pay not only for the section of property the railway line ran through, but also an additional sum for any work the property owners performed in grading the track. The Toohey family let it be known that anyone who bid against them for this contract would be doing so at their peril, but their threat didn't intimidate tavern owner Andrew O'Keefe (the same Andrew O'Keefe whose tavern had been demolished by a Protestant mob after the 1857 election).

O'Keefe certainly was an attractive candidate; he had both the equipment and the horses that would be necessary to do the job, and his price seemed more agreeable to the GTR than the one tendered by the Tooheys. After due consideration, the railroad awarded the contract to O'Keefe. However, before he could begin work, the Tooheys took action: they set fire to O'Keefe's stable, which resulted in the deaths of seven of his workhorses and one of his stallions. Then the Tooheys set fire to his hotel. Fortunately, the fire was spotted in time and put out before the tavernkeeper lost everything. Unfortunately for the hotelier, the loss of his horses meant that O'Keefe no longer had the means necessary to perform the job, with the result being the GTR had no option but to award the Tooheys the contract. Members of the Toohey family were arrested on suspicion of starting the fire but, per the usual, nothing came of it.[22]

And then there was the case of a man named William Cohalan, who had an argument with his neighbour, Mike Cain. The argument intensified. Cain then attacked Cohalan and held him until Cain's son arrived on the scene and proceeded to beat Cohalan to death with a board. Cain the younger escaped; Mike Cain was tried but, as with the previous trials in the community, he, too, escaped conviction.[23]

Still another crime was committed, this time against a man named Mitchell, who had newly moved onto the Roman Line and brought with him a new threshing machine. Some of his Roman Catholic neighbours resented this asset and stole onto his property in the dark of night and broke his machine to pieces.[24] And there was poor Sarah Harcourt, who, in May 1861, was set upon by a man named William Mahon, who beat her skull in with an oak shillelagh and left her to die.[25]

It was within this environment of extreme violence the Donnelly boys were raised. Merciless retribution was seen as the solution to all disputes and, apparently, it could be perpetrated without any fear of reprisal from the local courts or the constabulary. It certainly would have taken more command than a single parent possessed to raise a family of pacifists in Biddulph Township. And, consequently, once James Donnelly had left the family home, his boys had one fewer set of eyes upon them to prevent their getting into trouble. The dark clouds descended upon the family as a matter of course.

O n August 11, 1857, a little more than a month after the coroner's inquest had wrapped on the death of Patrick Farrell, and while James Donnelly Sr. was still hiding out from the authorities, Jim Donnelly (now sixteen years of age) and his young brother John (age ten), together with a friend, James Atkinson,[26] got into an argument with a woman named Ann Robinson. All three boys would subsequently be accused of having hit the woman. Robinson was knocked to the ground, where Atkinson then tore the hat she was wearing from her head. The three boys were charged with assault and, in a surprising change of pace for the Huron Court system, all three perpetrators were found guilty and ordered to pay the court costs. In addition, the two Donnelly brothers were fined ten shillings each, while Atkinson, who was considered the aggressor in the affair, was fined one pound.[27] While certainly not the Donnelly boys' proudest moment, they were still babes in the woods with regard to their actions, at least compared with the level of violence that was transpiring all around them by other factions within their community.

While the Donnelly boys were trying to cope with the absence of their father, James Donnelly was facing his own issues in attempting to adjust to prison life within Kingston Penitentiary. Upon his admittance on August 6, 1858, his name had been exchanged for a number — he was now prisoner number 4615, and his quarters were confined to cell number twenty-one, located on the first tier of the east wing.[28] The cell that was to be his home for the next seven years was small, as were all cells in the penitentiary, measuring six feet, seven inches in height by twenty-nine inches in width, and eight feet in length. The inmates were issued two sets of clothes upon their arrival with their individual prison number stitched onto the fabric. When Donnelly arrived, he received what was referred to as the "summer uniform," consisting of waistcoat, jacket and trousers — all made of denim, the sleeves and legs of which were coloured black on one side and white on the other. When winter came, the prisoners exchanged their summer uniform for one made of wool to keep them warmer during their outside labours, the sleeves and legs of this attire being yellow and dark brown.[29]

Like all prisoners in Kingston, James Donnelly was assigned to forced labour while at the penitentiary, either in the prison's tailor shop, cabinet factory, shoe factory, limestone quarry or stone-cutting shop. It's also possible that he was assigned to the farm, particularly given his background, which would have required him to work from dawn to dusk clearing a plot of one hundred acres that was owned by the penitentiary.

It is clear from the punishment records that have survived from Kingston Penitentiary that James Donnelly's penchant for noncon-formity had accompanied him into the prison. On July 16, 1859, he was caught talking while working. As a consequence, his regular prison food was withheld, and he was provided only bread and water for three meals. On November 28, 1859, he repeated the offence and, when caught, complained about it. The punishment this time was to be given only bread and water for six of his meals, and his bedding and mattress were removed from his cell for two nights. On February 19, 1860, he was put back on bread and water for three more occasions because he didn't wear a clean shirt that had been left for him in his cell, and also because, in an effort to keep warm, he had made a vest for himself out of a blanket. On March 9, 1860, he took bread and meat from the dining hall with him; this saw him put back on bread and water as his nourishment for his next four meals. And then, five days later, the same punish-ment was reinstated as a result of him talking at the breakfast table on March 14, 1860.[30]

As James Donnelly struggled to walk the line within the peniten-tiary, Johannah Donnelly spent whatever spare time she could find creating (and circulating for signature) no fewer than three petitions, which she sent to the Ontario government in the hope of obtaining an early release for her husband.[31] Although her pleas would ulti-mately fall upon deaf ears, James and Johannah had nonetheless been deeply appreciative of the backing that their community had provided, both during the time when James had been hiding out from the authorities, and in providing signatures for all of Mrs. Donnelly's appeals for clemency on his behalf. As a way of repaying this support, James Donnelly decided that his family should give back to the community. In June 1860, while still in prison, he directed Johannah to section off the northeast corner of their fifty-acre property and gift it to the trustees of Biddulph School, Section Three. To make the matter legal, some consideration had to pass between the two parties, and so the Donnellys received five shillings in exchange for the property.[32] A school, or at least a small building that could be used as a school, had been erected some years previously, and sat on the perimeter of the Donnelly property. It was less than a stone's throw from the Donnelly home, and came to be called, simply, the "Donnelly School." All who attended the school knew each of the Donnelly family members by sight, and each of the Donnelly children would attend the institution.

Despite the support, James Donnelly wasn't getting out of prison anytime soon. Johannah continued to do what she could to ease James's time behind bars, even making the 276-mile journey from her home on the Roman Line to Kingston to visit with her husband on at least two occasions, as the penitentiary record book for January 4, 1861, recorded the following: "The wife of the convict James Donnelly again came to see him. . . . this second interview between them."[33]

With her three petitions having changed nothing, and perhaps now having learned first-hand of her husband's living conditions while at the penitentiary, Johannah commenced to write a fourth petition to the provincial government, this time imploring them to grant her husband a full pardon:

That your Petitioner's husband, James Donnelly, was unfortunately the cause of the death of one Patrick

Farrell in an affray which took place at a Logging
Bee in the Township of Biddulph in the year 1857,
for which he is now undergoing a term of Seven
years in prison in the Provincial Penitentiary; four
years of the said term being now nearly expired.

Your Petitioner has been left during that time
with a family of eight children who are mostly
helpless, and dependent upon your petitioner. Your
petitioner humbly prays that your Excellency will
be pleased to take her helpless condition into the
merciful consideration of her husband's case, and
that finding the offence was committed without
malice or premeditation, and in the heat of passion,
your Excellency will be graciously pleased to
extend the clemency of the Crown to the said James
Donnelly, by granting him a pardon.

And as in duty bound Your Petitioner will Ever Pray,
Judith Donnelly[34]

Despite the final petition being signed by many heavyweights
from within the community (a police magistrate, a financier, a county
sheriff, several Catholic pastors, a coroner, a treasurer, a millionaire,
the deputy chairman of the Quarter Session, a renowned doctor, the
Master of the Middlesex Chancery, a county registrar, the postmaster, a hotel owner, the mayor, a judge and director of an insurance
company, an archdeacon and a rector),[35] this petition, like the three
that preceded it, would ultimately be denied.[36] This undoubtedly
came as bad news to James, who was continuing to trip up in the eyes
of the authorities within the prison. On January 18, 1862, he made
the mistake of laughing and talking to a teamster in the prison yard
and was forced to substitute five meals with bread and water.[37] And
then from February 21 to March 2, 1863, he suffered contusions to

the point of requiring hospitalization, which may have been a result of a fight or, more likely, according to Kingston Penitentiary Museum curator David St. Onge, "a job-related injury."[38]

While James Donnelly Sr. lay nursing his wounds within the hospital of Kingston Penitentiary, back on the Roman Line the harsh reality of life in Biddulph Township continued to assert itself. In February 1863, William Ryan attacked John Carroll to the point of causing permanent injury.[39]

By 1864, trouble was once again laid upon the Donnelly family's doorstep when eighteen-year-old William, together with an older friend, Michael Sullivan (aged twenty-seven), was charged with stealing six sheepskins from Patrick Ryan, a neighbour on the Roman Line. As the stolen fleeces were subsequently hidden in a shed on the Donnelly farm, Ryan also pressed charges against Johannah for receiving stolen property. Both William Donnelly and Michael Sullivan pleaded not guilty to the charge of larceny, while Johannah simply did not show up at court, no doubt having far too much on her plate to devote an entire day to an exercise in criminal justice. A bench warrant was issued for Mrs. Donnelly, but no one attempted to serve it to her. The trials were then postponed until the next Assizes but, in the end, none of the three people charged ended up being tried.[40]

Michael Maher, the man who had purchased the southern fifty acres of what had once been the Donnelly property, was proving unable to keep up with the mortgages on his property. And this, combined with the knowledge that James Sr. would be coming home soon from the penitentiary, caused Maher to start thinking about his own self-preservation. He found his exit strategy in the person of forty-seven-year-old Michael Feeheley, who was willing to pay Maher $300 for the southern half of Concession 6, Lot 18,[41] which gave Maher a $100 profit over what he had originally paid for the land. With money now in his pocket, Michael Maher packed his family up and left for the United States.[42]

In the meantime, Johannah and her boys continued their hard work on the farm. According to a local newspaper account, "The farm at that time was but partially cleared, and by incessant work she was only able to keep the place in order and grow food to supply a small and comparatively numerous family. Thus, the early lives of the Donnelly boys were made up of hardships."[43]

Back in Kingston, James Donnelly Sr. stepped over the line yet again, when, on September 27, 1864, he got into a quarrel with other inmates. When the guards separated the disputants, James refused to return to work. He was punished by having his bed removed from his cell and being made to consume only bread and water for six meals.[44] This, the seventh time he had been punished in six years, apparently had the desired effect, as there exists no further record of James Donnelly Sr. requiring any more disciplinary action while in prison. Eleven months later, he would sit down to give his only interview, a liberation interview conducted shortly before his release, from which the following excerpts have been drawn:

What do you think is the greatest privation that prisoners are subjected to in the Penitentiary?
The confinement to the cells on Sundays.

Do you think that the fear of confinement in prison or in the Penitentiary is sufficient to deter from crime?
Cannot say, he never heard about the like before his misfortune, dreaded his God more than earthly punishment.

What kind of punishment is, in your opinion, most efficient in maintaining the discipline of the Institution?

Thinks the chain. [A punishment in which a heavy chain was locked around the waist of a prisoner, making it difficult for him to move around.]

Have you seen or heard prisoners manifest feelings of revenge against the Officers or others employed in this Institution?
He has heard the like and very wrongfully.

What effect does the presence of visitors produce on the prisoners?
It [the visit of penitentiary chaplain] often tried his feelings as well as those of other convicts.

Do the prisoners hold conversations among themselves, and where is the most convenient place for conversing without being discovered?
They do when they get the chance. Has never heard more talk in other places than in the Roman Catholic Chapel.

What has been the general cause of your misfortunes and what has been the immediate cause of the crime for which you have been sent to the Penitentiary?
Liquor and passion [anger]. For killing a man but [it was] merely the effect of passion.

Do you think that your imprisonment in the Penitentiary has been beneficial to you in a moral and religious point of view and that you are better qualified to earn a livelihood now than before you entered the Institution?

Not more so than [when] he came hence. Is not so well qualified as before he came here, being further advanced in years.[45]

Twelve days after this interview, on Friday, July 28, 1865, the doors of Kingston Penitentiary swung open and prisoner number 4615 stepped outside. It had been seven long years, but he was now a free man. James Donnelly was coming home.

CHAPTER FOUR

LOVE AND WAR

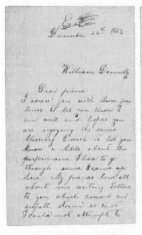

Letter from Margaret Thompson to William Donnelly,
Biddulph Township. December 24, 1873. (Library and Archives Canada)

In the four months leading up to James Donnelly's release from prison there had been a flurry of activity on the North American stage. President Abraham Lincoln had been assassinated, the American Civil War had ended, and Patrick Francis Healy had become the first African American to ever be awarded a Ph.D.[1] Eighteen sixty-five was turning out to be quite a year.

But it wasn't just the world that lay far beyond the thirty-two-foot-high stone walls of Kingston Penitentiary that had changed in the seven years since the Donnelly patriarch had been away. His more immediate world had also witnessed a major transformation. His sons had matured into young men during his absence: James

Jr. was now twenty-four, William was twenty-one, John was eighteen and Patrick was sixteen. His youngest sons, Michael, Robert and Thomas, who had been eight, five and four years of age when he had first been incarcerated, were now almost unrecognizable at ages fifteen, twelve and eleven, respectively. His daughter, Jennie, was now seven years old — a far cry from the babe in swaddling clothes she had been when he had last laid eyes upon her. Even his wife, Johannah, who was thirty-five when he went behind the wall, was now forty-two, but the stress of raising their eight children on her own, coupled with the demands of daily farming and household chores, had aged the poor woman considerably. And, of course, James Donnelly himself had changed. He was now eight months shy of turning fifty, an old man for farm work, which called for strength, energy and youth. His hair was now grey and, per his penitentiary exit interview, he felt less able to earn a living presently than he had when he first entered prison seven years previously, owing to being "further advanced in years." The concerns he held must have been compounded when it became obvious that some of his older sons, whom he had counted on assisting him with the labour on the farm going forward, were now expressing their intention to leave the family in order to head out and stake their own claim in the world.

This was particularly true of William, who had long dreamed of adventure south of the Canadian border. To be certain, the United States, with its impressive Constitution that proclaimed the sovereignty of an individual's right to the pursuit of his own happiness and the separation of church and state, must have seemed like the promised land to a young man coming into the prime years of his life. And then there were the tales of larger-than-life figures roaming the American territories that would only have added further fuel to the fires of the imagination of a such a young man. For example, in 1865, Wild Bill Hickok had engaged in the first ever fast-draw gunfight in the market square of Springfield, Missouri, where he gunned down Little Dave Tutt.[2] And the United States offered far more opportunity to earn money than did the Province of Canada,[3] which was still two years away from being considered a federation unto itself, and sixty-six years away from stepping out from under the rule of the British Empire. The United States, by comparison, had kicked out their British sovereigns the better part of nine decades previously, and each coast of the new nation radiated excitement, with seemingly boundless growth and burgeoning financial opportunities. Indeed, there wasn't much not to like from the perspective of a young Irishman who had spent all of his youth and young adulthood working farmers' fields in Biddulph County.

An incident that occurred less than a month after James Donnelly's return home may have hastened William's decision to head south. One of his childhood friends, Rhodace "Rhody" Kennedy, had suffered an accident on his family's farm, which resulted in his arm being cut off in a threshing machine.[4] William had accompanied the boy and his father, John Kennedy, by wagon to the establishment of a medical doctor in Lucan, William Quarry, who also served in the capacity of coroner for the town.[5] Temporarily leaving his son under the doctor's care at the physician's establishment (which happened to be the Biddulph Tavern in Sauble Hill), John Kennedy and William Donnelly started back toward the Roman Line. En route, the pair passed a small group of men and angry words were exchanged between the sixty-four-year-old Kennedy and thirty-four-year-old Patrick Hogan. The latter then attacked the older man, striking him three times and knocking him to the ground. By the time others came on the scene to intervene, old man Kennedy had suffered numerous facial bruises and a broken collarbone.[6] William Donnelly helped the old man up and assisted him back to his home, where John Kennedy convalesced for over a week.[7] The matter ultimately went before the local justices of the peace and Hogan was found guilty of common assault and sentenced to three months in jail.[8] However, when William Donnelly was subpoenaed to appear at the trial on October 9, 1865, it was entered into the record that he had already left for the United States.

Two years passed by uneventfully — and then 1867 arrived, bringing with it another wave of seismic change in North America. In the United States, Nebraska became the thirty-seventh U.S. state, and Alaska was purchased for seven and a quarter million dollars from Alexander II of Russia (which worked out to roughly two cents an acre). But the biggest news was reserved for Canada, which, as a result of the British North America Act, had finally received royal assent to form the Dominion of Canada. This served to unite the then–Province of Canada (Ontario and Quebec) with the maritime provinces of New Brunswick and Nova Scotia. It was the first step in making Canada, more or less, a country unto itself. And, to top things off, the man who had a direct hand in commuting James Donnelly's prison sentence, the former attorney general John A. Macdonald, had just been named the new Dominion's first-ever prime minister.

Concurrent with these international happenings came another round of changes within the Donnelly family. The family's oldest son, Jim, became the second Donnelly child to leave the family home. He had worked out an agreement with a man named Michael Devine, who had leased fifty acres of unfarmed land from the Canada Company, and who was willing to allow Jim to take over the property in exchange for $400 and Jim's pledge to clear the land and cultivate its soil.[9] Jim's intention was to farm the remainder of the land (the southern half of Lot 26, on Biddulph's Eleventh Concession),[10] in the hopes of making it prosperous enough that he would eventually be able to purchase the property outright. Later that same year, another family member, Pat Donnelly, also opted to move out of the family home in order to accept an apprentice-ship at a carriage works manufacturer in London, Ontario.[11] Pat would be the only Donnelly son who would never return home to live again. Not that the Donnelly homestead was ever wanting for residents; the family had a wide circle of friends, drawn ever wider by the fact that they never discriminated against people according to their class, or even their creed. While the Donnellys were Roman Catholics, they counted many Protestants among their friends, and made no distinction as to with whom they would be friends based on a person's religious beliefs.

Further, the Donnellys had a particular soft spot for outcasts — those who, through no fault of their own, had fallen several rungs down the ladder of social respectability. They had, evidently, taken in Bill Farrell, the young son of Patrick Farrell, the man whom James Donnelly had killed at the farming bee several years previously. Donnelly historian Orlo Miller indicated that this was largely an act of contrition on Johannah's part to atone for the sins of her husband in the matter.[12] This undoubtedly is true, and may well have been the counsel she received in the confessional, but it is also true that the Donnellys had a sincere desire to help people, especially those orphans or misfortunates of the township whom they perceived as being in need. An example of this would be Tommy Ryan, a local orphan, who would later be a factor in bringing the wrath of the parish priest down upon William Donnelly. Consequently, when the Donnellys learned that Sarah Farrell had remarried unsuccessfully and that she and her children had recently fallen on hard times, it isn't a stretch to believe that, the personal history of the two families aside, the Donnellys felt moved to do what they could to help ease her burden somewhat. And this included providing for Bill Farrell, who, in turn, would become quite loyal to his adopted family, and particularly to William Donnelly.[13]

In spring 1868, William Donnelly had returned from his three-year sojourn in the United States,[14] and taken up residence in London, Ontario. There, true to Donnelly family form, he was not that selective about the company he kept. Among those with whom he associated were John Graham and Margaret Morrison, a couple who ran a speakeasy out of the house they shared (according to one newspaper report, the pair were alcoholics[15]). One night while William was visiting with the couple, Graham brought forth a revolver he was particularly proud of and showed it to William. A wayfaring soldier who was also in the speakeasy that evening watched where Graham placed the pistol, and then surreptitiously put it under his coat and walked out with it. While Graham had been oblivious to the theft, William saw what had happened but chose not to say anything about it to Graham. Shortly thereafter, William once again left for the United States, and did not return to London until the fall.[16] Looking to further his education, he took his board in a house on Talbot Street, near where Graham and Morrison ran their speakeasy, and enrolled himself in an adult education school[17] where he studied law under attorney David Glass who, when William Donnelly wasn't available, would prove to be the go-to lawyer of choice for the various members of the Donnelly family in the years that followed.[18]

At some point during William's five-month absence from London, John Graham discovered that his revolver was missing. He remembered having once shown it to William Donnelly — and not much else. One day Graham spotted Donnelly walking along a street in London and ran out of his home to confront the young law student, demanding that he return the missing firearm.

"I don't have it," replied Donnelly.

"Well, who does, then?" asked Graham, his voice now rising.

"A soldier," replied Donnelly coldly.

"Well, *you're* going to get it back for me!" Graham demanded.

William Donnelly wasn't interested in having this conversation. "It is not my duty to restore it to you," he replied, and then continued on his way.[19]

Donnelly's attitude incensed Graham, but he was unwilling to try his muscle against him. Instead, he went to the London police station and had William Donnelly charged with larceny — this marked the second time in his life that William had been charged with this offence. However, the first time around he was a local lad of nineteen. He was now a well-travelled young man of twenty-four who had been studying the law and its loopholes. The prospect of going to court didn't intimidate him in the least.

The trial took place in the London Police Court on April 22, 1869. A local newspaper described the proceedings:

> The accused seemed fully to understand his position, severely pressed the witnesses with questions, and managed his case with an air of confidence which would do credit to many of the regular, but "single-barrelled," pleaders.
>
> His Worship — Your case is one which I think should be sent for trial.
>
> The accused — Yes, I was thinking of putting it back myself.
>
> His Worship — You are not obliged to plead before me, but what you say will be taken down, etc.
>
> The accused — I say "not guilty," of course. I know something about the affair, but I have nothing to do with it.
>
> His Worship — Mr. Clerk, take that down.
>
> The accused — He may take it down and welcome.
>
> His Worship committed him for trial, and refused bail for his appearance.[20]

William Donnelly's legal savvy had by now improved to such a point that he asked for (and received) an adjournment until September. The September trial was then postponed until October, at which point William Donnelly was acquitted.

At this point in his life, William Donnelly had grown into a solidly built, good-looking and intelligent young man who could speak up or down to any level, depending upon the requirement of the company in question. His club foot, which was bent downward and inward, meant that one leg was slightly shorter than the other, resulting in his having a slight hitch and shuffle to his gait.[21] His parents never had the money to spend on any medical treatment for his condition while he was growing up, with the result that he had simply learned to live with it and whatever limitations it brought to his daily life. The revulsion the affliction had brought to him from ignorant and cruel people throughout his life had the result of hardening him and sharpening his sense of humour.

It also caused him to invest his energy into other activities; rather than running and playing sports like most of his contemporaries, William read extensively and even learned to play the fiddle with some proficiency. Unlike his older brother Jim, or younger brothers Bob and Tom, who were hotheaded and often responded to any perceived offence with violence, William was far more cerebral, preferring to look long-term at things. This wasn't always the case — he was still a young man, after all — but as he grew older he preferred to defend himself using his brain rather than his brawn. After all, a punch to a man's face might hurt him for the moment, but a lawsuit would hurt a man's finances, which had the effect of wounding him for years. For this reason, William had spent considerable time in learning the intricacies of the law, and was completely at home in deciphering the formal and technical language contained in contracts and lawsuits. Given that most of his neighbours and contemporaries (and even members of his own family) were illiterate, his intellectual prowess drew a combination of secret admiration and resentment from many in his community. This was so indicated in the various nicknames that were bestowed upon the young man by those in Biddulph and London: "the lawyer" and "the plotter of the family" being but a few.[22] In time, William Donnelly became a young man with whom one didn't want to tangle unless one was willing to spend considerable time and money in defending oneself before various magistrates for the privilege. And while he had brains, he was also, like his brothers, a capable adversary physically who was not against using physical force and violence when he believed the situation called for it, particularly if any of his siblings were in a tough spot. Such attributes resulted in William being a magnet not only for many of the local girls his age, but also for many of the young men who looked to him as a leader of sorts; the type of fellow with whom they wanted to spend time, and whose lead they were willing to follow.

Two of William's closest companions during his youth were John Kennedy Jr. and his brother Rhody Kennedy, who lived three concession roads east of the Donnelly farm (near where Jim Donnelly was now dwelling). During their childhood, the boys were in and out of each other's houses constantly.

The brothers Donnelly and Kennedy were a dangerous mix, as during the time that William's legal savvy had seen him released on bail for the larceny charge, William and Jim Donnelly and two of the Kennedy brothers (Jack and Rhody) were charged with breaking into the Granton Post Office and stealing valuables that belonged to its postmaster. A report in the *St. Marys Argus* revealed the details:

> The usually quiet and orderly village of Granton
> has suddenly been infested with a gang of burglars,
> whose depredations have caused considerable
> alarm and excitement. On Wednesday evening or
> Thursday morning of last week the post office was
> broken into and pretty thoroughly ransacked. As the
> postmaster, Mr. Jamieson, deals in boots and shoes
> as well as taking charge of Her Majesty's mails in
> the village, the "swag" of the burglars comprised
> an extensive and miscellaneous assortment. Besides
> $20 in stamps, they also stole ten pairs of men's

calf-skin boots, seven pairs of women's prunella boots, as well as several pairs of other varieties. A lot of Canadian coppers kept in a box for change attracted their cupidity and were transferred to their felonious pockets. They magnanimously, however, left the box in the garden — empty of course. The suspicions are that there were two persons engaged in this nefarious business, as their tracks were plainly visible near the back window by which they effected their entrance. Three persons, two of whom are named Donnelly, the third Kennedy,[23] were apprehended next morning and brought before a magistrate, on the ground that they were prowling around the village all that night. They were discharged, however, for what reasons it is not clearly understood. The villagers loudly complain that the magistrate mismanaged the case, and it is even reported that he was not in a fit condition to sit on the bench.[24]

Having successfully ducked a conviction in the matter, Jim Donnelly decided it might be in his best interests to leave town for a while and set off for America, where it was said he worked in the lumber camps of Michigan, and eventually purchased an eighty-acre farm near Caseville.[25] During his absence, his brothers Mike, Bob and Tom put in what spare time they had working Jim's farm and tried their best to keep the buildings in decent shape.[26] William, in the meanwhile, had moved back into the family farm-house to help with the farm, becoming his parents' formal tenant and the principal caretaker of the family's fifty acres.[27] And, under William's guidance, and with the remaining family members pulling together, the Donnelly farm prospered.[28]

E ver since his release from prison James Donnelly Sr. had done his best to mind his own business. He got along with his fellow Roman Catholic neighbours, but he irked them as well by not toeing the factional line when it came to not associating with Protestants. He would, for example, drink in Orange taverns and shop in Protestant supply stores — and had even contributed money to the building of the Anglican Church in Biddulph.[29]

And then came the day when a logging bee was held at O'Keefe's farm in Biddulph. As O'Keefe was himself a member of the Roman Catholic faction, the neighbours who came to his farm to offer assistance that day were of the same faith, including James Donnelly Sr. Throughout the day, the men pushed and pulled, prying large stumps from the earth in an effort to rid the property of any impediments to the creation of gardens and fields.

At some point during the day two Protestant boys, Thomas and William Armitage, arrived at O'Keefe's to lend a hand. They were the sons of a local Protestant farmer and Lucan shopkeeper, John Armitage, and their presence at the farm did not meet with any disapproval initially, as the logging bee went on into the late afternoon without incident. As was customary, food was brought out to the men, along with jugs of whiskey, both of which served to take the edge off a day of demanding physical activity. At this point, William Armitage entered the O'Keefe farmhouse, perhaps to retrieve some more liquid refreshment for the men. Inside the farmhouse had gathered the wives of the men who were working outside. To his surprise, William Armitage discovered that the women all seemed keenly interested in everything he had to say and did what they could to keep him engaged in conversation inside the farmhouse. Suddenly he heard a loud noise coming from outside — the sounds of men running, thumping and yelling. William looked out the kitchen window and was horrified to see that his brother Thomas was being savagely beaten by several men. As he headed for the door the women moved en masse to block his way.

Hearing his poor brother's screams, William found a shillelagh in the house and threatened to strike anyone who barred his way. He burst through the front door and ran toward his brother. By this point, his brother Thomas was on the ground. Several men were kicking and punching him, while another group of men had gathered 'round to cheer them on. Suddenly James Donnelly Sr. broke through the crowd, holding in his hands a huge balk of wood. "I'll brain anyone who dares to lay as much as a little finger on either of the Armitage boys!" he yelled.

The men immediately stopped their assault of the boy and the circle of men slowly and grudgingly gave way, leaving space for Donnelly to come through and pull Thomas Armitage from the ground. According to one of the locals, "so much was Donnelly's word feared, they were allowed to depart unharmed."[30] James Donnelly's standing up to the mob may have earned him the undying respect of John Armitage and his family for the remainder of their lives, but it also caused several of those within his Roman Catholic faction to question his loyalty. His actions that day had effectively marked him as a potential outsider to this group — and the group was not pleased. Matters would worsen between the Donnellys and this faction over the years that followed, but this incident may have been the first fissure to appear between his family and the Roman Catholic community. It was decided that a message needed to be sent to the Donnelly patriarch.

In early December 1870, the Donnelly barn went up in flames.[31] This incendiary message was clear: move out of the community . . . or else. A similar threat had been made to a local farmer, Robert Owens, three years previously, when the same faction had burned down his barn. Robert Owens got the message and moved his family out of Biddulph immediately.[32] But Robert Owens wasn't James Donnelly. To Donnelly, his religious allegiance was never at issue — he was a Roman Catholic, who did his best to live by the Golden Rule revealed in Matthew 7:12, which states, "Therefore, all things whatsoever ye would that men should do to you, do ye even so to them: for this is the law and the prophets."

This was the Donnelly philosophy of life expressed in a sentence, and it would be passed down from the father and mother to their sons, who, over time, were quite willing to repay loyalty with loyalty, and kindness with kindness, but who also would repay violence with violence if that was what was offered them. Nobody was going to tell the family what to do or order them off their land. The Donnellys dug in. In the years to come their attitude would prove a costly one. For the moment, the Donnellys had enough manpower to stand their ground. They would use the insurance money they received from the fire to build a new house on their property, ostensibly spitting on the boots of those who had threatened them.

On February 2, 1871, John Donnelly, age twenty-four, decided to make a statement of his own. He had become engaged to Francis Dereham, the daughter of a couple who lived just five farms north of the Donnelly home. But rather than being married within St. Patrick's Church, the epicentre of the Roman Catholic faction that had burned his family's barn, John and his bride-to-be had opted to elope.[33] This was not well received — either by the church or by the Donnellys. Consequently, it was a rather shamefaced John and Francis who returned a week later to be married again, this time by a Catholic priest within St. Patrick's Church in Biddulph.[34] John's marriage proved to be short-lived, however, as shortly after John took over a pub in Lucan, problems occurred within the marriage (of what nature is unclear). And not long afterward, John decided to head off (like his brothers before him) to the United States.[35] His abandoned bride returned to her parents and eventually remarried, this time to a man named Harry Heard. William Donnelly helped Francis by managing the pub for a period of time during John's absence.[36]

In the 1800s, particularly in rural areas such as Biddulph, there existed no formal judges or police, at least not as we envision such occupations and organizations today. The justices of the peace, or magistrates, were the adjudicators, and were typically selected from among the more affluent landowners and/or businessmen in the area, whereas the constables (or sheriffs where applicable) were typically drawn from a pool of local artisans, small businessmen, tradesmen and farmers. The constables were responsible, once appointed, for serving warrants, attending court and escorting prisoners on a fee-for-service basis.[37] Such men were appointed to their positions by the local governing bodies, which made their legal duties susceptible to influence by various political factions. Indeed, according to author and Donnelly historian James C. Reaney, "In the days of oral voting, each voter was asked to swear allegiance to the Queen: while a great number of the Irish Catholic voters refused to do so, they were still allowed to vote. Moreover, the Irish Catholics in Biddulph wanted their own laws, and even their own constable, and their own magistrates."[38] Over the years they would eventually have these wants granted, which meant that people who had fallen out of favour with the ruling group could be arrested by the group's constables and tried by the group's magistrates. Consequently, once the Donnelly family fell out of favour, various members of the family began to be arrested for crimes they did not commit. Consider the case of Robert Orme, who, it was reported, had suffered a burglary:

> On Friday night last . . . the house of Robt. B. Orme, of Lucan, was entered by a burglar, who made off with a cash box containing the sum of $418. . . .
> The evidence of Orme was then taken, and was in substance as follows: That on the night in question he retired to bed, leaving a lamp burning on a chair at the head of his bed, and the cash-box, with $418 in it, beside it. At a late hour of the night he was aroused

from sleep by hearing a noise, as if made by the box
striking against the door. Thinking it was his brother
who made the noise, he called out to him by name,
but received no answer. He called a second time, and
still receiving no answer, he realized the nature of
the affairs, and at once sprang out of bed, seized his
pantaloons, and made after the burglar, who was not
more than twenty of thirty feet from him when he
reached the door. He gave hot chase, but the burglar
proved the fleetest runner, and far outstripped him
in the race, disappearing in the darkness. After
thinking the matter over he fancied the man might
have made for the station, to leave by the next train,
and in company with a friend, went in the that
direction to secure his detection if possible. Near
the station is a granary, raised from the ground, and
it occurred to Orme that the pursued man might
be hiding under it. So he determined to explore the
place, and, sure enough, had scarcely entered it before
a person started up and tried to make his way out.
In the hurry of his exit, the box again clinked against
a post or what other obstacle, and Orme could
distinctly hear the money rattle within. He attempted
to rush forward, but just then his forehead came in
contact with a beam, and in the concussion he was
almost stunned. The object of his pursuit escaped.[39]

The person Orme believed he saw in his room that night was
Tom Gray, a bartender at a local hotel. However, as Gray had been
observed earlier on the day of the crime in the company of his friend,
William Donnelly, it didn't take much prodding to have Donnelly
arrested as well.[40] As there was no evidence against him, however,
William Donnelly would ultimately be discharged, and when Gray

appeared at his trial on September 15, 1871, a grand jury decided that it wasn't possible for Orme to have been able to make a positive identification of the burglar in the dark of night, and so Gray was acquitted as well. Still, the Donnelly name had just been attached (however incorrectly) to another crime, and this had the effect of keeping the wheels of public opinion turning against the family.

The Donnellys, it must be said — perhaps as a result of seeing how the law was often misused by the powerful against innocents — would occasionally go out of their way to wryly undermine the institution so relied upon by those in authority who sought to buttress their power. This was particularly the case in the town of Lucan, where the affluent Stanley brothers held sway. A story that has been passed down with a large measure of amusement throughout the many generations of the McIlhargey family of Biddulph provides an example:

> At one time in Biddulph a man by the name of
> Kurb Farrell was wanted by the police on many
> charges. As he was a friend of the Donnelly
> family, they had [been protecting] him for some
> time. They had a concealed room above the kitchen
> that was reached through a trapdoor in the ceiling,
> which was almost invisible. After some time, it
> was reported that Bill Donnelly was going to be
> married. A week or so later a double carriage
> drove in to Lucan and in it were Bill Donnelly and
> his supposed bride (quite tall and with a heavy
> veil concealing her face) and a man and girl who
> were supposed to have been the groomsman and
> bridesmaid. Bill and his groomsman went into the
> hotel and treated everyone there, and then Bill and
> his supposed bride took the train for Detroit on
> their honeymoon. In a few days, Bill was back in

Lucan again and one of the first men he met was Barney Stanley, who was one of the men who had pressed charges against Kurb Farrell. Barney shook hands with Bill and asked him where his wife was.

"Oh," Bill said, "I can't be bothered supporting a wife. I left her in the States."

"Bill! That was Kurb Farrell you took away with you!"

"Now Barney, you don't think *I'd* do a thing like that, do you?" said Bill. It was, indeed, Kurb Farrell who had gone away with Bill and he got away free from all the charges.[41]

A real marriage took place on October 6, 1871, when twenty-two-year-old Patrick Donnelly wed Mary Ryan, a young lady whom he had been courting in London. Although both the bride and groom had been raised Roman Catholic, they were united in marriage within the Holy Trinity Church of England in Lucan.[42] This act removed any shadow of doubt from the minds of the Biddulph Roman Catholic faction about whether their attitude toward the Donnelly family had been warranted. To them, it was evident the Donnellys had drawn a line in the sand of their own choosing. On one side of it stood the great religious tradition of Roman Catholicism, and the faction that had carried it with them from Ireland across the ocean to be transplanted onto Canadian soil. It was this faction that had backed the Donnellys in their native Ireland and had stood with them again when the family made the three-thousand-mile journey across the ocean to the new world. And it had been this faction that willingly signed the petitions Johannah had circulated to commute her husband's sentence from manslaughter to seven years in prison, and who had hidden James Donnelly Sr. when he was running from the law after killing Patrick Farrell. And on the other side of this line stood the

Donnellys themselves, who in the eyes of this faction, had now essentially told them all to go fuck themselves.

As mentioned, William Donnelly was a man who typically thought matters through long-term before choosing to act. This character trait escaped him, however, in the matter of his affection for young Margaret Thompson.

Just to the north of the Donnelly homestead sat a plot of land that had been farmed since 1868 by a young man named William Thompson Jr. His father, William Sr., lived in McGillivray Township, eighteen miles to the west. At some point the senior Thompson had decided that, while his son was a fair enough farmer, his domestic skills left a fair bit to be desired. As a consequence, the patriarch had decided to send William's younger sister, Margaret, to her brother's farm on the Roman Line to assist him in taking care of the household. Margaret was eighteen years old, and hadn't been at her brother's farm long before she caught the eye of William Donnelly. After a few neighbourly discussions, the girl found herself strangely attracted to the young man, with his air of self-assuredness and keen sense of humour. They began to see each other, clandestinely at first, as, according to Donnelly historian Orlo Miller, the girl's father was virulently anti-Donnelly: "From all the available evidence, Thompson had a deep and implacable hatred of the Donnelly family."[43]

Perhaps the father's antipathy was understandable; after all, some of the Donnelly boys had already been charged with various crimes and, of course, William's father had been convicted of manslaughter. This certainly would not have been the family of first choice with which any father would select for his daughter to build a future. William Thompson Sr. quickly made his feelings about the budding relationship clear to Margaret, and, to his mind at least, his word on the matter was final. Indeed, his word was respected — initially, at least — as the couple would not be seen together in public from that day forward. However, the pair had continued to communicate their affection for one another through letter writing. Some of these letters have survived, but very few. None have survived from William Donnelly, as Margaret had taken to burning his missives immediately after reading them in an effort to conceal from her father any evidence that their relationship was ongoing. The physical separation from Margaret weighed heavily on William Donnelly, and he requested that she send him her photograph, which she did, along with the following lines:

April 22, 1873

Dear William,
    I was a long time about getting this picture
for you. You can keep it now, in hopes you think
as much of me as I do of you. At the beginning
of another term of our future summer, which we
can look back upon with pleasure, I desire to bear
testimony to the faithfulness with which you have
laboured for my benefit, and the kindness which you
have ever shown toward me.

Yours Truly,
Maggie Thompson[44]

In time, the idea of marriage began to percolate through the couple's minds. However, a marriage and future life together would cost money, a commodity that was in short supply in the Donnelly household. In an effort to augment the little money brought in from the family farm (which was largely spoken for in advance in order to ensure the upkeep of the property and to look after his parents' needs), William had decided to accept a job offer to drive a stagecoach for a friend of the family named Hugh McPhee. Driving a stage was an occupation to which William's club foot served no impediment, and his easygoing charm and professionalism instantly made him a popular driver among McPhee's patrons.[45] McPhee ran the Revere House Hotel in Lucan, and his stagecoach route extended from his hotel to the village of Exeter, a distance of some twelve and a quarter miles. McPhee had been so impressed with William's professionalism on the job that he soon inquired if any of William's brothers might be interested in driving for him. Not long afterwards Mike Donnelly was also hired on as a driver for the McPhee stagecoach line.[46]

The stagecoach business was a competitive one, as there were three other stage lines that made daily travels. All three travelled the Exeter-to-Lucan route, but two of them extended their route farther south into the city of London.[47] These latter two stage services were run independently by entrepreneurs Ted Crawley and John Hawkshaw.[48] In March 1872, however, Hawkshaw and Crawley opted to consolidate their stagecoach businesses in order to reduce competition and maximize profits, which then saw their stages competing for business against only McPhee's smaller stage line. Seven months later, Crawley sold his interest in the stagecoach line to his partner, John Hawkshaw.[49] As McPhee's stage ran only from Lucan to Exeter, while Hawkshaw's ran from Exeter all the way to London, Hawkshaw's was far and away the more profitable of the two remaining conveyance services. There was also a mail stage that made one run daily from London to Exeter, but as it did not deliver passengers, it was not in competition against any of the other stage lines.

While the consolidation of the two stage lines had served to reduce competition, the competition that remained became incredibly fierce. High-speed races took place between the McPhee and Hawkshaw stage services in an effort to pick up passengers before the rival stage could get to them. Fares were dropped to attract more patrons, and drivers who could (and were willing to) fight drivers from the competition were paid double the amount offered to drivers who were of a less pugnacious disposition.[50] Of course the Donnelly brothers, being young and full of testosterone, revelled in the rivalry. But at age thirty-one, Hugh McPhee wasn't interested in combat on the roadways and decided that his little stagecoach business wasn't making the kind of money that justified his degree of involvement and capital expenditure. He soon made it known that he would be willing to sell off his stages and horses if the price was right. Sensing an opportunity to become a business owner, and also knowing that higher profits could be made if McPhee's stage route could be extended into London, William Donnelly offered to buy the business from McPhee. McPhee accepted William's offer, and on May 23, 1873, William Donnelly, with the help of loans from his father and family friend and neighbour Patrick Whalen,[51] found himself the proud owner of the newly christened Donnelly Stagecoach Line. With his brother Mike agreeing to stay on as driver, William purchased new equipment and then aggressively pursued, and was ultimately awarded, the mail service contract to carry the mail from Crediton to Centralia. The contract didn't provide a lot of money, but it was enough to clear his feet of a good portion of the debt he owed to his father and Whalen. And the Donnelly stage service proved to be very popular with its patrons, as one passenger recalled: "It was often remarked that the Donnellys provided a far better service than their opposition, and you could always count on reaching your destination on time."[52]

Now the owner of a modest but growing business, and with money in his pocket, William Donnelly felt the time was right to revisit the subject of marriage with Margaret Thompson. He proposed to her in one of his letters, which prompted the following reply:

Dear friend,

I now wish to inform you that I have made up my mind to accept your kind offer, as there is no person in this world I sincerely love but you. This is my first and only secret, so I hope you will let no person know about it. But I cannot mention any certain time yet.

You can acquaint my parents about it any time you wish after the first of November next. Any time it is convenient to you will please me if it's in five years after the time mentioned. If it does not suit you to wait so long, you can let me know about it, and I will make it all right. Do not think that I would say you are soft for writing so often, for there is nothing would give me greater pleasure than to hear from you, but no matter now. I think soft turns is very scarce about you. If you have ever heard anything of the kind after me, I hope you will not attribute it to a desire on my part to give you pain, but regard it as thoughtless behaviour of youth; and that the blessing of God may ever attend it the sincere wish of your affectionate friend.

Margaret Thompson[53]

It must be remembered that at this point in Canadian history many marriages in rural communities were often arranged in advance by the parents of the prospective bride and groom for either economic or social advancement. William Donnelly was having none of that. He was making his own advancement economically with his new stage line, and being a business owner brought with it its own degree of social respectability. Consequently, his confidence was high when he decided it was time to approach William Thompson Sr. to request the hand of his daughter in marriage.

But it was not to be. Some of Margaret's friends, having heard of the couple's intentions, took it upon themselves to inform her father of the couple's plans.[54] William Thompson Sr. was beside himself with rage that his daughter had disobeyed his command to end her relationship with William Donnelly, and he was galled further still to learn that William Donnelly had the audacity to believe that he was now good enough to marry her. "I would rather see her going to her grave," he raged, "than she should have my consent to marry William Donnelly!"[55]

Seeing as how his word hadn't served as a sufficient deterrent before, William Thompson Sr. now decided that it was time for action. He promptly picked up Margaret from his son's Roman Line farm and whisked her back to the family home in McGillivray. There, her parents would be in a position to watch over their daughter's every move, and thus make certain that no contact could take place — either in person or via letters — between Margaret and William.

While William's intentions in his pursuit of Margaret Thompson were being thwarted, his younger brother Bob was encountering no such problems in the relationship department. Bob Donnelly was handsome and dangerous, a combination that had proven to be veritable catnip to the available women in Biddulph County (and later to the women in Glencoe County as well). Considered by some to be the best-looking of the Donnelly boys, Bob wore the most expensive clothing he could afford, and had a keen if mischievous sense of humour. He had been courting a young lady named Annie Currie, and on December 23, 1873, the couple were married in St. Patrick's Church. He and his new bride then moved to dwell in her hometown of Glencoe, in Ekfrid Township.[56]

Margaret Thompson, meanwhile, had grown rebellious under her parents' stern surveillance. She no doubt had heard of Bob Donnelly's marriage taking place on December 23, and, in an unguarded moment the very next day, Christmas Eve of 1873, Margaret dashed off an appeal to her beloved suitor, imploring him to take action:

December 24th 1873

Dear friend,

I wish to let you know a little about the performance I had to go through since I came up here. My friends heard all about me writing letters to you, which caused an awful storm so that I could not attempt to ask to go anywhere and, on that account, you will please excuse me for not writing to you.

Dear William, I would rather be in the grave than home at present, for the way my people abused me on your account hinders me of ever forgiving them.

I will never have anything like a chance of fulfilling my promise of marriage with you except you come and take me away by force. And if you think as much of me now as you did always, I trust you will relieve me before long. And if not, you will please send me my letters to Offa P.O. and I will try to put up with all. I burnt your letters when they commenced to abuse me about you, for they would surely get them if I did not do something with them.

Excuse my bad writing for I am in an awful hurry, as it is in the office I am writing it.

No more at present from your loving friend,
Margaret Thompson[57]

William Donnelly didn't need to be asked twice to come and rescue Margaret. But he couldn't just show up at William Thompson Sr.'s house and announce that he was there to take his daughter away — her father would shoot him before the words had left his mouth. And nothing good could come from his going there with a revolver of his own, as two adversaries with guns would probably end up using them and Margaret could get hit in the crossfire. William had to liberate Margaret from her parental prison, certainly, but how? This was not a legal brief that he had to figure out, or some adversary facing him in a court of law — this was a situation that required immediate action, and action of a sort in which consequences would be certain to follow.

After a while a thought came to him: in driving stage for McPhee part of his job had been to deliver subpoenas on behalf of the sheriff of Middlesex County.[58] In all instances, once the occupant learned that the law was outside of his or her door, the door would be opened, the subpoena would be served, and he would be on his way. Perhaps if the same procedure were enacted at William Thompson Sr.'s front door, Thompson might allow a small group of people to actually enter his home. Once inside they could grab Margaret and deliver her to safety — and to William Donnelly. The more he thought it over, the better the idea appeared. William decided that he would bring a small number of friends in on the venture. Their pretense for knocking on William Thompson Sr.'s door would be that they were county constables in search of stolen property. As it was winter, all of the group would be wearing mufflers and heavy jackets in order to break the cold. And if those mufflers were pulled up over their faces, it would conceal the men's true identities from Thompson. No harm had to come to anybody. For the plan to be put into action, all that was required was a sleigh and horses, which William already had, and some friends to serve as his accomplices, and he had those also.

Twenty-nine-year-old William pressed into service his younger brothers Mike (age twenty-three) and Tom (nineteen), along with friends and followers William Atkinson (a twenty-three-year-old blacksmith from Lucan), the cousins Daniel (forty-four) and James Keefe (twenty-one), Robert Corcoran (twenty-six) and Patrick Quigley (forty-one). In looking at the various ages of the posse members that William Donnelly had thrown together, we note that both Atkinson and Daniel Keefe were considerably older than William, and married men as well. But such was William Donnelly's appeal that they placed themselves willingly at his service.[59]

William had been specific about how the rescue plan should be implemented. He would drive the sleigh of "constables" to William Thompson Sr.'s house. The identity of his co-conspirators would be concealed by their pulling their mufflers up over their faces. The group would then exit the sleigh and proceed to the front door, while William remained behind in the sleigh. This would be done for two reasons: first, his gait as a result of his club foot would be a giveaway as to his identity; and, second, he was the most seasoned driver of the group, and, thus, needed to be at the reins in order for the gang to make a speedy getaway. His masked companions would knock loudly on the front door of the Thompson home, demanding admittance on behalf of the law. When Thompson opened the door, they would announce they had a warrant for a horse thief and needed to search his premises. This would give them entrance to the house. At this point they would search through all the rooms in the establishment, one of which was sure to contain Margaret. Once she had been located, the group would make a beeline out the front door to where William was waiting in the sleigh and they would all speed off back to Lucan.

What they would do at this point had not yet been broached. William would figure it out on the way back. With the plan and the accomplices now set, the only thing that remained was to pick a day to implement the plan. It was decided that the evening of January 9 would work best, and, when that day arrived, and at the agreed-upon hour, eight men climbed into a sleigh in Lucan and made their way nine and a half miles southeast to McGillivray, and the farmhouse of William Thompson Sr. They arrived a little before 8:30 p.m.[60] Per the plan, the men climbed out from the sleigh and pulled their mufflers up over their faces. They then walked to the front door and rapped loudly upon it.

"Open up in the name of the Queen!" one of them bellowed.[61] Michael Thompson, the eighteen-year-old son of William Thompson Sr., came to the door, and asked the masked men what they wanted.

"We're looking for a horse thief," one of them stated from behind his muffler, "let us in!"

Michael opened the door and allowed them in. At this point, his father entered the front room of the farmhouse to see what the commotion was about. "Get some chairs, boy!" William Sr. said to his son, and then bade the masked men to sit down. This had not been part of the plan. Nevertheless, the men did what they were told. William Thompson Sr. then pulled up a chair and sat down in front of them. During the act of sitting down, one of the mufflers had slipped off the face of Mike Donnelly.[62] The old man knew a Donnelly when he saw one, and immediately the jig was up. Still, he decided to play along with their ruse and, in all likelihood, might well have been expecting it. After all, he had already moved Margaret out of his house and into the Biddulph farmhouse of his son-in-law, James Toohey,[63] earlier that week. One of the masked men decided that it was time to assume control of the room. His first question was a non sequitur, however: "Have you got anything to eat?"

An awkward silence fell upon the room. The speaker's companions looked at him with silent disapproval — what did this have to do with rescuing Margaret Thompson?

"There are no women around," Thompson replied, "but there's a tavern about a mile away from here."

Another within the gang now found his voice. "Can I have an overcoat?"

The old man raised an eyebrow at the question. "I have scarcely enough to cover myself without giving you clothing."

Outside in the sleigh, meanwhile, William Donnelly was wondering what was causing the delay. His plan had called for the boys to be in and out by now.

Back inside, the requests from the group were becoming more bizarre: "Can we stay here tonight?"

"No!" replied a by now exasperated Thompson. "What exactly is it you're here for again?" The old man was now pretty sure that he recognized two of the other "constables" that were seated in front of him as being Tom Donnelly and Daniel Keefe.[64]

Mike Donnelly spoke up: "We have a warrant for a horse thief."

"Show it to me," challenged Thompson.

The men looked at each other again; an expression of "what now?" was revealed by their widening eyes. This had gone on long enough. The men stood up, en masse, and began searching throughout the various rooms in the house. It quickly became evident that Margaret Thompson was not there.

William Thompson Sr. was now on his feet.

"It's not a horse thief but my daughter you're searching for!" he yelled at them, a note of triumph in his voice.

The men did not reply. After inspecting the premises, the men turned and began to exit the house. William Thompson Sr. and his son watched them depart from the doorway.[65] They continued watching as the men climbed back into their sleigh, and, after exchanging a few words with the driver, sped off from the Thompson property. The old man was now certain that William Donnelly was aboard that sleigh. Once the sleigh was well down the road, William Thompson Sr. bolted from his house and hotfooted it south along the concession road toward the home of his nearest neighbour, the widow Ellen Fogarty. Looking over his shoulder, William Donnelly spotted Margaret's father running from his house and assumed that Thompson was headed to where his beloved was being hidden. He now turned his sleigh around and snapped on the reins to get his team running at a full gallop to Fogarty's house.

When the old man saw the sleigh barrelling down on him he started to panic. He quickened his pace until, finally, he was running as fast as he could toward Ellen Fogarty's house. He yelled out Ellen's name, hoping to alert somebody — anybody — to his predicament. In short order William's sleigh caught up to him and several men leapt from the conveyance to overtake Thompson just as he was approaching the front door to the widow's home. One of the men grabbed his arms, while another covered his mouth to prevent him from shouting. However, the older man broke free and, staggering toward Fogarty's front door, yelled: "Bring me an axe!"

Suddenly two shots rang out. One of Donnelly's men had evidently brought a gun with him that evening. The bullets may have been warning shots to back off the old man, but there was no stopping William Thompson Sr. now. He dashed into Fogarty's house and turned to secure the front door,[66] but before he could do so several of Donnelly's men pushed their way inside. One of the men grabbed Thompson while another took hold of the startled widow Fogarty, who had made it almost to the front door when her neighbour had come crashing in. William Donnelly now entered the house and, along with the rest of his men, began searching the rooms looking for Margaret Thompson. Finding nothing, they returned to face their captives in the front room. Ellen Fogarty was both scared and indignant. "What do you want?" she demanded of William Donnelly, who clearly was the leader of the group. Turning to Thompson, William said, "We want your daughter and we'll have her wherever she is." The old man was under no delusions about who was standing in front of him right now. In a fit of pique, he turned to William Donnelly and exclaimed, "That, Donnelly, you will never get!" Almost before he had finished his statement, one of the men from the group (whom Thompson later believed to be Daniel Keefe) stepped forward and punched Thompson square in the face ("the old man got a box in the ear," Fogarty would later recall) with the predictable result that the older man fell to the floor, a cut opening above his left eye. Recognizing that Margaret Thompson was not at the Fogarty home, the men were left with no choice but to depart without their prize. It was a long ride back to Lucan that night.

William Donnelly was despondent; not only had the rescue attempt of Margaret been a disaster, but his cover during the caper had clearly been blown. He knew another lawsuit would soon be heading his way as a result of his group's interaction with William Thompson Sr. that evening. And Margaret was still out there, somewhere, wanting desperately to be rescued. What would her father do to her now after what had just happened?

The group discussed options for several hours in Lucan, and then decided that there was one more Thompson residence that warranted investigation. Perhaps Margaret had been hidden at William Thompson Jr.'s house back on the Roman Line. It was an option worth exploring. Back into the sleigh went the men and travelled the three and a half miles northeast through the cold to the farm of William Thompson Jr. The young man, understandably, was both surprised and frightened when he opened his front door at 4 a.m. and in walked the eight men. They proceeded to search his house, and then his barn and outbuildings and, once again finding nothing, they retired to their sleigh and returned to Lucan.

The next evening William Donnelly and Daniel Keefe were walking along Lucan's Main Street when they spotted William Thompson Jr. in town. Donnelly called out to Thompson, saying, "I want to speak with you!" Thompson crossed the street to where Donnelly and Keefe were standing. William Donnelly made it clear to the young man that he wanted to know Margaret's whereabouts, and that he wasn't going to stop looking for her. According to Thompson, "He told me he had been at my father's and also at my place last night, and stated he would go there again . . ."[67]

It must be remembered that at this point in time, neither William Thompson Jr. nor Sr. knew anything about Margaret's letter to William in which she'd beseeched him to come and rescue her from her family. Consequently, the Thompsons were justifiably irate that the Donnelly brothers, in concert with a band of strangers, would invade their homes in the dead of night with the intention of abducting a member of their family. William Thompson Jr. then told William Donnelly exactly what he thought of him, and he didn't pull any verbal punches. That he would do so face-to-face with William Donnelly, and in the presence of Daniel Keefe, showed that his anger had superseded his better judgement. For while all the Donnelly boys were *capable* of violence, Daniel Keefe *was* violent. In short, he was a very dangerous and unstable person, particularly after drinking, and a man who had already served six months in Kingston Penitentiary for stabbing a man two years previously.[68] Fortunately, none of the parties took the matter any further that evening.

Throughout the weekend William Donnelly ruminated over the events that had transpired, and then, on Monday, January 12, still wanting to do right by Margaret, he drafted a pointed letter to her father:

> Mr. W. Thompson,
> Dear Sir,
> I address you at present in a more polite manner than that which you received on Friday night, of which I am the occasion. To make matters a little plain to you, I wish to let you know that I was in the crowd myself, and my sole business was to have satisfaction for some of your mean, low talk to your daughter that never deserved it — at least she never deserved it on my account. And now, Dear Sir, I want you to understand that I will have my revenge if it cost the lives of both families, which I am sure it will not, for I can get crowd enough in almost any town to carry out my design without any trouble, except a little law from you, but I do not care for that, as I have plenty of money to pay my way through all.

Dear Sir, in the first place I will show you how you were wrong in saying that there was letters passing from your daughter to me, as I defy her to say that anything of the kind ever happened; and secondly you were wrong in saying that I was a son of a bitch; and that you had sons could back you up in saying so. As far as your sons are concerned, there is one of them I would forever wish to be in friends with. But any time you feel inclined to have them or Mr. Toohey try their muscle, you will please drop a line to me, or some of your humble servants, and we will try and accommodate you. But, my dear sir, my opinion is that in all the friends that hang around you, either by birth or marriage, there is but two has got a principle — at present I will not mention names, but will simply say you are not one of them. For the long length of time your daughter was in Biddulph, I defy her or anyone else to say there was one word of marriage passed between us, and for that reason I would like to know what you abused her for and talked of me in the manner you have done, which a letter that I have in my possession will plainly show. Dear friend, I [hope] you will be prepared to receive me and my Adventurers before long again, and if you should succeed, as you say you will, in sending that crowd to Kingston, I have another ready to follow the same track until the job is completed. And, old friend, I want it impressed on your mind that if the business must be done on the way to church, I can get any amount of men to do it, so you may just as well stop getting yourself into trouble first or last. Your son William used some talk lately I shall never forget, and if he wants to dwell in peace on the Roman Line you had better tell him to be a little cautious, as I have a little money and plenty of good boys to see me safe through all my undertakings.

Give [my] respects to your daughter.

Answer if you like.

Yours,
W.D.[69]

On the heels of William Donnelly's letter followed one written on the same day from a man who was an acquaintance of both the Thompsons and the Donnellys (and whom at least one researcher believes to have been the Lucan postmaster William Porte),[70] who attempted to warn William Thompson Sr. of what he was getting himself into:

Lucan, January 12, 1874

Sir,

I beg leave to inform you that I have heard of the excitement that took place at your house on Friday night last, and as I am very intimate with Donnelly, I have had an opportunity of hearing a little more than others and, on that occasion, I give you a friendly advice. Donnelly told me there was no engagement between him and your daughter, and also that no letters passed between them. But this I do not believe, as I have a little more [information] than I will mention at present. But there is one thing sure, he and his crowd are bound on carrying out their intention, no matter what it may cost. Dear sir, as I am only a neighbour, I do not wish to meddle myself much in the matter, but will say the

Donnellys are a bad crowd to quarrel with, not only
them but the crowd that will almost die for them.[71]
And as I heard some of them make threats on your
son that lives on the 6th of Biddulph, I would advise
you to get on friendly terms with the whole party.

From a peace-making friend.
— P. Mc.[72]

The Thompsons, however, were not a family that was intimidated or placated by a letter-writing campaign. Besides, they had
more important things on their minds — William Thompson Jr. was
getting married. The happy family put the word out that their boy
would be tying the knot with twenty-three-year-old Mary Carroll,
a young lady who lived just across the road from his farm. The
Thompson family invited all their close friends to attend the union,
which was slated to take place on January 30, 1874.[73] Naturally,
the Donnellys were not invited. However, the community being
what it was, word eventually reached William Donnelly regarding
the forthcoming event.

Partly as a result of the Thompson family's treatment of Margaret,
partly as a result of their negative comments about him and his
family, and partly because the girl he loved had been deliberately
hidden away from him as if their affection for one another was
unworthy of serious consideration, William Donnelly had grown
to hate the Thompson family. And, after their heated dialogue
in the streets of Lucan, his displeasure had grown white-hot for
William Jr. For these reasons, the news of William-the-younger's
impending wedding had piqued Donnelly's interest. Moreover,
there was a sweetener of sorts that had been added into the mix,
as Mary Carroll was the daughter of Michael Carroll, whose testimony sixteen years previously in James Donnelly's murder trial had
largely contributed to the judge's decision to sentence William's

father to death for the crime.[74] And when further news reached William Donnelly that the bride and groom would be retiring after their wedding reception back to William Thompson's farmhouse — right next door to the Donnellys' farm — well, what an opportunity it was that had just presented itself!

There had long existed in Europe a wedding tradition that, perhaps understandably, has since petered out after passing through multiple generations in North America. Known as a chivaree (also spelled shivaree or charivari), it was typically a loud, over-the-top get-together orchestrated by friends and neighbours of the bride and groom. It consisted of lots of noise, drinking and merriment that was offered in benevolent, albeit raucous, celebration of a newly wedded couple's union and future happiness together — sort of a hazing to welcome the new "Mr. and Mrs." into the community of other married couples. Over the decades since the ritual had come to Canada, however, it had become corrupted into a loud and unruly mockery of a newly married couple, and was viewed more as an opportunity for drunken mayhem than celebration.[75] Consequently, after the official union of William Thompson Jr. and Mary Carroll, and after the newlyweds had returned to their farmhouse on the Roman Line for the night, William Donnelly and his brothers decided to head over to the Thompson farm and celebrate the couple's nuptials with them by hosting a chivaree. And so, in the early morning hours of January 31, William and his "adventurers" once again came calling.

And what a celebration it was — the Donnelly boys smashed almost every pane of glass in the Thompson farmhouse[76] and then proceeded to empty their guns into the walls of the house[77] and the farmhouse chimney until it collapsed.[78] From there they moved on to throwing stones and sticks at the dwelling.[79] When they finished this bit of merriment they then proceeded to tear down a rail fence from the front of the Thompson property and used it to build a bonfire around which they danced, screamed and sang into the wee hours of the morning.[80] The terrified couple didn't dare leave their house while this was going on. If the Carroll and the Thompson families had little regard for the Donnellys up to this point, they would have none after this incident. Newlyweds William and Mary Thompson would never speak with any of the Donnellys again.

Once the news of the Donnelly boys' chivaree reached the ears of old man Thompson, he decided that something had to be done. He had earlier merely threatened to send William Donnelly and his gang to Kingston Penitentiary;[81] but now he felt he had the ammunition to make his threat a reality. On February 2, he gathered up his son, William Jr., and the pair headed south to London to file a formal complaint against the Donnelly brothers and their cronies for having discharged a revolver at the senior Thompson during the night of their attempt to rescue Margaret. A London detective was quickly dispatched to serve warrants to William, Thomas and Michael Donnelly, as well as Patrick Quigley, Robert Corcoran, William Atkinson and Daniel and James Keefe, charging them all with the offence of "shooting with attempt to wound." And while William Donnelly dealt with how best to proceed with the new charges, his baby sister, seventeen-year-old Jennie Donnelly, became the next member of the Donnelly family to exchange nuptial vows, marrying James Currie, the brother of Bob Donnelly's wife, Annie. The marriage took place on February 9, 1874[82] — again within a Protestant church (the Anglican Grace Church in Bothwell, Kent County). The newlyweds then moved to Bothwell (and later to Glencoe) to live out the remainder of their lives. The fact that another Donnelly child had opted to be married in a Protestant church was not overlooked by the Roman Catholic faction in Biddulph. To them, it was yet another example of the Donnellys clearly signalling their non-conformity to the beliefs and code of what had once been their group.

It's quite possible that William, Tom and Mike would have been late in attending their sister's wedding, as the preliminary hearing for the Thompson affair took place on the same day. Of the eight men charged, two of the prisoners, Patrick Quigley and James Keefe, were (for some reason) absent from the proceedings.[83] Right from the start, William Thompson Sr. ran into trouble with his testimony. It was dark when the gang had arrived, and the men were wearing mufflers, which made absolute identification impossible. He also didn't know which of them had fired upon him — or even if the gun had been fired *at* him. To make matters worse, the widow, Ellen Fogarty, testified she did not hear any gunshots at all. His son Michael's testimony was even more confusing. So much so, in fact, that he could not remember how old he was, what clothing the men in his house were wearing that evening, what form of disguise they used, or any of their features.[84]

Warren Rock pleaded the case on behalf of the defence, and laid down the trump card of Margaret's letters, which proved that, rather than being an attempt to kidnap Margaret Thompson, William Donnelly and his companions had only been responding to her written request that he "come and take me away by force." Rock further stated that it was her own father who had kidnapped her, by taking her up against her will and stowing her in various houses between Biddulph and McGillivray. The weakness of the prosecution's case resulted first in the grand jury reducing the charge against the Donnelly squad from "shooting with intent" down to "common assault,"[85] and then, finally, at the trial that took place from June 16 to June 17, William Donnelly and his gang were acquitted.[86]

And while this was all very well and good for teaching a lesson to old man Thompson and bringing to light the way he had treated his daughter, there was still a lingering tension between those in the Donnelly faction and those within Thompson's. This was particularly true with regard to Thompson's son-in-law, James Toohey.

Apart from being the man who had hidden Margaret in his

home, Toohey had apparently also communicated his desire to fight with any member of William Donnelly's gang.[87] On February 10, one day after the preliminary hearing in the Thompson case, and while the jury was still deliberating the collective fate of the gang, three of its members, Daniel Keefe, James Keefe and Patrick Quigley, spotted James Toohey within Joseph Fitzhenry's tavern in Lucan. Within a matter of seconds, a fight had broken out. Daniel Keefe pounced upon Toohey, striking him as he was rising from his chair, but then the younger man quickly turned things to his favour, taking Keefe to the ground where he proceeded to blacken both of Keefe's eyes.[88] Eventually James Keefe pulled Toohey off his cousin[89] and the fight ended, but not before promises of charges and counter-charges were made.[90] However, that barroom altercation was simply the Biddulph way of settling things, and proved to be the ignominious end of the whole Thompson affair.

Having been thoroughly embarrassed by his nemesis in court, there was no way that William Thompson Sr. was going to allow Margaret to ever again see William Donnelly. In addition, Margaret must have been hurt that her private letters ended up going public (and being quoted in the London newspapers that covered the sensational "abduction" trial) for everyone to read.[91] The relationship between the two former friends and lovers was clearly over now.

The Toohey and Thompson families were deeply ensconced within the Roman Catholic faction of Biddulph, and their recent legal defeat at the hands of the Donnelly brothers only furthered that faction's resolve to do something about a family that was clearly now a liability. While there is no obvious direct connection, it is nonetheless interesting to note that shortly after the Thompsons had brought their charges against William Donnelly et al., in February of 1874 another Donnelly brother, Patrick — who had been living outside the township for several years already (and was far and away the most docile of the brothers) — was inexplicably charged with a robbery that had occurred in Lucan.[92] Patrick, along with another man, was formally arrested in London, but at the preliminary hearing witnesses came forth to testify that Patrick had been working at the time the crime was said to have been committed. He would be honourably discharged in the matter.[93] It may simply have been a matter of mistaken identity, but why he would be singled out at all was suspicious, unless it was done to send a message to the family that no matter where they lived in the province, the faction could reach them.

Wedding bells would chime again for another member of the Donnelly family on May 24, 1874, when twenty-five-year-old Mike Donnelly married eighteen-year-old Ellen Hines. Ellen had been raised in a Presbyterian household, and her parents ran a nursery garden and orchard. It is speculated that the Hines family had met Mike as he drove the Donnelly stage from Lucan to their hometown of London. The pair was married in the Church of England, another Protestant church.[94]

With all his siblings now married off (save for his older brother, Jim, and his youngest brother, Tom), William Donnelly discovered that the love he had been searching for lived only five concession roads away from his parents. Nora Kennedy, a girl with whom he had been friends for years, was one of three daughters born to John and Hanora Kennedy, and the sister of his old running mates John Jr. and Rhody Kennedy. While Nora's parents were no great fans of the Donnelly family, perhaps because they were part of the group that had by now started to ostracize the Donnellys, they always held a special affection for William. John Sr. had known him since William had been a young boy, and it had been young William who had assisted him when he had had his collarbone broken in the scuffle with Patrick Hogan some nine years previously. Both sets of parents blessed the union, and from that day forward William was fiercely loyal (a Donnelly trait that ran throughout the family) to Nora.

Nora's brothers, however, were not as welcoming as their parents had been, and this was particularly true of John Kennedy Jr. According to a newspaper account concerning the matter,

John Kennedy Jr. has never been good friends with Bill
Donnelly since the latter married his sister who was
her father's pet, and, being such, John feared his father
would leave all his property to her. He tried various
schemes for the purpose of getting Bill Donnelly into
trouble, offering on one occasion to steal a steer from
his father and make a present of it to a friend of his in
Westminster, in order that the theft should be saddled
on Donnelly, and, consequently, he would lose favor
in the sight of the old man Kennedy.[95]

This fear of being left out of the will consumed John Jr., and it
didn't take long before he had won his younger brother Rhody
over to his side in the matter. Undoubtedly, he confronted his father
with his concerns, and what his father told him clearly did little to
pacify him. Battle lines quickly became drawn in the sand, with
the new couple and their parents on one side, and John and Rhody
Kennedy on the other.

William, however, had no worries about the Kennedy brothers,
once commenting that John Kennedy Jr. "knew better than to
strike me."[96] Still, in order to keep the family peace, William did
not speak to the Kennedy brothers and limited his time inter-
acting with his father-in-law. Despite the fraternal objection, Nora
Kennedy and William Donnelly were married in a manner that was
approved of by both sets of parents — in St. Patrick's Church —
on January 25, 1875, during a ceremony presided over by Father
Gerard.[97] It is worth noting at this point that only two of the
Donnelly children's marriages had taken place within a Catholic
church; the remainder were conducted within Protestant houses of
worship, which further cemented the opinion of their enemies that
the Donnelly family were now beyond redemption.

While it was true that the Donnellys' list of enemies was growing,
it was also true that they still retained a large number of friendships

within the Roman Catholic community. James Donnelly Sr.'s old friend, Cornelius Maloney, for example, regarded the Donnelly family as being both benevolent and trustworthy. So much so that in March 1874, in return for their assistance at his farm and covering his needs for food, clothing and shelter (and the sum of one dollar to pass for "consideration," thus making the arrangement legal), he assigned twenty-five acres of his farmland to the family.[98] His reason for this rather odd arrangement was that a similar deal had been struck some years before between his brother William Maloney and their nephew, thirty-seven-year-old Dan Clark. Unfortunately, upon inheriting William Maloney's twenty-five acres, Dan had then spent whatever money the property yielded (largely on booze), totally neglecting the care of his Uncle William.[99] And, upon forty-seven-year-old William's death in 1872, Cornelius feared that he was now staring at a similar fate besetting him, and so he looked around for a more reliable alternative — and he found it with the Donnellys.

The deal he struck with fifty-eight-year-old James Donnelly understandably did not sit well with Dan Clark, who now looked poised to lose his additional security and a lot of drinking money. He began to publicly malign the Donnelly family, airing his suspicions that his uncle had been taken advantage of. Admittedly things looked suspicious when, on St. Patrick's Day in 1875, and not long after having given public utterance to his grievances against the family, Dan Clark turned up dead in a stable behind the Revere Hotel in Lucan.[100] The fact that Clark had been seen in the same bar as Jim and Tom Donnelly on the afternoon of his death did little to quell the suspicion that the Donnellys had somehow had a hand in it.[101]

An inquest followed, wherein testimony was heard from the local coroner, the bartender and other patrons who had been at the tavern that day. The presiding magistrate, Bernard Stanley, in assessing the evidence (particularly that of Dr. James Sutton, who had conducted a postmortem on the body), declared Clark's death to be accidental, the result of a fall he had taken within the stable.[102]

Be that as it may, it didn't stop tongues from wagging within the community that the Donnellys had killed Clark in order to secure his uncle's property for themselves.[103] Those within Cornelius's Roman Catholic faction did what they could to fan these flames of suspicion, and were evidently successful, for the old man soon sought out an alternative to the deal he had made with the Donnelly family. He came to an arrangement with Charles O'Mealy, who took out a *lis pendens*[104] on Maloney's property. However, after the inquest, this transfer was never actualized as Maloney had apparently been satisfied with the results of the inquest into the death of his nephew. The Maloney property would subsequently be entered into the Assessment Rolls under John Donnelly's name, and Cornelius would continue to live out his remaining years under the care of the Donnellys, ultimately passing away under their roof four years later, on December 29, 1879, at the age of eighty-four.[105]

James Donnelly Sr. was prospering. He not only owned a successful fifty-acre farm, but with the acquisition of the additional twenty-five acres of farmland from Cornelius Maloney, he could look forward to having even more bountiful harvests going forward. Unfortunately, his eldest son, Jim, was having trouble on the farmland that he had acquired. The Canada Company had first leased this particular plot of land in 1843, and between then and the time of Jim's possession, it had been populated by three legal lessees and one squatter, none of whom had been able to make a go of it.[106] The land had been vacant when Jim had moved onto it in 1867 and assumed the previous tenant's lease.[107] The Canada Company had no record of a formal lease with Jim, as whatever arrangement he had made with the former leaseholder had not been registered. Consequently, he was viewed in the company's eyes as a squatter, and on December 26, 1873, the Canada Company initiated an ejection suit against Jim Donnelly and his three brothers (Robert, Michael and Thomas, who had been farming the property during Jim's absence in the United States).[108]

Upon being notified of the Canada Company's intention to evict, Jim Donnelly immediately returned to Canada, where he quickly filed a counter-plea on February 9, 1874, which cost him $200.[109] From his vantage point, he had already paid Michael Devine (the lessee he had dealt with in 1868 when he first took possession of the land) $400 for the work that Devine had already put into the lot, so consideration had been exchanged. Moreover, together with his brothers, Jim believed that he had invested considerable sweat equity of his own into the property. He didn't believe that the Canada Company had the right to just sell it out from under him, particularly after all the additional work that he and his siblings had put into improving the land. Apparently it could, however, as Jim Donnelly's claim was denied, and the land was subsequently purchased by a local farmer by the name of Joseph Carswell,[110] who then moved onto the farm with his wife and nine children in March 1874.

The court's decision was a painful one for Jim Donnelly. While he owned a piece of property in Michigan, that didn't do him much good now that he was living back in Canada — where he owned nothing. He moved to the town of Lucan, where he took a job working for his brothers in their stage service,[111] but as he was the eldest son of James and Johannah Donnelly, working for his younger brothers made him feel like he was a charity case. He spoke frequently with his younger brother Bob, who, of all the brothers, was the one closest to Jim in temperament. Bob listened to his older brother's lamentations, and then decided to pay Joseph Carswell a visit. He inquired of the farmer if he might be willing to sell the property back to Jim in return for what Carswell had paid for it, in addition to compensating him for any improvements that Carswell might have made to the land. After speaking with Bob Donnelly, Carswell said he would accept the offer,[112] and Bob Donnelly returned to Lucan to tell Jim the good news. However, the reality was that Jim hadn't the capital necessary to follow through with such a transaction, particularly at the dollar value Carswell had placed on the improvements he had made. The matter appeared to be over.

And then a series of calamities beset Joseph Carswell. In December 1874 his straw stacks went up in flames.[113] On July 30, 1875, it happened again. Two of his horses were attacked with a scythe — one died as a result of the deep wounds inflicted by the attack, while the other had to be put down the next morning by Carswell.[114] The logical assumption was that Bob and Jim Donnelly were the culprits, as they were the only people in the township who were known to have a potential conflict with the farmer. While the Donnellys were never charged, in Carswell's mind they were the guilty parties. He claimed that he had followed tracks that he had seen from around his burned straw stacks and that they led toward the Donnelly farm.[115] The fact that a similar atrocity had been committed a few days prior to Carswell's horses being attacked when Usborne Township farmer George Armstrong, a man with whom the Donnellys had no issues, reported that the tongue of one of his mares had been cut out,[116] had no bearing on Carswell's beliefs. Carswell would grow so paranoid about the Donnellys, however, that when he ultimately lost his farm in 1879, he was convinced that the Donnellys were behind it. Indeed, his accusations became so bizarre and far-fetched regarding the family that even reporters from the local press were sceptical of his claims.[117]

Whether or not Jim Donnelly had a hand in the hostilities that were visited upon Joseph Carswell, he was certainly not above suspicion in such matters. Indeed, along with his younger brother, Bob, Jim was the one Donnelly brother most prone to violence. This would become evident a mere three months prior to Carswell's second fire, when, on the evening of April 5, 1875, Thomas Gibbs, a travelling fruit peddler, took a room for the night at the Revere House Hotel in Lucan. Gibbs, along with his young son John, had stabled their horse and wagon, which contained a generous supply of oranges and lemons, within the barn behind the hotel.[118] Early the next morning, Jim Donnelly entered the stable and spotted

Gibbs's unattended fruit wagon. Not having had breakfast yet, and checking to ensure that no one else was around, Jim ventured over to the wagon, leaned in and pulled out an orange — and then another. Unbeknownst to Jim, he was being observed by the fruit vendor's son, who wasted no time in running back to the hotel to tell his father that they were being robbed. Thomas Gibbs sprinted to the stable and saw that his son was telling the truth — Jim Donnelly was stuffing his pockets with the vendor's fruit. Creeping up behind Donnelly, Gibbs grabbed him by the shoulder.

"Leave them alone!" he declared. Donnelly spun around, surprised.

"Get your hands off me or I'll knock your brains out," said Donnelly.

But Gibbs wasn't playing around. He tightened his grip on Donnelly's arm.

Unfortunately for Gibbs, Jim Donnelly wasn't playing around either. He reached his hand into the pocket of his jacket and slipped on a set of steel knuckles. He then punched Gibbs squarely in the face, which dropped the fruit peddler to the floor of the barn, his face a bloody mess, his jaw broken. Young John Gibbs fled back to the Revere House tavern, where he yelled to bartender Richard Tapp that somebody was beating his father in the barn. By the time Tapp arrived at the stable, Jim Donnelly was gone and Thomas Gibbs was flat on his back, out cold.

Gibbs pressed charges and shortly thereafter Jim Donnelly was arrested and charged with assault and larceny. William Donnelly was said to have intervened on his brother's behalf, seeking to avoid the more socially unacceptable charge of theft. He was successful, as Jim Donnelly ended up being convicted only on the assault charge. After paying a one-dollar fine and $27.50 in court costs and damages to Thomas Gibbs, Jim Donnelly was free to go. But the violence and the lawsuits were only just beginning for the Donnelly family.

CHAPTER FIVE

HELL ON WHEELS

A replica of what one of the Donnelly stagecoaches looked like.
(Courtesy of Jackie Martens and the Lucan Area Heritage
& Donnelly Museum)

According to Oxford County historian W.B. Hobson, being a stagecoach driver was once considered a vocation that many young men aspired to.[1] It was a sign of social class, as drivers were well dressed, polite and able to rub shoulders with those who could afford to travel. And if stagecoach drivers were considered a cut above their neighbours socially, a person who owned a stagecoach line was considered to be just this side of high society. By mid-1875 the Donnelly stage service was holding its own against its competitors. William was the brains of the enterprise, but his partner in the business was his younger brother Mike, who was just as hardworking and professional. When the brothers had expanded their route to include trips into London, they required more drivers and, with four other brothers to choose from (Patrick still being gainfully employed in the carriage-making trade in London), John, Jim, Bob and Tom were available to be circulated into the rotation as required.

T he stagecoach industry had its genesis in England in the 1400s, but got its start in Biddulph in 1831, when Austin Steward started a stage service within the Wilberforce colony. Steward was a remarkable man: a former African-American slave, he would go on to become a businessman, an administrator and, ultimately, an author. It was Steward, in fact, who would christen the colony "Wilberforce" after the English abolitionist William Wilberforce. In 1831, the thirty-eight-year-old Steward had just arrived in Ontario to assist in the administration of the colony, which had been created by former slaves from the United States. According to Steward,

> Soon after settling in Wilberforce . . . I engaged
> to carry packages for different merchants in the
> adjoining villages, as well as to and from the
> settlement. Possessing a pair of excellent horses and
> a good wagon, I found it a profitable business,
> and the only one I could well do, to eke out the
> proceeds of my farm, and meet my expenses.[2]

Steward's stage service didn't last very long, however; in a foreshadowing of what would beset the Donnellys some forty years later, he would also become a victim of factionalism from within his own community. Not long after starting his stage service, a rival group from within the Wilberforce colony sabotaged Steward's enterprise by twice poisoning his horses.[3]

Consequently, by 1837, he had grown weary of the internal politics and left Biddulph Township for Rochester, New York.[4] However, Steward's pioneering efforts had established that a stage service could be a viable enterprise in the region.

The stagecoach businesses that would follow in Steward's wake were protean, with alliances frequently created and dissolved, and stage lines sold and purchased, according to the financial expediency of the moment. And that was how the stagecoach businesses would continue to operate within Middlesex County until the railroads expanded and eventually put them all out of business. When the plan was tabled to connect by rail the city of London and North Middlesex County to the northern counties of Huron and Bruce, the death knell had effectively been rung for the stage lines. The notion that their window of profitability was slowly closing had instilled within each of the stagecoach companies a heightened sense of urgency to make as much money as possible while the opportunity to do so still existed. Such anxiety led to fierce competition between the stage lines for passengers. According to a local newspaper at the time, "Opposition between the rival stages is very keen, and language the reverse of parliamentary is sometimes freely indulged in by the respective drivers when canvassing for passengers."[5]

The "rival stages" referred to in this instance were the Donnelly and Hawkshaw stages, but the greatest rivalry in the stagecoach wars was soon to come, when a newcomer to the trade by the name of Patrick Flanagan threw his hat into the arena in 1874. Flanagan believed that he had the perfect combination of business savvy and muscle to force his competitors out of business. The Flanagans ran a post office, a general store and a hotel/tavern (among other enterprises) at the crossroads where the London–Goderich road met the McGillivray and Biddulph town lines. Given that the Flanagan family owned most of the businesses within that region, this intersection was referred to by the locals as "Flanagan's Corners" (it had previously been known as "the Town of Ireland," or "Irishtown," and later would later become known as Clandeboye). When the family patriarch, Patrick Flanagan Sr., passed away in 1865, he bequeathed his various business interests to his four sons: Patrick Jr., John, William and James. But Patrick Jr. wasn't interested in continuing on in any of the family enterprises; he had his eyes set on a different business entirely. Finding a partner in Ted Crawley, Patrick Flanagan Jr. bought the Hawkshaw stage line. Needing a stable and a barn to house the horses and coaches, the new partners purchased what had formerly been an Anglican church, which stood just three miles north of Lucan along the shore of the Sauble River. This new base of operations was close to the Flanagan family's other business enterprises at Flanagan's Corners. Flanagan also had a satellite stagecoach office in Lucan, which allowed him to stable his horses in the barn behind the Queen's Hotel. By contrast, the Donnelly "Opposition Stage" (as the brothers had taken to facetiously calling their coach line) made use of the stables and barn behind the Revere House Hotel in Lucan, and their customers came from either the local hotels or from pickups at the Grand Trunk Railroad station.

Both businesses knew they were competing for the same customers and, to this end, they advertised their conveyance services extensively in the local papers. Both sides also knew things were going to get intense, as they dug in and prepared for war. And, given there were no constables along the Proof Line Road (upon which both stages travelled on their way to and from London),[6] they didn't have to wait long.

The first shot to be fired in what became known as the "stagecoach wars" occurred in January 1875. Patrick Flanagan had received word that two women in London were looking for transportation to Crediton. The latter destination had never been on the Flanagan (or Hawkshaw) stage route, which always ran directly from Exeter to London. To get to Crediton, the Flanagan stage would be required to make the run almost to Exeter (shy of Exeter by roughly five miles, making it a twenty-six mile trip from London), and then head due west for another seven miles. The Donnelly stage, by contrast, travelled daily to Crediton and had for some time.[7] To Flanagan, however, if tacking a bonus trip onto the end of his run to Exeter meant two fewer fares for the Donnelly stage, then he was happy to accommodate the ladies.

Small towns being what they are, news of Flanagan's intentions quickly reached the Donnelly brothers, who had been prepping their stage for departure from the City Hotel in London. Immediately upon hearing the news, Mike Donnelly hopped into the driver's seat of the Donnelly stage and, together with his brother John, headed over to pay Patrick Flanagan a visit. Flanagan had already assisted the two ladies into his coach when the Donnelly stagecoach suddenly arrived on the scene. John Donnelly quickly leapt from the coach, ran to the front of Flanagan's stage and unhitched the horses. Climbing down from the coach, Mike Donnelly informed Flanagan that the women would be taking the Donnelly stage to Crediton. Flanagan told Donnelly that wasn't going to happen, whereupon Donnelly stepped forth and belted his competitor square in the face, knocking him down into the street. The matter now being resolved, the Donnelly brothers went to the Flanagan stage, opened the coach door and escorted the two women back to the Donnelly stage. The Donnelly stagecoach left for Crediton just as Flanagan regained consciousness.[8]

Once the embarrassed stage owner had picked himself off the ground, he marched directly to the nearest police court and charged the Donnelly brothers with assault.[9]

A week later, under the cover of darkness, one of Flanagan's stagecoaches was pulled out from its storage shed and taken surreptitiously to a place a quarter of a mile out of town, where it was then chopped to pieces. The perpetrators were never discovered, although Flanagan had no doubt as to the identities of the culprits.[10]

While Patrick fumed and nursed his wounds, one of his brothers, John Flanagan, continued to run the family's successful general store at Flanagan's Corners. As with his brother Patrick, there was no love lost between John Flanagan and the Donnelly brothers as, apart from his business as a shopkeeper, he was also the silent financial partner of Patrick's stage line. One day John noticed that his supply of confectionary had run low and placed an order for more stock from a London wholesaler. The wholesaler, in a move of unequalled obliviousness, walked the package over to the Donnelly stage office for delivery to John Flanagan at his shop. The Donnellys must have known that the entertainment stock for the day had just gone up considerably. History has not recorded which of the brothers was tasked with delivering the parcel that day, not that it mattered, for as soon as a Donnelly walked into Flanagan's shop with the parcel, John Flanagan instantly refused delivery of it. When Donnelly pressed the matter, Flanagan took the parcel and threw it on the floor and then proceeded to stomp and kick it around his shop.[11] Donnelly laughed, left the shop, and then had the authorities serve John Flanagan with a summons to appear in court for smashing the parcel. The Donnellys later withdrew their charge and paid the miniscule legal costs,[12] perhaps considering the experience as having been a good bargain for a day's worth of cheap, painless entertainment.

Matters took a far more serious turn on February 4, 1875, during the height of one of the fiercest winter snowstorms ever to hit London and Middlesex County. Mike Donnelly was driving his stage toward London along the Proof Line Road. However, the sub-zero temperature, combined with the strong winds encountered on the trip that day, were proving to be more than even a seasoned stagecoach driver like Mike Donnelly could tolerate. Seated on top of the stage, he had no protection at all from the cold and the blinding snow, and so at some point during the trip, he stopped the stage, climbed inside the coach and pulled the reins of the horses in through one of the coach windows. Here, seated with his passengers, he proceeded to drive the team from inside the stagecoach. Approximately five miles north of London, just as his stage was summiting a small hill, a powerful gust of wind and snow hit the coach, blowing it off the road and down an embankment. When the stage finally came to rest at the bottom of the hill, Mike extricated himself and began to assist his passengers from the coach. However, as he was pulling out the last passenger, his horses suddenly bolted, knocking the woman back inside the coach, where she was now trapped. The spooked horses started running, dragging the fallen coach — containing its distraught passenger — behind it. The team charged its way through the scrub and snow with Mike Donnelly running as fast as he could to try to catch up to them. Despite the snow being almost thigh-deep, he was finally able to catch up to the horses and, grabbing their reins, he pulled as hard as he could until they eventually stopped running. At this point he was able to help the frightened woman (who was surprisingly unscathed) out of the stage. Mike's head sustained some bruises, but all the passengers were fine. He quickly arranged for another sleigh to deliver his passengers on to London.[13]

Five months later Mike Donnelly would be involved in another stage accident that didn't end as successfully. On July 1, 1875, the Flanagan stage was en route from Exeter to London. It was driven on this day by twenty-eight-year-old William Brooks, a driver of some experience, who was pulling in at various stops along the route — Mooretown, Flanagan's Corners and Lucan — to let out and pick up passengers. The Donnelly stage also happened to be travelling on the Proof Line Road that day with Mike Donnelly at the reins. Mike pulled his stage into the town of Lucan for a brief stop before continuing on to London. Brooks made a stop in Lucan as well, where he swapped out the horses for the stage, and then continued on his route to London.

Because the Donnelly stage had more stops to make, the Flanagan stage soon overtook it on the Proof Line Road. Mike Donnelly continued to follow behind Brooks as both stages made their way up the brow of Mount Hope, just outside of London. Both coaches passed over the crest of the hill at a modest speed (later approximated to have been five to six miles per hour), and, as they began their descent, Mike Donnelly moved his coach over to the left of Brooks's in an effort to pass. Brooks, however, wasn't having it. He quickly steered his stage over to the left until it was in the middle of the road, thus closing off the space that Mike required to pass him. Brooks increased his speed. Donnelly did likewise and had soon pulled up alongside Brooks.

Suddenly, the left front wheel popped off Brooks's stage and rolled off the road. Given the speed at which the carriage had been travelling, everything and everyone in the coach pitched forward violently as the front left corner of the stage crashed to the ground. A passenger who had been sitting up top in the driver's seat with Brooks was thrown from the stage and landed in front of the still-galloping Donnelly horses. Miraculously, he somehow escaped both the hooves of the horses and the wheels of the stagecoach. Brooks wasn't so fortunate; the violence of the abrupt stop had pitched him headfirst into the wooden crossbar that connected the horses' harnesses to the stage, which may have rendered him unconscious. Hopefully that was case, as he would not have wanted to be conscious for what happened next. His legs and arms became entangled in the reins of his horses and the spooked animals now took off in a full gallop, dragging the body of William Brooks behind them for a quarter of a mile until they eventually stopped in a state of near exhaustion.[14]

Mike Donnelly reined in his horses and jumped from his stage. He ran toward Brooks, as did one of Brooks's passengers, Robert Dempsey. A farmer who had been heading in the opposite direction in his wagon, Samuel Cobbledick, saw what had happened and pulled his wagon over to where Brooks's horses had stopped. He, too, climbed out and ran to the fallen driver. By the time that Donnelly and Dempsey arrived, Cobbledick looked up at them and said, "He's killed."[15] Donnelly and Dempsey untangled Brooks's body from the reins and placed it into the farmer's wagon.[16] Cobbledick then sped toward London, where doctors were summoned to examine the stage driver. Brooks's legs and arms were severely bruised and there was blood leaking from his nose, mouth and left eye. His skull had suffered a four-inch fracture that one of the doctors at the hospital was able to fit his entire hand into.[17] Unfortunately, there was nothing the doctors could do for the poor driver. He died shortly thereafter, leaving behind a wife and three children.[18]

A coroner's inquest was held later that same day. One of the passengers who had been on the Flanagan stage that morning, David Johns, a justice of the peace, testified, "I think the nut was loosened in Lucan by turning the wagon, and that it was shaken off during the [horses'] running. I think if there had been no running there would not have been an accident."[19]

Finally, John Lewis, the foreman of the jury, read their verdict:

> We the undersigned jurymen summoned upon the
> inquest held upon the body of William Brooks do
> hereby agree that the deceased came to his death
> from injuries received by being thrown from the
> Exeter Stage, which was caused by the fore wheel
> of said stage coming off, and that the deceased
> came by his death accidentally.[20]

Surprisingly, Patrick Flanagan, the owner of the damaged stagecoach and William Brooks's employer,[21] was allowed to sit on the jury. Unsurprisingly, the verdict didn't satisfy him. In fact, quite to the contrary of what the jury had concluded, he was convinced that the Donnellys had sabotaged his stagecoach, resulting in the death of his driver.

A little over a month later, on August 31, 1875, Robert McLeod, another of Flanagan's drivers who had known the late William Brooks quite well when the pair had both driven stage for Hawkshaw, found himself in a similar position to that of his late friend. Upon clearing a rise as he drove his stage north along the Proof Line Road toward Lucan, he spotted the Donnelly stage ahead of him. The driver of the stage was Tom Donnelly, who, at twenty-one years of age, was the youngest of the Donnelly brothers.

As the two stages continued their way north, McLeod saw an opportunity to pass his rival and did so, before settling in at a comfortable trot ahead of him.[22] McLeod had eight passengers in his stagecoach that day.[23] Tom Donnelly had ten, which consisted of seven within his coach and three more sitting on the driver's bench next to him.[24] The roof of the Donnelly stage was further loaded down with luggage from the passengers, while strapped to the rear of the coach were several barrels of vinegar that were to be delivered to a business in Lucan.

Both stages were scheduled to pull into the town of Birr, located six and a quarter miles south of Lucan. As the town came into sight, one of the ladies from within the Donnelly coach sent word up to Tom Donnelly that she would like to stop briefly to get a drink from the water pump that sat in front of the Swartz Hotel.[25] Happy to oblige, Donnelly turned his stage to the right and headed toward the water pump. McLeod, seeing that Donnelly had changed his position on the road, decided to move his stage over in an attempt to cut him off. The two stagecoaches proceeded forward with McLeod cutting farther and farther to the right and Donnelly moving farther to the right to avoid him. Eventually the Donnelly stage ran out of room and its right front wheel came into contact with a pile of rocks that had been placed around the water pump to anchor it, tilting the stage forcefully to the left. At this point McLeod's right rear wheel became entangled with the harness of one of the Donnelly horses, pulling the horse over and cutting one of its rear legs. This had the additional consequence of yanking the Donnelly stage violently to the left as well. There it hovered briefly, and then toppled over, knocking McLeod's stage over with it.[26] Both sets of horses and passengers tumbled onto the roadway, as well as the luggage that had been stored on top of the stagecoaches. To make matters worse, the vinegar barrels that had been fastened to the rear of the Donnelly stage now broke free, causing them to spill their malodorous contents onto the ground. Both stage drivers had jumped from their respective stages as they were falling over, but Tom Donnelly was the first to his feet.

"What did you do that for?" he demanded.

"I'd do it again if I had the chance!" yelled McLeod.[27] Soon the drivers' voices were drowned out by the yelling of their passengers and threats of legal action were freely bandied about.

One of the passengers from the Donnelly stage, a London farmer named John Cade, would later testify that

> [a]fter the stage upset, I got out and saw that
> both stages had turned over. Flanagan's stage had
> capsized about six feet in front and to the left of
> Donnelly's. I helped the passengers out, and then
> inspected the tracks of the stages. I found that
> both had come all right to the pump, and then
> Flanagan's had crossed over considerably so that
> Donnelly's stage was crowded onto the stones
> around the pump. Had Flanagan kept in his course
> without crowding Donnelly there was plenty of
> room, and to spare, for both stages to have reached
> the tie-posts at the hotel without injury. McLeod
> did not deny that the tracks were those of his stage.
> I have no doubt whatever that Donnelly could have
> got in safely to the hotel had McLeod not crowded
> him on the stones at the pump.[28]

Tom and his brothers viewed McLeod's actions as being both retaliatory and damaging: retaliatory in that they believed Tom had been run off the road solely as payback for Flanagan's belief that Mike Donnelly had run their driver William Brooks off the road; and damaging, as not only was the Donnelly stage damaged as well as their horses injured in the collision, but also two of their passengers, Louisa and Martha Lindsay, a mother and daughter, were now threatening to file a negligence suit against the Donnelly Stagecoach Line as a result of the injuries they sustained. The Donnellys were angry and wanted compensation for what they took to be a wanton attempt to damage their business.

Consequently, Mike Donnelly went before Magistrate Henry Ferguson in Birr to lay charges against Robert McLeod for malicious driving. Two days later, after having heard the testimony, the magistrate convicted McLeod, and ordered him to pay a one-dollar fine in addition to one hundred dollars in damages.[29] A few days later an irate citizen penned a letter to a London newspaper about what was now being perceived as a growing problem between the stagecoach lines: "It is too bad that the lives of the public are to be so endangered when they think proper to visit London and take the stage route, which for Lucanites is by far the shortest and most desirable route. The drivers are continually at war, get running races, and care little or nothing for either horse flesh, stages or those that are inside the stage."[30]

The magistrate's ruling was not acceptable to Patrick Flanagan, who refused to believe that his driver was at fault. And so, two days later, Flanagan instructed McLeod to appeal his conviction to the Middlesex Court of Quarter Sessions for that coming December.[31] Two days after McLeod filed his appeal, the Lindsay ladies filed their suit against William and Mike Donnelly, the owners of the Donnelly stage line, for negligence. The brothers felt confident that they would win this suit in court, particularly given that magistrate Henry Ferguson had just ruled in their favour. At their hearing on

September 25, 1875, they pleaded not guilty, and had their trial scheduled for the next quarter sessions in December.[32]

On Friday, September 17, yet another accident beset the Flanagan stage line, the result of either negligence (which might explain their prior two accidents with the Donnelly stages) or sabotage (which might justify their enmity toward the Donnelly brothers). The stage had set off from Exeter to London with twenty passengers and, according to the *Exeter Times*, "All went well until near Mooresville, when an axle of the stage broke as it was crossing a small bridge."[33]

The accident resulted in the stage, the driver, the passengers and their luggage tumbling off the bridge and falling "quite a distance."[34] September 17 would prove to be an action-packed day. Not only did the Flanagan stage suffer its third accident in as many months, but more drama was about to take place once the sun went down.

P at Donnelly was coming home from London to visit his parents for the weekend. On the way he was going to stop into Lucan to visit with his brothers after they had wrapped up their work for the day. The brothers had all agreed to get together at Levitt's tavern for a few drinks. There would be three elements that would be mixed into this family reunion that guaranteed it would culminate in violence that evening. The first, of course, was alcohol, which has a long-settled history of sparking trouble when consumed to excess. Second, loyal Donnelly friend James Keefe had agreed to join the brothers at the bar. Keefe, the reader will recall, had an active role in the attempted abduction of Margaret Thompson and, like all the Keefe brothers, almost seemed to welcome physical confrontations. And the third element was the arrival into the tavern of Joseph Berryhill.

It is unclear who exactly Joseph Berryhill was, or what he did. In reviewing what the various Donnelly authors have researched, we learn that Orlo Miller believed him to be a constable,[35] William

Butt is of the opinion that he was nothing more than a local bully,[36] while James Reaney[37] contended that Berryhill was an apple peddler and county strongman. It's entirely possible that Berryhill was a friend of Flanagan's, and was looking to mete out a little frontier justice to the Donnellys that evening. At the very least, we can assume that Joseph Berryhill was a big, strong man who, particularly when well into his cups, looked for any opportunity to throw his weight around.

Pat Donnelly arrived at Lucan's Revere House tavern that evening prior to his brothers and was soon joined by James Keefe. The pair were chatting over a couple of drinks when in walked Joseph Berryhill with two of his friends, Daniel Perley and Robert Taylor. The big man and his friends ordered some beverages and then ordered some more. After a short time, Berryhill, feeling no pain at this point, was evidently itching to assert himself. Looking around the bar, he announced in a loud voice (that presaged a similar challenge made famous by John L. Sullivan some years later) that he could lick anyone in the bar.

Donnelly and Keefe no doubt laughed into their drinks upon hearing this, which caught Berryhill's attention. He keyed in on Pat Donnelly, who, like his brothers, had a penchant for wearing the finest clothes he could afford, and who also happened to be the smallest of the Donnelly brothers.[38] Berryhill started in on him.

James Keefe looked up from his drink and told the strongman to shut his mouth.

Shifting his gaze to Keefe, who was just about his height, Berryhill pointed his finger at him. "I will lick you," Berryhill said.[39]

Keefe smirked, threw back his whiskey and returned the strongman's stare.

Berryhill and his friends finished their drinks and headed for the door. As they were leaving, Keefe called out to Berryhill, "I'll meet you to fight!"

The strongman ignored the statement and stepped out into the street. The trio now headed over to William Walker's Western Hotel to knock back a few more. They hadn't been gone long when Mike, Tom, Jim and William Donnelly showed up at Levitt's. They were quickly brought up to speed by Pat and James as to what had transpired and decided to head directly to Walker's. The Donnelly brothers intended both to witness James Keefe battle the town strongman and to serve as Keefe's backup, just in case Berryhill's two friends decided to get involved. As they approached the hotel, James Keefe picked up a hefty stone to better his chances in battle. Tom and Jim Donnelly did likewise. William Donnelly would later estimate that the time of their arrival was ten o'clock.[40] When the brothers reached the bar, William, Mike and Pat stood guard outside the front door (no charges would ever be brought against them for the incident that followed), while Jim, Tom and James Keefe went directly inside.

Immediately upon entering the establishment the men spied Joseph Berryhill leaning against the bar engaged in conversation with the tavern's proprietor, William Walker. Their entry was anything but subtle, and Berryhill turned from the bar to face his adversaries. He locked eyes with Keefe — and then it was on.

Keefe charged across the barroom toward Berryhill, who threw the first punch, which, unfortunately for the strongman, missed its mark. This gave Keefe the opportunity to take hold of the big man's coat with one hand, and strike him repeatedly on the top of his head with his other hand, which happened to be holding a two-and-a-half-pound stone. The headshots cut through both Berryhill's hat and hatband, momentarily stunning him. He might have fallen as a consequence, had Keefe not then grabbed hold of him by the beard, which had the effect of keeping Berryhill on his feet — or at least it did until Keefe yanked out a fistful of the strongman's whiskers in an attempt to pull him to the floor.[41]

"Give it to him — the son of a bitch!" yelled Jim Donnelly. Berryhill, having shaken off the first assault, grabbed Keefe and the two men grappled next to the bar for a moment, which was all the time Jim Donnelly required to grab hold of a solid wooden chair and bring it crashing down on Berryhill's neck and shoulders, which dropped the big man. One of Berryhill's friends, Robert Taylor, now rushed in to intervene, but Tom Donnelly grabbed him as he went running past and the two ended up tumbling to the barroom floor. Suddenly Jim Donnelly was there again, this time brandishing a heavy stone in his fist, and now proceeded to bring it down directly upon the head of Taylor, knocking him out cold. Berryhill's remaining friend, Daniel Perley, beat a hasty exit through the kitchen door. Both Jim and Thomas Donnelly then threw more stones at Berryhill, knocking out two of his teeth and loosening a third. The strongman continued to wrestle with Keefe on the floor of the tavern and, as Berryhill started to get the upper hand in the brawl, Jim Donnelly once again struck him with a chair, which sent the big man sprawling back to the floor. Keefe, together with Jim and Thomas, then started putting their boots to Berryhill, kicking him repeatedly until Mike Donnelly rushed in from outside and pulled them off.

And, with that, the fight was over.

Berryhill was by this point laid out on the floor, stunned. Blood was flowing freely from his mouth and from three deep cuts on the top of his head. His friend, Robert Taylor, was also supine; it would take a little longer for him to regain his senses than it did for Berryhill. Someone called for a doctor,[42] who arrived within minutes and assisted the two injured men into the kitchen of the tavern where he began tending to their wounds.

Of the assailants, only Tom Donnelly remained behind; James Keefe and his brothers had already left the tavern and headed out into the night. Tom ordered a drink, pulled up a chair, and sat and watched as Berryhill and Taylor, their heads freshly bandaged, staggered from the kitchen and then exited the tavern. Tom let his gaze travel about the bar for any signs of potential trouble and, seeing none, he slowly rose from his chair and left the establishment. After all, the night was still young — and the Donnellys were now feeling bulletproof.

Twenty-five-year-old James Curry, a member of the Four Battalion Rifle Brigade of the Lucan Volunteers' Militia, had been drinking heavily at the Western Hotel for some time that same evening. He had money in his pocket and had not been shy about flashing it around. Curry had been present when the fight with Berryhill had gone down and, after everybody had cleared out, he, too, left the Western to sample the wares of another tavern within Lucan.

As he was stumbling along the wooden sidewalk on his way to the next watering hole, he was blindsided by a man he later took to be Jim Donnelly, which caused him to tumble into a ditch. Startled by the occurrence, as even an inebriated person would be, he started to stand up — and that's when Tom Donnelly stepped in with a solid punch to Curry's chest, which sent him crashing back down into the ditch again. At this point two other men came forth and grabbed hold of his arms, yanking him up into a sitting position, and then Tom Donnelly rifled through his pockets, ultimately removing seven dollars and seventy-five cents. When Curry started to protest the theft, Jim Donnelly drew back his leg and kicked him square in the face, which dropped the militia man flat on his back. Curry thought he saw the Donnelly brothers, along with James Keefe and now William Atkinson, walking away from the scene.[43]

As the men approached the Dublin House tavern, they passed by one-armed Rhody Kennedy, who, by this point in time, was no longer on friendly terms with the Donnellys. William Donnelly had not spoken to any of the Kennedy brothers since shortly before his wedding to their sister, Nora, nine months previously, and he saw no reason to speak with a Kennedy tonight. Jim Donnelly, however, may have been feeling a touch sentimental. According to Rhody

Kennedy's account (which the reader must be cautioned not to accept at face value, given Kennedy's animus with the Donnellys and the fact that it was produced during a lawsuit against the brothers), as the Donnelly brothers walked past, Jim Donnelly approached his former chum and threw his arm over his shoulder. He told him about the brawl at Walker's hotel and obviously felt comfortable in the belief that Rhody had been too long a friend in good standing to betray a trust. Indeed, the Donnelly brothers and the Kennedy brothers had enjoyed some wild times together over the years. The Donnelly boys were always loyal to their friends and assumed, not always correctly, that these same friends, in turn, would always be loyal to them. Jim tightened his arm on Rhody's shoulder, drawing him in close enough so that he could lower his voice and still be heard.

"Rhody," he began, "I want to know if you would do *one thing* for me?"

"What would that be?" Rhody asked, not really sure where this was leading or — particularly given the feud between the two families — why Jim should now be asking a favour of him. He certainly wasn't prepared for Jim's response.

"I want you to burn out Patrick Flanagan's stage stable."

The stable in question was set in behind the Queen's Hotel in Lucan, not that far from where both men were standing at that moment.

"No, I won't do *that*," Rhody exclaimed.

Jim Donnelly then put his hand in his pocket and pulled out a five-dollar bill, perhaps the same one that his brother Tom had recently liberated from James Curry's pocket.

"Here, you can have this, if you go to the stable."

Rhody now recognized that Jim was serious. He immediately recoiled at the suggestion. "No, I won't. I never did the like — burning any man's stable!"

"You might as well earn the five dollars," Jim said, a smile playing about his lips.

"I won't do it!" Rhody said, adamantly.

Jim Donnelly shrugged his shoulders and released his grip on Kennedy, telling him to suit himself. "A week from Sunday night I am going to burn Flanagan's stables," he said, "and leave him not worth a shilling."

"If you do that, Jim, you will be sorry," Rhody cautioned him.

Donnelly walked away from his former friend, saying over his shoulder, "A week from Sunday you will hear of the place being burned to ashes."

"Jim, you had better not do it!" Rhody called after him.

Jim Donnelly paused in his tracks and then turned back to look at Rhody. "I will do it," he said matter-of-factly, "and then take Flanagan's life."[44]

And with that, Jim Donnelly turned and walked across the street to join his brothers and friends in the Dublin House tavern.

William Donnelly didn't hang around long at the bar that evening. Perhaps he suspected that Jim had consumed enough alcohol that he might think it a good idea to bring Rhody Kennedy along with him to the tavern in order to encourage the mending of some family fences. If so, William wanted no part of it. Whatever the reason, William, together with his brother Pat, decided that they had had sufficient excitement for one night and left their brothers behind in the bar. At some point after their departure, the group was joined by Bob Donnelly, as he, together with Jim, Tom, Mike, William Atkinson and James Keefe, would all be seen, both in the Dublin House and the Western Hotel that evening.[45] The brothers later spotted a friend, the Lucan veterinarian James Churchill, walking past the tavern, and hailed him to come in and have a drink with them. Upon entering the establishment, Churchill immediately detected that the mood among the brothers was not jovial. While putting a bully like Berryhill in his place was one thing, and rolling the town drunk who had been showing off his money was another, he noted that Tom Donnelly in particular was feeling agitated. Perhaps it was the booze. Or perhaps it was the fact that he couldn't shake from his mind the fact that Flanagan was behind Robert McLeod's lawsuit, or that the two Lindsay ladies had filed lawsuits of their own against his brother's stagecoach company, charging Tom with negligence as a result of an accident that wasn't his fault. Another round of whiskey only served to amplify his mood. As far as Tom Donnelly could see, the common denominator running through his family's legal and financial problems was Patrick Flanagan.

Jim by this point in the evening was completely drunk, talking much too loudly and on the verge of being problematic. After a while, Tom Donnelly said something to William Atkinson and the pair promptly got up and left the tavern. Churchill witnessed this and envied them their exit; Jim Donnelly was getting louder, which had the effect of making Churchill quite uncomfortable. After picking up the tab for another round for the lads, he decided that he would head back to his room at the Queen's Hotel. As he would recollect later,

> As near as I can tell it was then about half past
> ten o'clock p.m., and a bright moon shone. I left
> shortly after to go home at the Queen's Hotel.
> James Donnelly was worse of liquor and I wanted
> to get away. I went up Frank Street and round by
> Goodacre's shop. I passed Mason's Foundry [which
> was adjacent to the west side of the Queen's Hotel].
> I saw William Atkinson standing on the sidewalk
> in front of Mason's Foundry. I asked what he was
> doing there, and he said he was waiting for Thomas
> Donnelly. He said Donnelly had gone in round by
> Mason's Shop. I went round by Mason's Shop to get
> to my lodgings the back way. In going that way, I
> passed right past the south end of Flanagan's stables.
> My attention was attracted by seeing a person

getting up on a board at the northwest corner of the
Flanagan stable and lighting a match. The match was
lighted, and he was holding the match up toward
the barn, about as high as his head. Then the board
broke, and he fell about four feet to the ground and
the match went out. I called out and said, "Is that
you Pat?" The man called me by name and said, "If
you ever reveal this, I'll have your life!" He was then
about the same distance from me. I saw who that
man was — it was Thomas Donnelly. . . . [H]e stated
that he had "failed this time, but he would have his
revenge yet."[46]

What specifically Thomas Donnelly was looking to avenge is
unclear, but two weeks later Flanagan's stables went up in flames.[47]

CHAPTER SIX

TRIALS AND TRIBULATIONS

Tom (left) and Bob Donnelly (right), circa 1876. (Photo courtesy of Ely Errey on behalf of the McIlhargey family. By permission of Ray Fazakas, author of *The Donnelly Album* and *In Search of the Donnellys*)

On the night of the fire, Patrick Flanagan was so convinced that something bad was going to happen he had slept with his clothes on.[1] It was a little after midnight when he finally drifted off to sleep. Within an hour, intermittent flashes of light began to filter through his consciousness, causing him to awaken.[2] Shortly afterwards, the noises started. There was a commotion coming from outside, which immediately brought to the surface a fear that the stagecoach operator had been trying to suppress for the past few weeks.[3] He leapt out of the bed within his room at the Queen's Hotel and ran down the stairs and out into the street. Several men ran past him toward the rear of the building to join another group of men who were working feverishly to put out a fire in the stable. To Flanagan's amazement, he noted that Jim, John and Tom Donnelly were among them.[4] John Donnelly manned the pump[5] while Tom carried buckets of water to the burning stables to assist the men in putting down the blaze.[6] Several townsmen who had been early onto the scene had already rescued all eight of Flanagan's horses.[7] The animals were safe, but scared.

To the firefighters' collective horror, a wind now picked up, which started to blow embers from the burning stable onto the back of the Queen's Hotel. Within a matter of minutes, the hotel itself was engulfed in flames. Despite the heroic efforts of the Lucan townspeople, by morning both the stable and the hotel had burned to the ground. The cause of the fire was generally assumed to have been arson, but there had been no eyewitnesses to confirm this. However, the fact that three Donnelly brothers had been seen on the Lucan streets that evening, plus Churchill's earlier confession about what he had heard Tom Donnelly say on September 17, left no doubt in Patrick Flanagan's mind as to the identity of the arsonists. Nevertheless, the need to immediately re-establish his business was now the stagecoach line proprietor's highest priority; retribution against the Donnellys would have to wait for the time being.

B efore continuing, it's worth noting a story that has endured for over 140 years involving a brawl that took place between the Donnellys and a mob that was said to have been assembled by one of the Flanagan brothers. It is an astonishing tale, if true. Even if apocryphal, the fact that it has been readily accepted and perpetuated by various authors over the ensuing generations speaks to the fact that the Donnellys' reputation was such that it very well could have been true, which is impressive on its own.

The story first saw print when it reached the receptive ears of Donnelly author Thomas P. Kelley, who reported it as fact in his book *The Black Donnellys*, which was first published in 1954.[8] The tale would certainly be in keeping with the tenor of the times — the gathering of a mob to handle a problem (indeed, it foreshadows the manner in which a mob would be so assembled to interrogate friends of the Donnelly brothers and, ultimately, eradicate five members of their family a mere five years later). However, history has established that Kelley was never one to let the truth get in the way of a good story, and thus, the tale could easily be dismissed as spurious, or at least dubious, but for the fact that it has been related additionally by two other sources[9] (whose accounts, admittedly, may have been based solely upon Kelley's presentation), and so the author feels obliged to present it here, albeit with some measure of skepticism.

The story goes that after enduring so much misfortune at the hands of the Donnelly brothers, Patrick Flanagan had had enough. After the torching of his stables, and with no eyewitnesses present or willing to come forward to charge the Donnellys with the crime, it was time, he decided, to take matters into his own hands. Flanagan had many friends and acquaintances who championed his cause, and so it didn't take long for him to draw together a group of seventeen men the next morning, all hale and hardy types who had built considerable brawn from their daily work on their respective farms, and lead them to confront the Donnelly brothers.

These men gathered up whatever weapons they had at their disposal — shillelaghs, shovels, guns and, in at least one ambitious case, a rope — and advanced, like a military unit, toward the Donnelly stables, which were located in back of the Donnellys' favourite watering hole, the Revere House in Lucan.

The mob arrived at perhaps 6:30 a.m. as, according to Kelley, the Donnellys wanted to have their stage on the road to London by 6:45 a.m.[10] Jim and William Donnelly had just loaded three passengers into their coach — two women and a farm implements salesman — when the mob arrived. Jim Donnelly, who had just removed the halter snap of the lead horse from the hitching rail, was the first to notice them.

"We have visitors," he said calmly to William, nodding toward the eighteen men who had now reached the front of the Revere House, weapons in hand. William looked across from the stage to the men assembled on the road, nodded to his brother, and then opened the door to the stagecoach and stuck his head inside to have a quick word with the passengers.

"Stay in your seats, folks, this won't take long," he said. "The coach will be pulling out on time." With that, he closed the stagecoach door and walked to the stable. He exited a moment later carrying two shillelaghs and tossed one to his brother. The two Donnelly brothers then walked out to face the mob — two against eighteen.

Flanagan, clutching a shotgun, walked out ahead of his group. He wanted William Donnelly all to himself. As William locked eyes with his adversary, Flanagan's gaze suddenly shifted to the side of the Revere House — coming around the corner now were James Donnelly Sr. along with Mike, Tom, John, Pat and Bob, each armed with a shillelagh of his own. The Donnelly men now stood shoulder to shoulder, eight men ready for whatever Flanagan and his mob wanted to throw at them. Despite being considerably outnumbered, James Donnelly Sr. is said to have spoken the first words prior to the battle: "You gentlemen seem to be looking for trouble. If so, the boys and I will be pleased to oblige you."

Confusion now trickled throughout the mob; the Donnellys not only seemed to be expecting them that morning, but actually seemed to be looking forward to the encounter.

William spoke next: "Why the delay? Let's get started!"

This apparent alacrity on the part of the Donnellys gave the mob pause. They had clearly not anticipated that all the men of the Donnelly family would be present when they arrived that morning. Indeed, they had envisioned that the sheer size of their group would have been sufficient to force whatever Donnelly brothers they encountered into pleading for their lives. As Flanagan's men looked among themselves for a sign of what to do next, the Donnellys let out a collective war cry and charged into them, shillelaghs, fists and feet flying. Flanagan made a move to aim his shotgun at one of them, but quickly had it knocked from his hands while simultaneously receiving a blow from a Donnelly club, which sent him sprawling into the dirt. Within a span of ten minutes, the Donnellys had routed the mob, which eventually took to their heels with the Donnellys chasing after them.

William, it is said, then returned to the stage and climbed up onto the driver's seat. One of the female passengers was evidently hysterical at the carnage she had just witnessed and began shrieking in fear at the top of her lungs. "For God's sake, madam, shut up — I could have triplets with less fuss than that," he said, and then, nonchalantly, snapped the horse's reins and started the coach on its way to London.[11]

It is, again, a fantastic story; a sort of *Magnificent Seven* (or rather *Magnificent Eight*, counting James Sr.'s alleged presence in the battle), eighty-five years before the release of the movie. However, there are plenty of problems with the tale. To begin, in Kelley's version, the Flanagan in question is John Flanagan, Patrick's brother, whose stable was located in Clandeboye — not Lucan. And, while there exists a report that John Flanagan's stable had also been burned down (indeed, just three days before his brother Patrick's),[12] this was said to have occurred at Flanagan's Corners on October 1, not in Lucan on August 23, as Kelley reports.[13]

Next, for John Flanagan to have put together a mob of seventeen people from within Flanagan's Corners would have been quite an impressive feat in itself, as would convincing these same people to then walk the two and a half miles southeast to Lucan (almost an hour's walk). Moreover, that an event of this magnitude should have made none of the London newspapers (when other brawls clearly did)[14] is suspicious.

Finally, this was a period of heavy litigation between the Donnelly and Flanagan stage lines; that either party should pass up such an opportunity to bring charges of assault against the other seems bizarrely out of character for all those involved. This is not to say that such a tremendous display of martial prowess on the part of the Donnelly family could not have happened, but rather to suggest that one would be quite within one's rights in assuming that it didn't, and that there should have been at least some information from additional sources if it did. Kelley indicates that the story was related to him by a woman who, in her autumn years, was living in British Columbia, but who had been one of the passengers on the Donnelly stage that morning and who, therefore, had witnessed the altercation first-hand.[15] Presumably she shared it with Kelley, but no indication is given as to who this mystery lady passenger was, nor where she reported the incident (a letter, a newspaper or magazine interview, etc.). The author will therefore leave it to the reader to decide as to its veracity.

When the month of November arrived, so, too, did an arrest warrant for Tom Donnelly to stand trial for his alleged assault on Joseph Berryhill. The warrant was served on November 27, 1875, and indicated that he was to come to London to appear before a tribunal on November 30.[16] When November 30 rolled around, Tom Donnelly was present but Joseph Berryhill failed to appear, as did many of the witnesses who had been called. The trial was subsequently put off until December, and Tom was released into the custody of his older brother Mike.[17]

It was certainly old news to the Donnellys that James Churchill had switched allegiances, and that he had shared with Patrick Flanagan what he claimed to have witnessed Tom Donnelly doing on the night of September 17. This was hugely helpful information to Flanagan who, as a result of the fire and, perhaps, being humiliated in a public street fight, wanted desperately to file charges against the Donnelly brothers. However, Churchill's testimony didn't bother William Donnelly all that much; his knowledge of the law being what it was, he knew all that was needed to make Churchill's allegation a wash was conflicting testimony in the form of a denial from his brother Tom, which was easily obtained. What did catch him by surprise, however, was when in the early days of December he learned that Rhody Kennedy was going to testify that Jim Donnelly had threatened to burn down Flanagan's stable, and had even attempted to pay Rhody to do it. William might have wondered (and probably not quietly) just how stupid and reckless his two brothers could have been; after all, Kennedy's story, if true, would corroborate Churchill's and point the finger of blame directly at the Donnellys for the stable fire. While it was no secret that ill will existed between the Donnellys and the Kennedys, that in and of itself would not be sufficient to cast serious doubt over the veracity of young Kennedy's testimony. Indeed, Rhody Kennedy's impending report was going to be problematic.

But then something fortuitous happened: Rhody Kennedy encountered Bob and Tom Donnelly on the streets of Lucan. Both Donnellys knew how to push young Rhody's buttons, which they apparently did as Kennedy ended up either pushing or punching both of the Donnellys. Either action sufficed, as now the brothers could charge Rhody Kennedy with assault. This gave William the legal ammunition he required: evidence on record that Rhody Kennedy held enmity toward the Donnelly family, which would go some distance in compromising the value of any testimony that Rhody might provide that painted the Donnellys in a bad or illegal light. But perhaps it was Flanagan, more than Kennedy, who required a deterrent of sorts to prevent him from proceeding with any legal action against the brothers. If so, according to a London newspaper, he would receive it in the early morning hours of December 3, 1875:

> A murderous attack was made at Lucan upon a man named Patrick Flanagan who drives one of the stages between this city and that village. As was his wont, he had gone to tend the stage horses before daylight. No sooner however did he open the stable door than he was set upon by an unknown man who, with what he believes to be a club, knocked him to the ground, splitting his head open and rendering him insensible for some time.
>
> Medical assistance was obtained and the wounds inflicted dressed; and it is believed that, although severely injured, he will recover. Whether the fellow had any ill-feeling toward Flanagan or not is unknown, as from the suddenness of the attack and the darkness of the morning, Flanagan is unable to give any clue as to who he was and the scoundrel had decamped before any alarm could be given to the authorities, who are now however on the alert for him.[18]

The culprit was never located. The next day, December 4, Rhody Kennedy was brought before Magistrate Henry Ferguson of Birr, who convicted him on two counts of assault against the two Donnelly brothers and ruled that Kennedy be sent off to the London jail for twenty-five days.[19] Within a span of twenty-four hours, both the Kennedy and the Flanagan problems had been resolved for the Donnelly family, at least for the time being. But there were other legal fires now facing the Donnelly brothers that could not be so easily tamped out.

On December 13, James Curry brought his tale before a London Police Court magistrate. He was positive that Jim and Tom Donnelly had beaten and robbed him on the night of September 17. He further believed that Pat Donnelly had been involved in the assault, and the larceny as well. He charged all three brothers with the crimes. Unfortunately for Curry, three patrons of the Western Hotel came forth to testify that they had been drinking in the tavern with Tom Donnelly when they had observed Curry stagger in and declare that he had been robbed, which meant that Tom could not possibly have committed the assault. After listening to their testimony, James Curry left the court for the nearest tavern, where he promptly got drunk, and didn't bother to return to the courthouse, leaving the magistrate no choice but to dismiss the charges.[20]

On the same day that James Curry abandoned his case, Joseph Berryhill brought his case to court, charging James Keefe and Jim and Tom Donnelly with assault. Unfortunately, an important witness whom Berryhill had been counting on to testify on his behalf only made it as far as the courthouse steps. There he lay down for a nap, his blood alcohol level being far too high for him to be of service. The case looked lost until the strongman revealed to the court the severity of the wounds that had been inflicted on his head and shoulders as a result of the brawl, which prompted the magistrate to convict Tom Donnelly of assault and fine him twenty dollars as punishment, plus $22.25 in court costs.[21] Jim Donnelly and James Keefe would be summoned to court at a later date. And then, on December 28, the Flanagan stage line suffered another loss while in Exeter, when a person or persons unknown packed one of the company's stages with straw and set it on fire.[22] December had not been a good month for Flanagan.

During the twenty-five days of his sentence, Rhody Kennedy fumed and schemed to come up with a way to get back at the Donnelly brothers. With the use of only one arm, Kennedy had no intention of attempting to fight any of the brothers; his revenge would have to be through the courts. Upon his release on December 29, the only option he had come up with was to countercharge Bob and Tom Donnelly with assault. Both Donnelly brothers were promptly arrested but freed on bail, and summoned to be tried on January 13.[23]

The next day Rhody did what William Donnelly had suspected he might; he testified in front of justice of the peace Henry Ferguson, revealing that Jim Donnelly had conspired to commit arson when he had asked Rhody to burn down Flanagan's stables. Upon hearing the charge, William Donnelly stood up and, in a clever bit of legal manoeuvring, charged Rhody with perjury. Technically, William pointed out, Patrick Flanagan didn't own the stable that burned down; he merely leased it from a man named John Donohue.[24] Consequently, there were no "Flanagan's stables." Clearly, then, Rhody Kennedy was lying. To Kennedy's chagrin, the presiding magistrate accepted William Donnelly's interpretation of the law on the matter and decided to put both cases off until January 13.

The arrival of January brought with it an uneasy sense of foreboding. On January 4, 1876, the London, Huron and Bruce Railway (LH&B) officially opened for business — and business was brisk. Covering a distance of seventy-four miles, the LH&B represented both the novelty and the luxury of travel by train, and resulted in more and more passengers defecting from what was now considered to be the more outmoded conveyance of the stagecoach. Indeed, less than a month after its introduction, an Exeter paper reported that

> [n]orth and south, the passenger coach [of the train]
> is completely filled, and but little more crowding will
> demand another coach to be placed on the line . . .
> Since the opening of the railroad, the travel by stage

has fallen off so that the morning stages to London
are taken off entirely. . . .[25]

Every passenger that opted to travel by rail represented one lost to
either the Donnelly or the Flanagan stage, with the result that the
revenue of both businesses diminished and anxiety heightened as,
off in the distance, the dark clouds of change were gathering. And,
perhaps in a last act of defiance to the transportation change that
was taking place, the trestles of an overpass on the LH&B were
sawn through.[26] Understandably, the Donnellys were suspected of
having perpetrated the nefarious deed.

The Donnelly fortunes took a further turn for the worse in
January when the Lindsay ladies won their lawsuit against the
brothers for the accident in front of the Swartz Hotel. Louisa Lindsay
was awarded twenty dollars in compensation, while her daughter,
Martha Lindsay, was awarded fifteen dollars. The Donnellys were
additionally ordered to pay all the legal costs of the trial, which
came out to ninety-five dollars.[27] With the Donnellys now ruled to
have been at fault for the stage accident, Flanagan's driver Robert
McLeod's appeal suddenly took on new life. Upon returning to
court, the magistrate ruled in McLeod's favour, which cancelled
out his previous conviction, and the Donnellys were made to pay
his legal costs.[28] Despite the presence of the railway threat, Patrick
Flanagan's fortunes were now starting to look up.

On January 13, Rhody Kennedy's trial for perjury came before
Magistrate Henry Ferguson. Kennedy maintained his claim that
Jim Donnelly had attempted to entice him to burn down Patrick
Flanagan's stables. Jim Donnelly denied that he'd ever said any
such thing. Jim's brother, Tom, was then brought forth and backed
his older brother's play, stating that he had been with his brother
all evening and that no such discussion had ever taken place.[29]
With Kennedy's claim denied by two parties, Magistrate Ferguson
recognized that he was looking at a "he said/he said" situation.

Moreover, it was evident to Ferguson that this was a case that clearly involved two parties who intensely disliked each other, which would make the truth difficult to ferret out. He decided to release Rhody Kennedy on bail, and have the matter held over until the Middlesex Spring Assizes.

Perhaps seeing that the days of the stagecoach were quickly coming to an end, and after a year of dealing with the Donnelly threat on an almost daily basis, Patrick Flanagan decided to call it a day and cash out while there was still cash to be had. He sold his stage business to Lucan's Richard Bryant who, together with Hawkshaw's former partner, Ted Crawley, decided to make a go of it. They hired a new driver, Peter McKellar, and, being cognizant of the omnipresent threat of the Donnellys, Bryant and Crawley hired none other than Rhody Kennedy, who was now out on bail until his next court appearance in the spring, to ride shotgun for the stage line — just in case the Donnelly brothers got any ideas into their heads that the new owners would be a pushover like Flanagan had appeared to be.[30]

Despite the additional security measures, Richard Bryant met with little success. On January 16, a by-now familiar vandalism welcomed him to the stagecoach business when one of his carriages was surreptitiously removed from its shelter, taken a quarter of a mile away and then smashed to pieces.[31] Eight days later, two of the Donnelly brothers met up with Bryant's new driver Peter McKellar. Sometime around 6:30 a.m., McKellar, with his guard Rhody Kennedy riding shotgun alongside him, pulled his stage into Lucan to make a pickup at the Queen's Hotel. It was a cold morning, and when he arrived at the front of the hotel he called out for someone to bring him out a buffalo robe to keep his legs warm for his ride to London that morning. The robe was brought out and handed up to McKellar, who quickly wrapped the garment around his legs. McKellar then called out for any passengers who were looking to go to London. His raised voice drew the attention of John and Bob

Donnelly, who happened to be on the sidewalk across the street. Seeing that their old sparring partner Rhody Kennedy was aboard the stage, the brothers decided to head over and introduce themselves to Bryant's new driver. Rhody Kennedy began to shift in his seat as the Donnellys approached the stage.

"Come down off the stage and take drink," said a smiling John Donnelly.[32] Again, it was 6:30 in the morning.

McKellar declined John's invitation. Rhody Kennedy didn't say a thing. But the brothers weren't giving up that easily. Feigning surprise, John turned to Bob and shrugged his shoulders. He again addressed McKellar.

"If you won't drink here at Bowey's, then you must drink at McLean's!"[33] Bob Donnelly half smirked at his brother's suggestion. The vibe that McKellar was getting from the brothers was decidedly negative. He decided that waiting for any potential passengers to come out of the Queen's Hotel was only inviting danger and so, without reply, he snapped the reins of his team of horses and the stagecoach headed off down the street.

John and Bob then began running alongside the stage as it rolled along, but once it passed the front of the Central Hotel, the brothers knew that McKellar had no intention of stopping — and so they took matters into their own hands. Bob ran to the front of the stage and grabbed hold of the horses' heads, which brought the team to a full stop. John then leapt atop the wagon wheel on the opposite side from where McKellar was seated and, reaching over Rhody Kennedy, he grabbed hold of McKellar's buffalo robe with one arm, which not only locked up the driver's legs, but also effectively pinned one of McKellar's arms under the robe in the process. With his free hand, John struck McKellar. It was not a hard blow, but it did serve to secure the driver's attention.

"I'd like you to come down off that stage," John said menacingly.

McKellar tried to pull his legs free, but Donnelly had too firm a grip on the robe.

"McKellar, I'll have your life if you don't quit driving stage before a week — or any other man that would drive it," Donnelly threatened.

McKellar yanked his arm free from under the robe, his mitt coming off as he did so. "Let go of the horses!" he yelled.

Having delivered his message, John called to his brother, "Robert, let's go." Donnelly released his hold on McKellar's legs and jumped down from the wheel of the stagecoach and the two men ran off. McKellar looked over at Rhody Kennedy, who had been silent for the entire duration of the scene that had just played out. A wave of disgust washed over him as he steered the stagecoach out of Lucan toward London. He must have wondered just what sort of "guard" work Bryant was paying Kennedy for.

When the Bryant stage reached London later that morning, McKellar immediately sought out a friend of his by the name of Henry Brien and told him what had occurred between him and the two Donnelly brothers. Brien was a former county constable, and McKellar's story gave him cause for concern. He decided to accompany McKellar on the stage when the driver returned to Lucan later that afternoon. As an extra precaution, he tucked his service revolver inside his coat.

At some point later that afternoon on the Proof Line Road, the Bryant stage encountered the Donnelly stagecoach, driven by Mike Donnelly. Once again, insults and threats were directed at McKellar — and also at Brien, who, unlike Rhody Kennedy, had evidently felt obliged to stick up for the driver of the Bryant stage.[34] The unpleasantness would accompany the stagecoaches back to Lucan.

A little after 5 p.m., both the Donnelly and the Bryant stages returned to Lucan, with the Bryant stage arriving first.[35] After putting up their team of horses in the stable behind the Queen's Hotel, McKellar, Brien and Rhody Kennedy were about to head across the street to the Revere House tavern for a drink when the Donnelly stage rolled into town. Mike Donnelly took notice of the three men as he drove past and the look on his face when he saw them was such that Brien felt obliged to subtly slip his revolver to McKellar. After depositing his passengers at the hotel and securing his horses in the stable, Mike Donnelly walked directly over to where the trio was standing and challenged McKellar to fight. McKellar wisely said nothing and the three men walked across the street and entered the Revere House tavern, where they were joined by another friend, the Lucan tinsmith Henry Collins. After a little while the four men decided to leave the Revere House and headed over to drink at the Central House Hotel. As they walked along the sidewalk they yet again encountered Mike Donnelly, who was standing in front of the Central House when they arrived. They also noted that Mike's brother William was on the scene and was blocking the entranceway to the tavern. This did not look like it was going to end well.

Mike Donnelly reached into his pocket and pulled forth a roll of cash. He extended it toward McKellar, offering it to the driver if he would fight him. Despite having twice the number of men on his side, McKellar wanted no part of a fight with the Donnelly brothers. He brushed past Mike toward the hotel entrance, only to have his way blocked by William Donnelly. McKellar had had enough for one day; he pulled out the revolver that Brien had given him and pointed it at William Donnelly's stomach.

"Leave my way, you son of a bitch," he said, "or I'll put a ball through you." William smiled and stepped aside, and then watched as McKellar, Kennedy, Brien and Collins entered the establishment.

When the men left the tavern later that night, Henry Collins cautioned McKellar to be careful, which caused the stage driver to laugh. "Don't worry, I've got a good pair of legs," he said. He also had a good sense of self-preservation, for, a week later, he heeded John Donnelly's advice and quit his job as a driver for the Bryant stage line.[36]

The incident, however, prompted another round of legal wrangling, with charges and countercharges laid. McKellar and Brien charged Mike Donnelly with using abusive language and threatening McKellar's life.[37] William Donnelly, in turn, charged McKellar with pointing a revolver and threatening to shoot him.[38] For his part, McKellar denied that he even had a revolver with him on the night in question. The accusation and denial regarding McKellar pointing and threatening with a gun would take a little more time for Magistrate Henry Ferguson to process. He wrote to the London Crown attorney, Charles Hutchinson: "I have got into those unfortunate cases in and about Lucan . . . I am of the opinion that if something is not done there will be lives lost. Advise me what would be the best way to proceed."[39]

Brien then developed second thoughts about proceeding with his lawsuit against Mike Donnelly and attempted to withdraw it, but he was not permitted to do so by the magistrate. Mike Donnelly was subsequently convicted and fined five dollars, and bound to keep the peace for one year.[40]

In the meantime, Rhody Kennedy had decided to earn his pay to defend the Bryant stage by having himself appointed a special constable by the county authorities.[41] As a guard on the stage line; he had pretty much become the town joke. He was a guard in name only; with only one arm, he wasn't going to intimidate anybody physically and, while he could ride "shotgun," there was no way that he could shoot one. He lacked the brute strength and dexterity necessary to intimidate or to give pause to a would-be adversary. But being a special constable changed all that. The power to arrest somebody was, to Rhody Kennedy at least, the great equalizer; people now had to listen when he spoke and heed his commands. He now was a man who wielded legal authority. Looking to exercise his new power and to make a statement to the people of Lucan, Kennedy immediately obtained warrants to arrest both Bob and John Donnelly — Bob for having prevented McKellar's horses from leaving Lucan, and John for climbing up on the wheel of the stagecoach and threatening McKellar.

Upon picking up the written warrants on January 28, Kennedy found himself riding shotgun later that same afternoon on what would have been one of Peter McKellar's final stage runs. As the stage entered the town of Lucan and proceeded along its main street, Kennedy happened to spy Bob Donnelly. Rhody had McKellar stop the stage in front of the platform of the Central House Hotel. He climbed down and made his way toward Bob. As he drew closer he drew himself up and announced in a loud voice for all to hear that he was "placing Robert Donnelly under arrest." Bob was initially amused by his former friend's proclamation.

Rhody then took a firm hold of Bob Donnelly's arm.

A small crowd began to gather and Kennedy then made another loud declaration. "You, Robert Donnelly, are my prisoner in the name of the Queen!"

Bob's demeanour now changed from mild amusement to deadly seriousness. He subtly directed Kennedy's attention to his right hand, which was now holding a revolver. He spoke but four words, in a voice just loud enough for Kennedy alone to hear: "Let go of me."[42] Bob Donnelly, even without a gun, was naturally intimidating in a way that few men are, and that Rhody Kennedy could never hope to be. Rhody, of all people, having grown up with the Donnellys, should have known how poor his chances would be of (literally) single-handedly arresting Bob Donnelly. Instead of following Bob's directive, however, Rhody instead squeezed his grip even tighter on his would-be prisoner's arm. Unlike his brother William, Bob Donnelly had no interest in sparring verbally with any adversary; he instead struck Kennedy in the face with his gun — repeatedly. Rhody cried out as blood began streaming down his face. A crowd quickly gathered around the two men. From his vantage point sitting atop the stagecoach, driver Peter McKellar could see Rhody Kennedy being pistol-whipped. He immediately jumped down from the stage and started running to his guard's defence — which is when John Donnelly stepped out in front of him.

"Take one more step and I'll shoot you," he said.[43]

McKellar took heed of the warning and simply watched as Rhody took several more blows from Bob Donnelly's revolver. Blood now covered Rhody's face like a crimson mask and yet, despite the thrashing he was receiving, he refused to let go of his prey. To him, it wasn't just his aptitude as a constable that was now on the line, but his very dignity as a human being. He had to hang on to his prisoner — no matter the cost to him physically. Indeed, every time Bob attempted to jerk his arm free, Rhody pulled tighter on it. Jim Donnelly now appeared from out of the crowd of onlookers and grabbed hold of Kennedy's arm.

"Let him go!" he demanded.

With two Donnellys now involved, Rhody knew that any attempt to salvage his pride in the matter was now gone; he had no recourse but to yell for assistance. But nobody from within the multitude moved.

At this point, seeing that Rhody had no intention of releasing his hold on Bob, Jim kicked Rhody hard in the stomach, which dropped the newly minted constable to his knees, bending Bob over with him as he fell. With Jim continuing to kick Rhody, Bob struck him another blow with his revolver and then bit hard into his ex-friend's lip, which finally produced the desired effect: Rhody released his grip.[44]

Finally, someone came to the thoroughly beaten Rhody Kennedy's aid. County constable John Bawden bulled his way through the assembled throng and grabbed hold of Jim Donnelly's arm, yanking it free from Kennedy's. Taking note of the constable's arrival, John Donnelly now ran into the fray and, taking hold of Bob, pulled him out of the scrum and walked him briskly through the crowd and away from the area.[45] Bob Donnelly then left Biddulph until things cooled down. He would not return until June of 1877.[46]

The Donnelly brothers were making quite a reputation for themselves.

On January 31, 1876, the county Crown attorney recommended that Magistrate Henry Ferguson acquit Peter McKellar on the charge of pointing a gun at William Donnelly as the testimony was a wash, with one side accusing the other.[47] When Ferguson acted on this recommendation, it immediately opened the door for McKellar to lay a countercharge of perjury against William Donnelly, which he did on February 2, 1876.[48] William, who had opted for ten days in jail rather than paying the fine awarded to the Lindsay ladies, was released from his sentence on February 4, whereupon he was promptly rearrested on McKellar's charge, and committed for trial at the Middlesex Spring Assizes.

Rhody Kennedy then threw another charge on the pile, summoning William Donnelly to court on February 17 to defend himself against the charge of using abusive language during the incident in front of the Central House Hotel on the evening of January 24.[49]

William Donnelly had had enough of Rhody Kennedy, who, like a persistent gadfly, refused to go away no matter how many times one swatted at it. William filed a countercharge against Kennedy for using abusive language. Once again, because of the contradictory nature of the accusations, Magistrate Henry Ferguson felt compelled to write to the county Crown attorney, Charles Hutchinson, as to what course he should follow. Hutchinson advised that Kennedy should be acquitted.[50]

Ferguson, however, did not take the Crown attorney's advice this time around; instead he made Kennedy pay a $700 bond to keep the peace (which was a huge sum for the time). To ensure payment, he further ordered that Kennedy use a constable's assistance in obtaining guarantors for the bond — the constable that Magistrate Ferguson selected for the task turned out to be his own son, Charles

Ferguson — and then charged Kennedy for the constable's fees.[51] Kennedy was incensed at the magistrate's decision and, foolishly, his next step was to verbally and physically assault the first Donnelly he laid eyes on, which resulted in his being immediately sent back to jail.[52] He was released on bail shortly thereafter, and then had to appear for his trial in London against William Donnelly for using abusive language.

While in London, Rhody sought out Crown attorney Charles Hutchinson for guidance, and apprised him of his dilemma; he pointed out that Magistrate Ferguson had not only ignored Hutchinson's recommendation to acquit, but instead had imposed a massive fine upon him.[53] Hutchinson was not impressed that Ferguson had ruled contrary to his advice. And while the Crown attorney stewed about how he would deal with the matter, Kennedy proceeded to charge Bob and Jim Donnelly with assault for beating him up in the streets of Lucan. He further filed a charge for the assault he had witnessed the Donnelly brothers commit on Peter McKellar on January 24.[54] By the time Rhody had finished with his charges, Hutchinson had reached a conclusion as to how he intended to respond to Ferguson's action in the matter, and ordered the magistrate to reimburse Kennedy for the costs Ferguson had imposed upon him for having his son, Constable Charles Ferguson, assist him in finding guarantors for his bond to keep the peace. For its part, the police court reissued warrants to have Jim and Bob Donnelly arrested. But then, just as things were starting to break Kennedy's way, a magistrate in Lucan ordered him sent to jail for three weeks in consequence of his tirade after Ferguson had handed down his original verdict.

The situation in Lucan was now such that a plea went out from the local press for someone to come forth and deliver the village from the evils that had beset it:

It is a chance for a clever detective. Who will put a stop to this extraordinary state of affairs? Matters have now reached such a crisis in Lucan that nobody thinks of going out at night without a revolver, and the person who goes on another person's premises after dark goes at the risk of his life, for if the owner happens to be a nervous man, he may shoot first and make inquiries afterwards. Something should be done and done speedily, to stamp out the rowdyism which has been practised in the village with impunity for the last year or two, or the prospects of the village are not worth much.[55]

The call for a "clever detective" and for someone to "put a stop to this extraordinary state of affairs" was taken seriously, particularly by Patrick Flanagan who, despite now being on the sidelines of the stagecoach wars, still harboured a deep-seated hatred toward the Donnellys. Moreover, he had noted that the Donnellys had lost several court cases of late — even with William Donnelly at the helm. Had a potential Achilles heel just been exposed? Perhaps if such a detective could be enticed to come to Lucan to ferret out more crimes that the family could be charged with, the Donnelly brothers might well be sent to prison, or bled of all their ill-gotten gains to the point that they would have to leave Middlesex County. From Flanagan's perspective, it was certainly worth a try. To this end Flanagan reached out to a private detective named Hugh McKinnon,[56] late of the Hamilton police force. McKinnon already had a reputation as a ruthless and brutal man who had lost his job on the force due to his use of excessive violence. Here was a man who spoke the Donnellys' language, and who could (if one will forgive the metaphor) fight fire with fire.

CHAPTER SEVEN

HUGH McKINNON, P.I.

Private Detective Hugh McKinnon. (By permission of Ray Fazakas, author of *The Donnelly Album* and *In Search of the Donnellys*)

His most circulated photo depicts a proud (if not vain) and serious man, with over thirty medals pinned to his jacket and a walrus moustache that would have impressed Nietzsche. Private detective Hugh McKinnon was said to stand six foot three inches tall at a time when the average male height hovered around five foot six, and he weighed a rock-solid 225 pounds.[1] McKinnon was, as his photo bears witness, a well-decorated athlete, with a particular aptitude for Highland Games competition, excelling in the hammer throw, shot put and caber toss.[2] He won the International Games held in Toronto in 1875, where he was proclaimed the "best general athlete," and he would go on to win the heavyweight championship of North America in Charlottetown, Prince Edward Island, and then compete successfully in the United States, in cities such as Philadelphia, Baltimore, Washington, Brooklyn, Providence, Boston, Buffalo, Troy and New York, amassing some forty-three gold and silver medals in the process.

Born into a large (eleven children) Scottish Presbyterian family[3] he articled briefly at his brother's law firm before joining the Hamilton police force, where he eventually made detective. In addition to his law enforcement duties and athletic prowess, McKinnon appears to have been active socially, joining the Freemasons and various Scottish societies that existed throughout Ontario in the nineteenth century.[4] Unfortunately, McKinnon, who was married with a daughter, was also a philanderer and something of a hothead. He had acquired some measure of notoriety when he confronted a reporter on the streets of Hamilton who had written an article about McKinnon's brother — a city alderman — that accused him of embezzlement. McKinnon, who was a policeman at the time, demanded that the reporter publish a retraction. The reporter refused . . . and McKinnon beat him senseless right there on the street.[5] The reporter charged him with assault and McKinnon was removed from the force and left looking for a career. He was thirty-three, and clearly an imposing man physically, when he came to Lucan in February 1876, and he brought with him the ruthless ways of detectives from the cities who, in the mid-1800s, often operated as a law unto themselves.

He claimed to have arrived incognito, posing as "a sporting man who had not only a superabundance of muscle, but plenty of money."[6] His plan, at least according to several self-serving interviews that he later granted to the press in the aftermath of the Donnelly family murders, was to slip unnoticed into the establishments that the Donnelly brothers were known to frequent and clandestinely observe their behaviour and speak with the common folk around town to learn of any incriminating activities in which the Donnellys might be involved.[7] When this approach didn't pan out, his next step was to act in such a way that the brothers would believe he was their ally, and, therefore, take him into their confidence. Once he'd gained their trust, he was certain that he would be capable of obtaining confessions that he could then use to charge them with crimes and have them sent to jail. But how to do it? McKinnon said the opportunity presented itself one evening rather serendipitously:

> One day shortly after arriving in Lucan I was sitting in a barroom and heard a man railing at the Donnellys in a most violent manner. The opportunity was too good a one to be lost, so I immediately turned to the irate talker and rebuked him for scandalizing people who were not present to defend themselves, and to whom he dared not speak in such terms to their faces. One word brought on another, and finally I was obliged to end the discussions by giving the man an open-handed slap in the face. As soon as this incident reached the ears of the Donnelly boys, it convinced them that I must indeed be their friend, and I thereby gained their confidence.[8]

This, of course, was McKinnon's version. The Donnellys, however, had quite a different version. McKinnon, because of his being a new face in Lucan, and also because of his physical stature, stood out. Indeed, on the very first day of the private detective's arrival, Mike Donnelly had told a constable friend of his in London that a new detective had arrived in Lucan to spy on them.[9] As a consequence, the Donnellys eyed the new arrival suspiciously from the outset, often learning in advance what he was up to, as well as when he would be leaving and returning to Lucan.[10] McKinnon, however, was oblivious to his cover having already been blown, and believed wholeheartedly that his sly and cunning intelligence was gradually gaining him entry to the Donnellys' inner sanctum.

McKinnon, in all likelihood, rather than cleverly infiltrating the Donnellys' inner circle, simply hung around the taverns of Lucan and London in an attempt to surreptitiously gain some hearsay information on the Donnelly brothers' crimes; or, at the very least, to happen upon some leads that he might pursue. To this end, he took notes on some of the rumours he had picked up on:

- somebody was said to have given matches to the Donnellys on the evening that Patrick Flanagan's stables went up in flames
- somebody in Sarnia was said to have witnessed Thomas Donnelly attempt to burn Flanagan's stables on the night of the Berryhill fight
- somebody else was certain that the Donnellys had threatened on numerous times to burn down William Bowey's Queen's Hotel

McKinnon then made note of some thefts that were made in the area, perhaps the work of the Donnellys: some sheepskins and a tea shipment were missing. Another person was said to have paid a Donnelly family member's bail — why would he do that? Yet another person — the Lucan postmaster no less! — loudly proclaimed himself to be "a Donnelly man." What could that mean?[11] The detective was seeing a lot of loose threads, but no means of weaving them into a meaningful tapestry. McKinnon had even met clandestinely with Joseph Carswell, a man who habitually liked to point the finger at the Donnellys as being responsible for virtually all of his woes, and tried to convince the failed farmer to file charges against the family for the burning of his grain and the killing of his horses, but Carswell wanted no part of it.[12] In short, after five weeks of snooping around, McKinnon had nothing.

By the third week of February three new constables had been appointed in Biddulph — John Courcey, John Bawden and John Reid — to bolster the presence of local law enforcement throughout the township.[13] Having more constables was one thing: gainfully employing them to arrest the Donnellys was another matter entirely. Still, McKinnon did what he could. He reviewed the most recent charges that had been brought against various members of the family and looked to see if there were any legal loopholes that, if a Donnelly family member had been acquitted, might allow for him to be retried. He also looked through the testimony of these cases to locate where any additional charges might be brought to bear. To this end, he wrote to county Crown attorney Hutchinson:

> I have been for some time back engaged in ferreting
> out the perpetrators of certain crimes which have
> been committed in Lucan and its vicinity. I believe
> I have sufficient evidence in my possession to
> commit certain parties who have committed these
> crimes. I don't know if Pat Flanagan ever laid
> any information before a magistrate either for the
> burning of his stable or the attempted murder of
> himself. If he has not done so before the Police
> Magistrate in London, would you please write
> him to come in and do so at once. His address
> is McGillivray P.O. He resides in "Irish Town."
> I would also want Carswell who had his barn
> burned, stock killed and crops destroyed, to do the
> same, but we will attend to his case again.
>
> In the meantime, I presume you are already
> familiar with a great many circumstances connected
> with those crimes and offences which from time to

time have been committed in Lucan by the so called "Ku-Klux." When do your Assizes take place, and who is to be the Judge?

I am at presently in Stratford where I will remain until I hear from you. Please let me hear from you by return of mail — do not mention my name to any person but Flanagan at present. For the past three weeks I have been in Lucan, and so managed matters that only to those who should know was my real character known.

And so matters are, and so I desire them to remain for a few days yet.

Yours truly,
Hugh McKinnon
P.S. What has been done with Kennedy upon the last arrest by the Donnellys?[14]

It should be pointed out at this point that the Donnellys had absolutely zero affiliation with anything resembling what we presently know as the Ku Klux Klan. While the Klan had existed in the United States since 1865, it wouldn't make its way into Canada until 1924, when its first official Canadian branch would be started in Toronto. For reasons unknown, the London newspapers, particularly the *London Free Press*, had taken to referring to the Donnelly brothers and their friends as the "Lucan Ku Klux" ever since their failed rescue attempt of Margaret Thompson in 1874.[15] This is a peculiar epithet for the paper to label them with, particularly given that there is no record of the Donnellys ever harbouring any ill will toward African-Americans. Indeed, William Donnelly had gone on public record about the ill treatment of the Wilberforce settlers:

About thirty-five years ago, all the farms around the Sauble Hill were taken up by coloured people. Some of the folks who now call themselves law-abiders of Lucan lived at that time convenient to the Sauble Hill, and being eager to get the land out of the hands of the poor Africans, were willing to use any means to accomplish their ends. Accordingly, the plan was laid, and in the middle of the night, and in the depth of winter, those poor coloured folks, with honest hearts into them, were rooted out of house and home. Where this occurred is about half a mile from Lucan, and to their credit be it said the great part of those arrested for it are high-flyers in Lucan today [Donnelly is referencing none other than Bernard Stanley here, a man who had an active hand in driving out certain of the Wilberforce settlers from their homes, which Stanley coveted]. One thing [is] certain, none of our family were born at that time, except my father and mother, and they were never blamed for it.[16]

One could be forgiven for presuming that the leader of the Biddulph faction of the KKK would be made of sterner stuff. In any event, in McKinnon's eyes, as well as those whose only knowledge of the family was what they read in the local newspapers, the Donnellys and the Ku Klux Klan from south of the border were synonymous. As the private detective scanned the various arrest reports and court records on the brothers, looking for anything that they might be recharged with, the only previous charges that invited revisiting were Jim Donnelly's assault on Rhody Kennedy (when the latter had foolishly attempted to arrest Bob Donnelly on the morning of January 24), and John Donnelly's assault on stage driver Peter

McKellar. Regarding the latter charge, McKinnon noted that when John Donnelly's trial had been held in London on February 17, John Donnelly had failed to appear (he had been in Birr that day so he and his brother William could lay fresh charges against Rhody Kennedy for disorderly conduct). This decision by John had opened up the opportunity for his re-arrest. McKinnon applied for and received the necessary warrants to re-arrest John Donnelly, and then summoned the three newly appointed constables and revealed to them his plan of action to apprehend both Jim and John Donnelly.[17]

Two weeks would pass before the constables would act upon the warrants, however. It was McKinnon's desire to be in Stratford when the arrests were made, as he believed that his true identity was still undetected in the community, and he wanted to keep it that way. In addition, he knew of a forthcoming event that the two Donnelly brothers would be attending, which would bring them both together in one location in a very public setting. This, he believed, would better the chances of their arrests being made without incident. He couldn't have foreseen just how wrong this belief would prove to be.

The event that McKinnon had in mind was the wedding of twenty-six-year-old Thomas Ryder. Thomas was the younger brother of fifty-year-old Grouchy Ryder (who along with his late uncle Patrick was believed to have been involved in the Brimmacombe murder in 1857). The Ryders were a large Irish family that had been neighbours of the Donnellys on the Roman Line for over thirty years, with the result that William, John and Jim, along with several of their friends, were among the invited guests.

The wedding took place at St. Patrick's Church in Biddulph during the morning of February 24, 1876, with the reception to follow at Joseph Fitzhenry's hotel on Alice Street in Lucan. During the afternoon, Fitzhenry's Hotel filled up quickly, with the result that the overflow of wedding guests took their celebrating to the nearby Revere House tavern. The three constables, Courcey, Reid and Bawden, acting under their instructions from McKinnon, planned to arrest Jim and John Donnelly during the reception.

Armed with the warrant for Jim Donnelly, Constable Courcey first scoped out Fitzhenry's Hotel and, not spying his quarry there, moved along to the Revere House. Upon entering the establishment, the constable spotted Jim and William Donnelly among a crowd of revellers. When William walked away from Jim to mingle with some of the other wedding guests, Courcey saw his opening and made his move. He approached the oldest Donnelly brother, informed him that he was under arrest and then proceeded to walk Jim Donnelly out the front door of the hotel and onto the wooden sidewalk. Having Donnelly by the arm, Courcey marched him toward Fitzhenry's, where he knew his fellow constables would be waiting.

In the meantime, William Donnelly had noticed that his brother was gone, and asked one of the wedding guests where he had disappeared to. When William was informed that Jim had been taken out of the hotel in the custody of a local constable, he immediately went out the front door and into the street. Spotting Courcey escorting his older brother rather roughly along the sidewalk, William yelled out, "Jim! Don't be dragged along the streets by *that* fellow!"[18] William's words caused his brother to come to an abrupt halt.

And this is the point where things went sideways.

Jim Donnelly immediately pulled himself free from Courcey and began walking back toward William at the tavern. Courcey ran up and grabbed hold of him again but ended up being pulled along the sidewalk by his prisoner. When the pair had reached the Revere House, William Donnelly stepped forward and drew a revolver. Pointing it at Courcey, he said matter-of-factly, "I'll blow the heart out of you or any man that would take Jim — or any other one of the family."

At this point, Jim Donnelly jerked his arm free from Courcey's grasp and threw off his coat. He looked the constable in the eye and said, "There's no constable in Lucan able to take me!" Courcey had no desire to get into a fistfight with Jim Donnelly. He also knew that going for his holstered gun would not be wise, particularly given that William already had his gun out and trained on him. Seeing that his only option was to exit, he slowly backed away, turned, and headed off to confer with his fellow constables about the dilemma.

Jim and William then walked over to Fitzhenry's Hotel, ordered some drinks, and told their younger brother John about their encounter with the constable. None of the brothers believed the matter was over at this point, and so while they enjoyed themselves among their friends, they also kept an eye on the front door in case the law decided to return.

After Courcey had consulted with Bawden and Reid, the trio concluded that the best approach would be a full frontal assault — with three armed constables taking hold of the prisoners, there shouldn't be any trouble. There was strength in numbers, after all, and so it was resolved that they would head over to the Revere House and make the arrests as a group. They arrived at the tavern only to discover that the Donnelly brothers had left. With hastened strides the three constables made their way along the sidewalk to Fitzhenry's Hotel. Upon entering the establishment, they quickly scanned the room for Jim Donnelly.

John Donnelly had observed the trio's entry and, not realizing that the constables were looking to arrest him as well, walked directly up to Constable Bawden.

"Bawden, what's this about?" he asked.

"*You're* under arrest in the name of the Queen!" exclaimed Bawden, who immediately took hold of the surprised Donnelly's arm.

John Donnelly was in no mood for this and pulled his arm free. He had no problem with being arrested as he was confident that he could beat whatever the charge was. What he objected to was the fact the constables had waited until *this* day — a day when everyone was celebrating a wedding — to make their arrests. He offered to go with the constable on another day, once the wedding celebration was over. Bawden wasn't interested.

"You ought to mind your business — for this day at least," John Donnelly said, his temper now starting to rise. "When you arrested me before, I went with you like a man."

"Yes, when you *had to*," Bawden said disdainfully. Seeing that Bawden had hold of his prisoner, but might need assistance, Constable Courcey approached, and both men firmly took hold of John Donnelly's arms and began pulling him toward the front door of the hotel.

John Donnelly's temper was now at full boil.

"You son of a bitch!" he yelled. "If you don't let me go I'll kill you!"

Such a commotion, combined with such loud and colourful language, soon attracted the attention of the wedding guests within the tavern, many of whom were friends of the Donnellys. The crowd now encircled the constables. Fearing that Donnelly might break free, Bawden called out to the crowd: "I call for your assistance in the name of the Queen!" The irony of this pronouncement, made by a Protestant constable in a room full of Irish Roman Catholics, would not have been lost on the crowd. Several wedding guests did indeed step forward, but they were clearly on the side of John Donnelly, and were not about to see a fellow wedding guest, and a Catholic one at that, arrested by Protestant constables during what was supposed to be a time of joy and celebration.

Three wedding guests grabbed hold of John Donnelly and tried to pull him free of his two would-be captors, while the constables, for their part, attempted to pull him toward the front door. This tug of war occurred three times, with the constables pulling their prisoner almost to the front door of the hotel, and the wedding guests succeeding in pulling him back deeper into the tavern. Some of the wedding guests, James Keefe among them, began to throw kicks at the lawmen, which caused the constables, in order to protect themselves, to release their grip on the prisoner.

Now out of the clutches of the law for the moment, John Donnelly walked back toward the bar at the far end of the room — he had a drink to finish. However, no sooner had he reached the bar than Bawden rushed at him again. The constable attempted to tackle him, but Donnelly stood his ground and both men started grappling. That's when William Donnelly showed up — this time with a four-shot revolver in one hand and a shillelagh in the other. According to Bawden,

> William Donnelly presented his revolver close to my
> face and said, "You son of a bitch! If you don't let him
> go I'll shoot you!" I still held on and he fired at me.
> The shot did not take effect. William Donnelly fired
> again, and this shot at me was directed about four or
> five feet [past Bawden]. Then William Donnelly struck
> me several blows with a heavy cane.[19]

After William Donnelly's shillelagh had dug into his skull three or four times, Bawden fell to the floor, bleeding profusely and disoriented. Witnessing a fellow constable in trouble, Constable Reid now drew his service revolver. He took aim at the wild-eyed William Donnelly, who was standing before him with a weapon in each of his hands. Before Reid could squeeze the trigger, however, a shillelagh crashed into his nose, breaking it and sending him sprawling onto the barroom floor. The shillelagh was held by twenty-three-year-old William Farrell, the son of Patrick Farrell, the man James Donnelly Sr. had killed at the logging bee some nineteen years previously, but who now was fiercely loyal to the Donnelly family. Half dazed, Constable Reid fumbled on the floor for his service revolver. Although his eyes were watery from the blow from the shillelagh, he brought himself to his feet, raised the pistol and took a shot at somebody whom he hoped was Farrell. Seeing the revolver in the constable's hand, Farrell turned and started running toward the front door of the hotel. Reid proceeded to chase the young man and caught up with him in the hallway. He grabbed Farrell by the collar and proceeded to strike him repeatedly on the head with his revolver. Farrell, now doubled over, reached into his jacket and pulled out a revolver of his own. Reid pushed his man outside and moved in to grab him again. As he did so, one of the two men caught a foot on the tongue of a sleigh that had been parked in front of Fitzhenry's, which sent both men tumbling into the snowy street. As they fell, Farrell's revolver discharged, sending a bullet into the abdomen of Constable Reid. And then, flooded with adrenalin and perhaps in a moment of insanity, Farrell stood up, took aim and fired another bullet into the fallen constable.

Meanwhile, back in the tavern, Constable Bawden had regained his feet and resumed his fight with John Donnelly. As the two men continued to throw punches and wrestle, they stepped back and bumped into a woodstove that was heating the barroom and tumbled to the floor. Donnelly ended up on top of the constable and began pummelling him. When he thought Bawden had had enough, John picked himself up and walked over to the bar. His abandoned whiskey was looking rather welcoming at this point. Within seconds, however, the constable was back on his feet and again charging at his opponent from behind; the impact of his collision sent both men crashing to the barroom floor once again. William Donnelly now moved in and yelled, "Bawden, you son of a bitch! Let him go!"

Bawden had no intention of following William Donnelly's directive and clutched John Donnelly even tighter. William then struck Bawden again with his shillelagh. The blow caused Bawden to release his grip on John, who promptly freed himself and made a hasty exit from the tavern, his brother by his side. Once outside, John, William and Jim Donnelly were joined by their friends James Keefe and William Farrell. The five men quickly piled into a sleigh owned by Robert Keefe (James's cousin) and hightailed it out of town.

Back inside, Constable Bawden slowly rose to his feet and staggered to the front door of the hotel, followed closely by John Courcey. Upon seeing that John Reid had been shot, the two men quickly picked him up and rushed him to the nearest doctor. Reid would ultimately survive the ordeal, but for the moment, with two bullets in him and a substantial loss of blood, his prospects weren't looking good.

The news of the donnybrook at Fitzhenry's Hotel quickly rippled through Lucan, and when it reached the ears of Magistrate Bernard Stanley, he was enraged. A devout Protestant, Stanley was incensed by the fact that his three newly appointed constables, who were fellow Protestants, had been beaten by members of a Roman Catholic family at a Roman Catholic wedding reception. Moreover, as the largest business owner in Lucan, and a man with deep-seated political ambitions, Stanley was terrified that the Donnelly brothers were quickly giving the town he ran a bad name with their outrageous behaviour. They had to be stopped.

Taking note of the fact that the Middlesex Volunteer Militia were then engaged in their annual manoeuvres and drills within Lucan, Stanley pressed them into action to corral the Donnelly brothers. Among the volunteers that day who took part in the hunt for the Donnellys were two men who had encountered them before — James Curry (who had pressed charges against Jim Donnelly for assault on September 17) and Richard Tapp (who had been part of the inquest into the death of Daniel Clark).[20] Very few times in the history of the Wild West had the army been called out to pursue five outlaws, but this was, indeed, the case with three Donnelly brothers, along with their two friends William Farrell and James Keefe.

The members of the militia collected up their rifles, climbed into wagons and sped off in search of the five men. The predominantly Protestant townspeople of Lucan were in an uproar; there was talk of lynching the outlaws upon their capture.[21] What at the time amounted to an All-Points Bulletin was issued throughout Middlesex and the neighbouring counties for the apprehension of the fugitives.[22] Thomas Johnston, who was a constable in London at the time, recollected that

> [a] telegram came to London saying that the
> Donnelly boys were murdering everybody in Lucan,
> and assistance was wanted from the London police.
> Detectives [Harry] Phair and [Enoch] Murphy and
> myself went out to the village and found great
> commotion in the streets, but we found none of the
> Donnellys there except Mike, who was then living
> in Lucan. We went to his house and, although we
> had no search warrant, he made no opposition
> to our searching his house, and even showed us
> through it himself.[23]

William Donnelly was astute enough to know that of the five fugitives, he, James Keefe and William Farrell were in the most trouble legally. Jim and John Donnelly had merely resisted arrest; James Keefe had assaulted one of the constables, while William, for his part, had threatened one constable with a gun, discharged his firearm in a tavern full of people and then assaulted another constable with a shillelagh. As for William Farrell, he was a lost cause legally — he had pumped two bullets into a constable who, at the moment, was hovering between life and death. If Constable Reid died, Farrell would be hanged. These were the most serious charges any of the Donnellys and their immediate friends had ever faced.

In light of this, William Donnelly, James Keefe and William Farrell fled Middlesex County[24] (Farrell would never return). Jim Donnelly sought his sanctuary at the home of his friend Daniel Keefe, where he was later discovered by the militia hiding between two down-filled mattresses in one of the bedrooms.[25]

The military men proceeded to search along the Roman Line, going into and out of houses, hunting for John Donnelly. They finally spotted their quarry running through a field behind his parents' farmhouse and immediately fired a volley of warning shots in his direction, which brought his running to a halt. He put up his arms and surrendered to the militia. Jim and John Donnelly were arrested and taken back to London to stand trial.[26]

The local newspaper trumpeted the news of their capture:

LAWLESSNESS AT LUCAN.
THE DONNELLYS ON THE RAMPAGE.
TWO CONSTABLES SHOT YESTERDAY.
ONE OF THEM SERIOUSLY WOUNDED.
TWO OF THE GANG UNDER ARREST.
EXCITEMENT IN THE VILLAGE.[27]

The fact that only one constable had been shot during the fracas (despite the newspaper headline that two had taken bullets during the course of carrying out their duties), understandably did little to lessen the communal outrage at the crime. Receiving word that public opinion was now strongly against the Donnellys, Hugh McKinnon returned to Middlesex to continue with his plan to put all the Donnellys behind bars. He decided that he needed Rhody Kennedy free from incarceration in order to have him charge some of the other Donnelly brothers, and so he brought about Kennedy's release from jail.[28] Upon his release, Kennedy encountered Mike

Donnelly and, presumably, made some disparaging comments about the Donnelly family's latest predicament, which prompted Mike to use some colourful metaphors in his reply and, by one report at least, pummel young Kennedy yet again. Kennedy then charged Mike with using abusive language and assault, resulting in Mike Donnelly having to pay two more fines and being bound to keep the peace.[29] For his part, McKinnon saw to it that things went from bad to worse for the Donnelly brothers. James Curry was prompted to again charge Jim Donnelly with assault and robbery from their encounter in September 1875,[30] and Patrick Flanagan came forth to charge John and Jim Donnelly with arson.[31]

With his brothers facing another round of charges, and with newspapers such as the *London Free Press* painting the Donnellys as violent desperados, Mike Donnelly (perhaps with the help of his older brother William) decided to attempt some damage control (after all, they still had a stage business to run). On March 1, 1876, he wrote a letter to the *London Advertiser* that advanced the Donnellys' side of the Ryder wedding fracas:

To the Editor of the *Advertiser*:

Sir,

As there are always two sides to a story, and as I and my brothers have been misrepresented in connection with the above affair in one or two of the city papers, I deem it necessary, in justice to myself and my brothers, to make a few explanations in contradiction to the statements therein made.

In the first place, it has been represented that the Donnelly family are a terror to the neighbourhood in which they live, and no one dare to oppose them as stage drivers on the road between Lucan and London. This assertion I beg leave to contradict,

and have no doubt it is made for the sole purpose
of injuring my character and confidence in me as
a driver between Lucan and the city of London, a
position which I have occupied for the last five years,
and have with great care discharged the duties so as
to give general satisfaction to the public.

With regard to the late row at Lucan, I beg
leave to make the following statement on behalf
of my brothers: Reid and Bawden, although they
had a warrant for the arrest of them for some time
previous in their possession, failed to execute it for
weeks, although daily opportunity offered for their
doing so. But on the 24th February, there was a
wedding party being held at Mr. Fitzhenry's tavern
at which one or two of my brothers were present,
as was also William Farrell, and then and there, in a
most provoking and unjustifiable manner, Constables
Reid, Bawden and Courcey proceeded thereto for
the purpose of apprehending them and breaking
up the party, when a row commenced in which Reid
was represented to be fatally wounded and Bawden
cut badly about the head. But Bawden's wounds
were not of so serious a nature as represented in the
newspapers, for he was around the same evening as
hale and hearty as though nothing was the matter
with him. And he came to London the next
morning with the prisoners. Now, Mr. Editor, I and
my brothers have met with every kind of opposition
at the hands of a certain party residing in the vicinity
of Lucan for some time back, and every attempt
made by us to frustrate them has failed. They have
done our business much harm without any just cause.
All this is done in order to run us off of the road.

As far as the shooting business is concerned, the blame is as much attached to Constable Reid, who in arresting John Donnelly (after being arrested previously by Constable Bawden) was interfered with by the crowd. He then turned on Farrell and shot him twice, and beat him about the head in a fearful manner, leaving several gashes which will take some time to heal.

These, Mr. Editor, are the true statements of the case, and I make them in order that the minds of the public may not be altogether prejudiced against the "Tribe,"[32] as one of your local papers chose to term us.

Therefore, I hope and trust you will favour me by inserting this statement in your valuable columns, and by so doing oblige.

Yours respectfully,
Michael Donnelly[33]

The damage, however, had already been done to the family's reputation. The Donnelly stage business slowed to the point where Mike had to temporarily suspend daily stagecoach trips into London.[34] And to make matters worse, private detective Hugh McKinnon was just getting started. McKinnon convinced Constable John Bawden to file two additional arson charges against Tom, William and Bob Donnelly, as well as William Farrell.[35] William Esdale, a local drunkard,[36] was brought forth to charge Tom Donnelly with having robbed him approximately one year previously.[37] When another robbery occurred in McGillivray Township, McKinnon charged Tom Donnelly with the crime, along with Tom's friend, Alex Levitt, who owned the Donnelly's favourite tavern (and the Lucan depot for the Donnelly stage line), the Revere House.[38]

Bernard Stanley and his brother William Stanley were the presiding magistrates for these hearings and were only too happy to order that Levitt be held in jail while awaiting his trial. McKinnon also attempted to jail Tom Donnelly and, for some reason, his friend William Atkinson,[39] but with no evidence both men were released. The private detective, however, was now even more determined to jail every one of the Donnelly brothers, even endeavouring to have the St. Catharines police arrest Pat Donnelly — who was nowhere near Lucan. However, as there was nothing with which to charge Pat Donnelly, the St. Catharines police department refused McKinnon's request.[40]

The private detective was furious; he knew that the Donnellys — and Atkinson, too, for that matter — were guilty of these crimes, even if he couldn't discover any evidence against them. The backwards legal system in Biddulph and London clearly wasn't up to the task of taking care of their Donnelly problem, and so McKinnon believed it was time for him to employ some of his big-city methods of intimidation and interrogation (the very methods that had resulted in his being fired from the Hamilton police force).

First on his list was Mike Donnelly. Mike was proving to be a problem; not only was he still running the Donnelly stage business (albeit in a diminished capacity), but he was attempting to solicit support for his family in the local press at the very time that McKinnon was attempting to use the newspapers to condemn them. Consequently, McKinnon had Donnelly watched carefully. Anyone who visited with Mike was suspected of being a friend or a sympathizer to the Donnelly cause, and, therefore, someone to be eradicated. Such was the case with William Denby, a friend of Mike Donnelly's. As evidenced by the following article that appeared in one of the London newspapers in early March 1876, McKinnon had the Denby matter quickly taken care of:

On Saturday last a young man named Denby from
this city visited Lucan in company with Mike
Donnelly and spent the Sunday with him — in
a manner best known to themselves. During the
evening it became noised around that Denby was, if
not an active member of the Donnelly gang, at least
an ardent sympathizer, and on Tuesday morning the
Vigilance Committee interviewed Denby and escorted
him out of the village limits, reminding him of the
consequence should he be found inside the bar of the
toll gate in future — at least until the excitement had
died out. . . . Denby took the hint and has not been
observed in the neighbourhood since.[41]

Unfortunately for McKinnon and his newly formed "Vigilance
Committee," Denby was one of the people at the Ryder wedding
reception who had interfered with the constables in the course of
their duties to arrest Jim and John Donnelly. In his haste to run
Denby out of town, McKinnon had inadvertently released someone
whom the constables could have actually charged. A warrant then
had to be drawn up for Denby, but, thanks to McKinnon, there
was nobody to serve it to, as Denby was now safely out of town.
It was also proving fruitless waiting for Mike Donnelly to slip up,
and so McKinnon took it upon himself to arrest Mike Donnelly on
the charge of setting fire to Patrick Flanagan's stables. Although
he had no evidence that Mike Donnelly had been involved in the
crime, McKinnon had his constables apprehend Donnelly on
the street, whereupon the private eye took him to the London jail
in the hopes that the London police would hold him. However, as
the private detective had no evidence against Donnelly for the crime,
this attempt to incarcerate him was denied by the London authorities. Irate, McKinnon brought Mike back to Lucan and handed

him over to Constable John Bawden, who then handcuffed Mike Donnelly and, under McKinnon's orders, illegally imprisoned him within a room in the Central House Hotel.

With Mike now out of commission, McKinnon turned his attention to the associates of the Donnelly brothers, particularly the thirty-six-year-old Lucan blacksmith, William Atkinson. Atkinson might have escaped jail when McKinnon had taken him and Tom Donnelly to London, but the private detective was by no means through with him yet. It was his belief that, with the right persuasion, Atkinson would roll over on the Donnellys and offer up evidence of their numerous crimes that would lead to further arrests and convictions.

At 3 a.m. on March 2, William Atkinson and his wife Rebecca were awakened from their slumbers by the sound of someone pounding on their back door.[42] William rose from his bed and lit a candle. He groggily made his way along the hallway, past the kitchen, to where the loud noise was coming from. Upon opening his back door, he was startled to see Hugh McKinnon standing on his steps.

"Yes?" he asked, wiping the sleep from his eyes.

"Dress yourself," McKinnon demanded. "I want you."

Atkinson could scarcely believe his ears.

"I'm sorry?"

"Put out the lamp," said McKinnon matter-of-factly.

"No, I won't," said Atkinson. "What is this about?"

"I have a warrant for you," McKinnon replied testily.

McKinnon was not a man with whom Atkinson was prepared to argue. He returned to his bedroom and got dressed. When he returned to the back door McKinnon took his arm and walked him out of his house. Atkinson's wife, Rebecca, had followed behind her husband and, as she went to close the door after he and McKinnon had left, she noticed Constable John Bawden step out from beside the door and follow the pair. She further noted that there were several other men standing around in the shadows at the back of her house.

As Atkinson was marched along by McKinnon, Bawden caught up with them and took hold of Atkinson's other arm. The three men then continued along the wooden sidewalk. As they were walking, Atkinson noticed that four men suddenly appeared from out of the dark and fell in behind them. The walking continued until they were the better part of two blocks away from Atkinson's home, at which point Atkinson stopped abruptly and said, "Here boys, this has gone far enough."

McKinnon then let out a whistle and the four men who had been trailing them suddenly jumped upon Atkinson and threw him onto the road.

"Murder!" yelled Atkinson, in the hopes of waking someone who might cause the men to abort what they were doing.

Before he could yell out again, McKinnon caught him by the throat and began to choke him. Another from within the group came forth and tied a cloth around Atkinson's mouth, and still another tied a bandana over his eyes. While he was still lying on the ground and now with no means of appealing for help, a third man came forth and kicked Atkinson square in the ribs, the pain from which took his breath away. Atkinson was then picked up and led stumbling farther down the road until the group came upon a sleigh. Atkinson was thrown into the sled and two men climbed in on either side of him and took hold of his arms. He heard voices, but could not ascertain how many men there were nor their identities. The sleigh was pulled along by two horses to a spot near a bridge on the flats of the Sauble River, at which point Atkinson, still blindfolded, was yanked from the sleigh and marched over to the base of a tree. Two men continued to hold his arms, while two others climbed up into the tree with a rope. Someone then pulled the cloth from his mouth, allowing Atkinson to gasp in a huge breath of cold morning air.

McKinnon walked in front of his prisoner and revealed the purpose of his early morning visit.

"Now," he began, "I want you to tell me *all you know* about those Donnellys."

It was, in retrospect, a rather generic question to ask. Atkinson had been friends with the Donnelly brothers for years. And while he knew something of what the brothers had been up to as of late, he wasn't going to rat them out to McKinnon.

"I know nothing about them," he said.

Unfortunately for Atkinson, that was the wrong answer. He suddenly felt a noose being slipped around his neck.

McKinnon now phrased his statement in the form of a question: "Will you tell?"

Again, Atkinson said that he knew nothing about the Donnelly brothers.

McKinnon seemed almost pleased by the response. He looked up to the two men who were now standing on a thick branch of the tree, approximately ten to twelve feet off the ground.

"Pull him up!" McKinnon yelled, and Atkinson was suddenly yanked up by his neck four or five feet into the air. He would have heard the synovial fluid from between his vertebrae popping as his neck stretched, and felt the rope bite into his neck as the blood supply to his brain was slowly being squeezed off. In a panic, he was able to jerk his arms free and, in the process of trying to pull at the noose, he pulled the bandana from his eyes. Looking up he recognized the two men in the tree as being James Atkinson (no relation) and Arthur Gray, a man he knew worked at the Central Hotel on Lucan's Main Street. After he had been dangling for a short while, the men in the tree released the rope and Atkinson fell hard to the ground. Gasping for air, he looked around at the men who now surrounded him — again, he recognized the faces: Albert McLean, whose father owned the Central Hotel; David Atkinson (again, no relation), who was a Lucan grain retailer; and Thomas T. Atkinson, whom he knew to be David's brother. He also recognized the faces of Jacob Palmer, Alexander "Sandy" Reid and, of course, Hugh McKinnon.

It was immediately obvious that the men were taking their direction from the private detective. McKinnon now bent down closer to Atkinson's face and said, "*Now* will you tell on the Donnellys?"

"I don't know anything about them!" Atkinson exclaimed in between gasps. McKinnon scowled and then motioned for one of the men to cover Atkinson's eyes with the bandana for a second time.

Atkinson was terrified, and he had every reason to be.

"All right," said McKinnon, "then tell me where young William Farrell is at."

"I don't know," Atkinson replied, trying to be cooperative with his captors, "but I heard he went to Seaforth."

"And what do you know about the burning and cutting up of those stages?" McKinnon asked. Atkinson replied that he knew nothing about the losses suffered by Flanagan and Bryant.

McKinnon smirked. "You won't tell, eh?" The private detective then looked up to the men in the tree and yelled, "Pull him up, boys!" And up went Atkinson again.

This went on two more times, with Atkinson being strung up and then dropped to the ground, questioned, and then strung up again. Atkinson's neck was now raw and bleeding from the noose. He lay on the snow-covered ground for fifteen or twenty minutes after the last stranglehold in an attempt to regain his senses. When he finally came around, he again pulled the bandana down from his eyes and saw the faces of the eight men who now surrounded him.

"Do you know anything about some meat that was stolen recently?" McKinnon asked.

"No, I— I don't," Atkinson stammered. "I heard that the Donnellys were blamed for stealing two barrels of pork at Michael Carroll's — that's all, and that young Farrell was blamed along with them." Not wanting to be hanged again, he hoped that would satisfy the private detective. It didn't.

"Do you know anything about some sheepskins that were stolen from Henry Collins?" McKinnon queried.

"I do not," answered Atkinson. Thinking the worst was now over, Atkinson sat up and reached to remove the noose around his neck, whereupon he was promptly punched in the face by Albert McLean. He hit the ground hard, and blood began to stream from his nose. Again, Atkinson said he knew nothing about the theft of any sheepskins — and again he was pulled up into the air by his neck and left to hang for several seconds in an attempt to force him to reconsider his answer on the matter.

By this point it was obvious to McKinnon that Atkinson either really didn't know anything about the inner workings of the Donnelly clan, or that he was simply not going to betray his friends — despite McKinnon's torture tactics.

William Atkinson would be hanged by his neck no fewer than six times that morning in an effort to get him to confess his knowledge of the Donnellys' crimes, and it was eleven men — not eight — that McKinnon had amassed in his "Vigilance Committee" to secure his confession. When all was said and done, the men involved in Atkinson's kidnapping and torture — Henry Collins, David Atkinson, Thomas Atkinson Jr., Constable John Bawden, James Atkinson, Arthur Gray, Albert McLean, Alexander Reid, Jacob Palmer, Jim Hodgins and Hugh McKinnon — came away from their torture session with no more incriminating evidence against the Donnellys than they'd had before it began.

Atkinson was then driven back to Lucan where Constable Bawden locked him in a room within the Queen's Hotel. Unable to bring any charges against him, McKinnon decided to release Atkinson the next morning with the threat that if he ever reported to anyone what had happened he would be killed.[43] Atkinson didn't need to be told twice; he left Lucan and stayed away for the next six months.

At this point, Mike Donnelly had been illegally imprisoned within a room on the second floor of the Central House Hotel for four days. Neither his wife nor his family knew where he was, and he feared the worst was yet to come. Constable John Bawden had been the one selected to guard him while at the hotel-cum-prison. Bawden still nursed the wounds that had been inflicted upon him by John and William Donnelly at the Ryder wedding reception, and he had treated their younger brother with ruthless contempt during the four days of his confinement. Mike Donnelly waited and watched for any opportunity for escape.

That opportunity came on March 6. He waited until Constable Bawden fell asleep and then, somehow, was able to work one of his hands free from his handcuffs. Taking the key from the sleeping constable's pocket, Mike unfastened his other hand from the cuffs and then slipped the handcuffs onto Bawden's wrists and locked them into place. Donnelly then opened a window and jumped from the second floor onto the street below and disappeared.[44] The *London Free Press* made mention of his escape, but omitted the part about his having been detained illegally:

> Michael Donnelly, one of the Lucan gang of that
> name, escaped from a room in McLean's Hotel,
> Lucan, the place in which he was incarcerated
> for a week or more, on Monday morning last,
> by jumping from the second story window. The
> constable could not have been watching very
> closely at the time. But if Michael is innocent of
> the offences imputed to him (and he avers he is)
> then why take leave of his guardians in such an
> unceremonious manner?[45]

Throughout all the kidnapping, the torture and the illegal imprisonment, William Donnelly had been planning his next move. He was smart enough to know that being on the lam was no solution; he would have to face the music, but when he did he wanted a strategy that would better his chances for acquittal. He had, apparently, not left Biddulph at all, but had been put up at the home of a friend, Zackariah McIlhargey, in Elginfield, roughly two and three-quarter miles southeast of Lucan. Ely Errey, the great-granddaughter of Zackariah, recalled that the McIlhargey family passed down reports over the succeeding generations that shortly after the donnybrook at the Ryder wedding reception, William had come "riding in the laneway and around behind the barn in quite a hurry, shortly before the ones in pursuit came by. After they left, Bill came in the house and had a visit. No questions were asked."[46]

When he was certain that the constables and militia had stopped combing the local countryside looking for him, William saddled up his horse and, on March 15, rode alone toward London, where he surrendered to the sheriff of Middlesex County.[47]

Four of the Donnelly brothers were now in jail, and the list of charges that had been brought against them at the Spring Assizes in late March 1876 were, at first blush, absolutely staggering. True bills were brought in by a grand jury in the following cases:

- The Queen vs. Thomas Donnelly, arson
- The Queen vs. William Donnelly, shooting with intent
- The Queen vs. John Donnelly, assault on Constable Bawden
- The Queen vs. James Donnelly, assaulting Rhody Kennedy
- The Queen vs. John Donnelly, assaulting Peter McKellar

- The Queen vs. Thomas Donnelly, arson
- The Queen vs. James Donnelly, arson
- The Queen vs. Thomas Donnelly, larceny from William Esdale
- The Queen vs. James Donnelly, assaulting Constable Courcey
- The Queen vs. William Donnelly, assaulting Constable Courcey
- The Queen vs. James Donnelly, assaulting Joseph Berryhill
- The Queen vs. Patrick Donnelly, assaulting Joseph Berryhill[48]

Despite what would appear to be a mountain of overwhelming legal charges, by the time William Donnelly and his attorney David Glass[49] presented their cases for the defence, the above charges resulted in only three convictions — and the punishments, surprisingly, were relatively minor. Jim Donnelly was convicted only for his part in the assault upon Joseph Berryhill and was sentenced to nine months;[50] William Donnelly was convicted only of common assault for his part in the Ryder wedding melee and sentenced to nine months;[51] while John Donnelly was convicted of assault as a result of his fight with Constable John Bawden and sentenced to serve three months.[52] All three brothers were ordered to serve their sentences in Toronto's Central Prison. Of these three convictions, two were products of the fracas at the Ryder wedding reception, and the other resulted from the tavern brawl with Joseph Berryhill. None of the convictions had anything to do with any of McKinnon's sleuthing. His attempt to bring down the Donnellys through guile, kidnapping and torture had resulted in nothing.

CHAPTER EIGHT

THE WINDS OF CHANGE

Toronto's Central Prison, circa 1884.
(Toronto Public Library)

Toronto's Central Prison opened in 1873 in an area now known as Liberty Village. The village took its name from Liberty Street, which was the first thoroughfare that ex-convicts would walk upon after their release from prison.

Despite the area's present urban congestion, in 1876, when the Donnelly brothers had arrived at the prison to serve their sentences, the area was completely devoid of any residential or commercial development. The prison had been built exclusively to handle the overflow from Toronto's Don Jail, and opened its doors during a period of time when hard work and discipline were considered to be the perfect prescription for an inmate's rehabilitation. Of course, "hard work" meant free labour, particularly for manufacturers such as the Canada Car Company, who were the beneficiaries of the discipline the prison imposed on its convicts, which forced them into manufacturing railway cars for the company.[1] Rather than rehabilitation through labour, however, the prison would instead become known for its brutality, particularly while under the watch of its first warden, William Stratton Prince. Prince was an ex–military officer and a former chief of the Toronto Police. He also happened to be an alcoholic. Over time, word began to filter out from the institution regarding the ill treatment of its inmates; instances were reported of much-needed medical attention being denied to the prisoners, brutal beatings were carried out on an almost daily basis by the guards and, allegedly, clandestine evening burials took place, in which the bodies of convicts who ultimately succumbed to the extreme punishment they received were disposed of.[2] According to journalist Chris Bateman,

> Although it purported to provide honest
> rehabilitation, the jail quickly developed a
> dark reputation as a place of severe beatings,
> deprivation, and despair. The prison didn't have
> running water for its first five years — it would take
> ten years to get electricity. Minor transgressions
> resulted in whippings, protracted periods in
> solitary confinement, or "ironings," the practice of
> shackling men to a wall in a standing position until
> long after their legs gave way.[3]

The majority of the inmates doing time within Toronto's Central Prison had been found guilty of crimes against "property," with 36.7 percent of the inmates serving time for larceny, 15 percent for vagrancy, and 7.5 percent for drunkenness.[4] The Donnelly brothers, clearly, would have been put into the general population among the more violent offenders. We don't know if any of the Donnelly brothers were subjected to any of the prison's reputed brutalities, but we do know that one of them took matters into his own hands to get out of there in short order.

William Donnelly had served only one week of his nine-month sentence when he put his exit plan into action. Complaining of a pain in his spine, he developed a high fever after allegedly consuming a bar of soap.[5] The medical staff at the prison, genuinely concerned for his life, immediately transferred their sick prisoner out of his cell from among the general population and into the doctor's wing of the prison, which afforded him far more privacy and comfort.

Still, his condition did not improve. His wife Nora was called in, as the prison doctor believed any day might be his last. Perhaps out of fear that whatever he had might be contagious, and possibly fatal, William Donnelly, on April 30, 1876, after serving a mere eighteen days of his nine-month sentence, was discharged from Toronto's Central Prison on compassionate grounds, and, further, was granted a full pardon.[6]

Understandably, private detective Hugh McKinnon was apoplectic upon learning the news. William Donnelly had proven himself to be a hard fish to fry; not only was he an expert in avoiding punishment for his crimes owing to his legal manoeuvres in the courtroom, but now, apparently, he was equally adept at getting out of any punishment that the courts might deem fit to impose on him. In a fit of pique, McKinnon wrote to the Middlesex County Crown attorney, Charles Hutchinson, expressing his belief that the province had been duped by the clever Donnelly brother and arguing that William Donnelly should be sent back to prison immediately.[7] Hutchinson forwarded the private detective's letter on to the Ontario attorney general, Oliver Mowat. The attorney general wasn't interested. Hutchinson shared McKinnon's disbelief at William Donnelly's sudden mystery illness,[8] but it was too late. William Donnelly was a free man.

In truth, this episode was simply a demonstration of how technically precise was William's knowledge of the law, the Ontario prison system and the action/reaction nature of these mechanisms and institutions. It was largely a result of William's legal acumen and intellectual agility that not only William, but all the Donnelly brothers (save perhaps Pat, who never found bucking societal rules and regulations as irresistible as his brothers) enjoyed whatever freedoms they did. Indeed, the Donnellys experienced an unprecedented level of success in their court battles. Of all the charges the brothers had originally faced in March 1876, a fair number had been put off until later Quarter Sessions, or, in the cases of John, Jim and William, until after they had finished serving their prison sentences. And this was solely a result of William's (in combination with his attorney, David Glass's) legal machinations. And in each of these cases that were thus postponed, the charges were ultimately either dropped or resulted in acquittals, which flummoxed the Donnelly enemies and emboldened the brothers.

It was during this period of time that William Donnelly had earned the sobriquets "the lawyer" and the "most hated member of the family." And despite being used as pejoratives, the truth was these terms were a testimony to William's cunning and ability to successfully navigate the often rocky shoals of jurisprudence. He was hated by his adversaries because he continually outwitted them, causing them to lose face publicly and, in cases where the charges against the Donnellys resulted in acquittals, his opponents also lost the money that they had fed into the legal machine in their attempts to convict him. Consequently, while most of his brothers preferred the use of physical force to achieve their objectives, William had grown to feel most at home in the courtroom and would tend to direct most of his family's adversaries into this arena in order to better his chances of emerging victorious.

While William had no troubles in a courtroom, upon returning home to his wife Nora, he faced an uncertain future. The stagecoach business was diminishing with each passing week. He had been taken to (and returned from) prison by train, which only underscored the fact that the stagecoach had already been superseded by the new alternative in public conveyance. He decided that it was time to speak with his brothers about shutting down the business and looking for another line of work.

By June 30, 1876, John Donnelly's three-month stretch in Toronto's Central Prison was up and, like William, he returned to Biddulph.[9] And while the brothers discussed the viability of their future in the stagecoach business, their rival, Richard Bryant, was more decisive. He, too, longed to withdraw from the trade, but few, if any, prospective businesspeople were looking to purchase a stagecoach business now that the railroad was on the ascendant. And so, when Bryant discovered that William Walker, the proprietor of Lucan's Western Hotel, was interested in purchasing his stagecoach enterprise outright, Bryant couldn't act quickly enough. On July 10, 1876,[10] a transaction was hastily enacted. Walker had stuck his toe in the stagecoach waters before, when he, together with stagecoach veterans Patrick Flanagan and the ubiquitous Ted Crawley, had operated a short-run service coach that ran from Exeter to Crediton. Crawley also owned a piece of the Exeter-to-London stage line that had previously been operated by John Hawkshaw, and his interest in the enterprise had continued upon Hawkshaw's sale to Flanagan, and then to Bryant. However, he'd had a parting of ways with Bryant sometime in the spring of 1876,[11] which resulted in his quitting the bigger stage enterprise and returning to the smaller Exeter-to-Crediton stage service, which he continued to operate with Flanagan. As for Bryant, his health had been steadily declining ever since he'd injured himself falling from his stage the previous January, and, within a month of selling his business to Walker, Richard Bryant passed away.

The stage line that Walker now owned required a full-time commitment, which simply wasn't possible for the hotel owner.

There were already eight hotels competing for business in Lucan,[12] a town that had a population of slightly more than one thousand residents,[13] so Walker's time was already spoken for well in advance. The only way his new enterprise was going to work was if he could bring in a person to assist him with the running of the stagecoach service. He would eventually find such a person in thirty-four-year-old stage driver Joseph Watson,[14] who would come on board in December to drive stage for Walker.

Apart from the sale of Bryant's stage line, the summer of 1876 turned out to be a relatively quiet one in Lucan. William Donnelly by this time had moved out of the area, effectively divorcing himself from the family's stagecoach business. He had rented a forty-nine-acre hay farm on the Eighth Concession[15] and was giving serious thought to another line of work.

Mike Donnelly, the co-owner in the Donnelly stage business, likewise sought alternate employment and, after conferring with bondsman William McBride, and with the support of justice of the peace (and family friend) Patrick McIlhargey, he put forth an application to become a county constable. This never developed.[16] Mike, however, was in considerable need of a predictable and stable livelihood as, on February 8 of that year, his wife, Ellen, had given birth to their first child, a daughter they had named Catherine. The family rented a house in Lucan and, for the moment, Mike was content to stick it out with the stage business. Tom and John likewise continued to work for the stage line for the time being. Bob was still absent from the area (where he was exactly has never been determined), ever since beating Rhody Kennedy with his revolver on Lucan's Main Street.

The Donnelly Stagecoach Line limped along into November, with Walker's stage not doing much better. The Donnelly brothers by now had decided to terminate their stage business, as John and Tom Donnelly found themselves spending more of their time on their parents' farm on the Roman Line than they were in driving stage in Lucan. With Jim Donnelly still confined within Toronto's Central Prison, William Donnelly, being the second-oldest of the Donnelly children, felt it his duty to look out for his youngest brother, Tom. Tom was strong enough to be a good farmer, but, at age twenty-two, and having already tasted the fruits of working in the stage business, he, like many young men that age, preferred the life of the town over working in the fields of the farm.

In an effort to create gainful employment that Tom would welcome, William decided to pay a visit to William Walker and Joseph Watson. While they had been adversaries in the stage trade, Walker and Watson recognized that William Donnelly was no fool; they eagerly listened to what he had to say. In essence, Donnelly proposed a merger of the two stagecoach lines. Wouldn't that spread profits a bit too thin? Not at all, explained William. Neither he nor his brother Mike would be involved — just Tom. And in return, the two companies could pool their resources — horses (which the Donnellys, under William's stewardship, always had the best of) and coaches. Such a merger might result in increased business, less competition and more money, which would then be split between Tom and Walker. It was a deal that, in the final analysis, was simply too sound to pass up. With tongue planted firmly in cheek, the *London Advertiser* reported the merger:

> The hatchet is buried at last. The ceremony took
> place last week. Donnellys, Walkers, Watsons and
> the individual known as "Wicked Will" rushed
> into each other's arms; wept on each other's necks;
> bought stages from each other; exchanged whips,
> jack-knives, tobacco pipes, bowls, swore eternal
> friendship and are prepared to go to their necks
> in water for each other on occasion of the
> first thaw.[17]

As an active partner under the new arrangement, Tom Donnelly looked for another location to stable the Donnelly stagecoach horses. Henry Collins, the man who had told private detective Hugh McKinnon that the Donnellys had stolen his sheepskins, now stepped forward with an offer whereby Tom could lease stable space from him.[18] Tom Donnelly accepted, and with new money coming his way, Collins now thought the Donnellys weren't so bad after all. With Tom's immediate future now taken care of, William Donnelly returned to contemplating his own. He always had a passion for horses and a good eye for suitable breeding stock, which inclined him to consider starting his own horse breeding business.[19] He thought seriously about this, but couldn't quite give his mind over to it completely — at least not yet.

Hugh McKinnon may well have put William Donnelly out of his thoughts for the moment, but William Donnelly had not put Hugh McKinnon out of his. He knew what McKinnon and his gang had done to his good friend William Atkinson, and he was incensed by it. William wanted to get the self-cherishing private detective into the courtroom — William's domain — to answer for his transgressions in the matter. In the past, McKinnon had never lowered himself to appear on the witness stand, preferring to skulk about the periphery of the legal system, pulling strings like a puppeteer to have others do his legal bidding. The decision William would make, so typical of a Donnelly family member, would be based on loyalty to family and friends and redressing a perceived imbalance: the kind that always seemed to lead to something terrible happening. After all, things had just started to calm down in Lucan, peace had been made between the two stage lines, and all the Donnelly brothers but Tom had left town. Another year or so of such tranquility and, quite possibly, previous transgressions might well be forgotten, if not forgiven. But William Donnelly had other plans.

William had been in contact with Atkinson since May,[20] primarily in appealing to him to appear for Tom Donnelly's defence in his trial for arson at the Middlesex June Sessions. However, what William Donnelly really wanted was an opportunity to bring down McKinnon — and, given what had happened to his friend, he knew that William Atkinson had just the case to make this happen. Atkinson had been living with relatives in Michigan ever since the Hamilton private detective and his associates had hanged him by his neck repeatedly on the flats of the Sauble River the previous March[21] But by October, Atkinson was back in Biddulph and, after a few get-togethers with William Donnelly, he agreed to let William represent him at a preliminary hearing in Lucan. Donnelly proceeded to lay charges against McKinnon and his cronies on behalf of his client. Eleven men in total were charged with the crime before Magistrate James Owrey in London. All of them, with the exception of McKinnon, were respected members of the Lucan business community:

- David Atkinson, grain retailer
- Thomas Atkinson, cattleman
- James Atkinson (carpenter and constable)
- Jacob Palmer, carpenter
- Arthur Gray, bartender at the Central Hotel
- Albert McLean, the son of the owner of the Central Hotel
- Henry Collins, tinsmith
- James Hodgins, butcher
- Alexander (Sandy) Reid, shoemaker (also, like McKinnon, known for his prowess in the Highland Games)
- John Bawden, county constable and bricklayer
- Hugh McKinnon, private detective

During the hearing, Atkinson was brought to the stand and recounted in detail the harrowing experience he had suffered at the hands of McKinnon and his gang. His wife, Rebecca, testified that upon her husband's return home she saw a black mark and circular cut around his neck and that he was complaining of a pain his side as a result of a kick he had received. Another witness, Robert Mason, testified that he saw Atkinson in March, shortly after the incident, and that his neck was red and sore. Magistrate Owrey concluded that the evidence was sufficient to warrant a trial at the December Court of General Sessions of the Peace for the County of Middlesex. The defendants were then given bail and released. McKinnon was outraged and no doubt highly embarrassed to have had a very public light shone on his misdeed. In his comments to the London newspapers he referred to Atkinson's charges as "fraudulent" and "absurd."[22]

On the morning of December 15, Rebecca Atkinson once again gave her testimony. The court then adjourned for lunch — and William Atkinson disappeared. Constable Bawden had evidently stepped in and arrested Atkinson before he could deliver his testimony in the case.[23] Unable to locate Atkinson, the prosecutor in the case, the remaining witnesses for the prosecution who had testified in the preliminary hearing now lost their nerve to proceed. Consequently, the magistrate dismissed all the charges against McKinnon and his crew.[24]

Despite his ire at the underhanded way the defence had secured the acquittal, William Donnelly could only nod that McKinnon's move had been well played. But the magistrate's decision to acquit also exposed the Achilles heel of William Donnelly's overconfidence in the courts; if corrupt constables were in play, the scales of justice no longer tipped automatically to the side of the more legally astute. While this point may have been lost on William Donnelly for the moment, it would be remembered (and used to advantage) by his adversaries going forward. But William Donnelly also had to know there were two ways of administering justice — the first, of course, was his preferred way, through the courts, which in the Atkinson affair had proven to yield a most unsatisfactory result. The second way, however, was through the Donnelly family. And he could only shake his head at the thought that Jim Donnelly would soon learn of the Atkinson verdict, and that he was due to return home from prison in less than three weeks' time.

Jim Donnelly set foot on Liberty Avenue on December 30, 1876.[25] After nine months of incarceration, the eldest son of James and Johannah Donnelly was returning to Biddulph. Unlike his intellectual brother William, or his comparatively more moderate-tempered brother John, Jim was hotheaded. We don't know if he was subjected to any of the infamous punishments that were so casually meted out at Toronto's Central Prison: presumably he was, given his disposition. In any event, we can assume that he was an angry man upon his release.

His mood wasn't improved when, arriving back in London, he was promptly arrested on charges stemming from his resisting arrest at the hands of Constable John Courcey at the Ryder wedding back in February 1876, and for assaulting Constable Rhody Kennedy during the latter's attempt to arrest his brother Bob on January 28, 1876. On January 1, 1877, he was released on bail after his father and a friend of the family had posted an $800 bond[26] and he agreed to appear at future trials. As it happened, the evidence against him in both cases was surprisingly weak, and the charges would ultimately be abandoned.[27]

After catching up with his family, however, Jim was brought up to speed on the goings-on within the community, including his brother's thwarted attempt to get justice for William Atkinson. The names of the posse members who had hanged their friend were familiar to Jim. Indeed, several of them had been members of Lucan's Volunteer Militia, which had hunted him and his brothers down after the Fitzhenry wedding brawl.[28] Some have speculated that Jim Donnelly then went on a rampage of destruction; in other words, William had tried it his way in the courts and it didn't work out, so it was now time to try it Jim's way.

The first target was Sylvanus Gibson's planing mill and sash factory, the largest employer in the town of Lucan. Several of its employees had taken part in the hanging of William Atkinson, one of whom was James Atkinson, who had been one of the two men up in the tree pulling on the rope that had been wrapped around poor William Atkinson's neck. In addition, Gibson's factory provided employment to many of the members of the Lucan Volunteer Militia. Consequently, many Donnelly adversaries took a direct hit when it went up in flames during the second week in January[29] — the aforementioned James Atkinson lost $200 worth of carpenter's tools in the blaze.

Collateral damage from the fire saw the destruction of new milling machinery that had just been installed in the factory, in addition to a fair amount of lumber. The fire at Gibson's was large enough that it could easily have spread to other businesses in Lucan, including the Central Hotel, which was owned by the father of Albert McLean (the man who had punched Atkinson in the face as he lay on the ground). This would have taken out the employment of Arthur Gray, the bartender at the Central Hotel (the other man in the tree who had pulled on the rope around William Atkinson's neck). Fortunately for the town, the drifting sparks from the fire didn't spread to any other buildings.

Concurrent with the torching of Gibson's factory came damage to the shop and property of the butcher, Jim Hodgins. Once a week for three straight weeks his business fell victim to wanton acts of mischief. One week his shop was broken into and his meats tossed outdoors; the next week his shop windows were smashed out; the following week, the panels of his front door were kicked in.[30]

While it's certainly possible that these were simply random acts of destruction (after all, there were no witnesses to any of these crimes to say that they were all the work of Jim Donnelly), the connection between the people who owned or worked within these places with the Atkinson incident, Atkinson's own involvement with the Donnelly brothers, and the fact that all this destruction occurred after Jim Donnelly's return to Biddulph struck many in the community as being far beyond coincidental.

And the violence continued. The Lucan postmaster, William Porte, would note further incidents of arson in his diaries:

- Friday, March 9. Pieper & Hoggs' flax building and about $3,000 worth of flax and seed, and one horse burned between the hours of eight and ten o'clock this evening.
- Tuesday, March 13, 1877. James Maloney's Wagon Shop and all contents burned down on the Robins Corner between twelve and one o'clock this night — midnight.
- Saturday, March 17, 1877. Fire broke out in Collins' and Donnelly's Stable about half past eleven o'clock p.m. tonight. Fatally consumed one horse, burned harness, hay and grain belonging to stage.[31]

This last fire was clearly a strike against both Tom Donnelly and William Walker, and so would not have been perpetrated by either party. Why the main stage line would be victimized is uncertain, but the fire essentially ended Tom Donnelly's alliance with Walker and Watson. Each party decided to have new stagecoaches built and to run their stage lines independently of one another. Once again, however, the arsonists struck. On April 11, Tom Donnelly's stagecoach perished in flames.[32] In its report of this fire, the *London Free Press* mistakenly attributed ownership of the burned-out Donnelly stagecoach to Joseph Watson, which prompted Tom Donnelly to write a letter to the paper to correct the error:

To the Editor of the *Free Press*.

Sir,

    I notice in today's issue of your paper a news item headed "Incendiary Fire" wherein you state that "one of Mr. Watson's London and Lucan stages was burned while standing in the driving shed of the Montgomery House," etc. I beg you will have the kindness to correct an error which has crept into the above paragraph, whether accidentally or not on the part of your informant I am unable to say. The stage in question did not belong to Mr. Watson, nor has he any interest whatever in it. It belonged solely to your correspondent, neither Mr. Watson nor any other person having the slightest claim thereto except myself.

    Owing to this fact, I am of opinion that Mr. Watson will not turn many stones in order to find out the perpetrators of the dastardly act.

I am, Sir, &c.,
Thomas Donnelly.[33]

The paper was indignant at Donnelly's letter, and tagged its publication with an editorial response: "The information published in these columns was handed in by a responsible person. It matters not to us who was the owner of the stage, the act was one which should deserve condemnation."[34]

Tom Donnelly ignored the newspaper's rebuttal, and ordered a new stagecoach built, and, as he awaited its completion, Walker and Watson's stage line came into some additional misfortune. Two weeks after the burning of the Donnelly stage, a familiar mishap (similar in its details to the one that beset the Flanagan stage in July 1875) befell one of the Walker stagecoaches, when a nut came off during a run along the Proof Line Road, resulting in a wheel falling off and a passenger, seventy-year-old Joseph McGuffin, suffering a fracture of his spine, which left him paralyzed. He passed away shortly afterwards.[35] And then another familiar incident, reminiscent in its details to the one that saw Donnelly stage rival Patrick Flanagan knocked senseless in December 1875, was visited upon stage driver Joseph Watson when he was whacked upside the head with a hard object, perhaps a club or steel knuckles, which rendered him senseless.[36] He did not see his assailant and so no charges were filed after the assault. On Friday May 11, 1877, a fire consumed the stable behind Robert McLean's Central Hotel, where three of Walker's horses were kept. The three horses perished in that blaze, as did four belonging to McLean. The fire put McLean's stage service (which had run from his hotel to the Grand Trunk railway station) out of business.[37] That same night, the outbuildings located behind Bernard Stanley's hardware store were ignited, and only some of the building's contents were able to be pulled from the flames before the buildings were completely incinerated.[38]

The entire town of Lucan was now enveloped by a heightened state of anxiety; the quantity and severity of this recent rash of crimes were without precedent and seemed so reckless and random. Was any home or business safe? Guns were taken up by citizens and shop owners in order to prevent opportunistic theft. These weren't professional gunmen by any stretch of the imagination; they were culled from a pool of local artisans who happened to own guns and were willing to use them. A local barbershop belonging to William Berry secured the service of two armed men to watch over it. Lucan had turned into a war zone. The hired gunmen weren't particularly disciplined or keen-eyed either, as on at least one occasion a fellow armed guard was hit by friendly fire.[39]

On Saturday, May 12, 1877, Berry's barbershop was broken into and vandalized. One of the London newspapers reported that "everything in the shape of furniture, looking glasses, etc., was completely demolished."[40] The guard who had been appointed to watch over the shop was shot in the leg (perhaps the victim of friendly fire) when he happened upon the vandals.[41] It was as if the violence grew by what it fed on. While the Donnelly brothers had been rumoured to be responsible for a large part of the havoc that was now transpiring, the fact remained that the Donnelly stage business, too, had been targeted, which certainly wouldn't have come at their hands. In the case of Berry's barbershop, the building would continue to be targeted, being pelted with stones a little over a month later, as Berry was known to dispense more than haircuts out of his establishment.[42] The criminality in Lucan had now blown out of control and defied all explanation. It was as if the entire town had been targeted, rather than any specific targets within the town.

And then, on Tuesday, May 15, 1877, came the shocking news that Jim Donnelly was dead.[43]

Once again, we must break away from the narrative. The final hours of Jim Donnelly's life have been shrouded in controversy for well over 140 years, and historians and scribes have so muddied the waters on the matter that a critical examination of the various theories advanced on his death is warranted. In working with the London Public Library to check the newspaper reports on the matter, this author was surprised to learn that there weren't any references at all to either Jim Donnelly's death or his burial — even the staff of the library, who kindly pored over all the London newspapers from May 12 through till May 22, 1877, on my behalf could find nothing. The earliest reference to his death that came to light was a report published thirty-two months later in the *St. Marys Argus*: "James was said to have died from consumption, but those who were in a position to know, state that his death resulted from the effects of a pistol ball, while endeavoring to escape from [a] constable some years since."[44]

Right away, the researcher into the matter is given a conflicting report: Jim Donnelly died from either consumption (tuberculosis) or a gunshot. It's no wonder that the issue has seemed anything but clear over the years. Writers and researchers who have used the newspapers of the time as their starting point have understandably veered off in many different directions.

Starting from the disease of "consumption" mentioned in the above newspaper report, authors have gone on to claim other naturally occurring medical conditions as being the more likely cause of Jim Donnelly's death, such as "appendicitis."[45] However, problems immediately arise in reviewing such claims. Appendicitis and tuberculosis, for example, are two very different pathologies that seldom, if ever, present together; a ruptured appendix does not typically affect the lungs, and a tuberculosis of the lungs has no connection to the appendix.

The only known photograph in existence of Jim Donnelly. (By permission of Ray Fazakas, author of *The Donnelly Album* and *In Search of the Donnellys*)

In the four months since his release from prison there was no report (at least none that this author has been able to come across) that indicated Jim Donnelly had been suffering from the ravaging effects of tuberculosis. There were, for example, no reports of him suffering from dramatic weight loss, or excessive coughing. In the 1800s, consumption (so called because the disease literally "consumed" the body) was fatal, and typically was treated by bed rest in a colder climate, and a time span was then indicated regarding how long one had left to live, in order to give a patient time to put his affairs in order. A diagnosis of this contagious disease was essentially a death sentence that later would require those suffering from it to be institutionalized in sanitariums. However, the first Canadian sanitarium wouldn't come into existence until 1897 in Gravenhurst, Ontario. Prior to this, if you contracted the disease, you stayed (and died) at home. In 1867, consumption was the leading cause of death in Canada. In 1877, the tubercle bacillus, the bacterium that causes tuberculosis, was still five years away from being discovered by scientists.[46] There is no reference in any of the documentation that survives of Jim Donnelly having endured a long, drawn-out death as a result of tuberculosis. This doesn't mean that he could not have died from the disease, but only that there is no evidence of his ever having contracted it.

Interestingly, none of the Donnelly authors or researchers, or any of the local newspapers from the time, have ever indicated that a wake was held for the eldest Donnelly son — and this was peculiar for the Donnellys. However, if Jim Donnelly had, in fact, died of tuberculosis, rather than, say, appendicitis, it was believed (and rightly so as it turns out)[47] that the body of someone who died from the disease could be highly contagious, and so no public gatherings with the corpse and a quick burial would have been advisable. And, as a peculiar side note to the speculation regarding this lack of a wake, while there is a headstone within St. Patrick's cemetery with Jim Donnelly's name engraved upon it, thus indicating his burial there, it is intriguing that the original book of interments for St. Patrick's cemetery contains no reference at all to Jim Donnelly ever being laid to rest there.[48] An alternate reason for the lack of a wake that has been advanced over the years is that Jim Donnelly didn't die from anything so pedestrian as appendicitis or tuberculosis, but rather, as the *St. Marys Argus* reporter indicated back in 1880, as a result of a gunshot wound.

Understandably, if there was a bullet hole present in Jim Donnelly's body, any public (or medical, as in a postmortem) viewing of the corpse at a wake would make this evident, and suggest that he received the wound during the commission of a crime. This would be a further blight upon the family name, which would perhaps subject the family to paying restitution for any damages. But there are problems with this scenario as well as, indeed, there are with any version of the death of Jim Donnelly.

Orlo Miller, for example, suggested that Jim Donnelly may have been involved in the ransacking of Berry's barbershop and that, since shots were fired that hit the watchman that night, perhaps Donnelly could have been hit by one of these, or in shots returned by the watchman. This event was said to have occurred on the evening of May 12, or three days prior to Jim Donnelly's death. We know that George Gear (the watchman) had been shot in the leg that night by somebody; however, we don't know if Gear himself fired any shots in return, as there was no report of anybody else being hit. In any event, Miller speculates that this is the most likely death-by-gunshot scenario.[49]

None of the above explanations of how Jim Donnelly met his end are particularly convincing. Fortunately, two official documents containing information on the matter were revealed by a little more sleuthing. The first came via the good people at the London Public Library, who were able to unearth a copy of Jim Donnelly's death registration record with the Province of Ontario. This document was originally filed on May 19, 1877 — a mere four days after his passing, which makes it the earliest account of the event:

> *Name and Surname of Deceased:* James Donnelly
> *When Died:* May 15, 1877
> *Sex — Male or Female:* Male
> *Age:* 26 years [he was actually 35]
> *Rank or Profession:* Yeoman
> *Where Born:* Biddulph [he was actually born in Ireland]
> *Certified Cause of Death, and Duration of Illness:*
> Inflammation of the lungs, about 7 days
> *Name of Physician, if any:* Dr. Sutton
> *Signature, description and residence of Informant:*
> James Donnelly, Concession 6, Biddulph
> *When Registered:* May 19, 1877
> *Religious Denomination of Deceased:* Roman Catholic
> *Signature of Registrar:* H. Hodgins
> *Remarks:* [stamped] 008320[50]

With this official information as a starting point, I reached out to several friends who are medical doctors for their professional opinion on the cause of death cited in the death registration record, as "inflammation of the lungs" seemed to a layperson such as myself to be rather vague, medically speaking. The general consensus from the doctors was that Jim Donnelly most likely died of pneumonia. Doug McGuff, an ER physician in Seneca, South Carolina, wrote back to me indicating that

> [t]he diagnosis of "inflammation of the lungs" is
> also known as pneumonitis or, more commonly,
> pneumonia. Recall that in 1887 the germ theory of
> disease was not well-developed and the pathogens

causing pneumonia were not known. The diagnosis was made at autopsy by observing inflammatory changes in the lung both grossly and (sometimes) by microscopy. At the time most thought the cause was exposure to cold air — "you'll catch your death of cold" kind of thing. So, in a nutshell, pneumonia. Death over a seven-day period suggests pneumococcal pneumonia, as it was the most common and most virulent, and is what we vaccinate for when someone gets a "pneumonia vaccine."[51]

Dr. Anthony Drohomyrecky, from Bracebridge, Ontario, informed me that "while we treat a pneumonia diagnosis today with approximately ten days of antibiotics, in 1877, there was no treatment, and death was not uncommon."[52]

Despite the subsequent creation and application of antibiotics, pneumonia is still considered to be a life-threatening disease that claims four million lives each year.[53] Around the time Jim Donnelly died, it was, in the words of physician Sir William Osler (one of the four founding professors of Johns Hopkins University), "the most fatal of all acute diseases."[54] Indeed, from the late 1800s to the early 1900s, pneumonia was the leading cause of death due to infectious disease and the third leading cause of death overall.[55] Interestingly, for comparative purposes, during the American Civil War, Lieutenant General Thomas J. "Stonewall" Jackson experienced chest pain and difficulty breathing four days after having his arm amputated in a non-sterile field hospital. He was diagnosed as having contracted pneumonia and died three days later on May 10, 1863.[56] The period of time that elapsed from when his symptoms first appeared until his death was seven days — the exact same length of time that Dr. Sutton claimed to have been treating Jim Donnelly prior to his death.

The second official document in support of Jim Donnelly's death being a result of contracting pneumonia came to light during the course of the author's research when he was granted access to Bob Donnelly's case file from the London Asylum for the Insane. Just prior to his admittance to the institution (for a fourteen-month period) in 1908, he gave a private interview in which he stated categorically that his brother Jim had died of pneumonia.[57] This is significant, as it represents the only time a member of the Donnelly family spoke on record about Jim Donnelly's cause of death, and, as his interview was given in the strictest confidence (as one's asylum interview and records were protected, not unlike attorney-client privilege), there existed no reason for him to lie about the matter.

Harvard Medical School describes pneumonia as "inflammation deep inside the lungs caused by some kind of infection. As a result of the infection and the immune response to it, the tiny air sacs (alveoli) — where oxygen is absorbed into the bloodstream — fill with fluid, impairing the ability to breathe."[58] So, in all likelihood, Jim Donnelly died a slow, agonizing death, his ability to breathe diminishing with each passing day until his internal organs, deprived of oxygen, eventually shut down. Considering this in light of the volume of criminal activity in Lucan prior to his death, it stands to reason that, if Jim Donnelly did in fact commit any of the previous crimes indicated, he would not have been up to doing so in the seven days leading up to his death. This means he would not have been out and about on the night of May 12 to ransack William Berry's barbershop, nor would he have had the inclination to venture out on the evening of May 11, 1877, to set fire to Robert McLean's stables. Perhaps the steel knuckle shot to the head of Joseph Watson on April 28 was a possibility for his last hurrah, but even then, it would seem that Tom Donnelly, who was in direct competition with Watson in the stagecoach trade, would have made a more likely candidate of all the Donnelly brothers.

This is speculation, of course, but as in the case of the medical doctors' conclusions cited above, it is at least informed speculation, and that's all we can go on regarding the death of Jim Donnelly.

No matter how he died, the passing of Jim Donnelly represented a significant weakening of the Donnelly brothers as an oppositional force. Up to this point, their numbers and their willingness to use these numbers to support one another in everything from their stagecoach business to their legal scrapes had made them more or less an autonomous and viably independent group in the area. Jim's death saw this number and, thus, the brothers' strength, diminish palpably.

The number of their enemies, however, was on the rise. Not only did a growing faction from within the Biddulph Roman Catholic community oppose them, but, after the craziness that had gone down in Lucan recently, along with the violence in which the brothers had engaged during the stagecoach wars, a growing number of local Lucan businessmen (most of whom were Protestant) had come to view the family as a pestilence that needed to be eradicated. Talk of another "Vigilance Committee" forming had been bandied about in the local newspapers since at least February 1877.[59] To the higher-ups in Lucan, the Donnellys were bad for business. They had to go. And the death of Jim Donnelly, regardless of how it happened, represented a good start in that direction as far as they were concerned.

CHAPTER NINE

RAILROADED

Bob Donnelly, about the time a judge said of the Donnellys that he believed there were some good points in the Donnelly family. He "had no doubt they were generous and warm-hearted and would make warm friends. But there was no doubt they were bad enemies." (By permission of Ray Fazakas, author of *The Donnelly Album* and *In Search of the Donnellys*)

While there exists no record of a wake being held for Jim Donnelly, there undoubtedly was a funeral, and this would have brought all the remaining family members together — including Bob Donnelly. Bob, as mentioned, had been out of the vicinity of Biddulph since January 1876, after his pistol-whipping of Special Constable Rhody Kennedy. Unlike William, Bob shared his late brother's inclination to fight violence with violence. And he hadn't been home long when the violence in the community started up again. William Porte, the Lucan postmaster, would report the following:

- Tuesday, May 22, 1877. Three horses belonging to William Walker butchered in Tim Carey's pasture last night, two of them found dead, and shot the other one.
- Thursday, May 24, 1877. Fire set in Goodacre building behind Photograph rooms this morning about 12:15 a.m., but providentially discovered before doing any harm.
- Saturday, May 26, 1877. Attempt made to burn Oddfellows' Hall.
- Friday, June 8, 1877. Whalen Corners Post office burned last night.
- Thursday, July 5, 1877. Fitzhenry Hotel occupied by James [Maloney], together with stable, shed and Mr. Gleeson's stable burned this morning between one o'clock a.m. and daylight. Loss to Fitzhenry about $900. Gleeson stable about $200.
- Monday, July 9, 1877. Ben Blackwell's house occupied by Mike Donnelly burned about one o'clock a.m. this morning. Completely gutted. Shell left standing. Origin of fire a complete mystery.[1]

Porte made entries in his diary of no fewer than thirteen fires taking place in Lucan during the year 1877, which was three to four times the annual average based upon the previous three years.[2] That such a record of fires should occur only after Bob Donnelly had returned to Lucan is of course open to interpretation. The local press dubbed this period of time the "Reign of Terror":

> The "reign of terror" still continues in Lucan, and as yet no great effort has been made to secure the discovery of the rascals who have committed the

diabolical outrage of the past few weeks. Nor does there seem any prospect of an abatement in the lawlessness which has for some time existed. During the last week or two several thousand dollars' worth of property has been destroyed by fire, the origin of which, to the minds of all who reside in the neighbourhood, was clearly traced to incendiaries. In addition to this, some 15 horses, principally belonging to Messrs. Watson and Walker, stage owners, have perished, either by being burned alive or otherwise. The latest outrage, which appears to be the most fiendish of the series, was perpetrated between last (Monday) night and this morning. It appears that Messrs. Walker and Watson, having, as stated, lost several valuable animals by the burning down of stables, etc., were afraid to keep their horses in the stables overnight, and so put them out in a field. They did so, as usual, on Monday night, Mr. Walker putting three good animals, and Mr. Watson one, into a field adjoining the village. During the night, horrible to relate, some fiend, or fiends, in human form, visited the pasture and cut the [tails off] the whole of the dumb animals, at the same time frightfully mutilating their bodies. Finding it difficult to cause the death of Mr. Watson's horse by the process named, the scoundrels disemboweled him. The whole of the animals were found in a dead state this morning. These outrages have caused a great deal of indignation in the neighbourhood, and threats to hang the miscreants, should they be discovered, are freely indulged in. The authorities should lose no time in offering a reward for their arrest and conviction.[3]

The newspaper account referred to the first entry cited above from Porte's diary, which indicated that the horses belonging to the stagecoach owners Walker and Watson were targeted. The inference was obvious: the only entity that stood to gain from destroying Walker and Watson's means of transportation was their competition, the Donnelly stage. Popular opinion was the Donnelly brothers had killed the horses.

Horse mutilation has been one of the larger stigmas that has become attached to the Donnelly family name over the years. It is discomforting to contemplate, particularly given our vantage point of 140 years from when these barbarous acts were said to have occurred. However, it must be said in fairness to the Donnellys that this author has found no evidence to warrant such a charge. It is true that in the newspaper reports published after the murder of the Donnellys all sorts of atrocities were laid at the feet of the slain family. But it must be remembered that these comments were made by their enemies to justify the murders and also to influence potential jurors in the impending trials. The Donnellys had to be painted as inhuman villains, and the wanton killing and mutilation of horses certainly was a step in that direction. Immediately after the murders, for example, the London newspapers contained statements from nameless individuals who claimed that "it was necessary [to kill the Donnellys]. Our barns were burnt, our horses' tongues cut out, our cattle disemboweled, and no one was safe who ever said a word against the Donnellys"[4] and "they [the Donnellys] burned and cut, and were cut and burned."[5]

However, it must be pointed out that never once during their lifetimes were any of the Donnelly family members charged with the mutilation of animals. Even the press grew skeptical about many of the stories they were being fed about the family's alleged villainy. In the instance of Donnelly foe Joseph Carswell, the papers eventually began to preface his comments with caveats such as "We give it for what it may be worth"[6] and "Rightly or wrongly."[7]

Having heard from their enemies on the subject, it is important to hear from those who were related to the Donnellys or who were friends with them in order to get the other side of the story. As recently as 2001, Patrick Donnelly's grandson, Thomas Newman, felt obliged to hand-deliver a letter to the *Thorold News* about the matter, in which he stated, "It was rumoured at the time of the barn burnings and the bar brawls the Donnelly family was accused of cutting the tongues out of horses. My mother, Pat's daughter [Margaret], said, 'To beat up a man severely was of no concern to the brothers. Harm a horse? NEVER. They loved and respected horses.'"[8]

Another man who knew the Donnellys happened to be listening to a speech made in 1946 at the Middlesex Historical Society by London teacher Alice McFarlane. When she mentioned some of the crimes the Donnellys were said to have committed, she included the allegation that they cut the tongues out of horses. This prompted the man, eighty-three-year-old James McCormick, to stand up from his seat and yell out, "Members of the Donnelly family were accused of many things of which they were not guilty. The Donnellys might cut the tongues of people, but they would never cut the tongues of horses."[9]

Another man who worked for the Donnellys at their farm was John Casey, who recalled that the Donnellys "were very kind to animals and treated them as pets."[10] That the surviving relatives indicate the Donnellys had no qualms about assaulting people but drew the line at animals is telling, as is the fact that even the Donnellys' competitor in the stagecoach trade, William Walker, held no ill will toward the Donnellys for the horse killings — and he lost three of his animals to the butchery. Indeed, one month after his animals were killed, rather than accusing his rival Tom Donnelly of the crime, the two men (and former partners) teamed up one last time to lay a beating on a certain Frederick Allen. The details aren't known, other than that Walker was "disorderly and using abusive and insulting language," while Tom Donnelly was "fighting on the public streets."[11] We can presume that Allen said something, perhaps about Walker's loss of his horses (which had been in the newspapers) or about the declining stagecoach business, which set off Walker on a verbal tirade. When Donnelly found out what Allen had said, he decided that words weren't sufficient to teach the man a lesson and concluded the matter by beating the packing out of him on Lucan's Main Street. Both Donnelly and Walker were fined for the incident.[12]

Moreover, as evidenced by the last two entries in Porte's diary above, it wasn't just the Walker and Watson stage line that suffered from the recent "reign of terror," but other businesses in Lucan as well, including the Donnelly stage line. Consequently, not all these crimes could be said to be the work of the Donnelly brothers. In the case of the fire at Fitzhenry's in July 1877, the blaze consumed not only the Donnelly stagecoach, but also their horses that had been stabled there.[13] As William Donnelly would later state about the matter, "Fitzhenry's hotel and stables in Lucan were set on fire and burned to the ground, together with our new stage that stood in the stable. The Donnellys did not do this."[14]

The fire at Fitzhenry's had certainly taken the brothers by surprise as they had hired a security guard to stand watch over the stables and buildings. When Mike Donnelly arrived on the scene to help combat the blaze he noticed the security guard, a large and powerful Dutchman named Hocher, standing passively among the spectators as the stables burned down. Seeing as how this was the second Donnelly stage to go up in flames in as many months, Donnelly had some choice words that he directed at Hocher, letting his employee know exactly what he thought of his guard work thus far. This resulted in Hocher saying something in return, which caused Mike Donnelly to stop fighting the fire and start fighting with Hocher.[15] Donnelly's fists evidently articulated his point quite strongly — a warrant for his arrest was issued the next day, but he had already left Lucan. He was still out of town five days later when a person or persons unknown entered his home and set fire to it — Mike Donnelly's wife, Ellen, along with their seventeen-month-old daughter, Catherine, barely escaped from the blaze with their lives.[16]

And the fires continued. The next building to fall under the torch was the Queen's Hotel.[17] This marked the second time in the hotel's history that it had been burned to the ground. The stable behind the hotel was where the horses and equipment of the Donnelly Stagecoach Line were housed, which would have been a little too close to home for the fire to have been set by their hand. These last two fires had clearly targeted the Donnellys — with the passing of Jim, a group from somewhere on the periphery had now suddenly grown bolder.

Clearly something had to be done to curb the recent rash of crime and pyromania. In an effort to more effectively deal with the fires, the town of Lucan started its own volunteer fire brigade, purchased new pumps and hoses, and installed sunken water tanks along certain of the village streets.[18] In an effort to combat any future crime, the town installed streetlights,[19] built a new jail,[20] and appointed a man named Samuel Everett to be its village constable.[21] Everett's hiring was somewhat suspicious in that he had been brought in from outside the town to deal with the problems that were occurring within it. Coincidentally, like the private detective Hugh McKinnon, Everett also hailed from Hamilton, Ontario, where, again like McKinnon, he had been kicked off the police force.[22] He would, in time, prove to be perhaps the most corrupt constable in Lucan's history, which was no small achievement. He was eminently bribable, being willing to accept payoffs from people to arrest those against whom they held a grudge,[23] and he was receptive to bribes from prisoners to let them go[24] and to payoffs from criminals whom he had been sent to arrest.[25] It was also not beneath him to be inebriated when delivering a prisoner to the Lucan jail.[26] However, for reasons known only to the County's Court of General Sessions, he was evidently considered to be the perfect man for the job.

While the town of Lucan had taken steps to solve their crime problems, the stagecoach businesses had run out of options. As a result of the dominance of the railway and the repeated sabotage of their coaches and horses, the stage lines had ceased to be profitable. William Walker would be able to stay in the trade a little longer than his competition, as he also had the steady income that was generated from his hotel and tavern business, which he could infuse into his stagecoach enterprise as needed. Tom Donnelly, on the other hand, had no such backup. Only a handful of months after the fire, the Donnelly stage would make its final run.[27]

The stagecoach as a commercial enterprise had been operating in Canada since 1798,[28] but it had outlived its utility, and was now viewed as a relic of a bygone era. It had come to represent the days when the territories of Canada were pressed firmly under the thumb of European interests. The railroad, by contrast, coincided with (and to a large extent was responsible for) Canada becoming a country unto itself, as it served to join all of Canada together. Indeed, the construction of the Intercolonial Railway had been a condition written into the Constitution Act of 1867.[29] The railroad further provided an important link to commerce, connecting the smaller towns to big city markets, not only within Canada, but beyond into the United States. The railroad also delivered people to the smaller towns — and people meant growth: growth of potential markets for exported goods, more retail products to sell, new residents, businesses, taxes, prestige, power. And Lucan was a town that wanted all this, and the sooner the better.

During its construction, the London, Huron and Bruce Railroad had appealed to the towns and villages to buy shares in its railway line, which, in turn, would be matched up to 50 percent by the Ontario government. This would offset the expense of bringing the railroad through the area and connecting towns such as Lucan more directly to the outside world. Most communities jumped at the chance, but Lucan (and Biddulph Township) paused at this point; their town councillors and politicians wanted to weigh every angle of benefit against all potential risk. The people wanted it, to be certain, but money coming out of the public coffers was never a high priority for politicians — what if things didn't work out? Then they would be the ones who had bankrupted or financially crippled their respective town and township. Elections could turn on such a result. Besides, other municipalities on either side of Biddulph and Lucan had already agreed to buy shares in the railway line, which meant the railway had no choice but to go through their township. Lucan and Biddulph decided to wait and think about it. After taking considerable time, Biddulph voted against contributing any funding to the railway line. Lucan followed suit. Unfortunately, the LH&B Railway started and ended on lines operated by the Great Western Railway (Ontario), and Great Western wasn't in the charity business. When they got tired of waiting, they instructed their surveyors to move their survey stakes two miles to the west, and then extended their track such that it missed both Biddulph and Lucan completely.[30] Realizing the error of their ways, Lucan now said that it would gladly pay the subsidy, but it was too late.

The Donnellys must have laughed at how the men of influence within Lucan, such as Bernard and William Stanley, had shot themselves in the foot on this matter. The businessmen of Lucan had just taken a severe blow and hard feelings ensued. From the point of view of the Donnellys, however, any enemy of the town that had so pilloried their family and sabotaged their business couldn't be all bad. At least that's what Mike Donnelly must have thought, as ever since his family had been burned out of their Lucan home, he had been looking elsewhere for a different line of work. He soon found it within the very industry that had just squeezed his family's stage-coach line out of business. He accepted a job as a brakeman with the Grand Trunk Railway Company and moved his wife and children fifty-seven miles south of Lucan to the village of St. Thomas.[31]

James Keefe had been missing from Biddulph ever since he'd taken a stone and repeatedly beaten strongman Joseph Berryhill over the head with it inside Lucan's Western Hotel in September 1875. However, by August 1877 he had returned, and it was just the arrival the townsfolk of Lucan didn't need. Sure enough, Keefe quickly resumed his violent ways. The very month of his return Keefe made his presence known by beating up the local tinsmith (and a McKinnon posse member), Henry Collins.[32] For this he was fined for assault and breach of the peace. In December 1877 he punched out another man in Lucan and was once again fined for assault and breach of the peace.[33] With the Donnelly stage line on its last legs, Tom Donnelly found himself with progressively more time on his hands, and the return of his old buddy James Keefe meant that his time could be now be filled with some hell-raising — which, of course, was right up Tom's alley. One such occurrence came in January 1878, when Tom, James Keefe and a few more of their friends piled into a sleigh and headed south to the Elginfield Hotel.[34] They hadn't been in the establishment long before they started getting rowdy. Soon tables were overturned, glasses broken, furniture fragmented and barrels of ale and decanters of whiskey smashed open. One of the local newspapers reported the details:

> A few of the natives deliberately took possession
> of Glass' Hotel, Elginfield, London township and
> commenced a fearful scrimmage. Poor Glass had no
> chance whatever. Glass gives the names of three of the

"lambs" with whom probably our readers are already
familiar — Donnelly, Keefe and Feeheley. He says
the way they "cleaned out his decanters and tapped
his bottled ale would make any man shed tears."
During the row Mrs. Glass with a poker, and Mickey
with an axe handle, did all a properly constituted
landlady and an able-bodied hostler could reasonably
be expected to do, but alas! the good woman was
bowled down like a nine-pin, and Mickey retired
howling "wid a shanty over his eye."[35]

The owner of the tavern, Michael Glass, himself a justice of the
peace, quickly appealed to the Lucan magistrate Bernard Stanley
to send constables to arrest the crew. However, Stanley informed
him that his constables were already too busy in dealing with the
goings-on in Lucan, and that, since Glass was himself a magistrate,
he should get his own constables to do the job. Glass was furious at
this, but he brought no charges against Tom Donnelly, James Keefe
or any of their friends as a result of their trashing of his business.[36]

Among the Donnellys' neighbours on the Roman Line were
the Feeheley boys: twenty-year-old James and seventeen-year-old
William. The Feeheleys, like the Keefes, were wild, strong and
prone to violence. The previous fall, James Feeheley had gotten
into a fight in London in which he was stabbed repeatedly in the
stomach and kidneys, and yet still proceeded to beat his opponent
unconscious.[37] After recovering from his wounds, Feeheley was
back at it again, this time getting into a fight with twenty-two-
year-old Hugh Toohey, in which he blackened both of Toohey's
eyes.[38] The Feeheley brothers were prone to violence because they
had grown up with it; they came from an abusive home, which, of
course, meant that the Donnelly family had a soft spot for them.

The Feeheleys' father, Michael, had once been a friend of James
Donnelly Sr., even being one of his defence witnesses during the

latter's murder trial in 1857. But the two had since grown estranged, perhaps owing to Michael Feeheley's violence toward his own family. On two occasions Michael Feeheley had chased his wife Bridget and their two boys out of the family home with a butcher knife, causing them to take refuge with neighbours or with the priest at St. Patrick's Church. Another time he drove them out after beating Bridget with a horsewhip, and still another time he beat her with a stick of wood.[39] Michael Feeheley had also grown envious of the success of James Donnelly's farm, as his own farm was running him into debt (a fact that will come into play later in our narrative).[40] As a result of their unstable home life, the Feeheley boys spent a lot of time at the Donnelly farmhouse and became particularly close friends with Tom Donnelly.[41] But with children from scarred families come the emotional problems that such homes create within them, and reuniting the Feeheley brothers with the Keefes and the two Donnelly brothers who still lived on the Roman Line (Tom and John by this point in time) was, quite simply, bad news.

In early March 1878 James Feeheley and Tom Donnelly went into Lucan to hit the local bars. This was also the plan for local farmer Ned Ryan who, unlike Donnelly and Feeheley, was flush with cash as a result of having just sold his farm. With the proceeds from the sale Ryan had purchased another farm on the Roman Line, just two lots south of the Donnellys, and he still had money left over. As a result of his real estate success, he had come into Lucan that afternoon with eighty-three dollars in cash, a considerable sum to have in one's pocket in 1878. Upon entering Walker's Hotel, Ryan spotted his new neighbour, Tom Donnelly, seated drinking with James Feeheley. Ryan thought this represented a great opportunity for the new neighbours to get know each other. He approached the duo and, flashing his cash, began plying the pair with drinks. The trio ended up drinking in almost every bar that afternoon and on into the evening — all of it on Ryan's tab. And then, when it finally came time to call it a night, the three nuevos amigos headed out onto the street. A few hours later a very drunk Ned Ryan was found lying face down in one of the town ditches.

It was the new town constable Samuel Everett that discovered him and, after several attempts at trying to get Ryan up to his feet, Everett was about to drag him over to the town jail to let him sleep it off. That's when a cousin of Ryan's happened upon the scene. The cousin suggested to Everett that he would be willing to take Ryan to his house just down the street and let him sober up there. The constable agreed and released Ryan into his cousin's care. Before turning in that night Ryan turned to his cousin and declared, apropos of nothing, "My money's all right!" At which point he vomited, and then blacked out for the remainder of the evening.

In the morning, however, Ned Ryan discovered that his money was far from all right; in fact, it was missing. He thought he recollected someone grabbing him from behind and Tom Donnelly putting his hand in his pocket. He wasn't certain, but he thought he'd better track down Tom Donnelly and confront him about it. On his way he encountered James Feeheley and told him he wanted his money back. Feeheley was surprised, and then angered, by the accusation. He denied that either he or Tom had taken Ryan's money, and threatened the farmer with physical harm if he pressed the matter any further. Not to be put off, Ryan immediately tracked down Constable Everett and told him of his dilemma. To Ryan's shock, the constable flatly refused to arrest either Donnelly or Feeheley. From his perspective, there was no evidence of an assault or theft having taken place — no one had heard Ryan call out for help at any time that evening, and Ryan had been so inebriated that his ability to identify anyone was highly suspect.[42] Ryan was irate, but Everett was implacable; there was no evidence of any crime having taken place.

Constable Samuel Everett wasn't just unpopular with Ned Ryan, however. He had made many enemies during his short time in Lucan, foremost among them the postmaster, William Porte. Porte had been disgusted by the new constable's strutting, profiteering and boozing while on the job. On January 1, Porte had written about the town constable in his diary: "Tuesday, January 1, 1878. Our beast of a town constable made a regular blackguard of himself today at the Central Hotel. Drunk and insulting everybody who did not think as he did. . . . But hark, I'll tell ye of a plot, Baitherskin!"[43]

A plot? Evidently a comeuppance was heading the constable's way, and the conspirators, apparently, were named in a passage entered into Porte's diary the very next day: "Wednesday, January 2, 1878 — O'Donohue, Feeheley and Jimmy Keefe in town today. I know for what."[44] Clearly whatever the plot was, Porte knew about it. However, as nothing happened on January 2, it's hard to know what the plot might have been. The three men Porte mentioned were all friends of the Donnellys; John O'Donohue was the current owner of the Queen's Hotel in Lucan and was no fan of the town constable, while Feeheley and Keefe were young men who were always up for some excitement. By Porte's entry, no Donnellys were involved in "the plot" — whatever it was. Given that Everett had fallen out of favour with Porte, it may well have involved some attempt to publicly expose Constable Everett as being incompetent in the hopes of getting him to either step down in disgrace or be fired. That, most certainly, would have received Porte's blessing. In any event, the fact that no anti-Everett activity took place on that particular day didn't stop Porte from engaging in some anti-Everett activity of his own. He drafted a damning article about the constable and had it published in the *Parkhill Gazette*, a small newspaper in the village of Parkhill located thirteen miles to the west of Lucan. Porte did not sign his name to the piece (he seldom if ever allowed his name into print; when interviewed by the *London Free Press* about the Donnellys in 1880, he was referred to as "a close observer" of the goings-on within the town[45]). Retaining his anonymity was important, particularly as he sat on the Village Council, which had been the Lucan body that had hired Everett. Anonymity was also the reason Porte hadn't submitted his article to a London newspaper, where he would be easily identified. Within the article the postmaster drew attention to Everett's drinking on the job, his committing of misdemeanours and how the constable routinely abdicated his constabulary duties.[46] When Everett read the piece he became incensed, but not knowing the author of the article lived in Lucan, he charged the editor of the *Parkhill Gazette* with libel.[47] The editor, not looking to pay out any damages or legal fees, quickly confessed that William Porte was the author of the piece, whereupon Everett withdrew his lawsuit and went after the postmaster.[48] First he had Porte thrown in jail for public drunkenness,[49] and then spread false rumours that Porte had been the one who had been corrupt in *his* duties. This last allegation resulted in a postal inspector from Toronto travelling to Lucan to investigate the matter.[50] Everett may also have caught wind of whatever "plot" might have been in the works and that John O'Donohue was somehow involved, as he next turned his attention toward the proprietor of the Queen's Hotel, insulting and assaulting him.[51]

One of the younger hangers-on around Tom Donnelly and his friends was eighteen-year-old Thomas Ryan. Two years previously he had gotten into a scrape with a lad named James Carroll (a different James Carroll than the one of later infamy in the story).[52] Ryan was charged by Carroll with shooting rocks at him with a slingshot, and also for discharging a firearm in his direction, but was released on bail of somewhere between $800 and $1,000.[53] This payment was split, with half being paid by Thomas's father Patrick (who had been present at the bee when Patrick Farrell was killed), and the other half paid (for some reason) by James Donnelly Sr.[54] Not unlike the Feeheleys, Ryan had been looked after by the Donnellys as a result of some domestic problems within his parents' house. While in the Donnellys' orbit, Ryan came into contact with some of Tom's friends and proved to be malleable and easily influenced. If the author may dabble in speculation, it would appear that the "plot," as drawn up by Messrs. Feeheley, Keefe and O'Donohue (and perhaps Porte) would require Ryan to be arrested by Everett — nothing serious, but enough to warrant his being put in the Lucan jail overnight. At which point, the aforementioned men would break him out of jail, thus exposing the constable's obvious ineptitude.

While the details of the following incident are by no means clear, the gist of it is that on or around the beginning of January, Tom Ryan would need to be arrested. He would venture into Lucan and, within eyeshot of Constable Everett, pull forth a "double-edged fighting knife with a ten-inch blade."[55] Clearly such a weapon would be illegal to carry on one's person in town, but Ryan could always plead ignorance to this and, as he wouldn't stab anybody with the knife, any charges arising from his possession of the weapon would be minor. And so, on cue, Ryan produced the weapon on the streets of Lucan and Constable Everett moved in and promptly arrested him, depositing his young prisoner in the Lucan jail. As soon as Ryan was behind bars, however, a rumour circulated that a group of Ryan's friends were going to break him out. Upon hearing the rumours, Everett returned to the jail with a loaded shotgun, where he sat and waited for Ryan's supporters to make their move. When the clock struck 3 a.m. and nothing had happened, the constable decided that the rumour had been a bluff. He locked up the jail-house and went home to sleep. What happened next was reported in the local paper:

> The friends of the young man Ryan, it appears,
> waited till after three o'clock, when Constable
> Everett, deeming all idea of a rescue abandoned,
> retired to rest. With jimmies, crow-bars and other
> burglar-tools the "Biddulph and Lucan Lambs" soon
> made a hole sufficient to run a wheel barrow in,
> and in a very short time Tom Ryan was a free man.

The prisoner it appears was arrested on a charge of carrying a bowie knife.[56]

The "Biddulph" or "Lucan Lambs" was a pejorative, made in reference to the young men with whom Tom Donnelly hung around. It was first used by a writer at the *London Advertiser* in an article published on September 7, 1877, in reference to the statement of James Feeheley's father in defending the character of his son:

> Old Mr. Feeley [sic] was about yielding up his son to justice had it not been for the untimely interference of a leading Lucanite, who told the old man he could fix it all right with the constable. The old, old story was told again of "a *dacint* young man." "I tell yees I've known Mike since he was that high, and if it wasn't for the liquor he's as quiet as a lamb." . . . These Biddulph "lambs," however, have for years kept the community in an uproar. . . .[57]

But Everett always avenged a loss of face; he had, after all, shown both Porte and O'Donohue that he was not a man to cross. And he was not above fabricating evidence in doing so, just as he had when he made up stories about Porte's transgressions at the post office. And the Donnelly gang, those "Biddulph and Lucan Lambs," were now fixed firmly in his crosshairs.

E leven weeks later came the shocking news: someone had taken a shot at Constable Samuel Everett.

> Between eleven and twelve o'clock on Monday [March 18, 1878] night, Constable Everett, of Lucan, while entering his residence opposite

Stanley's mill, was fired at by some unknown person from behind the corner of a woodpile some fifty feet distant. The charge of buckshot, ten in number, hit the door about three inches from Mr. Everett's breast, eight of which became embedded in the door, and the other two went through the thick lumber into the hallway. The constable, for the first time in many months, probably, owing to the clear moonlight, had not his revolver in his hand, but notwithstanding this he made for the direction of the assassin, and found to his great surprise that there were no fewer than three on the stampede from their lair behind the woodpile. Mr. Everett chased them for some time through Mr. Butler's fields, but they had got too much of a start at the outset, and escaped — not, however, before he had taken measure of their figures.[58]

The "figures," of course, according to Everett, were members of the "Biddulph and Lucan Lambs." Indeed, the constable made a point of telling the press that he was "fully persuaded that the individual who fired the shot is one of the gang who were interested in the recent rescue of a prisoner from the lock-up," and then appealed to all law-abiding villagers to come to his assistance "and endeavour by every means in their power to ferret out the perpetrator of such a wanton and bloodthirsty deed."[59]

Nine days after the incident, the *London Advertiser* newspaper announced that Everett had found his shooter: "Yesterday afternoon an arrest was made in connection with the affair, Robert Donnelly being taken into custody on suspicion of being the party who fired the shot. It will be seen what developments an investigation before the authorities will lead to."[60] That Bob Donnelly should be named as the suspect was certainly a surprise; not only had he not been one of the "Biddulph and Lucan Lambs," but had, up until only four or five weeks previously, been living in Glencoe,[61] some thirty-nine miles away to the southwest, and had never had any interaction with Constable Everett. Be that as it may, Everett made time to speak to the local newspapers about how he had arrested the right man. Donnelly had been taken into custody on Tuesday, March 26. That evening or at some point the next day, Thomas Hines, the brother-in-law of Mike Donnelly, came to visit him in his cell. During their conversation, Hines either said or did something that was observed by Constable William Hodgins, who believed that it rose to the definition of "tampering with the prisoner"[62] and the constable promptly arrested Hines on that charge.[63] He was remanded for three days but bailed out by James Donnelly Sr. and another man named Maguire. When word of this reached the *London Advertiser* the newspaper released a story that Hines had attempted to break Robert Donnelly out of jail but had been thwarted in his attempt by the constable.[64]

The same day the *Advertiser*'s story came out (Thursday, March 28), John Donnelly rode into town and confronted Constables William Hodgins and John Bawden on the streets of Lucan. John already knew Bawden from their brawl at the Fitzhenry wedding reception, but he had not crossed paths with Constable Hodgins before. Hodgins was a genuine hard case: born in Ireland thirty-five years previously, he was a carpenter by trade and had been appointed constable nine months previously. He was tough and strong and could look after himself. Donnelly was thirty, his muscles hardened by decades of farm work, and, like all the Donnelly brothers, he knew how to fight. He had some choice words for Hodgins for telling the press that Hines had attempted to break his brother out of jail. The constable answered back in kind. Tensions escalated between them until Hodgins invited Donnelly to fight him. It was a challenge that John Donnelly could not pass up.

The pair then retired to a Lucan backstreet where, in front of the local blacksmith shop, they rolled up their sleeves and proceeded to pound each other nonstop for thirty minutes — an incredible amount of time to engage in a no-holds-barred fight. A crowd (estimated by the press to be in excess of one hundred people) quickly formed to witness the event, encircling the combatants as they exchanged volleys of punches. At one point someone from the crowd attempted to break up the match, but Constable John Bawden stepped forward and produced a revolver, declaring that he would shoot the first person who attempted to break up what he saw to be a fair fight. After half an hour the fight came to an end when one of the pugilists conceded that he was spent and had had enough.[65]

No clear victor was indicated in the accounts of either London newspaper, the write-up in William Porte's diary or in the court record that followed. In truth, after thirty minutes of all-out grappling, punching and kicking, it was more likely that terminating the encounter was a mutual decision on the part of both fighters. When Constable Samuel Everett learned of the brawl, he promptly charged both John Donnelly and Constable William Hodgins (for whom he had no love) with disorderly conduct in breach of village bylaw. The two were hauled before magistrate William Stanley, who convicted both of them of assault, fining Hodgins five dollars and Donnelly four dollars.[66] Presumably, Hodgins received the higher of the two fines for having instigated the match.

Bob Donnelly's case was set to commence in London two days later, on Saturday, March 30. It was a busy docket already, with no fewer than two murder cases to be tried at the Assize that weekend.[67] The Crown's case was presented by attorney Charles

Hutchinson, with lawyer Henry Becher representing Everett, and Queen's Counsel David Glass representing Bob Donnelly. The judge was Adam Wilson.

Donnelly had been arrested on March 26, which meant the Crown had only four days to prepare its case, and Hutchinson, in conferring with Everett and Becher, had indicated he thought their case against Donnelly was weak. Moreover, without any corroborating testimony, or a confession, he didn't like their chances in court. There were three sets of footprints that were discovered on the night of the shooting, after all, meaning that there was a one-in-three chance that they had the right shooter. In addition, the crime occurred in the dark of night; even when Everett gave chase he could see only the shapes of three men running away and they had their backs to him — how could he have picked Bob Donnelly out of these three with any degree of certainty? Plus, the three men had at least a fifty-foot head start on him, which would have made Everett's identification that much more difficult. The prosecution needed something more.

Hutchinson's words served to unnerve the constable and, unbeknownst to the Crown attorney, Everett sought further advice from several influential Lucan businessmen,[68] one of whom was said to be the magistrate William Stanley.[69] Everett was advised to place a spy in the jail cell next to Bob Donnelly's and encourage him talk to the prisoner; perhaps the spy could draw out a confession or some bit of evidence from Donnelly that would prove incriminating. One man, a local painter named Jacob Palmer, was selected for the job. Everett found another man, the painter-cum-watchman, George Gear, who was willing to testify that he had seen Bob Donnelly in Lucan on the night in question with a gun under his overcoat. Everett now had every reason to feel confident and, on Saturday, March 30, 1877, the Crown prosecutor presented his case. According to a report in the *London Free Press*,

In addition to the evidence of Everett, there was brought against the prisoner the damaging proofs that he was seen in the village in the night in question with a gun under his overcoat. And, further, it was proven that after the affair he had acknowledged the shooting, and said that if the gun had not hung fire he would have torn Everett's heart out.[70]

Everett's two witnesses had provided very damaging testimony. And then, for good measure, they further alleged that Robert Donnelly had claimed that "if he ever got out he would lay half of Lucan in ashes."[71] Given the problem that the townspeople had experienced with arson of late, such a statement shocked many members of the jury, who had lived through the fires, and caused the local newspaper to run Bob Donnelly's alleged claim as a headline in their reporting of the case:

"How Donnelly Incriminated Himself — He Threatens to Burn Lucan Down."[72]

The implication from the headline was obvious — the whole town would be at risk if Bob Donnelly was acquitted. Whether or not he had ever actually made such a statement was not, for the moment, even considered. During the trial, defence attorney David Glass brought to the attention of the jury the fact that both Gear and Palmer had participated in the hanging of the Donnellys' friend, William Atkinson, in an attempt to get him to confess knowledge of Donnelly family crimes. Clearly, these two men had an axe to grind — they held an obvious grudge against the Donnellys, and had almost killed a man in a prior effort to obtain incriminating evidence against them. Consequently, their testimony was unreliable. For his part, Gear denied his involvement in the hanging of Atkinson, but

Palmer offered an intriguing reply — he stated that, yes, he had been indicted for the crime, but that "he [Atkinson] is still alive; Mr. Glass got him to run away."[73] This caused a flutter of excitement in the court; did the Donnellys' defence lawyer have a hand in the disappearance of William Atkinson? This was certainly odd, but the matter was not pursued.

After listening to the testimony against Bob, the Donnelly family was convinced that their family member was being railroaded. The defence would have its opportunity to present its case the next day. William Donnelly, of course, had done what he could to aid his brother from behind the scenes. Presumably, he'd had a hand in coaching his brother in court etiquette and how to behave in a courtroom, as Bob had only appeared in court once before, in 1874, as the plaintiff in a transactional dispute.[74]

When it came time for the defence attorney to present his case, David Glass's defence consisted solely of attempting to provide an alibi for Bob's whereabouts on the night of the shooting. Three men were brought forward — Bob's father, James Donnelly Sr.; a neighbour, Patrick Whalen; and William McBride, a local carpenter who had been working at the Donnelly homestead — to testify that Bob Donnelly had been at the family farm on the evening of the shooting. James Donnelly Sr. testified that his son had been working with McBride on building a granary that day. Afterwards, James Keefe and John Hodgins had dropped by and stayed until 11:50 p.m., after which Bob went to bed.[75] McBride backed James Donnelly Sr.'s testimony, and Whalen confirmed that he had seen Bob present at the house earlier in the evening. The alibi witnesses were forthright, but as Lucan was only a little over three miles away, their testimony didn't rule out the possibility that Bob could have ridden into town in time to take a shot at Everett around midnight on that same evening.[76] The defence had hoped to have the young man that James Donnelly Sr. had mentioned, John Hodgins, added to the list of alibi witnesses who would testify, but nobody knew where he was. Glass tried to have the trial postponed until Hodgins could be located, but the judge overruled his request. William Donnelly's coaching had resulted in Bob looking relaxed and confident in the courtroom, as if he was innocent and therefore had nothing to worry about. This, however, seemed to irritate a reporter from the *London Free Press*:

> All during the trial the prisoner maintained a cool
> and easy demeanor, turning his eyes to the different
> parts of the courtroom, as if looking for someone
> and not caring in the least whether or not he found
> him. While the scene given above was enacted he
> frequently broke out in a broad smile, as though
> it were an excellent piece of fooling gotten up
> especially for his entertainment.[77]

After closing arguments, the jury retired to deliberate Bob Donnelly's fate deep into the evening of Saturday, March 30. There were four counts that required their consideration:

1. That he did shoot with intent to kill and murder.
2. That he did shoot with intent to maim.
3. That he did shoot with intent to disable.
4. That he did shoot with intent to do grievous bodily harm.[78]

They returned with their verdict shortly before midnight: Bob Donnelly was found guilty on the first count. Some confusion then ensued as to which count of the indictment they had deliberated on. The jury foreman confessed that they had not meant to find Donnelly guilty of the first charge — "shooting with intent to kill and murder" — but rather on the fourth count of "shooting with intent to do grievous bodily harm." However, by the time this was sorted out it was past midnight, and the judge refused to accept the verdict at this time. Consequently, the jury was ordered to be sequestered over Sunday and to re-deliver their verdict at nine o'clock on the morning of Monday, April 1, 1878.[79] This they did, at which point Judge Wilson delivered his sentence:

> [Judge Wilson] said it was very true that no charge had heretofore been brought against the prisoner; but still it seemed from the evidence that he was infected with the spirit that seemed to be the bane of the neighbourhood of Lucan. Now, he (the learned Judge) believed there were some good points in the Donnelly family. He had no doubt they were generous and warm-hearted and would make warm friends. But there was no doubt they were bad enemies. He did not wish to refer to any distressing family matters, but he could not help referring to the fact that the prisoner's father was once under sentence of death. And he could tell the prisoner that had the shot taken effect and killed Everett, Donnelly would most assuredly have been hanged. He then went on to speak in the kindest manner possible to the prisoner, assuring him that he was giving him the lowest sentence the law allowed, in the hope that it would prove of benefit to him and lead him to seriously reflect on the enormity of the crime and the serious results it might have entailed. He then sentenced him to two years in the Penitentiary.[80]

The entire Donnelly family was stunned by the verdict, none more so than Bob. He was immediately taken to the county jail by several constables to await the arrival of the train that would take him away to Kingston Penitentiary, the same prison that his father had entered to serve his seven-year sentence almost twenty years earlier.

CHAPTER TEN

THE NEW ARRIVAL

James Carroll, circa 1880. The chief antagonist of the Donnelly family.
(By permission of Ray Fazakas, author of
The Donnelly Album and *In Search of the Donnellys*)

In 1878, the Donnelly brothers, as a consolidated threat to the town of Lucan or anywhere else, were almost a distant memory. Bob was in the penitentiary, Jim was dead, Mike had moved to St. Thomas to work on the railway, William was living on a farm in Usborne township, and Pat had recently gone into partnership with Franklin Becker in Thorold, where "Becker and Donnelly" manufactured carriages and wagons, including cutters and sleighs.[1] Their sister, Jennie, had been living in Glencoe since her marriage in 1874 and was presently kept busy raising her two children, Robert David (born in 1875) and Johannah Honore (born in 1876). That left two brothers, John and Tom, who were now living with their parents in Biddulph, helping manage the family's acreage on the Roman Line.

For the most part, the Donnelly boys' "wild days" were behind them — their focus now was on settling down and creating families of their own. The brothers had experienced tragedies in this regard: Pat's wife Mary Ryan had died during childbirth on July 1, 1873 (the child would also sadly pass away on September 20, 1873); William and Nora had lost their first-born child, James, just two months after he was born in 1877; Bob and Annie had a child who passed away shortly after birth. Despite these soul-rending setbacks, the new Donnelly families were all young enough to try again and, with the exception of Bob and Annie, would eventually succeed in bringing new life into the world, despite the dire statistics of infant mortality in the 1800s.[2]

William, John and Mike were older now (thirty-two, thirty-one, and twenty-nine, respectively), and had, for the most part, already sown their wild oats. Pat, it seemed, never really had any wild oats to sow; he had been away from home during the stagecoach craziness, and had never really been of the same temperament as his brothers to begin with. Bob still had a wild side, to be certain, but Constable Everett and the Middlesex County Courthouse had taken care of that in short order.

That left Tom, who, while he had been part of the wildness perpetrated by his elder siblings, had never really been part of William's "Adventurers." However, being the baby brother, he had enjoyed the Donnelly reputation and perhaps longed to bask in its notoriety a little bit longer. He had his own small circle of friends who liked to get up to mischief with him, some of whom were prone to violence, admittedly, but it wasn't the same. Nothing could top the reputations that his elder brothers had earned as a result of their exploits, such as the attempted rescue of Margaret Thompson, the Ryder wedding brawl, or the stagecoach wars. People feared and respected the Donnelly brothers then. Now, for the most part, the Donnellys who had been responsible for engendering these feelings had all left and taken their reputations with them. It was a life of farming that presently loomed up as being the future for Tom Donnelly. No doubt, at twenty-four years of age, the youngest brother craved more of the excitement that had once enveloped his family. In truth, the enemies of the Donnellys in both Biddulph and Lucan had more or less achieved what they wanted — six out of the ten family members were now gone.

While Tom worked semi-contentedly on his parents' farmland, some of his companions, such as James Keefe, continued to run wild. In May 1878, Keefe, together with a buddy, John Cavanagh, spotted an unattended wagon hitched up to two horses in front of the Queen's Hotel in Lucan. This proved irresistible to the pair, who then proceeded to drive off in it, running the horses at top speed throughout the back roads of the township until the wagon was smashed and the horses were exhausted.[3] The man who had rented the wagon declined to press charges, but not so for a visitor to the town, John Flynn, who brought the matter to the attention of Constable Samuel Everett. Hearing Flynn's testimony, Everett decided to arrest James Keefe while the latter was heading to church at St. Patrick's that Sunday. Keefe was out on bail before the church service ended and, as he returned to St. Patrick's along with his brother, Patrick, and his stage-riding partner, John Cavanagh, the trio spotted John Flynn leaving the church service. They attacked him right there on the church steps and administered a horrendous beating. Both Keefe brothers and Cavanagh were promptly charged with assault. Their trial was set to take place in August 1878.[4]

By June, Constable William Hodgins, feeling confident after having given a good account of himself in his slugfest with John Donnelly three months previously, decided that he would make good on Ned Ryan's original warrant to have Tom Donnelly arrested for robbery. While Town Constable Samuel Everett hadn't believed there was sufficient evidence against Donnelly to make an arrest, Hodgins believed otherwise. He rode out to the Donnelly farm on the Roman Line and quickly spotted Tom in front of the house with his father. Dismounting from his horse, he announced to the pair his intention to arrest the youngest Donnelly brother. The Donnelly family knew horses, however, and could sense that Hodgins's mount hadn't yet been tamed enough to stay put unless his reins were secured to a hitching post. But when Hodgins attempted to tie his horse's reins to a fence post in front of the Donnelly home, James Donnelly Sr. told him that he wouldn't allow it. As Hodgins struggled to control his stallion, Tom Donnelly walked into the house and came out with a shotgun. He shouldered the weapon and pointed it at the constable.

"I'll blow your brains out, you son of a bitch!" he yelled.

Both Hodgins and James Donnelly Sr. froze.

"He isn't going to shoot you," said the elder Donnelly, loud enough for Tom to hear him. Constable Hodgins wasn't interested in sticking around to find out; he cautiously climbed into the saddle and rode south, away from the Donnelly farm, along the Roman Line. He would later say, "I thought Tom was trying to frighten me. That was the only time I had any difficulty with him."[5] The constable returned to Lucan empty-handed, but the Donnelly family had made yet another enemy. And the number of their enemies was about to increase again.

James Carroll was a man with a chip on his shoulder. A photograph reveals him to be heavy-set with a bushy goatee and strangely penetrating eyes. This last feature would later be described by a member of the press thusly:

> There is something to Carroll's face that will
> cause one to look at him a second time. On closer

observance it is found that his peculiarity of
expression rests in his eyes. They are small, dark
and restless, and very seldom look a man straight
in the face. This is almost invariably remarked by
all who see him. . . . He is a young man, being only
about twenty-seven years of age, although his beard
makes him look older.[6]

For the better part of eight years prior to his coming to Biddulph, Carroll had worked on the railway in the United States. There he had established a reputation for himself as being a tough and capable construction crew foreman, in charge of overseeing various track crews.[7] He further cultivated a competency in framing and building certain types of structures, such as barns and granaries. This vocation served him well, particularly upon his move to Biddulph, as it allowed him to interact with farmers within the community, and gave him entrée to make suggestions as to what farming equipment they should be utilizing for their planting and harvests. This was helpful to Carroll, who had recently become a salesperson for the Thomson and Williams Manufacturing Company, which was based in Stratford, Ontario, and specialized in farming implements. However, the reason for the young man's return had nothing to do with building or selling farming implements. He had returned to Canada solely to lay claim to his late father's estate.[8]

Until 1869, Carroll had lived on his father's farm in Stephen Township (which lay northwest of Biddulph) with his two younger brothers, William and Michael. Their mother Catherine had died in 1865,[9] leaving their father, Roger Carroll, on his own to do the best he could to work the farm and raise their sons. During the latter half of the 1860s Roger developed a romantic interest in a woman named Catherine Glavin, and soon the pair were married. Catherine had three daughters from her previous marriage, and the prospect of combining the two families was welcomed by Roger and Catherine. However, Catherine Glavin was not viewed by the Carroll boys as being a viable substitute for their late mother. They had no intentions, after all they and their father had gone through since her passing, of embracing their real mother's replacement. Eventually things came to a head, with the result that James, the eldest of the Carroll boys (and the most vocal of them in terms of expressing his opposition to Catherine Glavin), felt compelled to leave home for the United States. Roger and Catherine's union brought two more daughters into the world and, when Roger died in February of 1873, the men he had named to be his executors — his brother, Bartholomew Carroll, and his brother-in-law, John Delahay — dutifully followed the instructions contained in his will and named Catherine and her daughters as the primary beneficiaries. Roger's two youngest sons were to receive a small stipend of sorts, and James was omitted completely.[10]

Perhaps understandably, James Carroll fumed about the omission, and when his job at the railway eventually came to an end, rather than looking for another line of work, he decided that his financial prospects would be better served if he returned to Ontario and demanded what he believed was his rightful inheritance. The property his father had left behind was valuable: fifty acres on the Eighth Concession, and sixty-six acres on the Ninth.[11] The executors of his father's estate had been diligent in their duties; they had found a tenant who was willing to pay a significant amount to lease the properties from the estate, the rent from which was then divided amongst the beneficiaries named in Roger Carroll's will. Upon his return, James Carroll discovered that his two younger brothers were living with the executors — and indolent. Neither had bothered to learn a trade (which had been a stipulation within their father's will) and both still resented their stepmother, which meant that a natural take-charge personality like James Carroll could easily lead them in any direction he wished.

James hadn't been in Biddulph long before he paid a visit to the executors of his father's estate. As they were relatives, he believed he could sway them to see the error of his late father's ways, and amend the will to include him. Unlike his younger brothers, James was industrious and had a plan for the future. He initially proposed that he lease his father's properties — that would show the executors that he cared for the land and was willing to work it. Once they had witnessed this, Carroll reasoned, he would then table his proposition to be included in its ownership. In his first meeting with his uncles he stated his wish to lease the land starting that fall, after the current tenant had harvested his crops. But for some reason the executors sensed trouble with James and doubted his motives. Instead, when fall arrived, they leased the properties to someone else. Carroll threatened to take his uncles to court over the matter, swearing to make their lives miserable. He hired London lawyer John Joseph Blake and threatened to litigate the matter. Neither of his uncles wanted a court battle, and so they compromised: they offered to restructure Roger Carroll's will so that James Carroll was now included, and so that all proceeds from income derived from the properties would be divided equally among all the Carroll children. But this didn't change the fact that the land of James Carroll's father was still leased to someone outside the family. It would remain so for the next year, which meant James would have to wait a minimum of twelve months before he could attempt to enact phase two of his plan, which was to move to take possession of his father's properties outright.

Having flexed his legal muscle in Stephen Township, James Carroll headed southeast to Biddulph, where he took up residence a mile and a half north of the Donnelly farmhouse on the Roman Line, at the house of an uncle on his mother's side, James Maher. Carroll's younger brothers, who had up until this time been living at the homes of the executors, Bartholomew Carroll and John

Delahay, now followed their older brother into Biddulph, where they attempted to find employment as labourers on the local farms. Some work in all probability came their way courtesy of their big brother, as he had already started framing the odd barn in the community for extra money.

One evening that summer, a person or persons unknown crept into James Maher's stable and cut the tails off every one of his horses. Maher was justifiably furious at both the mutilations and the trespass, and told his nephew, James Carroll, that he believed this to have been the work of the Donnellys.[12] While there was no proof of this, Maher's cause in the matter was immediately taken up by his nephew. And, in speaking with several of his uncle's neighbours within the Roman Catholic community, he heard similar anti-Donnelly sentiments.

The most recent news in this regard, of course, was the incarceration of Bob Donnelly for shooting at Lucan town constable Sam Everett. In Carroll's eyes, the Donnellys were a bad and irredeemable bunch. In truth, the Mahers' anti-Donnelly sentiment had taken root many years previously. James Maher's wife, Ellen, was a sister of John Cain, who had purchased the southern fifty acres of what had once been part of the Donnelly property from its legal owner, Michael Maher. The whole issue over the property — the attempts to evict the Donnellys, the eventual sale of the southern fifty acres for two hundred pounds to Maher while the Donnellys were only made to pay fifty pounds for theirs — had planted deep-seated resentment among the Maher relatives well before this tail-cutting incident. Such family prejudices united by blood the relatives' hostility toward their enemies. James Carroll was part of that genealogy, and so this anti-Donnelly prejudice was taken up by him as a matter of course. And the fact that the Donnelly family lived only a mile or so down the road from where he was living with his uncle galled him. Such a family should be banished from the neighbourhood. At least, that was the Maher/Carroll perspective.

And if the Donnellys weren't bad enough on their own, the friends that they attracted to themselves were a further blight on the community. For example, John Cavanagh, along with James and Patrick Keefe, were tried on the morning of August 2, 1878, for their assault of John Flynn. Long-time Donnelly family friend Patrick Keefe was tried first before the magistrates William Stanley, James McCosh and Michael Crunican. He was found guilty and his punishment consisted of a mere three-dollar fine.[13] The trial of James Keefe and John Cavanagh was then scheduled to take place after the lunch break. When the court recessed, Flynn went to one of the local hotels to get something to eat and wait until the trial resumed. As he was sitting down and preparing to enjoy his meal, a brick suddenly came crashing through a window and struck him full force on the head. According to a newspaper report, "Flynn fell forward off his chair, falling on his face on the floor, the blood gushing in a stream from the ghastly wound. He soon, however, staggered to his feet and exclaimed, 'I'm shot! I'm shot!'"[14]

Flynn wasn't shot, but he had suddenly lost all interest in pursuing his prosecution against James Keefe and John Cavanagh. And without anyone to proceed with the prosecution, both Cavanagh and Keefe were discharged.[15] While the Keefes and Cavanagh had acted on their own in the perpetration of this crime, the fact that the Keefes were well-known associates of the Donnelly brothers further stained the family's reputation by association in the eyes of their enemies.

Later that same month, James Carroll landed a job to frame a barn in Biddulph and among those who showed up to help with the construction was Tom Donnelly. During the course of the day, some of the farmers gathered around Carroll as he organized the work to be done. As he had served as a foreman on railway labour gangs, organizing crews and delegating jobs was nothing new to Carroll. At some point during his delegating, Bob Donnelly's name came up, which caused Carroll's antipathy toward the Donnelly family to reveal itself. "Bob Donnelly got a light sentence," he announced to those around him. "His two-year sentence should have been twenty years!"[16] While Tom Donnelly hadn't been near Carroll when the comment was made about his brother, it was later brought to his attention by others who were at the site. Normally one to fly into action upon such provocation, Tom had other things on his mind presently — he instead filed the information away for future reference.

The most imminent thing on Tom Donnelly's mind was his forthcoming trip to Michigan. He would be heading there with his friend James Feeheley to pick up some extra money by working in the Saginaw lumber camps.[17] With a population of over a million people,[18] the Wolverine State offered the young men far more opportunity for good times than did the farmers' fields of Biddulph. Besides, Tom's late brother Jim had purchased some farmland there when he had worked in the same lumber camps in 1874,[19] and so the sojourn would afford the Donnelly family's youngest son the opportunity to look in on the property for the family.

About the time that the duo left Biddulph, Ned Ryan, who was still attempting to charge the pair with robbery, suffered a setback when his barns, along with the equipment he had within them, went up in flames. Ryan recalled Feeheley's threat from five months previously and concluded that Tom Donnelly and James Feeheley must have been the ones who were responsible for the fire.[20] It was a convenient if somewhat suspect recollection, as some members within the community believed that the barn had simply been struck by lightning, while still others voiced their opinion that Ryan had set fire to it himself in order to collect on the insurance money.[21]

September 1878 witnessed the Canadian federal election, and there was quite a backstory to it. The election was held on September 17 and resulted in the return of John A. Macdonald to the prime ministership of Canada. Macdonald and his Conservatives had been defeated in 1873 by Alexander Mackenzie's Liberal government as a result of a scandal that had occurred involving the prime minister and the Canadian Pacific Railway.[22]

The railway was the final stitch in the fabric of a united Canada, but railways (as Lucan found out) cost money, which had to come from somewhere. It was an enormous financial undertaking, particularly for a country of only three and a half million people. The great fear among Canadian politicians had been that, since the time of the American Civil War, American civil policy had clearly been one of expansion, and with catchphrases such as "manifest destiny" in the air, there existed among Canadian politicians a very real fear of annexation by Canada's neighbours to the south. Indeed, U.S. Secretary of State William Henry Seward had predicted that the entire North American continent "shall be, sooner or later, within the magic circle of the American Union."[23] This was a terrifying notion to a nation that was not yet a country. There was some worry for a time that British Columbia would opt to join the United States, but it would ultimately choose to join Canada's fledgling Confederation when Canada agreed to assume the isolated British colony's outstanding debt and further promised to build a railway that would extend from Montreal to the Pacific Coast within ten years' time.

But how to do it? The fear of the U.S. having a claim on its national railroad caused Canada's politicians to forgo the pursuit of any American investment in the enterprise in favour of an "all-Canadian route" that would see the railway blast through the Canadian Shield of Northern Ontario rather than pass through the American states of Wisconsin and Minnesota.

When America had been building its own railway lines, many capitalists had been attracted to the venture as a result of the U.S. government's promise of free but fertile lands that the tracks would be laid over in exchange for their investment. This was land that such investors could later sell for a considerable profit. However, no such enticement existed to encourage investment in the Canadian railroads — at least not initially. It's true that once the rail line hit Manitoba and the Northwest Territories there was valuable land to offer investors — but even if these acreages were thrown into a general pot, the amount of time required for any financier to see a return on his money was too long to be enticing. Moreover, money was required to blast through the Precambrian igneous and high-grade metamorphic rock of the Canadian Shield, and there was no return to be had on that. It was decided that the interests of a united Canada would best be served by the government putting the contract out to Canadian businesses for tender — and right away two syndicates stepped up to bid. The first was the Canadian Pacific Railway line, which was fronted by the Montreal capitalist Hugh Allan. The other contender was David Lewis MacPherson's Inter-Oceanic Railway Company.

The financial activities of Canadian political parties throughout the mid- to late nineteenth century were largely unregulated, with both the Liberal (Reform) and Conservative (Liberal Conservative) parties relying on corporate donations for their sustenance. And while John A. Macdonald was the leader of the country, he was also every inch a politician, with the result that ethical concerns often took a back seat to supplementing his and his party's coffers. And of the two parties bidding on the railway contract, it proved to be the one fronted by Hugh Allan that knew best how the political game was played. He offered John A. Macdonald and his Conservative government a $360,000 cash "donation" in return for the railway contract (approximately $8 million in today's dollars). This proved to be just what Macdonald's Conservatives were looking for from an aspiring railroad builder, and they awarded the contract to Allan's group. Allan's company would further receive a $30-million subsidy and large land grants valued at $20 million. In addition, the Macdonald government threw into the deal various tax exemptions and preferential treatment.[24] This most certainly was a return that justified the investment. It had been suspected that MacPherson's Inter-Oceanic Railway Company had some affiliation with American money, which was the reason, ostensibly, for his bid being rejected. However, while Allan claimed Montreal as his home, behind the scenes his backers were largely American, consisting of investors such as George W. McMullen and Jay Cooke.

When the payoffs and foreign influence were eventually exposed, Macdonald was forced to resign as prime minister and, during the federal election of 1874, his Conservative government was replaced by a Liberal government led by Alexander Mackenzie. Unfortunately for the Liberals, not long after Macdonald had abdicated, an economic recession hit the country and Mackenzie, as prime minister, along with his Liberal party, was blamed for it. They were going to face an uphill battle to retain control of the country as they entered the 1878 federal election.

The Donnellys, like most Irish Roman Catholic families in the North Middlesex riding, had been long-time Reform (Liberal) party supporters. The Protestants, particularly the wealthy businessmen in towns like Lucan, traditionally voted Conservative. The Protestant Stanley brothers, William and Bernard, were political heavyweights in Lucan, always stumping for the Conservative candidate in every election and expecting to have their interests looked after in return.[25] For the past eleven years the North Middlesex riding had gone Liberal under the candidacy of Reform party member Robert Colin Scatcherd, and he was the incumbent heading into the 1878 election. Tired of backing the losing horse, Bernard Stanley had used his influence to convince a Roman Catholic by the name of Timothy

Coughlin to run as the Conservative candidate in the riding, by which he hoped to draw a sizeable section of the Roman Catholic vote over to the Tory side. Stanley had previously crowed to the local press that he drove the Catholics to the polls like sheep to vote Conservative.[26] Running a Roman Catholic as the Conservative candidate turned out to be a clever bit of politicking; after all, the current Liberal prime minister, Alexander Mackenzie, didn't have a single Catholic in his cabinet — and this fact didn't sit well with those Catholics who had remained loyal to the Liberal party over the years. As it played out in the 1878 election, the Conservatives took Middlesex North by a very small margin (Conservative votes: 1,629; Liberal votes: 1,621),[27] and, further, were restored to power federally, with John A. Macdonald back at the helm as prime minister. But in the Donnelly riding (Voting Section No. 3, North Biddulph; Roman Line, Cedar Swamp Line), the Liberals won (Liberal votes: 79; Conservative votes: 40)[28] Voting Section No. 3 was Donnelly territory, and the Conservatives losing this seat had irked Bernard Stanley. He had no use for the Donnellys; the victory of their candidate had undermined his political strategy and his authority. The family's disrespect for Lucan's constabulary, their fights in Lucan's bars, their supposed involvement in the fire that had burned down Stanley's outbuildings, the sheer volume of legal charges that had been brought against them over the years — all had blemished Lucan's good reputation in Bernard Stanley's eyes and had hurt Lucan business.

The Donnellys, however, had seen through the religious veil that had concealed Stanley's politics; a Roman Catholic Conservative like Timothy Coughlin was, after all, simply a marionette for the Conservatives — a man whose strings were being worked behind the scenes by local big shots such as Bernard Stanley, and by the higher-ups within the Conservative party. Any of their Roman Line neighbours who thought they would be advancing the Catholic cause by voting Conservative in the recent election were delusional — and that included James Carroll and his relatives. In May 1878, during the height of the campaigning, one of the Donnellys' neighbours on the Roman Line, Grouchy Ryder, had made it known that he was going to switch his political allegiance from Liberal to Conservative. This apparently amused someone in his neighbourhood as, according to a news story that appeared in the *Exeter Times*: "Mr. Ryder, of the 6th or 7th concession of Biddulph, upon going into his stable the other morning, found the tail of one of his best horses clean shaved, and on it tied a placard reading, 'Vote for Coughlin.'"[29] Ryder, like his Roman Line neighbour James Maher, whose horses would suffer the same fate shortly afterwards, believed that the prank had been perpetrated by the Donnellys.

L ess than a month after the election, Tom Donnelly and James Feeheley returned to Biddulph, fresh from their lumberjack jobs in the United States. Tom hadn't been home long when news of a forthcoming farming auction was posted. Auctions were significant and much anticipated community events, as practical and necessary tools, equipment, feed and, on occasion, livestock could be bid on and often picked up for pennies on the dollar. Perhaps even more important than the auction itself was the fact the event doubled as a social function. Men, women and children from throughout the community attended, looked over some of the deals that could be had and caught up on the goings-on within the township. Consequently, on Saturday, October 12, 1878, a good crowd turned out for the event to inspect and bid on the items. Among the attendees were Tom Donnelly and James Carroll.

Undoubtedly, given that it was an all-day event on a Saturday, whiskey had been consumed by some of the farmers in attendance. This might explain why James Carroll's boisterous voice was soon heard weighing in on what had more or less become a familiar refrain; that Bob Donnelly should have been given a much harsher sentence for his shooting at Constable Everett.[30] Evidently someone from within his group suggested to the farm implements salesman that he might wish to keep his voice down, as Tom Donnelly was in the vicinity. Rather than quieting Carroll, however, the suggestion only served to make him louder. "I can lick all of the Donnellys!"[31] he proclaimed. And sure enough, Tom Donnelly just happened to be walking by at the very time he said it. Donnelly abruptly stopped, turned on his heels and went for Carroll. History has not recorded what words were exchanged between the two men at this point. It's safe to assume, however, that a liberal dose of colourful metaphors was employed, and, with women and children present, several farmers acted quickly to separate the two men and defuse the situation. Nevertheless, word of the Donnelly/Carroll encounter quickly spread throughout the community.[32] Upon his return home from the auction, Tom recounted Carroll's words in the presence of his older brother John, who was not impressed:

> I was vexed at what Tom told me Carroll said of
> Bob and myself. I was vexed at Carroll for speaking
> of Bob when I heard of it last summer. I had no
> quarrel with Carroll, but Tom told me that Carroll
> said he could "lick all the Donnellys," and I was
> mad about it.[33]

He was still mad about it the next day. He stewed a while and then resolved to take a walk along the Roman Line. He headed north in the direction of James Maher's farm, as that was where James Carroll was boarding.[34] He hadn't been walking long when he spotted his friends Patrick and James Keefe, walking toward him from the opposite direction. And walking with the Keefes that day was James Maher Jr., the sixteen-year-old son of James Maher and cousin of James Carroll.[35] Donnelly approached the trio. He had a message to deliver and got right to the point. "Where is Carroll, that *big fighting man*?"[36] he asked sarcastically. The teenager replied that Carroll was at the house of Dan and Eleanor McDonell, the latter of whom was Carroll's aunt.[37]

"Do you want to whip Carroll?" asked Patrick Keefe.

"No," Donnelly replied.[38] "I want to ask Carroll — civilly — what he was saying about our Bob and the whole family at the sale last night." Then, looking directly at Maher, he added, "but if he wants a fight, I'll make his big head soft."[39]

There was absolutely no ambiguity as to John Donnelly's intentions. As he would later recall, "I meant that I was able to lick him. I was willing to fight Carroll if he wanted to fight. As young Maher was Carroll's cousin, I did not care if Maher told Carroll what I said."[40]

From John Donnelly's vantage point, the time for talking was over. If Carroll had a problem with the Donnelly family then the two of them could meet and resolve the problem with their fists. When James Carroll arrived back at his uncle's farmhouse later that afternoon, James Maher Jr. immediately told him of the challenge that John Donnelly had now thrown at his feet. Carroll must have been somewhat apprehensive, for it was one thing to make a boast in front of a large crowd at an auction about how he could beat up the entire Donnelly family single-handedly, but quite another matter to say it within striking distance of John Donnelly — a man who had already proven his pugilistic mettle in a knockdown, drag-out, thirty-minute donnybrook with Constable William Hodgins.

The next morning, Monday, October 14, James Carroll awoke to find himself in a dilemma. He needed to collect some money from a client who had recently purchased a fanning mill from him.[41] Normally this would be a simple task, as the client lived only a short distance down the road from him on the Roman Line. The problem, however, was that so, too, did the Donnellys. Carroll knew that he would have to walk right past their house on the way to his client's, and that meant there was a very good chance John Donnelly would spot him. It's not that Carroll was scared of fighting (one couldn't lead a railway labour crew otherwise), it's just that there is no evidence he was very good at it.[42] After thinking over the matter for a while he came up with a solution. He had always had a talent for finding direct solutions to problems.

William Donnelly had arisen early that same morning within his home in Usborne Township and kissed Nora goodbye. He expected to be away for the better part of the day as he had promised his brothers he would assist them with the ploughing of their parents' fields. He drew his horse from the stable, threw his leg up over the saddle and rode west a short distance before reining his stallion south onto the Roman Line. Tom Donnelly had started the day early as well, and was already hard at work ploughing the field of his parents' twenty-five-acre lot on the east side of the road when William rode by on his way to the family farm. A couple hundred feet farther south and to the west, William spotted his brother John working a plough in the field beside his parents' house.[43] William would be at the front gate of the home in a matter of minutes.

Tom watched William ride by and left his plough, welcoming the break his brother's arrival represented, and started walking through the field toward the farmhouse. Upon reaching the entrance to the farm, William observed his mother Johannah out by the front gate milking one of the cows. He greeted his mother and exchanged nods of acknowledgement with John before directing his horse west, along the laneway that led to his parents' stables. After securing his steed in one of the stalls, he walked to the front of the farmhouse where his two brothers had by now gathered at the water pump. John worked the pump handle furiously, which resulted in a gush of water coming forth. Tom readily received the water into his cupped hand and lifted it to his mouth. Although it was early, the brothers had already been hard at work in the fields for some time that morning and had worked up a considerable sweat. Apart from general small talk, Tom and John wanted to know how their brother Mike and his family were making out in St. Thomas. Having visited with them recently, William brought his two brothers up to speed on Mike and Ellen's activities, as well as how their young daughter Kate was coming along.[44]

The break now over, John returned to the field at the front of the house to resume his ploughing. Tom and William remained behind at the pump a little longer, as William wanted to hear directly from Tom about what had transpired between him and Carroll at the auction.[45] However, no sooner had Tom presented his side of the story to his brother than James Carroll appeared in front of the Donnelly schoolhouse, walking north along the Roman Line. Carroll had evidently gotten up even earlier than the Donnellys had that morning, completed his transaction with his client and was now heading back to the Maher farmhouse. He was walking at a quick clip, clearly having no intention of stopping to chat. Tom took immediate notice of the new arrival and began to advance toward the roadway where Carroll was. William took hold of his impetuous younger brother's arm. The oldest Donnelly son had already divined the reason underlying Carroll's attitude toward the family.

"Don't mind Carroll," William said, "even if he challenges you to fight every day of the week. He wants *law*, not *fight*."[46]

Tom jerked his arm free from his brother's grasp. He hated being told what to do, particularly when it came to fighting.

"Go in the house," William ordered.[47] He knew his younger brother's temperament, and wanted him gone from the scene before anything that might lead to any legal trouble got started.[48] Tom fumed but held his tongue, turned and walked back to the farmhouse. There was no return on public brawling or in the rekindling of old fires. Keeping his eyes on Carroll, William walked over to the farmhouse and sat down upon the log steps at the front of the house.[49] He glanced over his shoulder at John ploughing the field.

It then dawned on him that, given the proximity of the field to the road — a distance of only about sixteen and a half feet[50] — when John looked up, he would be looking right at the man who'd boasted that he could "lick all the Donnellys." But before William could call out to his brother with the same admonition that he had offered moments earlier to Tom, John Donnelly had spotted James Carroll.

"Hey, Carroll!" John Donnelly called out. "I want to talk to you!"

Johannah Donnelly now leaned back from the cow she was milking to see who John was calling to. Carroll paused on the road.

"Well, I don't want to talk to you!"[51] Carroll said, attempting to deflect any discourse.

John Donnelly laughed. All that separated the two men was a distance of less than twenty feet and a split-rail cedar fence that lined the front of the Donnelly property. A wave of confidence suddenly appeared to come over Carroll, however. He took a step in John's direction.

"Jack, what were you saying about me yesterday?"[52] Carroll asked, an obvious indication that his cousin had delivered John's message from the day before.

"I was saying nothing yesterday that I couldn't say today," replied John, a smile playing about his face.

"I wish you would come out and try it," challenged Carroll. John Donnelly nodded, put his plough aside and started walking toward Carroll. He couldn't believe his good fortune. Suddenly, however, Carroll changed his mind.

"Meet me at Whalen's schoolhouse at two o'clock and I'll fight you," he said. John Donnelly's smile widened at the suggestion. He stretched out his arms and shrugged his shoulders.

"There's no one here but us right now. Let's have it here."

John had good reason to remember the hundred or so people who had gathered around him and Constable Hodgins when they'd had their set-to in Lucan not that long ago. He didn't want a similar sized crowd milling about for this encounter. Carroll now looked agitated. John Donnelly was getting closer. William was still seated on the front steps, but looking on with interest. He had every confidence in his younger brother's ability to handle himself.

"Hey, if you prefer," John Donnelly said, "you can get a man and I'll get another, and we can have it out here with no mobbing about it."

Gauging from artists' renditions of the Donnelly homestead that appeared in newspapers of the time, the split-rail fence that lined the property in front of the farmhouse, separating it from the road, stood perhaps four feet high. It would not have posed any impediment at all to John Donnelly getting to James Carroll. But by the time John had reached the fence, Carroll remembered the solution he had come up with earlier that morning. He reached into his coat and pulled out a revolver. He aimed it directly at John Donnelly, which brought John to an abrupt halt.

"You son of a bitch!" Carroll exclaimed. "If you come one foot farther I'll blow your brains out!"

The pistol was certainly a game-changer. James Carroll knew it — and so did everybody else. William Donnelly stood up. Johannah Donnelly leaned out still farther from behind the cow she had been milking to get a better look. Up until this point, the mother's presence had been undetected by Carroll. Her sudden appearance startled him.

"John, go on to your work," she said calmly. And then, fixing her eyes on Carroll and his revolver, added, "and never mind this blackguard."

John smirked, and turned to walk back to his plough. Carroll now trained his revolver upon Johannah.

"I'd just as soon shoot you as John," he said.[53]

Suddenly Tom Donnelly came charging out of the house. He picked up a large stone and threw it at Carroll, but it missed its target. He picked up two more and started out toward the road.

"Throw down the stones, Tom!" William yelled. But Tom was not heeding his brother's counsel on the matter this time.

"I'll fight you, Carroll! You coward!" he yelled. With three Donnelly brothers now staring daggers at him, Carroll was glad he had his revolver. Keeping the gun pointed in the direction of the Donnellys, he slowly started walking north on the Roman Line and away from their property. The farther away he got, the quicker his strides became. Tom, now on the road, was soon joined by his brother John, and the pair began yelling epithets at the now rapidly departing gunman, which Carroll later would recall included terms such as "thief," "coward" and "son of a bitch"; the latter term he believed he had heard Mrs. Donnelly yell at him.

After arriving safely at his uncle's farmhouse, James Carroll borrowed a horse and rode to Lucan where he charged the three Donnelly brothers with assault for throwing stones at him. He further laid a charge of abusive language against Johannah Donnelly. The brothers quickly countersued, charging Carroll with pointing a revolver and threatening to shoot. When the matter ultimately went to court, John and William Donnelly were found guilty and fined three dollars each, plus costs.[54] Tom Donnelly was acquitted.[55] Surprisingly, the Donnellys' charge against Carroll was dismissed — there was no proof that James Carroll's gun was loaded when he had pointed it at John and Johannah.[56] For her part in the matter, Johannah Donnelly was convicted for using abusive language. However, she would appeal the conviction (no doubt on the advice of her son William), and win the appeal, with the result that all her legal costs were charged to James Carroll.[57]

While John Donnelly had been sparring with James Carroll in the courts, he was still fighting for justice on behalf of his brother Bob, who was still behind bars in Kingston Penitentiary. Motivated by the success his mother had experienced when she had circulated her petitions to save her husband's life almost twenty years previously, John worked up his own petition on Bob's behalf and, on or around December 23, 1878, sent it along to the Governor General. The signatures he had affixed to his petition were impressive:

- William Ralph Meredith (London's Conservative member in the provincial legislature) and his brother Edmund Meredith (Biddulph Township's solicitor)
- William Glass (sheriff) and his brother David Glass (who had been the defence counsel in Bob Donnelly's trial)
- John McDougall (the provincial Conservative member for the North Middlesex riding)
- Bishop John Walsh (of the Roman Catholic Diocese in London)
- William Porte (the Lucan postmaster)
- James McCosh (a justice of the peace and Lucan business owner)[58]

He was further able to secure the signature of Constable John Bawden, the man with whom he had fought during the Ryder wedding reception. Surprisingly, despite the calibre of signatories in support of the petition, John Donnelly's appeal to release Bob Donnelly from prison fell upon deaf ears — Bob would remain in Kingston.

The year 1878 had ended on a bitter note. Johannah Donnelly's successful appeal and Thomas Donnelly's acquittal were small victories, but these had essentially been cancelled out by James Carroll winning his assault case against John and William Donnelly. Moreover, the Donnellys had now made yet another enemy in the person of Carroll. And although William Donnelly had thought that the family's wild days were behind them, he had to sense that, in truth, they were just beginning.

CHAPTER ELEVEN

THE PRIEST AND THE CLUB-FOOTED DEVIL

Father John Connolly. (By permission of Ray Fazakas, author of
The Donnelly Album and *In Search of the Donnellys*)

The Catholic faction within Biddulph had long ago concluded the Donnellys were outsiders to their group and had been disloyal to their cause. From their perspective, whether or not Bob Donnelly ever got out of the penitentiary was beneath their concern — particularly when they noted that almost all the signatures on John Donnelly's petition had come from Protestant hands. The Catholic community in Biddulph was far more interested in the changes that were happening within St. Patrick's Church — a new parish priest had arrived. The local press shared in their enthusiasm:

> Father Connolly, late of Quebec, has received the
> appointment of parish priest of Biddulph, [replacing]
> Vice Father Lotz, who has been called to London.
> The people of Biddulph speak in laudatory terms
> of Rev. Mr. Lotz as also of Rev. Mr. Logan, whom
> they say, came as near the right thing as possible, the
> only regret being they were not Irishmen; but this, of
> course, they could not help.[1]

The fact that the new priest was Irish was in itself cause for celebration within Biddulph's Catholic community. As the newspaper article attested, the parishioners of St. Patrick's had never had a resident priest who had hailed from Ireland, "this 'chosen leaf' of the 'land of saints and scholars,'"[2] but all that was about to change. Father John Connolly was an exceedingly well-educated cleric from the old country, having attended Maynooth College near Dublin, a very high-profile seminary that was well respected not only in Ireland, but throughout other parts of Europe as well. Father Connolly was a devoted student of ecclesiastical history, dogmatical and moral theology, natural philosophy, metaphysics, ethics, belles lettres and rhetoric, and was fluent in English, Gaelic and French.[3] He had also studied in Paris, France, a fact that made him appear very worldly in the eyes of his Biddulph parishioners, who seldom if ever ventured much farther east than Thorold. From Paris, the priest had crossed the North Atlantic Ocean to Quebec, where he served as a professor at one of the Church of Rome's diocesan institutions. He had received his ordinance from the Diocese of London in July 1878, but six months later, John Walsh, the Roman Catholic Bishop of London, having grown concerned at the problems within Biddulph township,[4] thought that bringing a fellow Irishman into St. Patrick's parish would be just the tonic for that troubled community. Father Connolly settled into the little brick parsonage next to the church and would live there for the next sixteen years, tending to the moral and spiritual needs of his congregation.

In examining a photograph of the man, he certainly looked the part of the benevolent parish priest — at least from our present-day vantage point. At fifty-nine years of age, with closely cropped, receding white hair and kindly eyes, Father Connolly looked like he had just walked off the set of *The Bells of St. Marys*. Given that he hailed from Ireland, and given his worldliness and erudition, it was little wonder that he was immediately and warmly embraced by the 130 families that made up the congregation of St. Patrick's.[5] Perhaps more importantly to the members of his flock, Father Connolly further represented a new set of empathetic ears that was ready to receive afresh the reports of the old trials and tribulations the good congregates from St. Patrick's had endured over the years. Moreover, his presence in Biddulph underscored the belief that St. Patrick's parish was an important part of God's plan. His was, after all, the sole capacity to interpret the word of God for his community's guidance and well-being. But first, he needed to get to know his parishioners. William Donnelly would later recollect that "[t]he first I knew or heard of Father Connolly was after he came here in the winter of 1879. The first Sunday [January 19] he said from the altar that he would visit all his parishioners, and he started to do this."[6]

And as the Reverend Father visited each farmhouse throughout Biddulph, a common lament among a large portion of his congregation was heard: that the Donnellys were a fallen family that was responsible for considerable crimes and misdemeanours in the community, both in the past and in the present. He also heard tell that the family had long ago turned away from their Roman Catholic brethren to follow their own path, which often led them into Protestant circles.

Father Connolly also made it a point to speak to Protestants — or least those Protestants who had influence in the community, such as Bernard and William Stanley. With the Stanleys, the priest had been able to swap tales of travelling in Paris (the Stanley brothers were among the few townspeople who had the means to have spent a holiday or two in Europe).[7] In addition, the Stanley brothers were only too happy to reaffirm the contention of many of the priest's parishioners regarding the evil that had attached itself to the Donnelly family.[8] Opinion and factions aside, for the Father was not a stupid man, the facts of the family's acts of destruction spoke for themselves. The patriarch of the Donnelly family had been sent to prison for manslaughter, and most of his sons had likewise served time of various durations. Indeed, one of the sons was presently serving a two-year stretch for trying to shoot the town constable. However, Father Connolly was also aware that factions existed within all communities, and, being Irish, he was no stranger to their existence within communities comprised of his fellow countrymen. He resolved to keep an open mind on the matter. This would prove no easy task, particularly when the Donnelly name kept coming up during his visits, more so than the name of any other family with regard to criminal activity. He would recall, "When I came here, and heard the depredations that had been committed by the Donnellys, I could hardly believe them."[9]

Some of his visits with his parishioners were brief, others lasted more than two hours. Slowly his conception of the Donnelly family took shape. He had wanted to give all his parishioners the benefit of the doubt, but it did appear that the Donnellys, above all other members of his congregation, were in the direst need of his counsel. And as the one name that kept coming up as being the ringleader of the family was William Donnelly, Father Connolly decided that his first Donnelly visit would be to William's house, in order to make his own assessment of the young man's character. And so, on a cold February morning, Father Connolly bundled himself up in a full-length wolfskin jacket and stepped out into the bitter Biddulph cold, where the son of parishioner Stephen McCormack was waiting in a sleigh to drive him to the home of William and

Nora Donnelly.[10] It was time he had a talk with this member of the family who was considered the "terror of the township."[11]

At this time William Donnelly was living in a small farmhouse in Usborne, which adjoined the northern boundary of Biddulph. The priest, unfortunately, had picked a bad day to visit, as William was away on business when the priest's sleigh arrived at the front of his house. As Father Connolly trudged through the snow on his way toward the front door, the Donnelly family dog, which evidently was quite large and territorial, became agitated by his wolfskin coat. The dog began barking loudly and aggressively, which put Father Connolly on the defensive. Hearing the noise outside, Nora Donnelly came to the door and did her best to restrain the animal. Having never laid eyes on Father Connolly before, Nora had no idea who he was or what his intentions were. The Donnellys, after all, had a lot of enemies by then, and so she had reason to be on her guard. Father Connolly announced his identity and then inquired if William was at home. Still struggling to retain the dog, Nora informed the priest that her husband was away that day. Father Connolly evidently had no desire to speak with William Donnelly's wife (despite her being a member of his congregation), and so returned to his sleigh and departed.[12]

Neither William nor Nora gave the matter much thought until they attended the priest's service at St. Patrick's the following Sunday (January 26). Father Connolly was evidently not just a man of the cloth, but also a man of pride — both in terms of the position that he occupied within his church, and in regard to how he believed a man in such a position should be revered. Such reverence was expected to be accorded him by his parishioners not only when they were within his church, but also when he visited their homes. Consequently, during his sermon that morning, the priest veered from his discourse to mention the occasion of his visit to William and Nora's home. What surprised the couple most was Father Connolly's recollection of the details of his visit. Without naming them directly, the priest told his congregation how he went to a certain parishioner's house where vicious dogs (plural) were ready to eat him alive, and how the woman of the house was oblivious to the fact that he was her parish priest (the wolfskin coat notwithstanding). He further felt obliged to mention that at most of the homes he visited the inhabitants always fell down on their knees and offered up a prayer in thanks for his visit. On this particular occasion, however, the female parishioner had been so ignorant of the proper protocol in greeting her Reverend Father that she had stood the entire time he was there[13] (the fact that Nora had been trying to control a large dog at the time of the priest's unannounced visit was never mentioned).

William and Nora were understandably put off at having being made an example of by Father Connolly, especially given the actual particulars of the occasion in question. But as the priest was, in fact, a priest, and also new to the township, William bit his tongue. But William Donnelly was not a stupid man either; he was well aware of what neighbours the priest had visited, and the anti-Donnelly stories with which they had plied him. He was also aware of Father Connolly's dialogue with the Stanley brothers in Lucan, and how nothing positive about the family would have come out of that particular conversation. Nevertheless, William decided to observe from the sidelines for the time being to see if the priest would be impartial or if he would be swayed by the one-sided testimony that was being presented to him by many of the family's enemies. Not long afterwards, William was visiting at the home of his friend James Powe, a thirty-eight-year-old farmer who lived on the Tenth Concession in Biddulph. As William was conversing with James and his wife, Father Connolly's sleigh arrived outside. The priest entered the farmhouse and spoke with the Powes. Not wanting to intrude, William stayed in the background until his presence was noticed by the priest and the Powes felt a formal introduction was necessary.

"Father, this is Mr. Donnelly," said James.

Connolly immediately looked down and stared at William's club foot. He then allowed his eyes to travel upward to William's face and commented somewhat disdainfully, "Oh, yes. You're *William* Donnelly." William would later recollect. "I came to the conclusion, from the way he looked down at my foot, that I had been particularly described to him."[14] The pair then conversed briefly. "We talked over the matter in general," Donnelly recalled, "and he said he hoped that in the future things would be better in Biddulph, and he intended to lay a good foundation with this end in view. He appeared quite friendly to me."[15] Perhaps as a result of his amiable repartee with their son, Father Connolly now felt comfortable paying a visit to William's parents on the Roman Line. To his surprise, the Donnellys had two boarders living with them: the first was Cornelius Maloney, who was now eighty-five years old, and who had been living both at his farmhouse (on Lot 17, Concession 6) and with the Donnellys since March 1874.[16] The second boarder was Bridget Donnelly, the twenty-one-year-old[17] niece of James Donnelly. Father Connolly was fascinated that Bridget had just recently arrived from Borrisokane, in County Tipperary, Ireland. Connolly himself had been born in Sligo, a county only 113 miles to the northwest of Borrisokane. As the Father had been in Canada since 1864,[18] he was delighted to learn from Bridget about what had been happening in that region of Ireland during the past fifteen years.[19] After discussing the state of the old country with Bridget, the priest proceeded to speak with James and Johannah. James Donnelly was now sixty-three years of age; Johannah was fifty-six.[20] Clearly the old folks were not a threat to anybody, and they had been loyal and regular attendees of St. Patrick's ever since their arrival in Biddulph in the 1840s. During their conversation, Connolly was direct.

"I've heard about the boys' bad doings. They should mend their ways or else I will straighten them out."

Johannah, however, knew what her sons had and hadn't done. "There are worse than my sons in the neighbourhood," she replied, "but a large crowd is against them."

The result of this, she explained, was that her sons were now being persecuted.[21] While this was true to a point, the reality was that the persecution hadn't gotten out of first gear yet. The Donnelly family understood that their enemies had the priest's ear far more often than they did, but they nevertheless believed that Father Connolly was a good and honest man who would have no trouble separating the wheat from the chaff once he took the time to get to know both sides of the story. And despite what the priest had been told, the Donnelly family had committed no crimes in the area for quite some time, and yet crime itself continued to flourish within the community. In one instance, near the end of February 1879, masked bandits broke into William and Nora Donnelly's home in Usborne, held them at gunpoint, tied them up and robbed them. The local newspaper reported the incident:

> On Friday night last about eleven o'clock three
> men entered the dwelling of Mr. William Donnelly,
> a respectable farmer of the Township of Usborne,
> adjoining Biddulph, and before he was well aware
> of the fact, proceeded to his bedroom, and securely
> bound his hands with what was evidently a piece of
> a train bell-cord. Upon being asked their intention,
> the robbers replied they knew there was $490 in the
> house, that they wanted it, and in case of refusal
> would burn the house down. Mr. Donnelly tried
> to impress upon them that there was no money in
> the house, upon which they fired two shots from
> a revolver over his head, the balls of which lodged
> in the wall, in rather close proximity to Donnelly's
> head. Donnelly can give no description of the

burglars (they being heavily muffled up), further than that one of them was about six feet high, the other about five feet seven, very stoutly built, and the third dwarfish in appearance.[22]

The thieves had rummaged through a trunk and found a pocket-book that contained $132 of sales notes that William had recently received. They stole this, but for some reason had missed thirty-eight dollars in cash that had been lying on the stand at the head of the bed. What had upset William more than the robbery, however, had been the fact that his wife had been ill for some time previously, and the robbers had threatened to shoot both her and a servant girl that had been attending her if the women did not cover their heads.[23] The trauma of the break-in, the shooting and the threats had caused Nora to relapse: "The missus was only three days after being confined, and the fright prostrated her for some time."[24]

One might think a crime of this severity having beset two members of Father Connolly's parish would have warranted a mention during his sermon the next Sunday. However, the man who had made it his mission to put down crime in the neighbourhood did not see fit to comment on it during any of his sermons. He made no mention of the robbery (despite the report of it having been published in at least two newspapers), nor of the delicate condition in which the experience had left a member of his congregation. And the crimes continued. Ellen Fogarty, whom the reader will recall had played unwelcome host to William Donnelly and his "Adventurers" during the Margaret Thompson affair in 1874, had been robbed of $240 by a group of men who matched the description of the ones who had burglarized William and Nora Donnelly's home.[25] And then there was the vandalism of a Protestant man's sleigh — which had occurred directly outside of St. Patrick's Church while Father Connolly was conducting a funeral service. This, particularly, had irked William Donnelly: "Young James Maher[26] and Jack Darcy stole the bells off a respectable Protestant man's cutter at the church gate, while Father Connolly was reading prayers at Mrs. Andrew Keefe's funeral. This theft was known to everyone, but the priest never reprimanded the young men in church."[27]

None of the three crimes indicated had been committed by any member of the Donnellys. However, at least one of these crimes involved members and relatives of the anti-Donnelly faction — and yet the wrongdoing was never acknowledged by the priest (this will become somewhat bewildering, given the way that the Donnelly family would soon be shown no mercy in this regard). And the violence continued — sometimes between fellow constables of the law.

The reader will recall that Constable William Hodgins had ridden out to arrest Tom Donnelly at his parents' home in June 1878 but had been thwarted when Tom got the drop on him by brandishing a shotgun. Hodgins didn't stew over the matter; he knew he would get another chance to bring Tom Donnelly in. And, in early April 1879, his chance arrived. The constable learned that Donnelly had returned from another tour of duty in the Michigan lumber camps,[28] and was stopping over in Brooke Township in Lambton County,[29] a community that lay forty-six miles to the southwest of Lucan. As Donnelly would be alone and weaponless, Hodgins decided it was the perfect time to take a second crack at enforcing the arrest warrant he had been holding on to for the past ten months. He boarded a train headed to Brooke Township and, once there, he placed the youngest Donnelly brother under arrest. Hodgins brought his prisoner back to Lucan and deposited him in the town jail to face charges for his alleged robbery of Ned Ryan in March 1878.

While Hodgins was pleased with his arrest, it was taken as a personal affront by Constable Samuel Everett. Everett had previously declared that there was insufficient evidence to warrant charging Tom Donnelly with the crime, so when Hodgins brought Donnelly in and locked him up in the Lucan jail, it was taken to be an overt display of disrespect for the Lucan constable's judgement and authority. On the evening of the arrest, both constables found themselves in the barroom within the Queen's Hotel in Lucan. At some point during the evening someone from within the bar asked Everett what he thought about Hodgins's latest arrest.

"I think it a very foolish thing to bring him in," Everett opined.[30] Then, raising his voice so that Constable Hodgins would hear, he declared, "Often I could have had Tom Donnelly, but *some men* want to make a big man of themselves by running him in."

It didn't take long for Hodgins to respond.

"Was it myself you had reference to?" he inquired, putting his drink down upon the bar.

"Yes," replied Everett.

"Then it is no such thing. I arrested Tom Donnelly because you dared not to do so."

Everett's temper flashed. "You talk like a fool!" he exclaimed. "You only made the arrest because you want my job! Well, you can have a chance to have my starvation job after my year is up and not before." Everett knew that he was only holding on to his job by a thread, particularly after his arrest of William Porte, who had been one of the village councillors who had hired him. Still, Everett did not like Hodgins's assertion that he had been afraid to arrest twenty-five-year-old Tom Donnelly. Cowardice was not part of the job description for a town constable, and Everett had no intention of losing his job to someone like Hodgins.

"I arrested Tom Donnelly before, and could do it again if necessary," he boasted.

"You dare not!" challenged Hodgins.

"You are a liar!" declared Everett.

"You are another," Hodgins replied.

Everett now decided to put the county constable in his place. With his finger pointing toward his colleague he approached him menacingly.

"You are a liar and a son of a bitch," said the Lucan constable.

"Don't put your hands on me! Go away from me!" Hodgins commanded, by way of warning.

"I could whip you on the ground you stand on," Everett said, "but I am not fool enough to lay myself liable to the law with such a slink as you are."

"You had better not," answered Hodgins, who was now on his feet, but backing away from his fellow constable. "And do not follow me!"

"I can go where I have a mind to," countered Everett, who then proceeded to chase Hodgins around the perimeter of the tavern no fewer than three times. On his third lap around the bar, Hodgins spotted Everett's constable's baton sitting on a table. He picked it up and whacked Everett on the head with it. He tried a second strike, but missed and hit the tavern's stovepipe. As the two men grappled with one another, a patron finally interceded and pulled them apart. Hodgins, in disgust, stomped out of the tavern.

Such was the state of law enforcement in Lucan in 1879.

Upon learning of Tom Donnelly's arrest, several members of Father Connolly's congregation had approached him with an "I told you so" postscript to their earlier statements to him about the family. Here, clearly, was fresh evidence that the Donnellys were a blight on the community and had no intention of changing their evil ways. The fact that the charge Tom Donnelly had been arrested on was over a year old and had been ignored by the town constable as being without foundation was, of course, never mentioned. The anti-Donnelly faction further warned their priest that he should shun the Donnellys from the sacraments of the Holy Church. While he had never personally witnessed any crimes committed by the family, Father Connolly nevertheless went on the record to state that

> [t]he Donnellys had been in the habit of committing
> depredations and stealing things from their
> neighbours. These articles or goods which were
> stolen they would leave with a neighbour, who
> would thus be brought into the mess, and for fear of
> personal violence to themselves and injury to their
> property, they would not disclose the crime or their
> knowledge of the theft. The Donnelly boys, by thus
> entangling different parties each time a depredation
> was committed by them, were enabled to gather
> a number of friends around them, who, although
> hating them in their hearts, were obliged publicly to
> befriend them, and were also afraid to give evidence
> against them.[31]

This was a rather incredible statement for Father Connolly to have made public as there was absolutely no evidence that such a manner of crime had ever been perpetrated by any member of the Donnelly family. Nor was there evidence of any of their friends "hating them in their hearts." The priest had clearly been told enough of such stories by enough people that, by this point, he now fully believed them. Consequently, when John Donnelly approached Father Connolly to go to confession, the priest, in a move of unexpected and (given the facts) unwarranted rebuke, denied John the Sacrament of Reconciliation: "A few days after Thomas was arrested for robbing Ryan, John Donnelly came to me to Confession. I refused to confess him, and told him I thought he intended to confess to an untruth, in order to free his brother and implicate others. He then went away."[32]

John Donnelly was hurt by this, as he had done nothing to warrant being turned aside so abruptly by the Father. Despite the slight, however, he perfectly understood why the priest had acted the way that he did. "Father Connolly is a fine man if let alone, but he should find out before believing them whether the stories are true or not."[33]

Meanwhile, James Carroll continued to stew about the Donnellys. Having caught wind of Ned Ryan's forthcoming trial against Tom Donnelly for larceny, and having come up short in his own lawsuits against the family, Carroll wanted another crack at them. He offered to represent Ned Ryan at his trial and, for some inexplicable reason, Ryan agreed.

It may have been one year, one month and two days since Ryan had allegedly been robbed, but on April 7, 1879, he was finally given his opportunity to present his case before Magistrates Patrick McIlhargey and James McCosh. William Donnelly had prepared the defence case for his brother, and had brought several witnesses to offer their testimony. With two magistrates, the contending parties and their lawyers, as well as the local press and the spectators who had lined up early to get into the courtroom to witness the legal battle that morning, the Tom Donnelly trial had clearly become quite the event in Lucan.

It ended almost as soon as it began.

James Carroll and his client were clearly not prepared. They had no witnesses to the alleged crime that they could call, and Carroll's strategy, such as it was, consisted of asking to have the trial postponed.[34] After a full year of waiting, this was the best the prosecution could muster. As for the defence, William Donnelly argued against a continuance; he had his witnesses ready to testify, his client was ready to proceed, and the prosecution had had the better part of a year to prepare its case. Having considered the evidence that Donnelly had amassed and contrasted it with the total lack of evidence that Carroll had presented, the magistrates ruled to acquit Tom Donnelly of the charge of larceny. William then requested and was granted a certificate of acquittal, so that the matter was closed — permanently.[35] Chalk up another legal win for William Donnelly — even if this one had come a little *too* easily.

James Carroll was beside himself; he was a man who hated to lose, but in fairness, his defence on Ryan's behalf had been really no defence at all. As he stormed from the Lucan Council Chamber, which had served as the venue for the trial, he walked past Thomas and James Keefe, who had attended the court proceedings that morning in support of their friend Tom Donnelly. Words were exchanged between Carroll and Thomas Keefe. Tempers flared — and suddenly a fistfight broke out. The two men brawled their way out of the building and into the street, whereupon Keefe took hold of Carroll's nose between his teeth and bit down hard enough that he almost removed it from Carroll's face. This was more or less the end of the fight; with Carroll bleeding profusely and clutching his nose, Keefe climbed on top of him and began raining punches down on his bloody adversary. Fortunately for Carroll, Constable Samuel Everett had caught wind of the battle that was going on and sprinted to the front of the courthouse. Pushing his way through the crowd, he grabbed hold of Thomas Keefe and yanked him from James Carroll. Everett pulled Keefe through the multitude of people toward the Lucan jail.[36] On his way to the jail, however, Everett's colleague, Constable William Hodgins, attempted to arrest him for having used abusive language toward him in the tavern of the Queen's Hotel. An argument ensued between the two lawmen and, upon Everett's depositing his prisoner in the lock-up, Hodgins whacked the town constable atop the head with his baton and threw him in jail. Once Everett posted bail, the courts were flooded with assault charges and countercharges: Hodgins charged Everett, Everett charged Hodgins, Carroll charged Keefe and Keefe charged Carroll.[37]

Meanwhile, in other Donnelly legal news, the Crown attorney Charles Hutchinson had heard some additional disturbing news about Constable Everett. Evidently the whack on the head he had received from Hodgins had jogged his memory about the night Bob Donnelly had supposedly taken a shot at him. Everett was now telling people he was no longer certain that it was Bob Donnelly who had shot at him from behind the woodpile that evening back in March 1878, and that he was now quite convinced that one of the prosecution's witnesses, the painter George Gear, had been lying when he testified that he had seen Bob with a gun under his coat that evening. Hutchinson decided to investigate the matter and wrote of his intent to Justice Adam Wilson, the man who had sentenced Bob Donnelly:

The Hon. A. Wilson, Toronto
April 29, 1879

Dear Sir,
Re: Donnelly
    I will make necessary inquiries respecting this
case. Everett will be in my office on Saturday, when
I will question him with reference to his assertion of
belief that Gear's evidence was untrue and made up
for the occasion. Lucan is in as bad a state as ever,
and unless it can be made very clear that Donnelly
was wrongfully convicted, it would seem a pity to
interfere on his behalf. I will write you again, and

Yours truly,
Charles Hutchinson, City Attorney[38]

This was certainly welcome news to the Donnelly family. That the man who had been shot at now had doubts as to the true identity of the shooter, and that he further believed that one of his star witnesses in the trial had lied under oath, emboldened their belief that Bob was innocent. John Donnelly resumed collecting signatures for another petition in the hope of getting Bob pardoned or, at the very least, having his sentence commuted. In the course of securing support, John approached Father Connolly, who must have been surprised at the news, particularly given how families such as the Mahers and Carrolls had adamantly insisted that Bob Donnelly not only did the deed, but that his sentence was too light. No doubt in spite of the protests coming from certain quarters of his parish, the priest believed that a good deed on his part toward the Donnelly family might bring them back into the fold and, thus, under his control. Father Connolly not only supported John Donnelly's petition, he reached out to the Honourable Hector Langevin — a Member of Parliament for Trois-Rivières, Quebec, and a friend of Connolly's from the days when he lived in that province — to support the appeal for clemency.[39] But even with Father Connolly's support and connections, the second petition had no effect on Bob Donnelly's sentence.

However, the matter gained momentum when Constable Everett then swore out a legal affidavit in which he stated for the record that he had no idea who had taken the shot at him and that the witnesses in his trial against Bob Donnelly had lied under oath.[40] Once again, Crown attorney Hutchinson sought answers, this time from the Lucan Justice of the Peace, James McCosh:

> May 9/79
> J.D. McCosh, Esq,
> JP Lucan
>
> Dear Sir,
>   A petition on behalf of Robert Donnelly, who is now in the penitentiary for shooting at Everett, has

been referred to me. It is supported by an affidavit
of Everett's; that he has discovered since the trial
that the evidence of George Greer [sic], painter, of
Lucan, was false, and made up for the occasion.
Greer swore that he had seen Donnelly on the night
in question near the scene of the shooting with a
gun concealed under his coat. I would like to know
something of this man Greer. Is he still in Lucan?
What character does he bear? Has he had any
difficulty with the prisoner or any of his family?
Did he volunteer the evidence? How did it become
known that he had seen Donnelly? Will you kindly
assist me in this matter and let me hear from you at
your early convenience and oblige,

Yours truly,
Charles Hutchinson, County Attorney[41]

While the legal experts contemplated whether or not Bob
Donnelly had been framed (and it was certainly starting to look that
way at this point), William Donnelly and his wife Nora had moved
from the farmhouse they had been renting in Usborne to a smaller
property on Whalen's Corners.[42] There, he continued his passion
and business of breeding horses.[43] John and Tom Donnelly, meanwhile, had returned to their parents' farm, and Father Connolly
had decided to start up the "Father Matthew Total Abstinence
Society of St. Patrick's."[44] Alcohol, the priest believed, seemed to
be at the root of a lot of the trouble in the district, and if his parishioners would swear off it, not only would their lives improve, but
it would also go a considerable way in reducing the various crimes
that were being committed. Many of his congregation joined his
abstinence society, including John Donnelly. Apart from the late
Jim Donnelly, none of the Donnelly family were particularly heavy

drinkers, so it wasn't a great leap for John. According to William Donnelly, "I have never been the worse of liquor in my life; John never tasted liquor; Patrick and Robert have had the pledge for a number of years; while James, when dying, refused to drink liquor, even on the doctor's order."[45]

Such a move was broadly welcomed by the businessmen of Lucan;[46] it appeared to them that Father Connolly was indeed a capable leader who was doing all the right things to keep his flock in line — or at least some of them. But still the complaints from certain sections of his parish against the Donnelly family continued to fill his ears. William Donnelly remembered that

> [h]e was continually visited by our enemies, who told him all sorts of stories against us, the effect of which kept him from sleeping at night, as he afterwards acknowledged to my brother John. In this way he was actually led astray, and formed a wrong opinion of us. For this reason, I do not altogether blame him, but I considered he should have brought us and his story-carriers face to face, and seen who was right.[47]

And then, on a Saturday night in mid-May, somebody stole James Kelly's horse from his stable on the Eighth Concession and rode it until exhaustion before abandoning the animal on one of the Biddulph concession roads. The next day Kelly told his priest about what had happened and, after the service, Father Connolly drove a wagon over to Kelly's to see the horse for himself.

"Do you know who took it out?" he asked.

Kelly shrugged his shoulders. "No."

"You *do* know — but you're afraid to tell me," said Father Connolly.

"No, Father," said Kelly. "I didn't see them."

And then, out of the blue, Father Connolly came up with a name. "This is Tom Ryan's work!"[48]

How Father Connolly came to this conclusion has never been revealed.

Tom Ryan, the reader will recall, was a young (nineteen-year-old) friend of the Donnellys, who had been broken out of jail by the "Biddulph and Lucan Lambs" the year before. He had never been a particularly close friend of the Donnelly brothers, like the Keefe brothers were, but Ryan was another one of those hard-luck kids to whom the Donnelly family had always felt partial and obliged to look out for. Indeed, William Donnelly recalled that Tom Ryan "used to make a home now and then at my place and my parents'."[49]

Father Connolly was aware that Ryan had spent time at the Donnelly household, which, from his way of thinking, meant that the young man was part of the "Donnelly gang" he had heard so much about. He decided to track Ryan down. Spying a group of teenagers walking along the Roman Line, the priest pulled his wagon over and interrogated them.

"Is Tom Ryan among you?" he asked. The boys answered in the negative.

"Do any of you belong to the gang?" Father Connolly inquired.[50]

"No, Father," answered one of the boys, who was soon supported in his answer by the remaining members of the group.

Satisfied that Tom Ryan wasn't in their company, the priest decided to head over to the home of Michael Powe, where he knew Ryan boarded. When he arrived at Powe's, the priest was in no mood for small talk.

"Where's Tom Ryan?" he asked pointedly.

Powe didn't know.

"You *will* discharge him from his work here," Father Connolly stated matter-of-factly, "and tell him that I want to speak with him tomorrow at my parsonage."[51] No further words were said.

The priest returned to his wagon and headed south back to St. Patrick's church.

Later that evening Tom Ryan returned to Michael Powe's and was told about the priest's visit and what was expected of him the next morning. To be singled out by the parish priest was worrisome to Ryan, who stewed about the news throughout the night. The next morning, rather than heading directly to the parsonage, Tom Ryan changed his course and headed to Whalen's Corners to consult with William Donnelly.

Upon arriving, he wasted no time in telling William of his dilemma. "Father Connolly blames me for the taking out of Kelly's horse, and wants me to go see him this morning," Ryan explained.[52] By now, William already knew of the priest's conversation with the young men on the road, and how Father Connolly had implied that Ryan was a member of the Donnelly "gang." While it was true that William Donnelly at one point in his life — back in the days of the Margaret Thompson incident — had attracted to him a group of "Adventurers," as he called them, these young men were simply his friends; he'd never been the leader of an organized criminal gang. The fact that Father Connolly believed otherwise — and that he believed that Tom Ryan was a part of it — rubbed William the wrong way: "I took it, from the way they [the boys on the road] told me and what our enemies said of us, that he was referring to us."[53]

Ryan told William that he was anxious to clear himself with the priest, but that he was nervous about speaking to him alone. He appealed to William to come with him for support. William agreed to the request and the pair proceeded to Lucan, where they believed they could find the priest. Upon arriving in town, however, they were informed Father Connolly had earlier boarded a train bound for St. Marys. Ryan and Donnelly then rode to the parish, where William composed a letter to the priest and left it for him at the parsonage. The contents of the letter, according to William, were as follows:

> I told Father Connolly I had been informed he was
> down the Cedar Swamp line [Eighth Concession]
> on Sunday evening, and openly accused Tom Ryan
> of taking out Kelly's horse. That he also asked
> different parties if their name was Ryan, or if they
> belonged to the "gang," and that I would like very
> much if he would explain to me what gang he
> referred to. Further, that it was my opinion that it
> was his sole objective to put us out of Biddulph.
> Also, that it seemed strange that the deeds of some
> of his parishioners were quietly smoothed over,
> while our supposed deeds were talked of by him
> and everybody else. I also told him about the parties
> stealing the bells from the church gate, and that he
> never drove around the road looking up that, or
> even spoke of it in the church. That the whole cry
> seemed to be "banish the Donnellys." I stated that
> Ryan and I had called on him that day and proposed
> to give him satisfactory proof of Ryan's innocence,
> and that we would lose no time in going to London
> and instituting an action against the proper parties.
> I ended by saying he could see Ryan any time at
> Michael Powe's, and that I would receive him at my
> own house at any time he found it convenient to
> call. He passed there several times subsequently but
> never called.[54]

By "proper parties" William made no bones about the fact that he meant "the priest, or Kelly, or whoever we could prove as accusing Ryan, for I felt justified in defending myself or a friend against anyone who maligned us."[55] He further claimed that there were "a half dozen respectable people" who knew that Ryan had been elsewhere at the time the horse was stolen, and that the priest was treading on thin ice legally with his accusations.

William's reflex to hit back when threatened had served him well in the courtroom — but it was the completely wrong approach to take in dealing with a man like Father Connolly, who took the content of his letter as a horrific impertinence. So angry did Father Connolly become, in fact, that he was still hot under his clerical collar some eight months afterwards, as indicated by this sampling of what he said to the local press:

> "I considered it to be a very impertinent epistle to be addressed to a priest."[56]

> "Mr. William Donnelly sent me a sharp, incisive letter, which might be a good one to write to a politician or business man. He was naturally a talented young man, and capable of writing a good letter — if he were a newspaper editor it would be a good reply, but it was not a good letter for a priest. . . ."[57]

> "William Donnelly, like many sons of Irishmen, is a little too smart."[58]

> "Such epistles would not intimidate me."[59]

And then His Reverence heard something that added fuel to the fire: "I heard that William talked and said he was going to drive me from the country."[60] The good Father, alas, had no means to filter hearsay, and carried this rumour along with the thought of William Donnelly and his infernal letter with him into the pulpit at St. Patrick's, where, on Sunday, May 18, 1879, he announced,

"I received a threatening letter from two parties who came to my house, one of them William Donnelly — a cripple and a devil!"[61]

While it was true that William Donnelly had threatened legal action against anyone (including the priest) who would accuse Tom Ryan of horse theft, he had never once threatened to run Father Connolly out of town or to hurt him in any way. Nevertheless, this apparently formed the content of a good part of the priest's sermon that Sunday. When word reached William Donnelly that the priest had implied he had threatened the Father's life, he was shocked: "[Connolly] said he didn't care if he got a bullet put through his heart, he would do his duty. I am satisfied from these words that lots of people believed I had threatened in the letter to shoot him, which I never did."[62]

The priest went on to mention the theft and riding of Kelly's horse, and then offered up a curse to the party who did it. "Mark my prophecy," he told his congregation, "the guilty party will be a corpse inside of a month!"[63] If this was a litmus test to determine the true identity of the culprit, then no one from within Biddulph could have perpetrated the crime, as no deaths would be reported that month. Still, the enemies of the Donnellys could scarcely believe the positive turn of events; their priest had just told them that his life had been threatened by none other than William Donnelly! Who could possibly sympathize with those damned Donnellys now? They were clearly against Father Connolly — which meant that they were against the Holy Church of Rome. If there had been any doubt before, the fact that the priest called William Donnelly a "devil" had removed it. And, to put a sharper point on the matter, Father Connolly also made it known that, henceforth, he "should have nothing more to do with them [the Donnellys]."[64] He had just set the lead for others in the community to follow. If he was having nothing to do with the family, then neither should any of his parishioners.[65]

For his part, William Donnelly, while not believing he had done anything wrong, nevertheless believed that Father Connolly had blown the matter out of all proportion. He thought a sit-down with the Reverend Father might clarify matters: "I asked two different men to see the priest and try and arrange a meeting between him and myself, so that we could settle the misunderstanding," Donnelly later told a reporter, "but they told me that it was no use in their going to Father Connolly, that he would not listen to them."[66]

The priest had effectively excommunicated William Donnelly from St. Patrick's Church. While William could live with being shunned by Father Connolly and certain members of his congregation, being referred to as a "cripple and a devil" immediately got his back up. William decided that if Father Connolly would have nothing more to do with the Donnellys, he, at least, would have nothing more to do with him. In a familiar show of support, William's brothers followed suit. Henceforth, they would only attend church outside of Biddulph.[67] Whatever the content of the letter (and only William Donnelly's summation of it has survived), it is clear that the priest was concerned for his own safety. Whether this consternation was a result of what he read in the letter, or simply his own mind reading more into it than was intended (augmented by a lot of anti-Donnelly sentiment from the family's enemies), is not for us to know. What we do know is Father Connolly felt vulnerable and in need of protection. According to William Donnelly, "He must have had an idea that I was going to do him bodily injury, because he warned his parishioners that, as Irish Catholics, they were in duty bound to protect their priest."[68]

It may well have been this sense of duty that prompted certain parties from within the Roman Catholic community of Biddulph, such as James Maher, to give voice to the idea that a vigilance committee of sorts ought be created in order to rid the community of the Donnelly family.[69] It's not known if Father Connolly was in complete agreement with this sentiment, but we do know that he now believed he needed a group that would support him and would band together for the purpose of ferreting out and suppressing crime in the area. Not wanting to overstep his bounds legally in the formation of such a company of kindred spirits, he sought the counsel of John J. Blake (the same London lawyer who had assisted James Carroll in his lawsuit for inclusion in his late father's will) as to how best to proceed.[70] He didn't want to create a holy posse; he merely wanted to bring his parishioners on board for a cause that would help to deter crime in the community, and also let any would-be adversaries know that he had backup at the ready should he ever require it. By June 1879 Blake had put his finishing touches on the document, and Father Connolly brought it back to St. Patrick's and placed it within the church for his congregation to sign. It read as follows:

> We the undersigned Roman Catholics of St. Patrick's of Biddulph solemnly pledge ourselves to aid our spiritual director and parish priest in the discovery and putting down of crime in our mission, while we at the same time protest as Irishmen and as Catholics against any interference with him in the legitimate discharge of his spiritual duties.[71]

From the pulpit Father Connolly spoke of the new declaration; it was a society, he said, of those who disapproved of criminal activity and who supported him in carrying out his calling in the parish. Good people had nothing to hide, and so anyone who signed thereby also agreed to have their properties searched at any time if it was believed that stolen property was being hidden there.[72] Moreover, any of those who declined to join his society by refusing to sign the declaration he considered to be both backsliders and sympathizers of the "gang." And if any of those who didn't sign the declaration became sick, they could send for William Donnelly to administer to them — not him.[73] The priest left the document out for his parishioners to sign for at least two more Sundays. The signatures he collected numbered ninety-four in total. Some were enemies of the Donnellys, such as Patrick Flanagan, John Kennedy Jr., and James Carroll; others were friends of the family, such as some of the Keefes, Michael O'Connor and Michael Collisson. The Donnellys, however, were conspicuous by their absence — not one of them signed the pledge.[74] Apparently, James Donnelly Sr. had initially intended to sign the document, believing that if the family abstained from doing so, others in the parish would think they were guilty of the crimes that their enemies had accused them of. However, William Donnelly had talked him out of it:

> I told him there were men in that society who would
> not hesitate at anything to get our family in trouble;
> that they would steal something, hide it on the
> farm, come in a body and search for it, find it, and
> then have him sent to the penitentiary for a crime
> he never committed. He agreed with me in this and
> never joined, neither did any of the family.[75]

William and his brothers were joined in their boycott of St. Patrick's Church by several of his friends, including Thomas Keefe.[76] Unfortunately, in the bigger picture, all this meant was that there were now fewer voices heard to offset all the negative testimony about the Donnellys that swirled around Father Connolly's head. The society he had created, in the meanwhile, was stuck in neutral. Indeed, the priest had not done much beyond getting signatures to pledge support for him and, essentially, to say that they were against crime in the community. In fairness, Father Connolly hadn't the time to spearhead an anti-crime committee; his priestly duties dictated the saving of souls as his priority, not the location of stolen material goods, and so he spent his time tending to his priestly duties — catechism classes, communions, temperance meetings, church bazaars and hearing confession.[77] Some within his congregation had wanted him to do more, to take the initiative in banishing the Donnellys altogether. Before long, the priest's anti-crime society was languishing. But then Tom Donnelly did something that would rouse several of those who had signed the priest's pledge to put James Maher's idea into motion. They would create a Vigilance Committee of their own — a committee that had no intention of sitting idle.

CHAPTER TWELVE

THE COW AND THE FIDDLE

The Cedar Swamp Schoolhouse: where the Vigilance Committee
held their meetings to plan the Donnelly family's downfall.
(Photo by author)

W illiam Donnelly was done with St. Patrick's, done with
Father Connolly and his anti-crime society and, more or
less, done with Biddulph. He busied himself breeding horses at his
farmhouse at Whalen's Corners and, like his brothers John and
Tom, continued to assist his parents with the chores at their farm.
He was no longer involved with the Roman Catholic community in Biddulph — and that was fine by him. He most certainly
was not looking to further his reputation as a tough guy, perhaps
because he already had passed through that stage of his life and, if
anything, was rather looking to lose that particular status. While
he was always the first one called upon by family and friends if they

279

were in trouble, and always the first one to defend his family (his upbringing, particularly during his father's absence in Kingston, had assured this would always be the case), he often shook his head at what he considered to be the juvenile behaviour of his younger brothers, particularly Tom.

Of course, William was thirty-five, married, self-employed and renting his own farmhouse; Tom was twenty-five, single, working for his parents and living in their house. Apart from their "family-first" loyalty, the two brothers had little in common. William was intellectual; he had attempted to broaden his education and possessed a humorous sense of irony regarding the human condition. He would even name one of his favourite horses after the club-footed poet Lord Byron.[1] Perhaps owing to his own disability, he understood that there were other equally if not more effective ways to deal with a problem than merely subjecting it to brute muscle. There is no evidence that Tom shared any of his older brother's beliefs in this regard. The brothers, naturally, were different people with different interests that were commensurate with their age and life experience. Consequently, when William learned that Tom intended to cause trouble for both Ned Ryan and Father Connolly, William opposed his younger brother's plan: "I warned him that he was doing wrong when he replied that Father Connolly had never tried to protect him in any way, and that he was going to torment both Ryan and the priest now."[2]

To Tom, Ryan was a fellow who needed to be taught a lesson — "Ryan had persecuted him," William would later recall, "and [Tom] wanted to pay him back in his own coin."[3] With regard to Father Connolly, in Tom's eyes the priest had enacted a double standard; he had not once spoken to his congregation about the injustice of Tom being dragged to court to defend himself against a bogus charge, and yet had no problem in berating his brother William in front of the congregation for pointing out that the priest had fingered the wrong man for the theft of Kelly's horse. While Tom was upset about this, to William the issue with the priest was already behind him. And, to his mind, Ned Ryan had already been taught his lesson when he'd been defeated in court — these weren't battles that needed to continue. And being one to weigh well the potential consequences of an action beforehand, William understood that any aggressive step made by his family would too conveniently play into their enemies' hands. Tom's was not a plan that smacked of intelligence. But then, the youngest brother was never known to be the brains of the family.

It was now August, the month in which farmers threshed their wheat. It was a big job, requiring a special machine that few farmers in the district owned. Instead, they relied on borrowing or renting a thresher from some of the wealthier farmers in the district, who normally would make them available once they had finished tending to their own fields. Tom Donnelly knew that Ned Ryan needed a threshing machine — and he was going to see to it that he didn't get one. Ryan had engaged Martin Curtin, a farmer in the district who owned a threshing machine, to thresh his wheat for him. When Tom Donnelly found out about the arrangement, he took Curtin aside and told him in no uncertain terms that he was not to thresh for Ryan. Father Connolly would later be told by Ryan that Tom Donnelly had actually threatened Curtin directly, saying that Curtin's machine would be destroyed if he attempted to employ it on Ryan's behalf. As much as he envied his older brother William's reputation, Tom Donnelly had developed one of his own — he was viewed as a man who never made an empty threat. Curtin informed Ryan of his talk with Tom Donnelly, and apologized that he would be unable to thresh for him.[4]

Ryan was now in a predicament; if he couldn't thresh his wheat, there could be no harvest and no money to be made from his months of tending his fields. He needed that money to pay his mortgage on his farm and to survive. But nobody with a threshing machine was willing to go against the edict of Tom Donnelly. Ryan believed that his only recourse lay with Father Connolly. The priest was the one who had made the most noise about putting down crime in the community: he was the one who had formulated a society for that very purpose, and, quite clearly, what Tom Donnelly was doing — with his threats and the loss of income that his threats represented to Ryan — was criminal. According to Father Connolly,

> Ryan . . . reduced to extremities, appealed to me. Previous to this I, in company with Mr. Coughlin, M.P., had made strenuous efforts to obtain the release of Robert Donnelly from the Penitentiary, where he was confined for shooting at Constable Everett. In my effort, I was guided mainly by the opinion that I could by this means win over the Donnellys to become respectable neighbours and peaceable subjects. Not doubting but these disinterested efforts on my part would be remembered by the family, I had not the slightest suspicion, but if I asked them they would give their consent to Curtin threshing Ryan's grain. Impressed with this belief I went to Thomas Donnelly and asked him as a personal favour to me to allow Curtin to thresh for Ryan. After hesitating, he said he would ask John. I went to John, who promised to give me an answer before Sunday, and I went away, fully believing that they would oblige me. I waited patiently, but when Sunday came and I saw nothing of John, I felt that my efforts and advice had no weight with them.[5]

The men who had signed Father Connolly's anti-crime charter had watched the Tom Donnelly/Ned Ryan incident unfold closely; this, they believed, would be the moment when the priest would overtly declare war on the Donnellys and send his holy troops into battle against them. Instead, they looked on incredulously as Father

Connolly, cap in hand, had asked — asked! — if Tom Donnelly would please change his mind, and then was told to wait and someone else would get back to him. What kind of "anti-crime society" was this? Who could take it seriously from this point forward? It was decided among these men that a "proper" society needed to be formed. It would be composed of those of a far more militant bent who had signed on with the original society, but who were now disgusted by its lack of teeth. These people weren't interested in being members of a Father Connolly fan club; they wanted the Donnellys out of Biddulph.

It may have been true, as evidently the priest would later believe, that this group of dissenters, or one very similar to it, had existed prior to his arrival at St. Patrick's, and well before he had created his own anti-crime group.[6] If so, it was more an association of grumblers than a formal society. That all changed now. The leaders of this new group were, not surprisingly, those who had the strongest bias against the Donnellys — men such as James Carroll and John Kennedy Jr. — along with men such as Martin McLaughlin, Patrick Breen and John Heenan, who legitimately shared the priest's intention to diminish crime in the community, but who believed that this intent should be backed by action. The group was privately referred to by its members as the "Biddulph Peace Society" but the local press would later give them the same name as McKinnon's posse — the "Vigilance Committee." Its members were given official positions,[7] an oath was sworn,[8] the Bible kissed,[9] and a building was then selected to be their private meeting place. They began to recruit members to their cause under two conditions — first that they were trustworthy and not likely to expose the group's existence to anybody from the outside; and second, they shared one common goal: to drive out or put down the Donnellys.[10] According to William Donnelly,

> I once heard of a member of the Vigilance
> Committee trying to get his brother-in-law to join.

He was apparently telling the brother-in-law the
nature of the oath. The brother-in-law remarked it
was a hard oath, especially when a man was sworn
not to speak to or keep company in any way with
the Donnellys, although they had never injured
him. The brother-in-law never joined. It will be seen
from this that the society was formed for no other
purpose than to make war against us.[11]

The Peace Society's meeting hall of choice was a small brick
schoolhouse, located on the Swamp Line concession road that lay
just two concession roads east of the Roman Line. Both McLaughlin
and Breen were trustees for schools in the community, with Breen
being the trustee for the Cedar Swamp School, which undoubtedly
was how the society was granted access to it. The school owed its
appellation to the fact that it stood near a swamp that was lined with
old cedar trees. The building itself was a sturdy wooden structure,
sided with yellow brick, that was erected in 1874 and still stands
to this day. In 1879, it had a large front porch that opened into a
main classroom. At the rear of the classroom two doors separated
the classroom area from a small room that was used as a teacher's
study.[12] It was in this backroom that the leaders of the Peace Society
would meet to decide its most pressing resolutions. The new group
would conduct its first meeting within its walls in late August 1879.

As word began to trickle out about the group and its clandestine
meetings, some members of St. Patrick's thought it was related to
the priest's anti-crime group, and showed up to attend what they
thought were more official meetings of the group to which they had
pledged their support at the church. They were quickly disabused
of this notion. William Donnelly was told that

[a] respectable farmer went to join, believing they
were organized on Father Connolly's simple basis,

but on entering the schoolhouse John Kennedy
approached him with a book to have him sworn.
He refused to take the oath and was immediately
shoved out of the room. Another proof of a second
society being in existence is this: Martin Collisson,
a respectable farmer, living next door to the priest,
signed his name to the declaration in church, but
after the meetings started at the schoolhouse he was
continually tormented by men who attended the
same to come and join them, which he refused to do,
as he understood it was a sworn society. No one was
allowed to attend their meetings who had not taken
the oath, although Father Connolly's form called for
no oath, but simply a signature.[13]

At the first meeting of the Peace Society the problem of Tom
Donnelly was discussed. Even for those members who were not
necessarily anti-Donnelly, but who were sincere in their desire to
diminish crime in the neighbourhood, the thought that a fellow
farmer, as well as their parish priest, had to beg permission from
Tom Donnelly to thresh grain, was unacceptable. This was particularly galling to the farmers within the group who saw parallels
between this and what they or their parents had witnessed first-hand
back in Ireland, where the Catholic serfs had to beg, cap in hand,
their Protestant landowners for permission to work their fields in
order to eke out a living. Who was Tom Donnelly to decide who
could or could not harvest their own fields? Sometime later William
Donnelly would learn just how heated that first meeting of the Peace
Society became, and he recalled, "I was told by a man who was a
member of the committee that he had to use physical force at one of
their meetings to defeat a motion to lynch my brother Tom."[14]

Fortunately, cooler heads ultimately prevailed on how best
to resolve the threshing problem of Ned Ryan. Ryan had friends

within the Peace Society, and they decided, collectively, that they would make a guarantee to Martin Curtin that if he threshed for Ryan and anything happened to his machine, they would cover the cost of repair or replacement and further compensate him for any time he'd lost while the repairs were being made. With his machine thusly insured, Curtin accepted their offer and agreed to thresh Ryan's wheat.[15]

However, upon his arrival at Ryan's farm, Curtin discovered that some of the farmer's sheaves had been filled with pieces of iron.[16] This was brought to the attention of the members of the Peace Society and immediately, and perhaps justifiably, they concluded Tom Donnelly was the culprit.[17] Curtin next took his threshing machine to the farm of Daniel Ryder, but the next morning discovered his machine had been broken to pieces.[18] However, a curious thing then transpired which shed some doubt on Tom Donnelly's supposed involvement. Martin Curtin had approached the Peace Society about collecting on their guarantee of paying him for any damages and lost time. Here, William Donnelly picks up the story:

> But Dan Ryder stood up at the meeting and said,
> "No, we ain't going to pay Curtin for this damage.
> I saw him running away in the night after breaking
> his own machine!" He explained that he had heard
> a noise during the night, and getting up, went out
> and saw Curtin running from the barn where the
> machine stood. Curtin lived immediately across the
> road from Ryder's on a rented farm. His lease had
> expired, and he was disposing of all his stock and
> effects, and evidently wanted to destroy his machine
> in order to avail himself of the priest's[19] security,
> which was equal to the value of the machine. This
> story was related to me by Dennis McGee, a member
> of the Committee, in the presence of William

Blackwell and his wife and his brother-in-law, Isaac
Hodgins, at Whalen's Corners.[20]

The reprieve for the Donnellys would prove to be short-lived,
however.

William and Mary Thompson counted their cows one evening
in late August and discovered that they were missing a
heifer. Given that the Donnellys were their immediate neighbours
to the north, in addition to the animus they had held toward
the family ever since being chivareed by the brothers five and a
half years previously, the Donnelly family became their primary
suspects. Encountering James Carroll, Mary Thompson told him,
"I heard a cow bawling at Donnelly's place which sounded like my
cow!"[21] William Donnelly considered this to be a rather humorous
statement, and later recounted, "Mrs. Thompson stated she heard
a cow bawling all day Monday in Donnelly's stable, and that she
recognized the bawl as that of *her* cow. The stable is 100 rods from
Thompson's house, so that she must have pretty fine ears."[22]

As a rod converts to sixteen and a half feet, this means that Mary
Thompson was able to distinguish her cow's particular "moo" from
that of the other cows on the Donnelly property[23] from a distance
of 1,650 feet (which is the equivalent of four and a half football
fields lined up end to end). Be that as it may, Carroll felt confident Mary Thompson's story about her cow being missing from her
farm was true. And he had good reason for this belief: his younger
brother William, along with recent Peace Society member William
Feeheley, had been the ones who had deliberately chased the heifer
from Thompson's property in order to cause more trouble that the
Donnellys could be blamed for.[24] James Carroll wasted no time in
convening an immediate meeting of the Peace Society to deal with
the matter.

The Society had by this point grown to approximately twenty members, who took their direction from an inner sanctum that was composed of a handful of men — James Carroll and John Kennedy Jr. among them. William Thompson, already a member of the Peace Society, was brought forth to tell of the theft of his cow:

> The meetings were held at the Cedar Swamp
> Schoolhouse on the ninth concession; it was the
> recognized place of meeting of the Vigilance
> Committee. The first meeting I attended was about
> the time I lost the cow. I was there, Anthony Heenan,
> John Kennedy, I think, James Carroll. I think there
> might have been twenty there. I have met Martin
> McLaughlin, Thomas Ryder, Patrick Ryder Sr.,
> Patrick Ryder Jr., Patrick Ryder, James Maher Sr.
> and James Maher Jr. The object of the meeting was
> to support law and order and help to find things that
> were lost. I have always understood that it was the
> intention to punish guilty parties only so far as the
> law would allow. The Donnellys were the subject of
> considerable discussion.[25]

Despite Mary Thompson apparently having heard her missing cow lowing from somewhere upon the Donnelly property earlier that day, the Society members concluded that it had probably already been butchered and its meat hung to dry within a chimney.[26] They decided that the best course of action would be an early morning raid on the Donnelly farm to conduct a thorough search of the property. This would accomplish two things: first, a show of numbers would reveal to the Donnellys that there was a "new sheriff" in town that would no longer tolerate their cock-of-the-walk attitude and criminal behaviour; and second, they might just find the remains of Thompson's cow, and thus have the evidence they required to arrest and convict the family. If these efforts were successful, the Donnellys could be excised from the community permanently; their days of intimidation and corruption would be over. Since William Thompson owned the heifer that was missing, it was decided that he should be the one to ride to Lucan that night and request a search warrant from the local justice of the peace, William Stanley. Thompson recalled: "I went to Mr. Stanley, J.P., of Lucan, about my cow; he stated that his opinion was that I would be justified in going on [the Donnelly property] and looking for the cow. And if they objected to the search, I was to go and get a warrant."[27]

During Thompson's departure to Lucan, James Carroll brought forth Constable William Hodgins to present to the Society. Hodgins was then informed about the need to arrest Thomas Ryan, who, they believed, had recently gotten away with stealing Kelly's horse. However, there was another charge the Society wanted to see him arrested on: Ryan had recently used abusive language to one of the members of the Society, and, given that they were the new power players in the area, this was unacceptable. And then, just for good measure, they wanted Ryan charged (perhaps as an accessory) with stealing Thompson's cow.[28] Hodgins agreed, and said that he would secure an arrest warrant for the young man by morning. The Society members then sat back and waited. Come dawn, the Donnelly family would finally be put in their place. And, while the Society members waited through the night, forty-nine-year-old James Quigley, a farmer who lived on Concession Road Five just behind the Thompson property, saw a lone heifer slowly meander into a pasture that adjoined his farm and the Thompsons'.[29]

At 5:30 a.m., the Peace Society members were on the move. It's not known with exactitude how many members headed out from the Cedar Swamp Schoolhouse that morning — William Donnelly would later claim a total of forty,[30] whereas Society member James Carrigan would testify under oath that he saw thirty-five men.[31] Either number represented overkill to effect the arrest of Thomas

Ryan. Most brought weapons of some sort: shillelaghs, walking sticks that doubled as cudgels, and one at least was carrying a rifle.[32] One of the Society members, Michael Carroll, drove a wagon, within which he had concealed a gun.[33] They went first to the farm of Michael Powe, where they knew that Thomas Ryan was employed. Several of the group grabbed hold of Ryan, while, from his wagon, Constable Hodgins produced his warrant and announced that the young man was under arrest for having used abusive language toward Pat Dewan, a member of their Society. He further announced that Ryan would be charged for stealing Thompson's heifer. Feeling every bit of their strength in numbers, the group then threatened Michael Powe for having hired Ryan, which unsettled the seventy-year-old farmer. Ryan was pushed into the constable's wagon, which then headed off for Lucan where Ryan would be thrown into jail.[34] With half of their mission now complete, the mob headed west to the Roman Line, where they turned south and marched on toward the Donnelly property.

James Quigley, in the meantime, had also risen early and decided that he would head over to William and Mary Thompson's to let them know about the cow he had seen wandering about in the pasture between their two properties the night before. As he approached their farm, however, he spotted the same cow and drove it back onto the Thompson property.[35] He told Mary Thompson the news and took her out to show her the animal. It was her cow all right, but it was too late; the train had already left the station. Her husband, along with thirty-eight or so other men, had already arrested Thomas Ryan for the theft, and were now approaching the Donnelly farmhouse.

Within the house slept sixty-three-year-old James Donnelly, his fifty-nine-year-old wife Johannah, and their thirty-two-year-old son John (Tom was not at his parents' home that morning). Also in the house that morning were two houseguests: James Donnelly's twenty-one-year-old niece Bridget and twenty-year-old Thomas

Hines (brother-in-law of Mike Donnelly). Shortly after 6 a.m., John Donnelly was wakened from his slumber by the voice of his cousin Bridget.

"Johnny! Johnny, get up!" she yelled, "there's a lot of men at the barn!"[36]

John sprang from his bed and threw on some clothes. Quickly tying up his boots, he hastened his stride through the main room and exited outside through the kitchen door. He walked directly toward the granary, where the mob had now gathered. Johannah Donnelly followed him outside. Half the mob were poking around the barn, the remainder gathered at the stable and lean-tos that sheltered the Donnelly livestock. Taking notice of John Kennedy Jr. and William Thompson, John Donnelly walked straight up to the two men as the mob closed in around him.

"Boys," he said in acknowledgement, "what do you want?"

William Thompson spoke up. "I have lost a cow."

"You'll find no cow here," Donnelly replied.

John Kennedy Jr. now stepped forth. He had a shillelagh in his hand. "We have not searched the granary yet," he said, gesturing toward the small building in which the Donnellys stored their animal feed and threshed grain.

"Search the granary then," said John Donnelly, "and be sure and make a good search."

Kennedy nodded toward James Carroll, who now stepped out of the crowd. The two men walked around the structure and looked within it. They returned to where John Donnelly was standing. Something about John was unsettling to them. When they had appeared in full force earlier at Powe's, they could sense the fear in the farmer and, of course, in Ryan. They were getting no sense of this from John Donnelly. Indeed, Donnelly was now looking at both Kennedy and Carroll — the two leaders of this unruly mob — as if they were buffoons. Donnelly looked around at all the good Catholics who had signed their priest's anti-crime document. Forty men looking for a missing cow — *was this what it was all about?* He had to stifle a belly laugh at the thought. Watching the sullen-faced James Carroll skulking around the granary looking for a "stolen cow" that wasn't there was almost too much entertainment for so early in the morning.

The concern that William Donnelly had expressed to his father now looked to be a prophecy that was playing out before John Donnelly's eyes: *I told him there were men in that society who would not hesitate at anything to get our family in trouble; that they would steal something, hide it on the farm, come in a body and search for it, find it, and then have him sent to the penitentiary for a crime he never committed.* It might well have ended up that way had William Feeheley and William Carroll been brave enough to hide the cow within the Donnelly family's barn instead of simply driving it out of Thompson's pasture. Suddenly John Donnelly remembered Father Connolly in his pulpit cursing the man who had stolen James Kelly's horse. "Go to the priest," Donnelly said laughingly, "and have him *curse the man that took the cow!*"

"We have the man that took the cow," Carroll said. "He's going in the buggy up the road."

The reference to Thomas Ryan's arrest was lost on John Donnelly, who simply snorted, turned and, together with his mother, walked back to the farmhouse.

After standing around the granary for a few more minutes, the group made their way to the front of the Donnelly farmhouse. Some of them walked to the water pump in the front yard and primed it to get a drink. In the meantime, John Donnelly had gone back into the house and told his father what was going on. James Donnelly was angered at the news and, pulling on his pants as he walked out the front door toward the mob, approached the group at his water pump. John Donnelly followed him.

"Boys, what brought you here?" he demanded.

"I have lost a stolen cow," answered William Thompson.

"Well, if you think the cow is here, do not leave one straw on top of another," said James Donnelly. "Make a search for her."

Again, James Carroll spoke up. "We need not, for we have the thief."

This raised an eyebrow from the Donnelly family patriarch. Looking over the size of the mob, he worried whether their prisoner might end up getting lynched before he had a trial.

"Well if you have him," said Donnelly, "make sure you give him the benefit of the law."

"You harboured the thief — Thomas Ryan!" yelled James Harrigan from within the mob.

"I would harbour your father's son," said James Donnelly.

If they already had the cow thief, thought James Donnelly, then why were they at his place? Surely, they didn't think *he* was hiding any stolen property! Now James Donnelly wanted answers. He turned to face James Carroll. "What do *you* want?" he asked suspiciously.

"We don't want anything," James Carroll replied, puffing out his chest. "Only to show you we are not afraid of *you*."

Carroll needed forty men with him for backup and he wanted James Donnelly to believe he *wasn't* afraid of him? James looked wryly at his son, John, who likewise had caught the irony of Carroll's statement. James Heenan, stepped forth from the group and now approached the two Donnellys.

"This work will be put down!" he yelled. "And *we will* put it down!"

Now it was James Maher's turn to vent his spleen. He walked up to John Donnelly and pointed his finger at Donnelly's chest.

"Who shaved my horses' tails?" he asked pointedly.

"I don't know anything about your horses," said John Donnelly.

Another member of the mob yelled out, "Who rode Kelly's horse?"

"It was Tom Ryan!" declared another.

"It was not," John Donnelly said disdainfully.

"I will have satisfaction," Heenan yelled, pointing his shillelagh at John Donnelly, "if it is in twenty years!"

Thomas Hines was hiding in the house. "I was afraid to go out," he would later recall, "the parties appeared pretty wild." He hadn't heard anything of the dialogue that took place by the granary, but now that the group was beside the house, he could hear everything that was said. "Several persons spoke to Carroll about things being stolen," he would later testify, "and if they would go to the priest and curse the man that took their cow, the cow would soon come back."

At this, John Donnelly piped up, "If the priest did curse the man that took the cow, my belief is that Carroll here would be the man that would be *first* taken up."

Carroll scowled.

James Donnelly offered a far more direct solution. "If you don't like us, you can kiss my ass."

"You can kiss my ass!" yelled John Darcy.

Looking around at the group, James Donnelly now broadened the invitation: "You can *all* kiss my ass!"

James Carroll now walked up to James Donnelly.

"How would you like a few kicks in your ribs this morning?" Carroll asked menacingly.

Donnelly was unfazed by the threat. "I have seen the day I could give you a few kicks in the ribs."

Carroll's face flushed at the remark.

"You'd best hold your tongue," Carroll threatened. "We could break your bones at your door here and you couldn't help yourself."37

"I was a man when you weren't able to wipe your backside," the old man replied.

As a man who had spent seven years in Kingston Penitentiary alongside some of the most cold-blooded killers in the province, James Donnelly was not the least bit intimidated by James Carroll.

James Donnelly now looked around at the assembled throng and declared, "I have no stolen cow, and I'll arrest every man of you for trespass."[38]

"We will make you keep quiet," a faceless voice bellowed from within the crowd. Another man raised his club in the air and yelled, "If I ever come here again I won't be going away as peaceable as I am now!"[39]

James Donnelly had had enough of dealing with what he considered to be a group of paper tigers. "I will be here if the devil would burn the whole of you," he said. "I am not in the least afraid of you." With that, he turned his back on the crowd and he and John returned to the farmhouse.

This certainly hadn't turned out as the mob had planned. Not only did the Donnellys not have the missing cow, but they had not been rattled in the least by the Peace Society. While some of the Society members began to remonstrate about what their next step should be, John Kennedy Jr. spoke up, suggesting that they should proceed to the home of his brother-in-law William Donnelly.[40] After all, just because the cow hadn't been discovered at old man Donnelly's farmhouse, that didn't mean that it wouldn't be found at the home of another member of the family. The mob poured out through the Donnellys' front gate onto the Roman Line, where, heading north, they encountered Thomas Marshall, a teacher at the Donnelly School who was just arriving to prepare for his morning classes. He was startled by the size and coarseness of the group, which he described as "a body of men, between forty and fifty in number, having clubs and bludgeons in their hands."[41] The teacher paused in his tracks as the horde approached.

"In the name of God, where are you all going to?" he asked.

"We're looking for a heifer," someone from within the group answered.

Given the size of the mob, Marshall was bemused. "Has every one of you lost a heifer?"

"No," came the curt reply from someone.

"Have you looked through the woods for the cow?" asked Marshall, "before turning out like this?"

"We know the cow is skinned" came the reply, "and we are trying to smell the meat down the chimneys."[42]

The mob pressed on, eventually passing the farm of James Keefe Sr., who happened to be at his front gate when the group was passing by. He was surprised to see the councillor of Biddulph Township, Patrick Dewan, in among them.

"What are you men doing?" asked Keefe.

"We are looking for a stolen heifer," Dewan replied.

"I do not think the cow is stolen at all," said Keefe. As the mob continued past his gate, Keefe noticed a rifle propped up against the front seat of the wagon that was driven by Michael Carroll.[43]

The Peace Society's plans had been poorly organized from the start. At the moment it seemed that they were more a group on parade to impress than a society on patrol to eradicate crime. So far that morning they had threatened an innocent farmer, Michael Powe, arrested the wrong man in Thomas Ryan, been embarrassed by old James Donnelly and his son John and turned up no stolen cow. They had no intention of raiding any other houses in the district, preferring instead to target the home of another Donnelly family member who lived three miles away. And even this tactic was poorly planned. To begin, the mob was taking a very leisurely route to William Donnelly's house by heading north to the end of the Roman Line, and then east to Whalen's Corners. Their travel was further delayed when the men decided to split up and have breakfast at two of the farmhouses they passed along the way. And, finally, when John Kennedy Jr. had announced where they would be heading next that morning, he did so in a voice loud enough that Johannah Donnelly could hear him. Given the delicate condition of William's wife, Johannah decided that she had better warn her son of the mob of armed men that was now heading in his direction. She had her son John hitch up a team of horses to one of the farm wagons and then, unlike the Society members, she took a back route that was much more direct, arriving at William's house while the Peace Society members were still consuming their breakfasts. William, now forewarned of what was heading his way, had plenty of time to prepare for the arrival of the gang. He pulled out a revolver, loaded it and stepped outside his front door to wait for the mob to arrive.

As William Donnelly watched the roadway he had already decided that he was going to protect his wife and property at all costs. "I had made up my mind to demand their authority for searching my place, and, if they could not show it, I intended to shoot the first man entering the gate,"[44] he later said. He had been waiting for some time when the mob finally came into view. Forty men, he reckoned, most of them armed with some sort of weapon, were walking along the road toward his house. Still he waited, revolver in hand, as they verged nearer. Finally, the mob was across the road in front of his house. There they paused and conversed in hushed tones among themselves. William watched coolly, almost with detached interest. Like his father, he evidently felt no fear of the danger the group posed. James Carroll and Martin McLaughlin took a group of men with them and walked a little farther down the road, where they entered the blacksmith shop of Edward Sutherby. Sutherby owned the house that William and Nora rented from him, and had been a long-time friend of the couple.

"We're looking for a stolen cow," said Carroll, by way of introduction.

Sutherby thought he was joking. "It would be better if you were cutting thistles or ploughing," Sutherby said. Then, realizing that the men were serious, he asked laughingly, "Surely you do not expect to find a stolen cow here in my shop?"

Martin McLaughlin by this time had had enough of being laughed at that morning. He approached the blacksmith and, brandishing his shillelagh, hissed, "We will visit you at all hours — when you least expect it."

Sutherby shook his head dismissively. "You're a very respectable-looking crowd, indeed," he said sarcastically.[45]

With that, the men left to join John Kennedy Jr., Ned Ryan and the rest of the gang across the road from William Donnelly's house. Nothing had happened in their absence; the throng had clearly been given pause by the sight of William, gun in hand, staring back at them. John Kennedy walked along the side of the road until he spotted an overturned log. He sat down upon it and stared at William. William scanned the faces in the crowd and, noting the lack of direct eye contact, concluded that the men had lost their nerve. He then directed his attention back to John Kennedy Jr. Kennedy was a big, powerful man who had been given the nickname "Bull" by his friends, owing to his imposing physique.[46] But seeing him sitting on a log across from his house with no intention of doing anything, William Donnelly would later tell a reporter he thought that a more apt nickname would have been "Sitting Bull."[47]

William then went inside his house. He re-emerged moments later with a violin tucked under his chin and started to play it. He later told the Toronto *Globe*, "I took the fiddle to the door and played the well-known march of 'Bony Crossing the Alps,' which I considered very appropriate to the occasion."[48]

The tune was played to draw a facetious contrast between Napoleon and his soldiers crossing over the Great St. Bernard Pass in the Swiss Alps on their way to invade Italy and John Kennedy Jr. and his lethargic mob, who were too unnerved to even cross the road. It's doubtful that any of the Peace Society's members who were present caught the intended irony of the piece. John Kennedy suddenly stood up and marched off. Slowly his gang turned away from William Donnelly, who was still playing his fiddle, and began to trundle off down the road back toward the Roman Line. As they walked away, William recognized a member within the mob as being worthy of a jab. "I called to one of them if he was looking for his mother, whom he had left in a poorhouse in Ireland to die — although he was rich in Biddulph," he said.[49]

Johannah Donnelly then joined her son outside and shouted her own disparaging comments at the crowd. She recognized certain faces within the gang as being among the multitude of hard-luck cases she had taken in and fed over the years when they'd had no one else to turn to — and this hurt her. She was particularly upset to see people like Martin Darcy among the group, as he was a young man whose father, Dennis, she said, "was the decentest [sic] man in Biddulph!"[50] She was still upset later that evening after she had returned home. At dusk, she ventured across the road to speak with her neighbour, Mary Carroll, and lamented, "Is this not a pretty way we are treated?" During her conversation with Mary, Johannah mentioned that another of their neighbours, nineteen-year-old James Ryder (known locally as "Young Grouch") had ridden out to William's house that afternoon in a horse and buggy in support of the Peace Society. This had shocked her. "Grouch was there with the rest," she said. "I will go out to the road and meet young Grouch — and put a blush on his face and make him lie back in his grand buggy!"[51] She was venting now. But her outburst had been born from a union of pain and puzzlement that she had been feeling lately, one she could not quite account for. Somehow a change in the Donnellys' immediate environment had taken place. It had occurred slowly, almost imperceptibly, at first. But if it was slow it was also progressive, much like drops of water filling a bucket, until, finally, things were no longer the same.

The Donnellys had known James Ryder's parents, Patrick ("Grouchy") and Julia, for over three decades. The Ryder family, with seven children (James, Michael, Patrick, Mary, Morris, William and John), was almost as large as the Donnellys'. Such a big family required a big property, and the Ryders owned one; their farmhouse sat on one hundred acres, just three lots to the north and across the road from the Donnelly property. Patrick Ryder had also acquired half of the Maloney brothers' property from Dan Clark (before his untimely demise). Since Cornelius Maloney had essentially given James Donnelly the other half of that property, the Ryders and the Donnellys were immediate neighbours, and such was their relationship that no fence between their two properties had ever been required. But while the Donnellys owned less acreage, their properties were more profitable, owing largely to the work ethic the family had embraced. Their success had resulted in a sense of envy and resentment festering in the mind of Grouchy Ryder. This resentment gave way to anger, with Ryder believing that a Donnelly had cropped one of his horses' tails during the previous national election campaign. Then there was the fact that Grouchy, along with some of his brothers (James, John, Daniel and Thomas), had switched his political allegiance from the Liberals to John A. Macdonald's Conservatives, further separating their family from the Donnellys, who had remained steadfastly Liberal all their lives. Consequently, the Ryders now had more in common with other neighbours, such as James Maher. And they had begun to talk more frequently with Maher's nephew James Carroll. The friendship between the Donnellys and the Ryders had ended . . . only the Donnellys weren't aware of it yet.

CHAPTER THIRTEEN

DIVINE OUTLAWS

St. Patrick's Church. (Courtesy of Jackie Martens and the
Lucan Area Heritage & Donnelly Museum)

***

Johannah Donnelly fretted about the strange turn of events. That several of her neighbours, people she had shared good times with and formerly considered to be her friends, would join in a mob to express their contempt of her and her family was bewildering. Her sons, however, weren't quite so nostalgic. Their approach had always been to meet adversity head on, or, to use Tom Donnelly's phraseology, to pay back their persecutors "in their own coin." To this end, William wanted the mob that had shown up at his parents' property arrested and tried on a charge of trespass. However, as none of the gang had set foot on his property, he couldn't be the one to lay the charge; this would have to be done by another member of his family, on whose property the trespass had so brazenly occurred. Neither James nor Johannah wanted to get involved in any protracted legal battles, which made John the best candidate to represent the family's interests in the matter. William instructed his brother to go to the offices of the Crown attorney, Charles Hutchinson, and share with him the details of the case. Hutchinson, as evidenced by a letter he wrote later that same day to justice of the peace John Peters, clearly believed that a crime had been committed:

Sept 10/79
John Peters,
Esquire, Justice of the Peace

Dear Sir,
The bearer, Mr. Donnelly, has a complaint for trespass to lodge against a number of men, who appear to have acted in a very unjustifiable way, and are clearly liable to be punished. I have advised him to go to you, as a magistrate sure to act as you think right without that fear of consequence which seems to prevent the Lucan justices from doing their duty.

Yours truly,
Charles Hutchinson,
Clerk of the Peace[1]

John Donnelly (and James and Johannah) had recognized only some parties of the forty or so that had come onto their property, and he set about composing a list of names of the individuals that he wanted charged with the crime. James "Young Grouch" Ryder's name was conspicuous by its absence and was omitted in large part because Johannah still believed that the two families were friends. The final list was: Terry McDonald, Pat Breen, Mike Blake, James

Carroll, James Harrigan, Pat Dewan, John Kennedy, John Keenan, Ed Ryder, John Ryder, John Darcy, James Martin and James Kelly.[2]

Upon receiving the news that the Donnellys were taking them to court, the Peace Society members involved in the alleged trespass gathered together to prepare their legal defence. They approached James Carroll's lawyer, John Blake (the brother of one of the accused trespassers in the case, Peace Society member Michael Blake), for representation. Blake, the reader will recall, was the attorney who had assisted Carroll in the latter's challenge to his uncles for inclusion in any profits earned from his late father's estate. As the attorney had also drafted Father Connolly's anti-crime society document, this anti-Donnelly faction was proving to be a reliable and steady stream of income for the barrister, and so he readily accepted their offer of employment once again. He earnestly set to work on examining the weaknesses of the Donnellys' case.

In the meantime, Lucan constable Samuel Everett had fallen out of favour with his employers at the town council. William Porte clearly had no use for him, but now the other members of council had come to share the postmaster's views. The final straw had been during a period of fiscal tightening, when they had asked the town constable to include among his duties the lighting of Lucan's street lamps. It was assumed that a well-lit main street would prove to be a deterrent to potential criminal activity occurring during the evenings. Therefore, the council reasoned, the duty of lighting the street lamps fell within the town constable's duties. Everett thought otherwise; he was being paid a salary, and had been for some time, to do exactly what he had been doing — and nothing more. There was no financial incentive for him to be climbing ladders and lighting lamps every night, and so he refused to do it. The council was angered by his decision and voted to suspend his salary, which they did,[3] and then elected to fire him for insubordination. But Everett sued the corporation of Lucan and the magistrate ruled that the constable was within his rights to forgo the lighting of the Lucan street lamps. Any salary that had been withheld from Everett was ordered to be paid to him.[4] However, the town council was also within its rights to fire him. Everett, then, received his back pay and then found himself out of a job. He continued to live in Lucan and watched from the sidelines as his rival, William Hodgins, was promoted to his old position of Lucan town constable. This appointment was bad news for the Donnellys, as it meant that the official "law" of Lucan was a member of the Peace Society, a decidedly anti-Donnelly fraternity. Hodgins had acquired his job on merit, it was true, but in which direction he would decide to exercise his authority was anyone's guess.

O n September 6, 1879, the Peace Society, with Father Connolly in tow, attended court in Lucan when the case against young Thomas Ryan was presented before magistrate William Stanley. As the Thompson cow theft charge had turned out to be baseless, the charge that had been brought against Ryan had been for using abusive language toward the councillor of Biddulph Township, Patrick Dewan, who, like Constable Hodgins, was an active member of the Peace Society. Ryan had been released from jail as a result of two people (John Kennedy Sr. being one of them) putting up bail for the young man[5] — a move that could not have pleased his son, Peace Society member John Kennedy Jr.

Councillor Dewan was sworn in and stated in his testimony that Ryan had called him names and threatened to cut his heart out. Having heard Patrick Dewan's version of events, Magistrate Stanley called upon defence attorney William McDiarmid to present Ryan's. McDiarmid put his client on the witness stand and began his defence presentation by asking Ryan what had happened on the night in question. Ryan answered that while he was at Dewan's that night, and did indeed call Dewan a few choice names, he had never once threatened him.[6] Before McDiarmid could pose a second question to his client, however, Father Connolly jumped to his feet and yelled at McDiarmid, "You're trying to make him perjure himself!"[7]

This, understandably, brought the proceedings to a halt. Magistrate Stanley ordered that the good Father should refrain from any more interruptions in his court. Once things had settled down, Stanley ruled that he was acquitting Ryan on the charge of threatening, but would find in favour of the prosecution that Ryan had used abusive language. He fined Ryan a paltry sum and ordered the case dismissed.[8]

Father Connolly was beside himself with rage. The previous Sunday he had used his pulpit to declare that he would attend the trial, and if the magistrate didn't deliver justice in his verdict, the priest would have him punished for it.[9] In the event, "justice" turned out to be a small fine. Hardly justification for Ryan's arrest by a mob, or the threats they had levelled at his employer, Michael Powe. Powe had also attended Ryan's trial and, now believing that his employee had been vindicated, he decided to talk to Father Connolly about the matter. To Powe's surprise, he discovered that the verdict had done nothing to lessen Thomas Ryan's guilt in the good Father's eyes. In fact, according to the priest, all the trial had done was make public what a weak-kneed joke the Lucan law courts had become. And if the magistrate didn't see fit to punish Thomas Ryan, Father Connolly would. He demanded that Powe immediately discharge Ryan from his employ.

"I can't, Father," Powe pleaded. "Ryan's time isn't up, and if I put him away I'd still have to pay him all his wages."

"How much would that be?" asked Father Connolly.

"About thirty dollars, Father," answered Powe.

The priest snorted. He knew that the young man probably wasn't owed more than twenty dollars. But thirty dollars would be money well spent if it included the purchase of a train ticket that would send Ryan far away. He put his hand in his pocket and pulled out some bills. Counting off thirty dollars, he handed the money to the farmer.

"There," said Father Connolly. "I want you to drive Ryan and his trunk of belongings to the railway station in Granton tomorrow morning and see him started away out of the country."[10]

Powe agreed to the priest's demand and, upon reaching his farm, delivered the news to Ryan that he was now unemployed. True to his word, early the next morning Powe loaded Ryan and his belongings into his work wagon and started out toward Granton. En route to the railway station, however, Ryan asked Powe to stop in briefly at his friend William Donnelly's place. Donnelly recalled what happened next:

> When they came to my place, Ryan got out of the
> buggy and laughed at Powe, and told him to go
> home and said he had never made twenty dollars so
> easily in his life. The following day I drove Ryan to
> Lucan, and got him a job with some men who were
> travelling with a threshing machine, as I did not
> consider it right to have the boy banished away for
> nothing, all his relations being very respectable, and
> he was quite willing to work for a living.[11]

When word of Ryan's duplicity, and of Donnelly's role in it, returned to Father Connolly, his ire at William Donnelly reached new heights. He was so upset, in fact, that those within the Peace Society decided they had better look into resolving the matter personally. Society member James McGrath volunteered to drop in to pay a visit to the travelling threshing machine employer with whom William Donnelly had arranged for Thomas Ryan to work. Upon meeting the man, McGrath told him straight out that he should fire Ryan immediately. The head of the threshing company refused his request, whereupon McGrath threatened him.

"How would you like to have your machine burned some night?"

"I'm not discharging him," the man replied. And then, fixing McGrath with a steely stare, he said, "And I'd like to see you try your hand at burning my machine."[12]

Both the priest and the Peace Society had been thwarted by the cunning mind of William Donnelly again. After stewing about the matter for a few days, Father Connolly, perhaps at the behest of his parishioner John Kennedy Jr., decided that he should pay a visit to Kennedy's father to reprove him for having bailed Ryan out of jail. However, John Kennedy Sr. was having none of it.

"I had a good right to bail the boy out," Kennedy said. "Ryan's father had stood for my son Joseph when he was christened, and once in Lucan, when some of the Society were trying to kill my son[13] in a quarrel, Ryan's cousins and his uncle, Robert Keefe, saved him. I consider him a quiet, harmless boy if he was let alone."[14]

Not making any headway on the subject of Thomas Ryan, Father Connolly changed the subject to his pet peeve. "What are you going to do with your son-in-law?" he demanded.

"William Donnelly?" asked Kennedy in surprise. "What do you want me to *do* with him?"

The priest lost his temper. "He's a devil, the biggest devil I ever met, and Ryan is another — and I want you to keep Donnelly away from your house!"

"I'll do *no such thing*," Kennedy answered.

"Well, then," said the priest, "if anybody takes sick in your house, and you send for me and Donnelly is here when I come, I'll take the patient in the yard and prepare him for death sooner than enter the house he is in."

Now it was John Kennedy Sr.'s turn to get angry. "I have known William Donnelly since he was a child, and I never saw anything wrong with him. He is always welcome in my house while I have one. And, as to Ryan, I will go his security any time it is needed!"

Father Connolly was both furious and astonished that one of his parishioners should flat-out disobey his fiat. He left John Kennedy Sr.'s home in a rage. The next Sunday he again used his pulpit to condemn his adversaries — he told his parishioners that none of them were to hire Thomas Ryan, then he blamed William Donnelly for thwarting his attempt to drive Ryan out of the country. He went on to decree that none of his congregation were to employ any strangers to the area (presumably in reference to the threshers who had employed Ryan) and that he was determined to do away with all arsonists, ex-convicts and evildoers. These were the kind of people he believed would support or otherwise enable a person such as Thomas Ryan.[15]

While the Peace Society members had proven themselves willing to lay charges, and their town constable willing to make arrests, their cases against the Donnellys always seemed to unravel once they got before a magistrate. Plans were therefore put into motion to better ensure their success in the courtroom. It was decided that they would require another constable who could devote himself to arresting the Donnellys, and a justice of the peace who would rule to have them convicted. This required following the proper channels, of course, and would take some time but, particularly once they had their own magistrate in place, the outcome of any future legal matters would be certain to shake out in their favour. To this end, the Peace Society began the process by looking among its members for a candidate who could serve in the position of full-time constable. His duty would be to dedicate himself solely to the Society's primary objective of getting rid of the Donnellys. After a promising start, the ex–town constable Samuel Everett had proven to be a disappointment; while he had successfully prosecuted Bob Donnelly, which resulted in the latter being hauled off to Kingston Penitentiary, he hadn't done anything since. He wouldn't even press charges against Tom Donnelly for his robbery of Ned Ryan. The fact that the recently elected Lucan constable William Hodgins was a member of the Peace Society was certainly a benefit to the cause, but he could only devote so much time to pursuing and arresting the Donnellys. Most of the other county constables had the same problem: they had farms to run, which made their constabulary work somewhat part-time and seasonal. The Peace Society needed a man who could devote his time solely to the *real* crime problem in the community — the Donnellys and their gang members. To the Society, James Carroll was such a man.[16] He had no farm to work, he had no wife and children to compete for his attention and he was quite passionate about driving the Donnellys out of the township. When approached with the proposition, Carroll expressed his willingness to take on the job, and so the Peace Society had their lawyer, John Blake, draft up a formal petition for Carroll's appointment as county constable.[17] It read as follows:

> To William Elliot, Esquire
> Judge of the County of Middlesex
>
> The humble prayer and petition of the undersigned
> inhabitants of the Township of Biddulph showeth
> as follows:
> Whereas, for some time past, certain evil-minded
> persons in the Township of Biddulph have been
> violating the laws and acting in such a manner
> as to endanger the persons and property of the
> peaceable portion of the inhabitants thereof. And
> Whereas, from there being but a few constables in
> said Township it is difficult and often impossible to
> have warrants or other process of the local Justices
> of the Peace executed, and in Consequence thereof
> compelling injured persons to either refrain from
> taking legal proceedings in the address of wrongs
> or go to the expense of laying complaints before
> Justices of the Peace in the city of London. And

> Whereas your petitioners are of opinion that much
> of the above cited inconvenience would be obviated
> by the appointment of James Carroll of said
> Township as a constable therein.[18]

Affixed to the end of the petition were the signatures of fifty-six men, all connected to the Peace Society. The petition passed and James Carroll was officially appointed a county constable on September 20, 1879.[19] Upon leaving the courthouse after his appointment, Carroll encountered two other local constables, William Hodge and Charles Pope. Pope is an interesting side figure in the story; born in the United States to African-American parents, he was a resident of Waterloo, Ontario, and, apart from his detective work, he was a chimney sweep by profession. By all surviving accounts he was very popular, and had a well-earned reputation as a very honest and thorough constable. He knew without being told the reason underlying Carroll's appointment.

"I understand you are a constable," Pope said. "You are in a position to catch *them* now."

Carroll smiled at the thought. "Yes," he replied. "I'll be the cause of the Donnellys being banished out of Biddulph!"[20]

On the same day as Carroll's appointment, thirteen members of the Peace Society travelled to Lucan to stand trial on the charge of trespassing on the Donnelly property. Attorney John Blake's opening tactic for the defence was to bring to the stand a man who would attest to the sterling character of those charged with the offence. In Blake's eyes, there was no better character witness than Father John Connolly. When the priest took the stand, he gave witness that the men who now stood accused before Magistrate John Peters were "all respectable farmers" and "some of them are leading men in the township."[21] He supported their search of the Donnelly property, indicating that he had been "sent to that neighbourhood partly for the purpose of putting all lawlessness down."[22] The prosecution then called their witnesses to the stand: Thomas Hines and James and John Donnelly. Hines mentioned that he had been at the Donnelly house that morning and could hear the yelling and the threats made by the Peace Society members, which he admitted had scared him. However, when John Donnelly took the witness stand and started to give his version of events, Father Connolly once again felt compelled to stand up and interrupt the proceedings. According to William Donnelly,

> While my brother John was giving his evidence Father
> Connolly contradicted him (I don't remember what it
> was), but John answered, and said that if he (Father
> Connolly) "had attended to his spiritual affairs, and
> had not organized that society, the present law suit
> would never have taken place." It was quite evident
> that the priest was working on behalf of the accused.[23]

Magistrate Peters decided to postpone the trial, and ordered it to be resumed one week later, on September 27. Seizing the moment, Constable James Carroll now approached Magistrate Peters and presented Ned Ryan to him. He had Ryan relate he had been robbed by Tom Donnelly a year and a half ago, and now was looking to press charges. Magistrate Peters, not realizing that this very case had already been tried, gave Carroll the warrant he requested.[24] Carroll then approached his fellow Peace Society member Constable William Hodgins, and borrowed both his revolver and a pair of handcuffs.[25] He further asked Hodgins for the warrant he had been holding for some time to arrest James Feeheley, who had been with Tom Donnelly on the night in question. He wanted this second warrant not for the purpose of making an arrest, but rather for leverage. James Carroll had plans for Feeheley.[26]

The day after his outburst in court, Father Connolly delivered his sermon from the pulpit within St. Patrick's Church. James Donnelly attended the service and, afterward, was offered a ride home in the wagon of James Keefe Sr. Father Connolly had witnessed Keefe's neighbourly act — and was incensed by it. His parishioners knew without any hint of ambiguity on what side of the fence their priest stood with regard to the Donnellys, and to have a member of his very own congregation offer a kindness to a member of this family — particularly after John Donnelly had told him to mind his own business in front of a courtroom full of people — was an outrage to the Father. The priest stewed about Keefe's act of betrayal for two days and then decided to confront the farmer about it. He climbed into his wagon and drove the five miles to James Keefe Sr.'s farmhouse. Keefe barely had time to utter a greeting when Father Connolly opened up on him.

"How dare you carry old Donnelly home in your wagon?" demanded the priest.

Keefe, like John Kennedy Sr. before him, was at first startled by the question. However, he wasn't startled long. "*Your* Vigilance Committee is composed of murderers, blackguards and thieves!" declared the old man. He pointed at the Roman Line that Father Connolly had travelled upon to get to his farm. "Old Donnelly and I helped to make that road before the greater part of them were born. I've always found him a good neighbour and warm-hearted friend, and I will carry him wherever I have a horse to draw him!"

The two men were soon joined by James Patton, a thirty-eight-year-old teacher at the Donnelly School, who had heard the farmer arguing with the Father and decided to intervene. His efforts were ignored by the priest, who then turned his ire toward the matriarch of the Donnelly family. "Johannah Donnelly is not worthy to receive the blessed sacrament, and she will yet die in the ditch!"[27] Connolly declared. James Keefe had heard enough and indicated that the conversation was over.

When asked later why the priest would say such a thing about Johannah, William Donnelly replied, "I judge he had formed a bad opinion of my mother from the stories he had heard. My opinion was that he wanted to turn everybody against us, and would like to drive us or anyone who assisted us out of the township."[28] But it wasn't just Father Connolly who was pressuring the Donnellys' neighbours on the Roman Line not to associate with the family — a campaign was already underway by the Peace Society to ostracize the family. As William Donnelly would recollect:

> William McLaughlin, a near neighbour and a friend,
> was going to have a threshing, and asked my father
> to send him a couple of men to help at the same. We
> owed him this assistance, as he had been helping my
> father to thresh. The old man willingly promised to
> do so, but the next morning early McLaughlin sent
> word over for the men not to come, giving as a reason
> that William Thompson, Mike Carroll and other
> members of the Vigilance Committee had come to
> him the night before, and threatened that if any of the
> Donnellys were at the threshing they would not come.
> They also asked him not to "neighbour" with them.
> So, it will be seen that they were bound to turn all the
> neighbourhood against our family.[29]

William Donnelly saw trouble on the horizon: the fact that the Society members were spreading poison about his family to their neighbours, that they now had their own constable and the services of a good lawyer, and were more concentrated and organized than he had initially believed them to be was ominous. Things were going to get a lot worse; he felt it in his bones. Having tried to set up a meeting with Father Connolly twice and failed, he took it upon himself to write another letter. This time he sent it over the priest's head to the Bishop of London, John Walsh. Once again, we must turn to William Donnelly to discern the letter's contents:

> I then came to the conclusion that unless something
> was done towards doing away with this Society, it
> would never end well. Accordingly, I wrote a letter
> to Bishop Walsh. In brief, I told His Lordship about
> the Society being formed by Father Connolly; that I
> understood the members were sworn to each other;
> that I believed they were in direct opposition to my
> family. I told him that our name was continually
> referred to in church in connection with crimes, but
> that the names of others known to have committed
> crimes were never even hinted at, two or three of
> which I instanced. I told him now that young Hugh
> Toohey had broken his father's ribs, but that Father
> Connolly never spoke of it to the people. I stated that
> the priest was prejudiced against us, and I wished
> His Lordship to bring Father Connolly and I face to
> face before him and decide who was in the wrong.
> I referred him to some of the most respectable men
> in the township, viz — Patrick Nangle, Stephen
> McCormack, Dennis [Darcy], John [McIlhargey],
> Michael Crunican, J.P., James Keefe and Robert
> Keefe, as to whether they thought we were guilty of
> all the crimes laid to us. I begged of him for God's
> sake to do something towards disbanding the society,
> for I was sure it would end in murder.[30]

When Bishop Walsh received the letter, he was in a position to assert his influence in the affair and, thus, bring a stop to the conflict before it escalated out of control. Rather than doing this, however, he merely shrugged his shoulders and handed William Donnelly's missive over to Father Connolly. That was it. A meeting at this juncture might well have prevented the dark tragedy that was looming in the distance. Father Connolly's reaction, perhaps predictable at this point, was to use his pulpit to chastise the author of the letter and the manner in which William Donnelly had addressed the Bishop:

> Father Connolly threw out insinuations as to the
> way in which I had addressed my letter to the
> Bishop. He meant to convey that I had not been
> respectful in my language to His Lordship; that is,
> that I had not addressed him as the dignity of his
> position demanded. Well, as for that I can say that I
> only received a poor education at best. While I was
> a boy my father spent seven years in the Penitentiary
> for an unlucky stroke he gave in liquor, and during
> that time my poor mother was not able to clothe us
> so that we could attend school regularly. Therefore,
> any mistake that I may have made in my letter
> was simply for the want of knowledge about such
> matters, and was not by any means intentional. I can
> say for the letter, however, that if it was published
> tomorrow, the public would find more sense and
> truth in it than they would in many of the addresses
> delivered in Biddulph church during the past year.[31]

The priest was particularly irked by William Donnelly's claim in the letter that several respectable members of the Father's parish had evidently disagreed with the Reverend Father regarding his assessment of the Donnelly family's criminal history. Connolly confronted each of these men individually, inquiring "What kind of *men* are you?" before again putting himself front and centre. "Do you want to put me out of the country?" The men replied that while they hadn't given William permission to use their names, they nevertheless had only good things to say about him.[32] The letter was thereafter ignored by the priest.

Armed with Constable Everett's handcuffs, revolver and warrant, James Carroll was now actively searching for Tom Donnelly. He had learned that Donnelly was helping thresh at the farm of sixty-six-year-old farmer Mitchell Haskett, which lay two concession roads southwest of the Donnelly property. Haskett was a Protestant (Church of England), who had been a friend of the Donnelly family for many years. He had been the one who had accompanied James Donnelly when he surrendered himself to the authorities in Goderich after eleven months on the lam for the killing of Patrick Farrell. Other farmers were present in the field assisting with the threshing that day as well — John Kent and William Simpson, among others. All were Protestants with whom the Donnellys were friendly. In truth, their circle of Roman Catholic friends had almost disappeared by this point, thanks to the proclamations of Father Connolly and the intimidation and threats of the Peace Society. The Donnellys, then, had welcomed the fellowship.

There was nothing of fellowship on Carroll's mind, however, when, on the morning of September 25, he brought his buggy to a halt in front of Haskett's farm.[33] His arrival had been conspicuous, made all the more so when he stepped down from his buggy and drew his revolver. He knew that Tom Donnelly was perhaps the most capable fighter in the Donnelly family and he wasn't taking any chances. Cocking his pistol, he called for the men to stand back and announced that he was there to arrest Tom Donnelly. Donnelly had been eyeing Carroll warily since his arrival. He stepped forth from the field. "Read the warrant!" he demanded.

Carroll produced his warrant and read it aloud, and then, with his weapon still trained upon Donnelly, he walked toward his adversary. Donnelly held forth his hands and Carroll quickly snapped the handcuffs around Donnelly's wrists. With his prisoner now defenceless, Carroll's confidence rose. He began to shove Donnelly roughly toward the buggy. Tom Donnelly complained at how tightly Carroll had cinched the handcuffs around his wrists. Carroll responded by giving his prisoner another shove. Carroll was clearly enjoying this. Too much so, thought the men who were witnessing the arrest. As Carroll gave Tom Donnelly another powerful push toward the wagon, Donnelly lost his footing, whereupon Carroll drew his baton and threatened, "I'll give you this over the head if you do not get in!" The men had seen enough. John Kent stepped forward and said derisively, "You might as well kill the man at once while we're all here." Carroll's eyes widened at the suggestion. Kent then attempted to bring Thomas Donnelly's jacket to him, whereupon Carroll pointed his gun at Kent.

"Stand back or I'll shoot you!" he yelled.

The revolver, understandably, gave all the men pause. Carroll, sensing that there would be no trouble from the farmers, pushed Tom Donnelly up into the buggy, hopped in alongside him and started the carriage off toward London.

It would not be the last time Carroll would put Tom Donnelly in handcuffs.

Upon reaching London, Tom Donnelly was released on bail that was paid, in part, by Haskett, and the balance by the ex–Lucan constable Samuel Everett — the very man who had refused to serve Ned Ryan's warrant to Donnelly a year and a half previously. He still believed the charge to be questionable. Donnelly was ordered to be tried before magistrate John Peters in Lucan on September 27, 1879.[34]

Two days later, Magistrate Peters had two trials to preside over: Tom Donnelly's alleged robbery of Ned Ryan and John Donnelly's charge of trespass against the thirteen members of the Peace Society. Both were adjudicated quickly: the magistrate ruled against John Donnelly when it was revealed that, in his anger, James Donnelly had blurted out to the Peace Committee that they should "make a search" for the missing heifer and "do not leave one straw on top of another." That, said Magistrate Peters, constituted permission granted. There was no trespass. The thirteen Peace Society members were acquitted.[35] An interesting thing came of the court case, however. The local press now knew of the existence of the Peace Society and what it was getting up to and announced its existence and purpose to its readers:

> A number of the residents to the number of
> forty banded together and formed a "Vigilance
> Committee," invested with power similar to
> Judge Lynch's, for the summary treatment and
> disposition of all offenders against the property
> or persons of anyone in the vicinity.[36]

The veil having now been drawn back on the Society, its existence was no longer a secret. It also now had a new name: the "Vigilance Committee." It would be referred to by this moniker henceforth.

Next to appear before Magistrate Peters was Tom Donnelly and his accuser Ned Ryan. Just as before, James Carroll may have brought Tom Donnelly to court, but he still had been unable to find any witnesses to corroborate Ryan's account of the alleged robbery. With only the contradictory testimony of the two principals in the trial, Magistrate Peters had no choice but to acquit Tom Donnelly of the charges.[37] It was the same result as when Ryan and Carroll had attempted the same prosecution against Tom Donnelly the previous April. One would think two legal defeats within five months on the same case would have been more than enough. But one would be in error for thinking so. "I will carry it further," Carroll vowed.[38] And so he would.

Carroll appealed to his problem-solving attorney, John Blake, in London. Blake, in turn, accompanied Carroll and Ryan to the office of the Crown prosecutor for the Middlesex Fall Assizes: Malcolm Cameron. Cameron listened to the men and agreed to enter their charge among those of other cases that would be tried in October.

Cameron's duty obliged him, particularly since there had been no preliminary hearing, to notify Crown prosecutor Charles Hutchinson:

> Before deciding to present the bill in this case to the Grand Jury, Blake and Ryan told me that there had been an investigation before the J.P.'s and that the case had been dismissed — but dismissed because the J.P.'s were afraid to commit Donnelly on account of the well-known character of the Donnelly tribe — that it was a very gross case and that justice would be defeated if a preliminary investigation were insisted on. And so, I reluctantly submitted the bill, and now it must take its course. From all that I can learn they are all a bad lot and a few months in gaol would do them all good.[39]

With Cameron's support, the indictment was presented before the Grand Jury, which returned a true bill on the charge, and, by ten o'clock that same evening, James Carroll had yet another warrant for the arrest of Tom Donnelly. Carroll rode over to the home of fellow Vigilance Committee member and Lucan constable William Hodgins, and told him of his plan to arrest Tom Donnelly the next morning. Hodgins may well have remembered the occasion when he had tried to do likewise and ended up having a shotgun aimed at him, and so he offered to tag along with Carroll to make the arrest. They believed that Tom was staying over at his brother William's house and, knowing how the Donnelly brothers always stood up for one another, neither wanted to risk any resistance to the capture, such as had occurred at Thomas Ryder's wedding reception.

Early the next morning, both men loaded their guns and rode out for William Donnelly's house at Whalen's Corners. William Donnelly was in the loft of his barn when the constables arrived around 8 a.m.[40] He had watched them ride in, secure their horses, and then meander about his property. He watched as they walked to his front door and heard them tell his wife Nora that they were looking for his brother Tom. And he continued to watch as they remounted and rode their horses north toward Usborne. William then left the barn, saddled up a mount of his own and rode south to warn his brother.[41] Mary Thompson (she of the chivaree and lost cow fame) saw William ride up to his parents' farm and head out into a potato field on the property where his brothers John and Tom were working.[42] William told his brothers that Carroll and Hodgins had been at his home that morning looking for Tom, and that the two constables would no doubt soon be coming for him here on the farm. William then climbed back into his saddle and rode home.

Upon leaving Usborne, Carroll and Hodgins rode their horses south along the Roman Line. They dropped in at James Maher's farm and shared breakfast with him before riding farther south to the farm of William and Mary Thompson, which sat on Lot 17, right next to the Donnellys' property. It was about eleven o'clock in the morning by this point. Looking onto the Donnelly property, the constables spotted Tom Donnelly working in his parents' field. Cautiously, like lions encircling their prey, the two men led their horses along a western lane that lay between the Thompson and Donnelly properties. According to Constable Hodgins, "We then left the horses tied and went to arrest him [Tom Donnelly] — Carroll went one way and I another. When I and Carroll parted, I went southwesterly to the woods — thinking to catch him there and cut off his escape."[43]

James Carroll, meanwhile, made his way onto the Donnelly property and reported what happened next:

> I crossed the fence into Mr. Donnelly's fields, and
> went across a fall wheat field expecting to get on
> [Tom Donnelly's] track to follow him up. I had not

gone a great distance when I saw Thomas Donnelly
going in the opposite direction to when I first saw
him. He did not go far when he commenced to run.
I then ran after him. John Donnelly could see me
chasing Thomas Donnelly all the time. John then
started to run towards the stable. I next saw John
come out with a horse — Sorrel in colour — short
ears and white face. Thomas Donnelly came up
running to where he was standing with the horse.
Thomas Donnelly got on the horse and rode away,
out to the road, then south on the road.[44]

Carroll was furious that Tom Donnelly had escaped — and that
John Donnelly had assisted him with the getaway. "You had no
business to give that horse to enable Thomas to escape from being
arrested!" Carroll yelled.[45] John Donnelly facetiously told him that
he had no idea what he was referring to; that his brother had merely
gone to Lucan to have his horse shoed at Thomas Kenny's blacksmith shop, and that Carroll should follow him there. "I will make
it hot for you when I get to Lucan!" said Carroll threateningly.[46]

Carroll quickly saddled up and rode out after Tom Donnelly, but
his prey was long gone. Hodgins, for his part, gathered together a
posse of sorts from a group of fellow Vigilance Committee members
who happened to be threshing in a nearby field.[47] A portion of this
group stayed behind to keep an eye on the Donnelly farmhouse if
Tom should return,[48] while the rest rode with Hodgins to scour the
surrounding countryside for him. James Carroll visited the places
where he believed Tom Donnelly might take refuge.

Later that day, all the search parties met up in front of William
Donnelly's house and conducted another search of his premises.
Then the posse stopped in at Edward Sutherby's blacksmith shop
at Whalen's Corners, presumably to ask him if he had seen Tom
Donnelly come or go from William Donnelly's house. These men,

the reader will recall, had invaded the smith's shop on a prior occasion when they were searching for William Thompson Jr.'s missing heifer. As that had come to nothing, Sutherby was growing somewhat exasperated by having gangs of men randomly bursting into his place of business and asking him questions about the Donnellys and various supposed crimes in the neighbourhood — particularly when whatever charges they brought against the Donnellys always seemed to end up being dismissed.

"Would it not be better for you to quit quarrelling with the Donnellys?" he asked.

Carroll almost spat out his answer. "I will have the Donnellys out of Biddulph if it costs me my life!"[49]

Carroll's hatred of the Donnelly family had now grown into an obsession worthy of Captain Ahab; his statement above had become his mantra. Unable to locate Tom Donnelly, the next day Carroll arrested John Donnelly on the charge of aiding a felon to escape from arrest.[50] Carroll had attempted to pump John for answers as to Tom Donnelly's whereabouts, but John was saying nothing. Further, John voiced his suspicions to Carroll about the latter's competency at his new job of constable; after all, Carroll had known that Tom was living with his parents, and yet he went to William Donnelly's house first. And then, rather than going directly to the Donnelly farm, Carroll went to Usborne for two hours.

"If you had come down early in the morning you might have got Tom quite easily before he knew anything about it," taunted John, before adding, "I am not afraid of this case. I will beat you on it."[51]

And John Donnelly had a point; almost immediately there were problems with the charge. Crown attorney Charles Hutchinson wrote Magistrate James Grant that Carroll had placed the cart before the horse; that John Donnelly could not have assisted a "felon to escape" unless Tom Donnelly had first been found guilty of the felony he was charged with.[52] It was looking like more like a persecution than a prosecution.

For six days, Tom Donnelly had successfully eluded the searches by Carroll, Hodgins and the members of the Vigilance Committee. However, on October 15, perhaps upon the recommendation of his brother William, he had decided that his best bet was to surrender to London sheriff William Glass (just as William had done after his role in the fracas at the Ryder wedding reception). The decision turned out to be a prudent one, as Tom Donnelly didn't have to wait long in jail. He was bailed out the same day by his father and the old farmer Mitchell Haskett.[53] Magistrate John Peters ordered Tom Donnelly to appear for trial at the next Assizes.

Meanwhile, the John Donnelly case was turning into a tire fire: he was bailed out on October 17, because there could be no trial on the charge of assisting a fugitive escape until Tom Donnelly had, in fact, been found to be a fugitive. Magistrate Grant released him on bail and put the matter over until October 23 in Middlesex County Court. Throughout the week, Vigilance Committee attorney John Blake worked feverishly to find any witnesses who could corroborate Ned Ryan's charge of robbery. None were acceptable to the Crown attorney.[54] On October 23, when there was still no indication of any progress in this regard, Crown attorney Hutchinson again released John Donnelly on bail and put his trial over until the next Assize.[55]

The fate of the Ned Ryan case was by now obvious even to its most ardent supporters: he was never going to get a conviction against Tom Donnelly. The case was silently dropped.[56] With the decision to abandon the larceny charge against Tom Donnelly, the charge against John Donnelly for helping his brother escape from being arrested was also dead in the water. James Carroll and the Vigilance Committee needed something else — but none of the Donnellys had broken any laws. The Committee required some sort of leverage to drive the family out of the township. After conferring about a next step, it occurred to one of the Committee members that, on a technicality, John Donnelly could be charged with perjury. After all, he had sworn under oath on September 20, 1879, before Lucan magistrate John Peters that the members of the Vigilance Committee had trespassed onto his father's property without permission. The recent ruling in the matter had clearly indicated that he was wrong, which was why his charge was dismissed. Swearing under oath to a falsehood was the very definition of perjury — and so it was decided that they would bring a new charge against John Donnelly on this very infraction.

Committee member Michael Blake, the brother of the Committee's attorney, John Blake, brought the new charge against John Donnelly before Magistrate William Stanley.[57] The case was tried on October 30, 1879, and five members of the Vigilance Committee spoke as one that they had heard not only John Donnelly, but also his father, grant them permission to search on the Donnelly property that fateful day in early September. While this was good, they needed the legal transcript of John Donnelly's testimony to the contrary in order to establish perjury, which they hadn't brought to court. Without it, their allegations were merely hearsay. Magistrate Stanley held off on rendering a verdict until he could consult with the Crown attorney. Hutchinson's recommendation was delivered to Magistrate Stanley in early November — John Donnelly should be acquitted:

> Dear Sir,
> Re: John Donnelly Perjury
>
> I have been from home or would have replied
> sooner. I have read the evidence in this case. I don't
> think you can properly commit the defendant on the
> evidence. . . . I think you had best dismiss the case.
>
> Yours truly,
> Charles Hutchinson, County Attorney[58]

Magistrate Stanley did just that. And John Donnelly was a free man — if only for another two weeks.

Father Connolly was livid at what he perceived to be the Lucan magistrate's miscarriage of justice. From his pulpit he again railed against the Lucan judiciary, calling them "perjurers" and pointing out the callous indifference they displayed to crime in the community.[59]

And while the Donnellys had not committed any crime in quite some time, criminal activity was ongoing in the region — even a random flip through the pages of the *London Free Press* between April and August 1879 would reveal the occurrence of assaults,[60] larceny[61] and drunk and disorderly conduct.[62] Such criminal activities, one might assume, should also have been addressed by Father Connolly from his pulpit, or one might assume that the perpetrators of these crimes would have been ardently pursued by new constables, such as James Carroll and his Vigilance Committee of thirty or forty men — given their pledge sheets and secret oaths sworn to eradicate crime in the area. However, none of the crimes indicated (or others that the author has left out) were deemed as important to the well-being of the residents of Middlesex County as was making a second attempt to convict John Donnelly for allegedly committing perjury during his trespass case against the Vigilance Committee members. Consequently, on November 20, 1879, James Carroll obtained a warrant from Magistrate James Grant and had John Donnelly arrested for the *second* time on the same charge. Only this time the complainant in the case would not be Ned Ryan or Michael Blake, but James Carroll himself.[63]

Five days later, John Donnelly and his accusers gathered in the courtroom before magistrate James Grant. Vigilance Committee members John Kennedy Jr., William Thompson Jr., Michael Blake, James Maher and James Carroll were then called upon to give testimony that John Donnelly had lied under oath when he claimed that they, and the group they were with, had trespassed upon his property. However, where in the previous trial they had overlooked bringing in the original court transcript of John Donnelly's testimony, this time around they had looked for it but couldn't find it. Magistrate Grant wrote to Crown attorney Hutchinson, indicating that he had believed that the transcript had been filed at Hutchinson's office and that he would await word back from the Crown attorney before passing sentence in the matter. Magistrate Grant then ordered John Donnelly to post bail until a trial could be set to take place in the courthouse in London.[64]

When Charles Hutchinson learned that John Donnelly would soon be brought to court for a third time — on the same charge — he sent off a letter to Grant expressing his concerns:

> It matters not who brought the charge of perjury —
> whether Carroll or somebody else — the fact is that
> Donnelly has been subjected twice to prosecution
> before a magistrate on the same charge. I do not say
> this is illegal, but I do say it is inadmissible unless
> there are very particular circumstances to justify
> it, which I do not think exist in this case. I think
> you had no right to accept oral evidence or copies
> of examinations in lieu of the original documents.
> The only legal evidence of Donnelly's oath and
> testimony where the alleged perjury was committed,
> is the original deposition signed by him, and attested
> by the Justice of the Peace — you had no right to
> convict in the absence of the original deposition. I
> am not aware of the examinations being filed in my
> office. They have no occasion to be so, as it is not
> necessary, nor is it the practice for magistrates to
> return examinations when cases are dismissed.
> There will be no possibility of proceeding with
> this case vs Donnelly, without the original sworn

deposition on which the prosecution is based — and it is your duty to see that it is returned to me, and filed with the other papers in the case.

Truly yours,
Charles Hutchinson, County Attorney[65]

While the Committee's efforts to convict the Donnellys in court had stalled, its members now ramped up their campaign to ostracize the Donnelly family from the community. According to William Donnelly,

First-class neighbours that we had before this would not come near the house nor "neighbour" with my father's family in any way. On one occasion two neighbours went to collect oats for the priest and called at every house on the Roman Line except my father's. I considered they were afraid of the Vigilance Committee and also that Father Connolly wished them to keep away from us. Many a time I have seen my poor old mother sit down and cry on account of the way the family were being treated. She often used to say she thought the people were afraid of the priest, and for that reason kept away from her and the rest of us.[66]

And it continued: James Feeheley was warned not to be seen in the company of the Donnellys;[67] the Kennedy sisters were ignored at a local dance by the members of the Vigilance Committee owing to their sister Nora's marriage to William Donnelly;[68] a farmer who was to breed his mare with William Donnelly's stallion was threatened by John Kennedy Jr.;[69] a friend of the Donnellys received a letter threatening that his livestock would be shot if non-Committee members were seen in his home.[70] And, of course, Father Connolly had started his own campaign within St. Patrick's parish to discourage any of his congregation from socializing with the Donnellys.

It must be remembered how severe such a censure was in small communities in the nineteenth century. The local church was the hub of community activity — it brought people together in marriage and buried them in death; it brought comfort to the afflicted and direction to the despondent. It was also where people went to have their social opinions formed — it was, particularly in the 1800s, their Facebook, Twitter, Instagram, CNN or Fox News, radio and Google, all rolled into one. Consequently, if the parish priest spoke ill of someone or some family, then that family was immediately considered to be outcasts and pariahs. And this is exactly what had happened to the Donnelly family since Father Connolly's arrival in Biddulph. One of the local papers summarized the ostracism of the family thusly: "It appears that they [the Donnellys] have been denounced from the Altar as outlaws, not only as civil but divine outlaws."[71]

And when the priest's views were reinforced by a Committee that was essentially a private militia unit, even those who knew better eventually came around to the more official line of thinking. With each passing week, the Donnellys became more and more isolated, while their neighbours within the community gradually began to welcome and encourage their eradication. Perhaps it was *schadenfreude*: the Donnellys had had it too good for too long; they didn't tip their hat to anyone — even the parish priest — and went about their business as if they didn't have to follow the same rules as everybody else. For as long as people could remember, the Donnelly family had always been independent, self-motivated and self-confident. The children had survived without a father in their home for seven years and had built a rather prosperous farm largely on their own. They then went on to start a successful stagecoach line from scratch. The boys were very popular with the local girls and always wore the best clothes. Many, if not most, of the local boys (and men) were scared to fight with them. The law didn't seem to apply to them, and they seemed to possess no fear of it. Now, however, the tide had turned, and the Donnellys were revealed to have gotten a little too big for their britches. They needed a strong lesson in humility. Or so the Vigilance Committee and a growing number of their neighbours believed.

This pervading attitude was not lost on the brighter of the Donnelly children. When Patrick Donnelly, now living in Thorold, Ontario, had returned home for a visit, he immediately picked up on the prevailing sentiment that was being directed at his family from the community . . . and it worried him. He suggested that perhaps it might be a good idea for his parents to move from the region. But neither his father nor his mother had any intention to move. They had been through too much and had worked too hard to make the land they lived on their own. Besides, where would they go at this stage in their lives? The only other property they owned outside of Biddulph was in Michigan — a piece of land they had inherited from their son Jim Donnelly upon his passing — and neither James nor Johannah had any intention of moving to the United States.[72] Besides, they weren't going to be run off by the likes of James Carroll and his cronies, particularly when they hadn't done anything wrong. Patrick was still concerned about the matter when he arrived back at his home in Thorold. He put pen to paper and wrote to his parents, stating his fear that something bad was going to happen to them if they didn't vacate the area.[73]

William Donnelly thought it might be wise for his parents to take out extra insurance on their property. His father shook his head; nobody was going to burn them out — he'd shoot them before they could strike the match required to do it. To underscore his seriousness about the matter he then proceeded to show William his arsenal — a shotgun, a rifle and two revolvers, all of them loaded.[74] This was unsettling to William; in all the years he had lived in Biddulph, he had never known his father to sleep with loaded guns in the house. There was clearly a dark sense of fore-boding that had now descended upon his family — and William wanted no part of it:

> I wrote to Father Flannery,[75] of St. Thomas, telling him of all the trouble, and how Father Connolly was opposed to us through the influence of our enemies. And saying I was tired of Biddulph, and would be very thankful to him if he would use his influence in getting me work elsewhere, no matter how humble it might be. Father Flannery answered the letter very kindly, saying that he would give me a recommendation whenever I required it. He added that he was sorry my enemies had caused such an ill feeling between Father Connolly and I.[76]

And while William was looking to move out of town, James Donnelly Sr. felt protected — not only by his guns, but by his sons. Thomas and John were living with him, William was but three miles away, and Patrick and Michael were close enough that they could be home within twenty-four hours if required. Besides, Bob's sentence was due to end in a few months, and he wouldn't allow anything untoward to beset the family. James Donnelly further believed that he still had enough friends in the community who would forewarn him if anything violent was heading his way. Nobody was going to run him off his land.

CHAPTER FOURTEEN

DEATH AND LIBERATION

Mike Donnelly in his early twenties, about the time he married Ellen Hines.
(By permission of Ray Fazakas, author of *The Donnelly Album*
and *In Search of the Donnellys*)

On the evening of September 15, 1885, Special Freight No. 151, drawn by locomotive No. 88, was heading west at a good clip along the Grand Trunk Railway line. It would shortly pass St. Thomas station. At approximately 9:30 p.m., the engineer, William Burnip, took a look out at the track that stretched on in front of him and, it's safe to assume, the last thing in the world he expected to see was the rear end of an elephant. But there it was: an elephant (and it was said to be the biggest one in the world) running away from him, westbound on the Grand Trunk Railway line. Burnip immediately whistled for his brakemen to turn the big handwheels at the end of each boxcar to stop, or at least to slow, the progress of the locomotive, while he pulled hard on the Johnson bar in an attempt to drive the engine into reverse. But it was too late — he had come upon the beast too quickly. The train collided with the animal with such force that both the engine and one boxcar were knocked clean off the tracks. Jumbo the elephant, late of his triumphs as a performer in Barnum & Bailey's Circus, and of his being a former royal amusement in London, England (where he used to give rides to Queen Victoria's children, as well as future dignitaries and statesmen such as Theodore Roosevelt and Winston Churchill), died ten minutes later.[1]

The city of St. Thomas, where this tragedy took place, would, for some reason, later come to embrace its macabre connection to Jumbo the elephant, erecting a four-metre-high, thirty-eight-ton statue to the memory of the poor creature. Even today, tourists to the city are invited to "Come and take your picture with a life-sized statue of the most famous elephant in the world! Jumbo, 'The King of Elephants!'"[2] However, the identity of St. Thomas, Ontario, hadn't always been known as the death site of the world's biggest pachyderm.

It used to be known as "Railway City," and a weather-beaten highway sign just as you enter the region gives some faded evidence of this, declaring St. Thomas to be "The Railway Capital of Canada." It's hard to envision this now, as weeds and goldenrod currently grow through the rusted railway tracks of St. Thomas, obscuring its once-mighty role in the iron horse trade. At its peak, however, St. Thomas was considered the axis point of several prominent railway lines, which facilitated an easy and direct transportation of goods and materials between Canada and the United States. The city further served as the primary stop on the shortcut between Detroit, Michigan, and Buffalo, New York. Over eight different railway lines once ran through St. Thomas, bringing in more than 100 trains a day.[3] St. Thomas had grown along with the railway: founded in 1810, it achieved village status in 1852, town status in 1861 and, finally, city status in 1881.[4]

It was, in fact, its status as the Railway Capital of Canada that had prompted the Canada Southern Railway (CSR) to make St. Thomas the site of its headquarters. This, in itself, drew more people to the town who sought jobs in the railway industry or within the multitude of businesses that grew out of it.[5] In other words, if you wanted to work in the railway industry in Canada, St. Thomas was where you wanted to be.

When Mike Donnelly had taken a job as a brakeman for the CSR, it made sense for him and his family to move to St. Thomas. He hadn't regretted the move. Indeed, things had been looking up for Mike Donnelly ever since he had arrived there in early 1878. The headquarters of the Canada Southern Railway (CASO Station) were conveniently located just a mile and a bit north from his home on Fifth Avenue. And it was an impressive headquarters, having been designed in an Italianate style by the Canadian architect Edgar Berryman. The building was 354 feet long by 36 feet wide, and boasted two levels — the bottom level was the train station proper, which allowed for entrance and egress of the passengers from the trains that came into the station, while the upper level housed the CSR headquarters. The ceilings in both levels were the better part of twenty feet high. Over 160 windows brought sunlight into the building and over 400,000 bricks went into its construction. Of all the CSR's railway stations (and there were thirty-one of them built across the province), the St. Thomas station was the largest.[6] All in all, it was an impressive step up from the farmers' fields of Biddulph Township for Mike Donnelly. And, given the town's two schools, fire brigade and easy and convenient access to almost any place in Ontario via the railway, it looked to be a pretty good place to raise a family. This was important to Mike and Ellen, as, in addition to their daughter Kate, the family had increased in April 1879 with the addition of a son, James Michael Donnelly.

Unlike his parents back in Biddulph, Mike and his family were popular with their St. Thomas neighbours and coworkers.[7] Mike had done well with the railroad, working as a brakeman for the Canadian Southern Railway, a dangerous job to be certain, but one at which he excelled. The job required him to walk along the tops of the boxcars as the train was moving to check the couplings and turn the handwheels that would apply the brakes when needed; a sudden shift or pitch of the train had sent many an ambitious brakeman fourteen feet down to his death between the wheels of trains over the years, but Mike Donnelly was strong and sure-footed enough to have escaped this fate, even when the walkways atop the trains had been covered with ice during the winter months.

He had put all that Biddulph nonsense behind him several years ago, and was, it seemed, enjoying himself. This is not to suggest he had mellowed at all; he'd had a few fistfights since coming to work for the railroad, certainly enough for his fellow railwaymen to have assessed him as a "good fighter."[8] But these fights had been unavoidable, as the railway workers were hard men who only respected and obeyed the orders of other hard men. But shy of these very infrequent bouts, Mike Donnelly's rough stuff was all in the past.

In fact, this author could find only one instance of him having settled a matter with his fists since moving to St. Thomas, and that was when he had come to the aid of a friend and co-worker who was being hassled by two railway workers. The co-worker, James Muir, had backed his train into the depot but had accidentally backed it up too far, causing the rear wheels of the locomotive to slip off the tracks. Muir was immediately confronted about the mishap by a man named Tom Tremellon, who was the boss of one of the railway labour crews. Soon Tremellon was joined by a man named Greenwood, and the talk became heated. This caught the ear of Mike Donnelly, who came to the scene to defend Muir. Donnelly was arguing with Tremellon about the incident, when Greenwood stepped forth and said something. Whatever he said, Donnelly's response was to slap him hard across the face. Neither Greenwood nor Tremellon said anything more. The situation was defused. Greenwood, however, had a roommate who also worked for the railway, twenty-two-year-old William Lewis, an American who was employed as a labourer on one of the construction crews of the railway line. When he learned what Mike Donnelly had done in his defence of Muir, Lewis declared that if he had been there he would have thrown Muir into the gravel pit. He berated his friend for allowing Donnelly's slap in the face to go unanswered. He vowed that if his friend was unwilling to do anything about it, then he would.[9] Mike Donnelly was unaware of his threat, of course, and probably wouldn't have cared even if he had been made aware of it.

Mike Donnelly's job required a fair bit of travel along the CSR line, with stopover destinations being any one of the many towns that dotted its route from Niagara-on-the-Lake in the northeast to Windsor in the southwest.[10] On December 9, 1879, Donnelly's train pulled into the station at Waterford, a village which sat about fifty miles east of St. Thomas. It had started to rain on this day — an anomaly for the month of December in Southwestern Ontario, when snow is the typical form of precipitation. As a result of the rain, several of the railway workers had decided to call it an early day and headed off to knock back a few drinks at Slaght's Hotel, which was the village watering hole.[11] Donnelly happened to be boarding at Slaght's, and so the idea appealed to him. He told his friends and fellow railway employees James Muir and James Marrs that he would meet them in the hotel's tavern.

William Lewis was also in Waterford. Like the others, he had decided to head over to Slaght's. He left his boarding house and was already drinking in the hotel bar by 6 p.m. that evening. According to James Marrs, there were about five or six people at the bar when Mike Donnelly walked in. He spotted a coworker, Francis Perry, and called out, "Let's have a bowl!" The two men then stepped up to the bar and ordered their drinks. While they were waiting, Mike struck up a conversation with some of the local patrons, one of whom was an older man whom he had never seen before. The old man was a harmless drunk, but with a sharp sense of humour that

Mike found appealing. As they conversed, Marrs drank a glass of beer while William Lewis threw back a shot of whiskey and closely observed Mike Donnelly and the old man. The old man boasted that he "had lots of money to lose" and proposed a bet. Mike laughed and took his watch out of his pocket and held it up in his hand.

"I have no money to bet, but I'll put my watch up," he said, still not sure what he was betting on.

"I have a dog that could whip any dog in Ontario!" the old man exclaimed.

Mike was quite fond of dogs, and had a bulldog of his own back at his home in St. Thomas. "I have a bulldog that could whip any dog of his own weight in Ontario," he replied.

The old man shrugged. "I have no dog at all," he confessed. Mike was bemused and had no idea where this conversation was going now. "But I could myself whip any dog," the old man added, and then inquired, "Do you want to know how?"

Mike Donnelly took a sip of his drink and widened his eyes, communicating to the old-timer to continue. "I'd take my clothes off — a dog will not fight a person with his clothes off." Mike laughed, and then added, "Well, if you can't lick my dog you could not lick his master," and then finished off his drink.

The next thing Mike Donnelly knew, William Lewis was standing next to him at the bar. "You don't want to hop onto that man," he said, a hint of a threat in his voice.

Mike looked at the old man and then turned to Lewis. "I don't know that anyone wants to *hop onto* him," he said, before adding, "and I didn't know that it is any of your business."

"You're always shooting off your mouth," Lewis said.

Mike, who didn't know Lewis, now caught the drift of where this was going. He removed his jacket. "Do you want something of me?"

Lewis's eyes narrowed. "You don't want anything of me," he said.

"I don't know that you could hinder me," Mike said. Lewis suddenly moved to throw a punch, but Donnelly trapped Lewis's wrist with one hand and grabbed him by the throat with the other. He then proceeded to walk Lewis hard into a wall in the tavern. James Marrs quickly stepped between the two men and told them there was no need for any trouble. Lewis glared at Donnelly, who gradually released his hold, and, turning his back on Lewis, returned to the bar. He had barely started a conversation with another man at the bar when Lewis marched up behind Donnelly and struck him in the back of the head. Enraged, Mike Donnelly wheeled and grabbed Lewis by the coat, spinning him with some force into the wall behind the bar. Donnelly had hold of Lewis with both hands. And that's when he felt the steel blade of the knife enter his body.

William Lewis had unfolded the blade of his pocket knife prior to approaching Mike Donnelly at the bar and, as soon as both Mike's hands had grabbed hold of him, he had reached into his pocket and pulled the weapon out, driving it into the femoral vein of Donnelly's right upper thigh, near the groin. The knife opened a one-inch wound in the vein and continued to travel upwards into Donnelly's abdomen.[12] Lewis withdrew his knife and a cascade of blood followed its removal. Still holding on to his adversary, Mike Donnelly looked down to see a steady flow of crimson now issuing from his groin area. He also saw the blade of the knife in Lewis's hand and knew he wasn't long for this world. He released his grip, turned and steadied himself on the bar.

James Marrs now ran to him. "My God, neighbour," Mike said through laboured breaths, "I'm stabbed." Marrs was now joined by James Muir. Both men tried to assure him that he would be all right. Mike looked at his two friends. "Boys, I am gone," he said.[13] His breathing suddenly became laboured. Mike pushed himself away from the bar and, with his two friends closely in tow, slowly shuffled toward the tavern washroom. He kept his feet until he reached the washroom door. There he collapsed into his friends' arms, who then carried him into the washroom and laid him down upon its floor. Somebody ran for the nearest doctor, Alexander Duncombe, who was on the scene within ten minutes — but by then Mike Donnelly was dead.

With the knife still in his hand, William Lewis stayed at the bar until the news of Donnelly's death was confirmed. Then he left the building and returned to his boarding house, where he encountered fellow railway man Robert Brooks. "I had a row with Donnelly — and I fixed him," he said.

"A row?" asked Brooks. "About what?"

Lewis ignored the question and pulled out the bloody knife. "This is the thing that did the business."

Brooks immediately left for Slaght's Hotel. In the meantime, Charles and Freeman Slaght, the bartender and owner of the hotel, respectively, ran to inform Constable Thomas Henry about the killing. The constable picked up two associates and then proceeded to where Lewis was boarding. According to Constable Henry,

> I found him at Mrs. Best's sitting down to his supper. Garlow was with me. Sandford went behind and took hold of him. He wanted to know "what this was for?" I told him "for stabbing Donnelly." He said, going up to the lock up, "it was done in my own defence." I think he said, "it was not more than he deserved."[14]

William Lewis was arrested and his trial scheduled for May 1880 at the Norfolk County Spring Assizes, where Justice Matthew Crooks Cameron would preside.

The news of Mike Donnelly's death was telegraphed to both his wife, Ellen, in St. Thomas, and to his family in Biddulph. The news was crushing to the late man's parents and siblings. Ellen was devastated. Her children, fortunately, were too young to comprehend the severity of what had happened to their father. With all the negative things that had been happening to the Donnellys in Biddulph, Mike's death represented a further piling-on to the already wounded soul of his family. Luckily, Mike had joined the Order of Foresters shortly after he had moved his family to St. Thomas — an organization that provided life insurance to the widows and orphans of its members. Ellen was thus able to claim $1,200 after her husband's death from his policy.[15] While the money would certainly help short-term with the financial burden Ellen now faced in raising her children alone, it did nothing to reduce the magnitude of her loss.

Mike Donnelly's corpse was taken to London, and then to Clandeboye, by train. There it was placed on a wagon and driven to his parents' farmhouse on the Roman Line where they laid his body upon his mother and father's bed for the wake prior to burial. The wake brought many friends into the Donnelly home: the O'Connors, the Kents, the Keefes, some of the Feeheleys and other neighbours and family came and went from the house. Mike's brother Patrick arrived from Thorold and his sister Jennie from Glencoe, where they joined with James, Johannah, William, John and Tom to honour the memory of the fifth child of the family. Only Bob was missing, which agonized Bob, but there was no way the authorities in Kingston would release him from the penitentiary, even on the grounds of compassion, to attend his brother's funeral.

And while he wouldn't dare attend either Mike Donnelly's wake or funeral, County Constable James Carroll nevertheless watched with intense interest the goings-on at the Donnelly farmhouse during this period. For a better view, he stayed the night on the upper level of the residence of fellow Vigilance Committee member William Thompson Jr.,[16] where a window faced south toward the Donnelly farmhouse. It was important for him to observe who was sympathetic to the Donnellys, and so he watched. And watched.

At 11:30 a.m. on December 12, 1879, Mike Donnelly was laid to rest next to the body of his late brother Jim in St. Patrick's cemetery. According to the Lucan postmaster, William Porte, it was a large funeral. Porte also felt compelled to note that most of the attendees that day were Protestants.[17] Be that as it may, the funeral service was performed by no less a Catholic than Father John Connolly. It marked his first direct contact with the Donnelly family since visiting with them on their farm almost a year before. He must have been sympathetic, because Tom Donnelly asked to see him for a word after the service. The priest listened to the young man, who, shattered by his older brother's death, was willing to do whatever was necessary to get right with the Church. But Tom may have had an additional reason to seek counselling, for he had received news that on December 7, 1879, seventeen-year-old Flora McKinnon, from Ekfrid Township, had given birth to his son.[18] Tom, of course, wasn't married, and had no desire to spend the rest of his life with Flora. There would later surface a report that Tom had once intended to marry a girl (perhaps upon discovering that she was pregnant) and had even received two hundred dollars from her family to follow through with it; however, he never did.[19] It's entirely possible that Tom Donnelly did not believe that the girl had been pregnant with his child, and, thus, had backed out of the arrangement. However, Flora McKinnon's father would go on to register the name of the newborn child as Tom Donnelly Jr., and cite the father as being one Tom Donnelly, a farmer from Biddulph, which narrowed the odds of it being anyone else's child but Tom's down to zero.

It's not known if this subject was broached with Father Connolly during this meeting, but it certainly would have been weighing heavily on twenty-five-year-old Tom Donnelly's mind around this time. Many of his problems in the past were a direct result of drinking, he told the priest, and Father Connolly offered the youngest Donnelly son the opportunity to join his Temperance Society, to change his ways, to start heading in the right direction and to get closer to God. Tom accepted his offer, and both men left their meeting feeling better about their respective futures in Biddulph.[20]

James's and Johannah's relationship with Father Connolly also had improved since the funeral; at least they were speaking with the priest now, and were partaking of the sacrament of communion within St. Patrick's.[21] Indeed, on Christmas Eve, James and Johannah Donnelly went to confession at St. Patrick's and afterwards Father Connolly had invited Johannah into his office to speak with her privately:

> For two hours she was in my office on Christmas
> Eve, giving me the history of her whole life in
> Biddulph. She received the Sacrament, and the last
> words she spoke to me as she went away were,
> "Father Connolly, I am going to get not only my
> boys, but all Biddulph boys to reform."[22]

Such good Christian fellowship between the family and the priest was welcomed by the Donnellys, but it posed a serious problem for the Vigilance Committee. Their mission had been to drive the Donnelly family out of Biddulph, and this desire had gained some serious traction of late. William and Tom's unanticipated feud with Father Connolly had bolstered their cause over the past year. This had been augmented when John Donnelly had exchanged harsh words with the priest while in court. This falling out between the priest and some Donnelly family members had played into the Vigilance Committee's hands, imbuing their vendetta against the family with almost a divine purpose. The Committee, then, had been counting on Father Connolly continuing to back their play with regard to the family: to continue to brand them all as evil and demand that they be driven from the neighbourhood.

But now, inexplicably, Tom and John were part of the priest's Temperance Society and the Father had welcomed the parents back into the church. The priest actually seemed pleased that he had turned a corner with the Donnellys, which meant that all the poison the Committee had laid down about the family was now being diluted; their efforts were losing ground. This goodwill and fellowship had to stop. The Donnellys were weaker now as a group: Jim was dead, Mike was dead, and they had never been more vulnerable. Now was the time to increase the pressure on them, not welcome them back into the fold. The inner sanctum of the Vigilance Committee, men like Carroll, Thompson and Kennedy, needed to figure out what their next step was going to be in order to get their pet project back on track. And they needed to do it quickly.

The loss of Mike had seriously weakened the Donnelly family, not only reducing their number but taking a devastating toll on them emotionally as well. Christmas 1879 had been a particularly tough time in this respect as it was the one time of the year when all the Donnelly family members made the effort to come together under one roof. Mike's absence was felt particularly keenly then. Perhaps to mitigate their suffering somewhat, an old family friend, the London constable Harry Phair, had presented James Donnelly Sr. with a little bulldog puppy as a gift (the dog may well have been the one owned by Mike Donnelly). James Donnelly welcomed the new addition into the family home and named him Jack. The puppy was immediately showered with affection, not least of all from Jennie, the family's only daughter.[23] Four days later, however, sadness crept back into the family home when the Donnellys' long-standing houseguest, Cornelius Maloney, passed away. His wake was held within the Donnelly farmhouse, as Mike Donnelly's had been three weeks earlier.[24] The Donnellys could be forgiven if they felt that their home had seen enough death for a while.

The Vigilance Committee decided that they needed to take stock: they had two constables in their group, Carroll and Hodgins; an excellent lawyer in John Blake; and a sympathetic magistrate in Granton J.P. James Grant. But even with all this legal firepower at their disposal, they had thus far come up empty-handed in securing any meaningful convictions against the Donnellys. Indeed, the best they could muster was to have their cases put over to a future date rather than suffer the indignity of an outright acquittal. This was where the problem lay. They needed a magistrate who would do his job properly: one who would be willing to do what *they* told him to do. The Vigilance Committee held a meeting to nominate one of their members to serve as Justice of the Peace. William Casey, best known for his unpunished role in the Brimmacombe murder, seemed to them a worthy candidate to sit in judgement of criminal activity.[25] And by the end of December, Casey had been sworn in and the Committee had their own magistrate.[26] They now had a means to arrest, a means to prosecute and a means to convict at their beck and call. This meant they could abandon their previous tack of attempting to re-prosecute old cases against the Donnellys in favour of finding new crimes with which to charge them. And two weeks later they believed they had found just such a crime that would allow them to make full use of the legal machine they now had at their command.

B ob Donnelly sat within his two-and-a-half-by-eight-foot cell. He was wearing his winter-issue prison uniform — half green, half yellow. His hair was cropped short. His cell was unlit. He hadn't had many visitors over the past twenty months, and that was fine by him. He hated visitors — people feeling sorry for him or family members who would show up for an hour and then leave for months. In prison you had to put all the things you loved out of your mind and keep them there, as thinking about them would drive you into a deep depression, and depression was viewed as a weakness when you were behind bars. It was better not to have visitors — particularly family visitors — at all. Letters were similarly a waste of time. However, there was one thing happening within the penitentiary that had allowed Bob Donnelly to possess some small glimmer of hope for an early release. Kingston had incorporated a new system — "remission" — which could see months trimmed off a prison sentence in response to an inmate's good behaviour while they were behind the wall. According to Cameron Willis, the operations supervisor for Canada's penitentiary museum,

> Basically, every inmate was given a certain amount of days off their full sentence — so if you were sentenced to a minimum two years, 730 days, the earliest you could be released would be after 585 days or so. Prisoners accumulated "good time" at the rate of six days a month until they had a total of seventy-two days. At that point, they began to earn remission at the rate of ten days a month. No inmate earned remission while in the punishment cell, and they earned only half remission (for conduct) while in the hospital. Any offences against the rules and regulations could result in days of remission being taken away — it was not unusual for prisoners caught talking or with contraband to lose a day or two.[27]

It was the introduction of "remission" into Kingston Penitentiary that did what John Donnelly's petitions did not — get Bob Donnelly out of prison early. He had accumulated enough "good time" during the course of his sentence to be released four months early. During the twenty months he had thus far been incarcerated, he had never once caused a problem. Unlike his father, who had been incarcerated in Kington in the 1850s, Bob was never once written up in the punishment register. He never got out of work because he was sick, and never once spoke to any fellow inmate when he wasn't supposed to. He ate the slop — meals of brown bread; stews made from potatoes, carrots and turnips — for the better part of two years and said nothing. He endured two "Christmas" celebrations while in prison, so called because the inmates got to eat puddings, turkey or goose, and specially prepared vegetables for one day only, as if that were a viable substitute for not seeing one's family during that time of year. He performed the hard labour — blacksmithing, construction, breaking rocks, tailoring, farming, roofing and excavation — as all healthy prisoners were supposed to do, and he did it to the best of his ability, which was considerable owing to his strength. He was up and at attention every morning at 6:30 a.m. and spent only a few hours each day outside his cell for work — less in the winter months when work availability diminished owing to the severity of the weather and lack of available light. Despite being innocent of the crime of which he had been convicted, he never once pitied himself; all he wanted was to do his time and get out.[28] This was reflected in the terseness of his answers during his prison exit interview, conducted on January 7, 1880. A sample of his responses include:

> *Is the conduct of the Officers and others employed*
> *in the Institution humane and kind toward the*
> *prisoners?*
> Yes. Mr. Stewart is not, however, so kind as he
> might be.[29]

> *What do you think is the greatest privation that*
> *prisoners are subjected to in the Penitentiary?*
> Liberty.

> *Do you think that the fear of confinement in prison*
> *or in the Penitentiary is sufficient to deter from crime?*
> Yes.

> *What kind of punishment is, in your opinion,*
> *most efficient in maintaining the discipline of the*
> *Institution?*

The cats [cat o'nine tails].³⁰

*What effect does the presence of visitors produce on
the prisoners?*
Do not like to see them.

*Do the prisoners hold conversation among
themselves, and where is the most convenient place
for conversing without being discovered?*
Yes.

*Did you receive a good religious education when
you were a child?*
Yes.

*How did you obtain your livelihood before being
sent to the Penitentiary, and what do you propose
doing after you are liberated?*
By farming. Same.

*What has been the general cause of your misfortunes
and what has been the immediate cause of the crime
for which you have been sent to the Penitentiary?*
Not guilty. No cause.

*How often have you conversed with your clergyman
in the Penitentiary on religious subjects and during
the time of your confinement here have you made
any progress in your religious instructions?*
About six times. Yes.

*Do you think that your imprisonment in the
Penitentiary has been beneficial to you in a moral*

and religious point of view and that you are better
qualified to earn a livelihood now than before you
entered the Institution?
Yes. Yes.[31]

Three days after his interview, on January 10, 1880, Bob Donnelly walked out of Kingston Penitentiary.[32] He exited the institution from the North Gate and headed toward the train station; his pace may have quickened at the thought of being reunited with his siblings and parents in Biddulph the next morning. Physically, he had been liberated; "the cats" had never once touched his flesh during the twenty months of the sentence he served. But he was about to enter a period of his life that would ultimately scar him in a way that Kingston Penitentiary and all its punishments could never approximate.

His visit home was understandably emotional but surprisingly brief. After visiting with his parents and brothers, he undoubtedly then paid his respects at the gravesite of his late brother Mike. He was spotted briefly in Lucan by the postmaster William Porte,[33] and then Bob and his wife Annie headed thirty-seven miles southwest to Glencoe, where they could visit with Bob's sister Jennie, her husband James Currie (Annie's brother) and their children (Robert, Johannah and James), and where they would live for the next several months. Bob, like Patrick, had put Biddulph behind him.

CHAPTER FIFTEEN

THE NIGHT PAT RYDER'S BARN WENT UP IN FLAMES

The Donnelly Schoolhouse, where the Keefe/Quigley wedding took place on the Roman Line. (By permission of Ray Fazakas, author of *The Donnelly Album* and *In Search of the Donnellys*)

Grouchy Ryder watched as three of his children — twenty-three-year-old James, twenty-year-old Patrick Jr. and eighteen-year-old Mary — dressed up in their finest clothes and headed out of the house and across the road to attend the afternoon wedding of a popular local couple: Martha Keefe and Michael Quigley.[1] The date was Wednesday, January 14, 1880, and the wedding was set to take place within the Donnelly schoolhouse with the reception to follow at the farm of the bride's father, Robert Keefe Sr.

The Donnelly brothers, William, John and Tom, had been invited to the wedding, but at this point, so soon after the death of their brother Mike, none of them felt much like celebrating.[2]

Besides, there would also be guests there, such as James Ryder, who were members of the Vigilance Committee — or, if not members, were at least sympathetic to their cause — and the presence of such people at the festivities would do little to lighten the Donnelly brothers' mood. At one o'clock that afternoon, Bridget O'Connor arrived at the Donnelly farmhouse. Bridget and her parents, Michael and Mary, and siblings, Mary, Thomas, Johnny and Patrick, had been long-time friends of the Donnellys. Bridget, at age seventeen, had already proven herself to be a talented seamstress, and would lend her talents to the Donnelly family from time to time. Her thirteen-year-old brother Johnny was also popular with the family, always available to help them out at the farm. Michael O'Connor was a good man to know as well, as he ran an illegal alcohol dispensary out of his home in Lucan. This made him popular in some quarters, but he also had incurred the wrath of some others in the community who were of a more puritan bent over his side business.[3] Bridget was visiting the Donnelly home on this day to deliver two petticoats she had made for James Donnelly's niece, Bridget Donnelly.[4]

Like the brothers, both Bridgets were wondering if they should attend the wedding. Given that the venue was the Donnelly Schoolhouse, which was no more than a stone's throw from the Donnelly home, its proximity, as well as its social component, was tempting. Ultimately, however, both girls decided they would just stay home.[5] The Donnelly brothers, on the other hand, eventually decided the wedding might be a good thing to break them out of their funk. Besides, their friend, Thomas Keefe, would be attending, and his sense of humour always made them laugh, and laughter had been a commodity that had been in short supply of late. The boys finally got dressed and headed across their front yard to the schoolhouse. They would be returning home late from the reception, and since Thomas Keefe would be with them, they most likely wouldn't be back until sometime the next morning.

James Donnelly, meanwhile, had been feeling under the weather for the past two weeks and had developed a chronic cough.[6] Consequently, he was going nowhere that evening and probably would be retiring early. Johannah occupied herself by knitting some socks.[7] Once it got dark, Bridget O'Connor was invited to spend the night, which gave the two younger women time to talk about the goings-on within the community and any future plans they might have. In time, the topic of the Quigley-Ryder wedding came up, and both women seemed pleased that the Donnelly brothers had gone to the event.

"They're having a good time at the wedding," O'Connor stated.

Bridget Donnelly smiled and nodded in the affirmative. "They *are* having a good time," she replied.[8]

Bridget Donnelly then baked some cakes and the foursome shared tea[9] prior to turning in at eleven o'clock that evening.[10] The wedding guests by this time were half a mile up the road at Robert Keefe's farm celebrating the wedding reception. Despite their earlier misgivings, the Donnelly boys were actually enjoying themselves. Patrick Ryder Jr. returned home sometime after midnight, followed sometime later by his siblings Mary and James.[11] Despite the slow but steady departure of the wedding guests, the reception would continue until the better part of 4 a.m. that morning. It was at that time that Thomas Keefe noticed a strange light flickering over the horizon from somewhere south on the Roman Line: "They were dancing at the time I saw the fire."[12]

Grouchy Ryder's barn was ablaze. Once the wedding guests recognized what was happening, the reception ended. Grouchy Ryder, already awakened by the light of the fire, hurried outside with his son, Morris, to assist their livestock out of the barn and away from the flames: "I ran out as soon as I could get dressed. I ran to the stable and called to let out the horses and cattle. . . . The first person I saw after going out to the fire was my son, Morris, who was engaged in driving out the cattle from the burning buildings."[13]

According to Bridget O'Connor, James Donnelly was the first of the Donnelly family to see the blaze: "Mr. Donnelly got up first; I heard him get up a little after four o'clock in the morning. I heard a wagon pass as the clock struck four. . . . As the wagon was passing, the dog barked loudly for some time . . . light came in at the window. Mr. Donnelly came in and said, 'The schoolhouse is on fire!'"[14]

The two girls got out of bed and ran to the window. Both Bridget and James Donnelly initially thought the fire was coming from the schoolhouse, but Bridget O'Connor pointed out the smoke was rising above the schoolhouse, which meant its source was behind it, somewhere across the road, perhaps at Pat Ryder's farm.[15] James Donnelly agreed. "It's Mr. Ryder's — his fine building is gone!"[16] But the damage was much greater than that; not only had Pat Ryder's barn gone up in flames, but also his granary, his sheds and his entire harvest from the fall, which included fifteen tons of hay, twelve hundred bushels of oats and four hundred bushels of barley and wheat.[17]

Patrick Ryder was beyond "grouchy" later that morning. He was absolutely furious. Who could have done this? And why? A few members of the Vigilance Committee dropped by later in the morning and were certain they had the answers to his questions. What family, after all, had a reputation for arson? And weren't most of the sons of that family home this week? And didn't the mother of the family not that long ago rail against Grouchy's son James for being a member of their Committee? It seemed pretty obvious who the guilty parties were. Given that both his younger brother, Thomas, and his son James were members of the Vigilance Committee, it didn't take Grouchy long to see their side of things. The Donnellys had to be the guilty parties. All their making good with the local priest was now out the window; the Committee had a new charge to lay at the family's doorstep: arson!

Later that morning Grouchy Ryder hitched his singed horses up to his wagon and, with three Committee members on board, headed south along the Roman Line. On the way, the men spotted some of the Donnelly brothers out in front of their parents' property. "*They* burned my barn," Ryder said to the men in the wagon as they passed by the Donnelly homestead.[18]

Ryder and his passengers were heading directly to visit with the Vigilance Committee's latest acquisition, the magistrate William Casey, who they knew would be willing to provide warrants to their constable James Carroll for the arrest of all the Donnelly boys. And Casey did not disappoint. He immediately drew up arrest warrants for William, John, Tom and even Bob — despite the fact that Bob was 135 miles away to the southwest in Glencoe at the time of the fire.[19] It didn't matter. All the Donnelly brothers, save perhaps Patrick (who was living in Thorold), could now be put behind bars where they belonged. But Magistrate Casey, James Carroll, et al. quickly learned that there was an obvious problem with all the warrants that they had just prepared; namely, that the Donnelly brothers had all been at the wedding reception at the time of the fire, and, thus, in the company of many witnesses who could provide alibis for them. There was no way they could have been the arsonists. The charges wouldn't stick.

Father John Connolly had been visiting with old friends in Quebec when he received news of the Ryder barn burning. He immediately caught the next train and returned to Biddulph. Back at St. Patrick's, he summoned the Ryder family for a meeting and was told the fire was the work of the Donnellys. William Donnelly recalled:

> The Ryders had a private meeting with him in
> connection with the fire. They were seen at his house
> by William Toohey, school trustee. . . . "Damn the
> schoolhouse," he [Father Connolly] added, and
> "Damn the wedding," which, he said, was the cause
> of the fire, and at the same time he spoke in ridicule of
> the "simple gaudy little bride."[20]

This last reference particularly irked William Donnelly. The bride and groom were good friends of his, and the priest's comments struck him as being beneath the dignity of Father Connolly's calling. But William Donnelly's opinion on the matter was inconsequential; the priest wanted the guilty parties punished for the deed.

The Vigilance Committee called an emergency meeting. Father Connolly attended. The problem was tabled and a resolution proposed. While the Donnelly sons might have had alibis, their parents did not. It would be no big task to amend the warrants to now charge James and Johannah Donnelly, rather than their sons, with the crime of arson.[21] According to Grouchy Ryder, "My reason for suspecting Donnelly of burning my barn was Mrs. John Carroll told my daughter Mary that my son 'would not be long riding in a buggy' — and this buggy was burned in the building. She further said that Mrs. James Donnelly made this threat. This threat alarmed me."[22]

William Donnelly believed the priest's involvement set the wheels in motion for what happened next: "I have no doubt that Father Connolly approved of having my father and mother arrested."[23]

Father Connolly once again used his pulpit to good effect: he offered a $500 reward for private information leading to the detection of the guilty parties and, with great melodramatic flourish, he called for a ball of fire to fall from heaven upon the house of the arsonists.[24] According to the priest, "I felt it to be my duty then to declaim the burning of the barns from my pulpit, telling my people about it, but never once mentioned the Donnellys."[25] He didn't have to. Any gaps in the priest's narrative were willingly filled in for the benefit of the curious by the Vigilance Committee members within his congregation. It didn't take long for the entire parish to know who the priest believed was guilty of the crime.

The insinuations rubbed at least some of his parishioners the wrong way, however. When congregation member Mrs. Patton, the wife of a teacher at the Donnelly School, told the priest that

James Donnelly Sr. was too old to have perpetrated such a crime, she was cut off sharply by the Reverend Father — "James Donnelly is capable of doing anything," he said curtly.[26]

James Carroll made his move to arrest James and Johannah on Monday, January 19, 1880. He rode out to the Donnelly farm where he produced his warrant and took the family patriarch prisoner. To his surprise, he learned that Johannah Donnelly had left Biddulph earlier that day to visit with her daughter Jennie in St. Thomas. There, the Donnelly ladies were going to spend some time with Ellen Donnelly (Mike Donnelly's widow) and her children. At least, that was the plan. However, once James Carroll caught wind of it, he immediately secured a wagon and headed south to St. Thomas. There he met up with the local police chief, James Fewings, and, together, the men arrested Johannah and returned her to Biddulph to stand trial for the burning of Ryder's barn.[27] Soon both James and Johannah were hauled before the Vigilance Committee magistrate, William Casey, who demanded a $1,000 bond to release them on bail. This was paid by George Hodgins and James Keefe Sr. (the same James Keefe who had incurred Father Connolly's wrath for daring to give James Donnelly a ride home from church the previous September). The Donnellys' trial was set for January 22, 1880.

I n the days leading up to the trial, James Carroll was having trouble finding any witnesses who could place the elder Donnellys at the scene of the crime. All he had been going on was hearsay from some of the Donnellys' neighbours, such as Grouchy Ryder's daughter, Mary, who thought she had heard that Mrs. Donnelly had threatened her brother James as a result of his involvement in the missing cow fiasco. While it certainly was true that Johannah Donnelly had spoken of how angry and disappointed she had been at her property being searched by a mob of people, none of her neighbours could recall her ever threatening James Ryder. Consequently, when

January 22 arrived, Carroll and Ryder went to the Lucan courthouse with no evidence to support their prosecution of the older couple.

At 2 p.m. that day the trial opened before magistrates James Daniel McCosh and William Casey. The prisoners were called and asked their respective names.

"James Donnelly," replied one of the prisoners.

"Julia Donnelly," replied the other.[28]

The charges were then read into the record and the two prisoners were asked how they pleaded. Both answered, "Not guilty."

The formalities now out of the way, the magistrates turned to James Carroll and Patrick Ryder to present their case for the prosecution. Not wanting to risk having the case dismissed, Carroll immediately requested an adjournment in order to procure witnesses. He claimed they had not had sufficient time to prepare their case but would be able to do so if they could have a four- or five-day postponement of the trial. The two magistrates, one of whom was in the Committee's pocket, granted the constable's request, and the trial was set to resume in five days' time in Granton.[29] James and Johannah were then released on bail and returned home.

William Donnelly and his brothers did what they could to reassure their parents that Carroll and Ryder had no case against them. But that was little comfort against what the old folks had already suffered: the indignity of being publicly accused of the crime, of being jailed and then dragged into court to answer for it, to say nothing of the ongoing censure they had to endure from their community.

James Carroll, meanwhile, was wracking his brain in an effort to come up with some way of tying the senior members of the Donnelly family to the crime scene. There had been no witnesses who had seen anybody commit the incendiary act, which meant he needed another line of attack. And then it came to him: Grouchy Ryder had mentioned his daughter, Mary, had heard that Johannah Donnelly had been ranting to her neighbours about Ryder's son James. All Carroll needed was for one of these neighbours to testify that Johannah had threatened to take revenge in some way against the Ryder family, and he could establish motive. He first approached Donnelly neighbour Mary McLaughlin, who had indeed spoken with Johannah on the evening in question, but Mary refused to testify.[30] Failing here, Carroll next went to the Whalen farmhouse — the Donnellys' immediate neighbours across the Roman Line — and tried to enlist Ann Whalen's support for the prosecution, but she also refused. Carroll bristled at her refusal; he attempted to pressure her into compliance, at which point Ann's husband, Patrick, picked up an axe and chased the constable from the property.[31]

Having no luck securing witnesses of their own volition, Carroll's next step was to obtain subpoenas that would force these witnesses to take the stand. In this he was far more successful, and thereby secured the cooperation of Donnelly neighbour Mary Carroll (no relation), Bridget Donnelly and Bridget O'Connor. The latter two were a bit of a Hail Mary attempt on Carroll's part, but he hoped once they were on the stand their testimonies in providing alibis for Mr. and Mrs. Donnelly on the night of the fire could be proven false and, thus, by negation, they would help to bolster the prosecution's case.

Back to court went Carroll, Ryder and the Donnelly parents on Tuesday, January 27, 1880, this time before magistrates William Casey, James Grant and Philip Mowbray. Carroll decided that his opening gambit should be to put the alleged victim on the stand — Grouchy Ryder — a move that immediately blew up in his face. For when Ryder testified, he admitted that "none of the Donnellys was at my place on that night or during the fire."[32] Since Mr. and Mrs. Donnelly could not have set fire to his barn without being on his property, why, then, were they being charged with the crime? Ryder confessed that his only reason for suspecting the Donnellys at all had been hearsay, the result of something his daughter had told him she'd *thought* she had heard.[33] Carroll had to think of something to stop the damage his client was doing to himself, but he needed more time. He asked for, and yet again received, an adjournment. All parties, including witnesses, were ordered back to court to resume the trial two days later, on Thursday, January 29, 1880.[34]

William Donnelly was getting antsy; he had seen the toll all this was taking on his parents, but he couldn't yet use the one weapon he had to protect them — his legal savvy — until the prosecution had actually presented some evidence. And, so far, the only evidence Carroll had presented had imploded. William didn't believe either of the two Bridgets would have anything to say that would be of value to the prosecution, but Carroll and Ryder seemed quite confident something was coming now that they had gotten Mary Carroll on board. William would have to wait until his parents' third appearance in court to see what she had to say and, thus, what opportunities to counter-strike might present themselves.

When court resumed in Granton that Thursday at 10 a.m., James Carroll called forth his star witness, Mary Carroll, to testify as to what she had heard Mrs. Donnelly say about James "Young Grouch" Ryder. This she did — and Ryder's case slid even farther off the rails. When Mary Carroll was asked to confirm that she had heard Mrs. Donnelly say that young Grouch "wouldn't have his buggy for long," Mrs. Carroll categorically denied ever having heard Johannah Donnelly say any such thing: "Mrs. Donnelly *did not* say that Ryder would not have his buggy long — I am positive of this. She said nothing of burning anyone; did not speak of Ryder, but of his son — whom she called 'Grouch' — because he was searching [on her property for the cow] with the rest."[35]

It will be remembered that Grouchy Ryder had testified under oath that his only reason for suspecting the Donnellys at all had been this very point — which Mary Carroll had just now refuted. The prosecution case was deteriorating now before Carroll's eyes; it was the Ned Ryan court fiasco all over again. The two Bridgets were next called to the stand, one after the other, and gave testimony that was identical in its essence — that Mr. and Mrs. Donnelly had not been out of the house during the night of the fire. This was easy for them to recollect, particularly in the case of Mr. Donnelly, as he had been bedridden with a bad cold and his coughing had kept the girls up all night.[36] Magistrate Mowbray had heard enough: he had seen no evidence that Mr. and Mrs. Donnelly had even been near Ryder's property on the night in question. Moreover, there was absolutely no motive that had been introduced into the proceedings to even suggest why the Donnellys would have been inclined to commit the crime of arson against their neighbour. Mowbray wanted to acquit right then and there. William Donnelly watched the proceedings closely:

> They were brought before three magistrates at
> Granton — Messrs. Grant, Mowbray, and Casey . . .
> The evidence did not in the slightest way implicate
> my parents, and Mr. Mowbray regarded the charge
> as absurd and unwarrantable, but could not prevail
> on his brother magistrates to discharge them. Casey
> was a member of the Vigilance Committee, and Grant
> was influenced by Jack Kennedy, they being near
> neighbours. Hence their antipathy to our family.[37]

James Carroll, sensing his opportunity to convict the Donnellys was slipping away, made a desperate move to right the sinking ship of his prosecution against the old couple. Yet again, he asked the court to grant him additional time to procure more witnesses. Over magistrate Mowbray's objection, the two other magistrates decided to give James Carroll one more chance to make a go of his case. The trial was adjourned to be resumed in Granton on February 4, 1880.[38] Before adjourning, however, the Donnellys' lawyer, William McDiarmid, stood up and addressed the court. He wanted the magistrates — and all the Donnelly family's persecutors — to know they were done being passive little "lambs." They would, of course, return to court on February 4, 1880, but he wanted it understood that if at that time Carroll and Ryder could not produce their witnesses and prove their case, then he and his clients were going to go on the offensive. As William Donnelly later explained, "Mr. McDiarmid told Ryder at the trial in Granton that my father was going to bring an action against them for malicious arrest. I consider that they were afraid of the old man breaking them in a law suit, and becoming desperate, arranged with the inner ring of the Society to destroy the family."[39]

With all their legal muscle, the Vigilance Committee had never considered the fact they themselves might be vulnerable to the law. William Donnelly no doubt had supported McDiarmid's decision; his parents had been through enough already. It was time the family pushed back. The Donnelly policy, albeit unofficial, had always been to meet law with law. A lawsuit for damages was the proper thing to pursue in a matter where the family was clearly suffering from malicious (and needless) prosecution. And it was a lawsuit that could be easily won. This would not only help the Donnellys financially (by seeing them recoup their considerable court expenses), but also serve as a weighty deterrent to the Vigilance Committee in bringing any more baseless charges against the family. But, unbeknownst to William, his family and their lawyer, none of their recent court cases had really been about infractions of the law; the Vigilance Committee had brought forth their various prosecutions for no other purpose than to drive the Donnelly family either into jail or out of Biddulph. They had taken the Donnellys to court almost as a courtesy — they had delivered a message in legal garb that it was time for the family to go. The Donnellys, with their threat of a countersuit, had clearly not gotten the message. To the Committee's mind, they were through with the courts; it was time to move on to Plan B.

CHAPTER SIXTEEN

FINAL DAYS

James Donnelly Sr. had a strange sense of foreboding prior to
the murders. (By permission of Ray Fazakas, author of
The Donnelly Album and *In Search of the Donnellys*)

James Carroll's first impulse after the most recent adjournment
had been to try to salvage his case. He was a proud man, like
all the principals in this drama, and hated to lose — particularly to
the Donnellys. The thought that the only time he had won a case
against their family had been when he had charged the old woman
with using abusive language — and then had the magistrate's
decision reversed on appeal — had only underscored his incom-
petence in the legal arena. The prospect that all his legal efforts
on both the Ryan larceny case and the Ryder barn burning case
had been for naught, and that he was going to lose his case against
the Donnelly parents (and that he might well lose a countersuit

to them as well), was humiliating. Still, he was obsessed with arresting only Donnellys and, to use Orlo Miller's phrase, he was "monumentally uninterested" in any other case that he, in his capacity as county constable, might pursue. Indeed, in the several months that he had been a constable, the only arrests and court appearances he had made had been ones involving members of the Donnelly family.

On January 30, 1880, he had written a letter (evidently in reply) to Constable James Fewings (the same Constable Fewings who had assisted him with the arrest of Johannah Donnelly in St. Thomas) indicating that he was abandoning his case against the Donnelly parents, but was preparing to start another one against their son Bob:

January 30, 1880

Sir:

As regards the arson case against Mr. and Mrs. Donnelly it will, I fear, fall to the ground. There has been four adjournments already,[1] and Wednesday next has been set as the final day. I have made no arrest yet of any of the sons but will I think pretty soon. I will wait no longer for Robert to be caught. I am getting a case against him for arson with some proof which will I hope return Robert to Kingston for a long term of years. I expect in about two weeks to have a case with evidence strong enough to prove that Robert is the man who two years ago burnt out a farmer of this township against whom the Donnellys had a dreadful spite.[2]

You will excuse me for not writing sooner but I wanted the fire case over as I fear it will amount to nothing.[3]

That Carroll was now looking to rumours that had circulated from two years past for anything that would bring charges against members of the Donnelly family reveals his desperation. However, at the next meeting at the Cedar Swamp Schoolhouse, Carroll's plan was quashed. The word from the inner circle was "enough." They'd spent enough time chasing dead-end lawsuits against the family; they'd spent enough time pressuring neighbours of the Donnellys not to associate with them anymore; they'd had enough of sending constables to other townships to make arrests; and they'd had enough of sifting through old case files to find potential openings for re-prosecutions. It was time to act to put the Donnellys out of the picture permanently. The only question remaining was "how?" It would be easy to kill them, of course, but to do so with no blowback to their Committee would be a challenge, given the very public nature of their persecution of the family.

Someone from within the Committee then recalled an incident from the previous September that occurred during the time that the Donnellys had been suspected of stealing Thompson's heifer. An electrical storm had swept through the community and a lightning bolt had struck James Donnelly Sr.'s two-seater buggy. A large number of the more superstitious St. Patrick's parishioners had believed it had been an act of God. Never mind that lightning had also struck William Kent's house and burned it down, nor that Thomas Courcey's barn and stables had suffered the same fate that night — the fact that a lightning bolt had descended from the heavens and hit the Donnelly property was the point.[4] And hadn't the priest recently, in light of the Ryder barn burning, called forth from his pulpit for a ball of fire to strike the home of the perpetrators?[5] Things were starting to fall into place. If a "ball of fire" were to hit the Donnelly home and kill everyone inside, who could say that it wasn't the hand of God at work again? Fires were certainly not uncommon in Biddulph and, thus, wouldn't arouse suspicion. Indeed, if William Porte's diary entries are to be believed, fires had been on the ascendant in the area of late, rising from only one in 1878 to (not including the ones indicated above) three in 1879.[6]

The priest clearly believed the Donnellys had been the guilty party in the Ryan barn burning. And despite the complete lack of evidence in support of his position, and no doubt after lengthy prayer, Father Connolly believed God had spoken to him, transmitting His desire as to how the guilty parties would and should be punished. The Father had then broadcast the message he had received from his pulpit. The Vigilance Committee, then, would not be committing any crime by killing the Donnellys — quite the contrary; they would merely be tools in the Almighty's hands to enact His bidding. All the parishioners would know was God had decreed a ball of fire would hit the house of the evildoers and then the Donnelly home had gone up in flames.

The priest certainly wouldn't be able to accuse the members of the Vigilance Committee of having done anything wrong as he had been the one who had expressly communicated God's intention of how the matter would be dealt with. In one fell swoop, all the Vigilance Committee's problems with the Donnelly family would be swept away; they would no longer have to pursue the arson case against the parents or dig through old court records to charge the sons. And, most certainly, there would not be any countersuit coming their way from the family. Yes, the Donnelly farmhouse had to burn, but simply setting fire to it would not necessarily mean the death of the Donnellys — they might escape from the flames. But if the family was already dead inside the house before the torch was put to it, the fire would then conceal the crime. Less than a month after the murders, William Donnelly would state his belief publicly that this was precisely the Vigilance Committee's plan: "I have no doubt that if it had not been for the providential escape of young [O'Connor] from our burning house to tell the story of the butchery, the people would have believed that our family were the guilty parties, and that Heaven's vengeance had fallen on them in the way wished for by the priest."[7]

Just for insurance, the Vigilance Committee needed to come up with a witness who would provide cover for them once the crime had been committed. This witness needed to be credible and seemingly impartial in his account of how the fire might have started in the Donnelly home (which meant that Carroll, Kennedy and Thompson were out, as they had a well-publicized history of enmity with the Donnellys). It was decided that their own magistrate, William Casey, would fit the bill. And he readily agreed to come forth after the deed had been done and state that he had witnessed the men of the Donnelly family driving their wagon past his house on the very evening of the fire and that they had clearly been drunk. In such a condition, they may well have inadvertently set fire to their own house. Casey not only agreed to say such a thing to his fellow Committee members, but would in fact state it when he stepped onto the witness stand during the coroner's inquest in March 1880:

> I saw Mr. Donnelly, Thomas Donnelly, and the boy
> passing the night before, about sundown. I thought
> they were driving too fast for the roads. I couldn't
> tell which was driving, I took no particular notice.
> From the rate of speed that they were going and the
> state of the road, I concluded that they had drank a
> little too much liquor, and for that reason, I thought
> that the burning was accidental when I heard of it in
> the morning.[8]

But then there was the problem of the murder itself. The Donnellys always seemed to have their guard up, and there were weapons in the Donnelly home, as Constable Hodgins found out when Tom Donnelly had pointed a shotgun at him not that long ago. It was decided that an inside man was required, somebody who could spy on the Donnellys for the Committee without rousing suspicion. The group could not afford to have the family tipped off; the Donnellys would not go down without a fight. And so, a stealth attack committed in the dead of night, when no one would (or could) see it coming, was to be a necessity. This inside person would let the Committee members know when the Donnellys were most vulnerable. A friend of the family would make a good candidate, as he could enter the property and take stock of how many people were inside and what sort of weaponry was close at hand for the family. However, this qualification narrowed the field of potential candidates considerably, as to be a friend of the Donnellys required proven loyalty over many years. The family may have offered kindnesses to strangers, but seldom friendship. Friendship had to be earned, and those who had earned it weren't the kind to break their bond of trust with the family. The Keefes were out; they had been friends with the family for too long and were too loyal. The young Ryan lad was out of the township now. This left only the Feeheley boys — James and William. While they had been loyal to the Donnellys, in truth, they were only loyal to the expediency of the moment. If it served their interests, they might well come aboard.

While James Carroll had nothing to offer William Feeheley in return for his betrayal of the family, that wasn't a big problem, as William Feeheley had already been attending meetings of the Vigilance Committee.[9] He wasn't a part of their inner circle by any means, but Carroll was confident he would pretty much do what he was told. The problem was William wasn't as tight with the Donnellys as was his brother James. James and Tom Donnelly were actually good friends. But how to get James to switch allegiances? That's when Carroll remembered the warrant he had tucked away since receiving it from constable William Hodgins some five months previously. The warrant for James Feeheley dated back to the Ned Ryan robbery and Carroll had intended to use it as leverage when the time was right. Now appeared to be the perfect time to put its influence to the test; after all, the threat of arrest might just appeal to Feeheley's sense of self-preservation enough that he would do the Committee's bidding. Carroll now set off in search of his prey. James Feeheley would later recall that

> I had a conversation with Carroll about the Vigilance
> Committee. And he said the bad doings would have
> to be stopped. If the Donnellys were in it, they would
> have to be stopped. Carroll also told me to shun the
> Donnellys. I then asked Carroll if he had a warrant
> for me. He said he had, and I asked him what for?
> He said that was his own business.[10]

Carroll's threat apparently did the trick as, after his meeting, the Vigilance Committee now had their Judas Iscariot in the person of James Feeheley. But Feeheley might not have been as hard to turn against the Donnellys as the Committee may have originally thought. He had evidently been harbouring a grudge against at least one of the Donnelly brothers for some time. Francis West, a man who would later bring to light the Feeheley brothers' duplicity with the Donnellys, recalled hearing James Feeheley say, "'One of the Donnellys nearly beat me dead once, but I have had good satisfaction since. . . . I helped put one son of a bitch out of the way and know who finished four more.' I then asked him whom he had helped put out of the way. He then replied, "'It don't make any difference to you.'"[11]

James Carroll's directive to Feeheley was that he was to enter the Donnellys' home on a particular night and take stock of who was in the house. He was then to bring this information back to the constable — the Vigilance Committee would handle it from there. Feeheley was also made privy to the fact that a group of men were going to make a raid on the Donnelly farmhouse, but, as far as he knew, the Committee members were only going to remove the

Donnelly men from the home and then, employing a tactic out of private detective Hugh McKinnon's playbook, they would hang them until the Donnellys confessed to setting fire to Ryder's barn.[12] At least that was the story the inner ring of the Vigilance Committee had passed along to its outer ring. Only the inner ring knew, per Carroll's letter above, that they had no intention of pursuing the Ryder arson charge against the family any further. If it had been stated that they had intended to murder the family, some of the men they required to do the deed might drop out or, worse still, talk. They couldn't risk this, and so the true plan was only known to a few of the men. Once the murders went down, everyone in attendance would be complicit, and therefore would know to keep their mouths shut for their own good.

James Feeheley would learn what was really going to happen to the Donnellys from his uncle (and inner circle member) John Cain. He had been passing his uncle's house on the Roman Line in the company of James Keefe when his aunt, Sarah Cain, waved him to come over. She walked James into the house to have a word with his uncle John, while Keefe was told to wait outside. A few minutes later Sarah and James Feeheley emerged from the house, and both were crying. As Keefe and Feeheley resumed their walk along the Roman Line, Keefe turned to Feeheley and asked him what the problem had been back at the farm that had so upset him.

"My uncle told me that I am not to stay overnight at the Donnellys anymore, as something awful is going to be done to them," he replied.

"What is going to be done?" asked Keefe. But Feeheley refused to say another word on the subject. At his next opportunity, Keefe told John Donnelly about what he had seen and heard, but Donnelly simply laughed, not correctly reading the severity of the situation.[13] Sometime later, Committee members Martin Darcy and James Carroll invited a farmer from the community, John Doherty, to meet them at John Cain's house. If Doherty had been apprehensive about joining a sworn society, he was absolutely repulsed by what happened next. Their host removed a shillelagh from above his stove and declared to the trio, "By God, I will bury this stick in Tom Donnelly's skull before a week!"[14] Doherty recoiled. "I will have nothing to do with putting a stick in anyone's brain!"[15] he exclaimed, and immediately made his exit from the premises. It was clear that a simple interrogation of the Donnelly family was not on the Vigilance Committee's agenda.

On Sunday, February 1, 1880, John and Margaret Armitage invited James and Johannah to their home for dinner.[16] The Donnellys were always welcome guests at the Armitage home on the Fourth Concession Road, as James had saved two of their sons from a vicious beating and perhaps death at the hands of some Biddulph farmers some years back. The details of the two families having dinner together prior to the murders are scant, unfortunately. However, given the fate that was soon to befall the Donnellys, in addition to what they had endured from among their Roman Catholic brethren in the community of late, the comfort of fellowship between old and loyal friends — even though Protestant — would have at least have given the old couple an all-too-welcome break in the tension that had enveloped them.

Meanwhile, William Donnelly had grown worried about his parents. The strain of having their neighbours turned against them, the invective of the parish priest, the repeated persecution by Carroll, the vilification of their family by the Vigilance Committee, the bleeding of their funds to pay bail, the borrowing of money from friends to cover court costs, Johannah being arrested in front of her daughter and daughter-in-law and dragged back to Biddulph, the trials and postponements — they all had taken a collective toll on both James and Johannah Donnelly, and particularly Johannah. She, who had done so much to ease the burden of so many in their time of need over the years,[17] had now been abandoned. Who would step forth to ease her burden now, in this, *her* time of need? The answer was a short one: nobody.

The Vigilance Committee's membership had grown in light of the propaganda that was being spread after the burning of Ryder's barn;[18] word had travelled through the underground that something bad was in the works for the Donnellys, and that it was best to stay away. Johannah felt it deeply when the parish priest, whose relationship with the family had looked for a time to have been repaired after the death of her son Mike, was now not willing to lower himself to offer her any consolation. In fact, Father Connolly was instead actively speaking out against Johannah's family to their few remaining friends. This certainly was not a woman who was baying for the blood of her enemies, as later reports from her killers' relatives would tell the press, but rather an old woman sitting at home silently enduring the pains of a broken heart and a grieving soul. It is hard not to empathize with the pain her oldest surviving son must have felt in seeing her this way. William's mother had once been a strong and fiercely independent woman, the backbone of the family. She was now a shell of her former self. She was drained emotionally. With their trial set to resume in two days, William decided that he should drop in on his parents to see how they were holding up. Upon entering the house, he saw his mother sitting alone by the stove. "She always wore under flannels," William recollected, "and upon this occasion she had on a red flannel skirt, her chemise and petticoat, and a small breakfast shawl over her head. She looked rather fantastic."[19] Her eyes had weakened. She wore spectacles now.[20] She had always welcomed his wit and so, seeking to bring a much-needed smile to his mother's face, he made a joke about how she was dressed:

"Mother go and dress yourself, for if Barnum came here and saw you now he would have you at any price," he said with a smile.[21]

Rather than laugh, or even acknowledge the teasing, his mother began to weep. "It is easy for you to talk," she said. "My poor old heart is broken. If you were pulled around the country in the way Ryder and Carroll is pulling me and your father, you would not feel like laughing."[22]

This was *not* the effect William had intended. He later recalled the strange, almost prophetic dialogue that then followed between him and his family members:

> I felt as though she had a foreboding of something
> wrong about to happen, and I had to leave the
> house. On going into the yard, my father said, "Put
> out the mare and wait and have some dinner with
> us." I said I was in a hurry, and he said a second
> time, "wait." And added, with one of his well-
> known good-natured smiles, "It may be the last
> time we would ever have dinner together as the
> Ryders and Carrolls might have me in London gaol
> tomorrow." Something seemed to detain me and
> then my mother came to the door and said, "Why
> did you not bring Nora [William's wife] over with
> you?" I felt very down-hearted, as if something was
> hanging over me which I could not account for. I
> told her to cease crying. She replied, "When you and
> all the rest of the boys were children I often took
> the light at midnight to look at you taking a happy
> sleep, full of the hope that I might live to see you
> all men and be happy myself, but that hope has left
> me, and my mind often tells me that Carroll will
> someday get his ends of us."[23]

William recoiled at the thought. "You had better go up to Father Connolly, and ask him to use his influence to induce the Ryders to stop the prosecution," he said.[24]

The tears now flowed freely from his mother's eyes; her unofficial excommunication was a wound from which she would never recover. "Sure he knows the way they're using us without me going to tell him," she said pointedly.[25] The old fire flashed briefly in her eyes. There it was: that old Donnelly sense of independence reasserting itself. William Donnelly knew his mother too well; there would be no appeals to outside help on this matter. She would simply find the necessary strength from somewhere deep within herself to carry on. That had simply always been the way with her.

William walked back into his parents' house and talked over with his father the strategy to be employed upon their return to court. While he was confident in their legal counsel, William McDiarmid, he wanted a real pit bull in his parents' corner when it came time to launch their countersuit. To this end, he had drafted a letter on his father and mother's behalf to be sent to Edmund Meredith, the London lawyer who had represented both John and Tom Donnelly in the past. The Donnellys, under William's direction, were hoping to employ Meredith to launch their counter-offensive litigation against Grouchy Ryder for damages. William sat down with his father and outlined the points he had hit in the letter and left it for him to sign and post the next day. He said goodbye to his parents and promised he would be present in the courtroom with them when the trial resumed in two days' time. As he was leaving, his cousin Bridget came to the door and asked him if he had answered a letter that he had received from her mother back in Ireland. William nodded. "That's right," Bridget replied smilingly, "she will be glad to hear from all of us." Again, William felt a strange sense of foreboding, as if he shouldn't leave the homestead. As he mounted his horse, Tom came out of the house, calling to him that he would be coming to his place on Wednesday to pick him up so they could head to Granton together on Thursday morning for the trial.[26] William agreed to the plan and then rode back to his home at Whalen's

Corners. He had no way of knowing that his visit with his family would mark the last time he would see any of them alive.

Later that evening, a neighbour dropped in to visit with the old couple. Who it was has been lost to history, but he evidently expressed concern about the welfare of James and Johannah should they remain in Biddulph. "Wouldn't it be better for all concerned if you would pack up your traps and leave the place?" he asked.

James Donnelly nodded. "Yes, I believe it would. And as soon as this trial about the barn burning is over I intend to leave."[27] Certainly, if James and Johannah had been planning on leaving the community after their final appearance in court that week, and if Carroll was no longer willing to proceed with the arson case against them, the entire tragedy could have been prevented, if only each had known of the other's intentions.

The morning of Tuesday, February 3, 1880, passed at the Donnelly home without much happening out of the ordinary. James sat down to review the letter that William had drafted:

Mr. Meredith:

Sir,

On the 15th of last month Pat Ryder's barns were burned. All the Vigilance Committee at once pointed to my family as the ones that done it. Ryder found out that all my boys were at a wedding that night. He at once arrested me on suspicion, and also sent a constable after my wife to St. Thomas. The trial has been postponed four different times, and although we are ready for our trial at any time, they examined a lot of witnesses, but can't find anything against us.

Ryder swore that we lived neighbours to each
other for thirty years, and never had any difference,
and had no reason for arresting us, only that we are
blamed for everything. The presiding Magistrates
are old Grant and a newly made one, William Casey,
who is married to Ryder's cousin.

They are using us worse than mad dogs. Mr.
McDiarmid is attending on our behalf, and says there
is a good chance against Ryder for damages. They
had the first trial in Lucan, and then adjourned to
Granton simply to advertise us. We have to appear
tomorrow again, and I am informed they are going
to send us for trial without a tittle of evidence. If so, I
will telegraph you when we start for London, to meet
us at the City Hotel, and get us bailed to take our trial
before the judge. And I want you to handle the case
on our behalf, and if there is any chance for damages I
want you attack them at once, as they will never let us
alone until some of them are made an example of.

There is not the slightest cause for our arrest, and
it seems hard to see a man and woman, over sixty
years of age, dragged around as laughing stocks.

Yours truly,
James Donnelly, Sr.[28]

He dated and signed the document and placed it in his coat pocket.
He would mail it that afternoon when he and Tom went into town.
They had to head to Lucan for a few reasons that day. First, they
needed to pick up some items for the farm at John Armitage's general
store there. Second, they had to borrow a cutter from the O'Connor
family. And, finally, they needed to pick up thirteen-year-old Johnny

O'Connor, as his parents had agreed he could stay overnight at their farm in order to watch over their livestock while they were away at court the next day. Later that afternoon, under the watchful eyes of strategically placed spies, James Donnelly Sr. and Tom Donnelly left their farm and drove their sleigh toward Lucan.

Once the pair had arrived in town, they secured their team of horses to a hitching post and entered Armitage's store. After selecting the necessary items, James Donnelly walked up to the counter. John Armitage asked him if would be paying by cash or wanted the items charged to his account. James considered the question, smiled and expressed a sentiment similar to what he had shared with his son the day before: "Charge this to the Queen. Perhaps I'll never return to pay you again."[29]

James Sr. and Tom then left the store and walked over to the post office, where they exchanged greetings with William Porte and mailed the letter to Edmund Meredith. From the post office, the pair then returned to their sleigh and headed down Lucan's Main Street to the O'Connor home to pick up Johnny and the cutter. It was now 3:30 p.m. To their surprise the men learned that neither Johnny O'Connor nor the cutter were there. William Donnelly had already picked up the O'Connors' cutter and taken it back to his house on Whalen's Corners. Johnny O'Connor was away working at the home of a family friend, William Hutchins. His sister Bridget volunteered to go fetch her younger brother for the Donnellys. James and Tom chatted for a while with Michael and Mary O'Connor, and soon Bridget had returned with her younger sibling in tow. Johnny said goodbye to his parents and climbed aboard the Donnellys' sleigh, settling down between Tom and the old man. The trio then set off for the Roman Line.

From here on out, our story is one of tragedy. There were witnesses to what would follow, certainly, but just as certainly, few would ever speak about it publicly. Johnny O'Connor would speak about it, and, later on, James and William Feeheley would share what they had witnessed, albeit grudgingly. Consequently, the recollections, though accurate, are partial, like electrical flashes of activity, that serve to briefly shine light on certain moments rather than illuminating an entire event. Be that as it may, when these partial fragments are placed side by side, a reasonably clear picture of what transpired on the night of the murders comes into focus through the smoke and the soot, the clubs and the guns and the blood.

NOTES ON TEXT

PROLOGUE

1   "He did not sleep any last night though he had slept 5 or 6 hrs.
     the night previous. He was extremely apprehensive of danger this
     morning and was so much afraid of a plot being made to burn
     him up and that his head would be cut off." Province of Ontario,
     Clinical Records, Robert Donnelly, Casebook 1162; June 24, 1908.
     RG 10-280: London Psychiatric Hospital patients' clinical case
     files, Robert Donnelly, File Number 295. Archives of Ontario.

2   All information about the London Asylum for the Insane's buildings,
     doctors, rates and therapies was drawn from "Restoring Perspective:
     Life and Treatment at the London Asylum." "The London Asylum
     for the Insane." https://lib.uwo.ca/archives/virtualexhibits/
     londonasylum/index.html (accessed August 30, 2020).

3   For the weight of the spittoon, the author located a description
     of one of a similar vintage to what would have been present in
     Bob Donnelly's room: "Antique 1800s Large Heavy Solid Brass
     Saloon Spittoon Cuspidor 11.5 LBS," https://worthpoint.com/

worthopedia/antique-1800s-large-heavy-solid-brass-427211127 (accessed February 15, 2020).

4 "He [Bob Donnelly] was extremely apprehensive of danger this morning and was so much afraid of a plot being made to burn him up and that his head would be cut off. Fearing that Attendant Reid was going to do this, he threw the spittoon at him, hitting him on the shoulder." Robert Donnelly, Casebook 1162, June 24, 1908. RG 10-280: London Psychiatric Hospital patients' clinical case files, Robert Donnelly, File Number 295. Archives of Ontario.

5 "He appeared to Dr. Forster as being more disturbed and was put back to bed." Robert Donnelly, Casebook 1162, June 24, 1908. RG 10-280: London Psychiatric Hospital patients' clinical case files, Robert Donnelly, File Number 295. Archives of Ontario.

6 Physician's Certificate Re: Robert Donnelly, prepared by James Sutton, M.D., June 11, 1908. Robert Donnelly, File Number 295. Archives of Ontario.

7 Physician's Certificate Re: Robert Donnelly, prepared by Thomas Hossack, M.D., June 15, 1908. Robert Donnelly, File Number 295. Archives of Ontario.

8 Physician's Certificate Re: Robert Donnelly, prepared by James Sutton, M.D., June 11, 1908. Robert Donnelly, File Number 295. Archives of Ontario.

9 Physician's Certificate Re: Robert Donnelly, prepared by Thomas Hossack, M.D., June 15, 1908. Robert Donnelly, File Number 295. Archives of Ontario.

10 Application No. 7842, Province of Ontario, Statement, Questionnaire/Interview with Robert Donnelly by James Sutton, M.D., Lucan, May 26, 1908. Robert Donnelly, File Number 295. Archives of Ontario.

11 See "Bond for The Maintenance of Robert Donnelly, June 15, 1908," which indicates that Bob Donnelly paid $2.75 per week, which suggests he had a private room. See also "P & A Hospital For Insane Series, Province of Ontario, June 15, 1908," which indicates same, as well as stating that Donnelly is a "Hotel Keeper" and "supposed to own an estate to the value of $10,000.00."

London Psychiatric Hospital patients' clinical case files, Robert Donnelly, File Number 295. Archives of Ontario.

12   See Admittance Record, Province of Ontario Hospital for the Insane, Correspondence File No. 1011, June 15, 1908, "Admitted by Dr. Harris at 12:00 a.m." London Psychiatric Hospital patients' clinical case files, Robert Donnelly, File Number 295. Archives of Ontario.

13   "Sent to Ward: Inf." London Psychiatric Hospital patients' clinical case files, Robert Donnelly, File Number 295. Archives of Ontario.

14   For references as to Bob Donnelly being fifty-five years old, see *London Free Press*, September 29, 1908; also "Inventory and Valuation," "Receipt," "London Asylum, Re: Robert Donnelly, an Eloper, Report of Elopement" documents. London Psychiatric Hospital patients' clinical case files, Robert Donnelly, File Number 295. Archives of Ontario.

15   Regarding Donnelly's birth month being October, but uncertainty of the day of birth see question and answer No. 3: "Age: 55; Birthday and year: October — records lost in burning homestead." London Psychiatric Hospital patients' clinical case files, Robert Donnelly, File Number 295. Archives of Ontario.

16   See Province of Ontario Ward Admission Records for April 12, 1908 ("Partly bald — a few gray hairs in whiskers") and December 4, 1908 ("Part bald and gray hair, a little long"). London Psychiatric Hospital patients' clinical case files, Robert Donnelly, File Number 295. Archives of Ontario.

17   Province of Ontario Ward Admission Record for April 12, 1908. London Psychiatric Hospital patients' clinical case files, Robert Donnelly, File Number 295. Archives of Ontario.

18   "List of Clothing Received with Patient On Admission." London Psychiatric Hospital patients' clinical case files, Robert Donnelly, File Number 295. Archives of Ontario.

19   Province of Ontario Ward Admission Record for April 12, 1908. London Psychiatric Hospital patients' clinical case files, Robert Donnelly, File Number 295. Archives of Ontario.

20   London Psychiatric Hospital patients' clinical case files, Robert Donnelly, File Number 295. Archives of Ontario.

21 The buildings, located at 850 Highbury Avenue in London, became the London Psychiatric Hospital, and the facility closed its doors permanently in 2001. Several of the original buildings remain.

22 Letter from James Michael Donnelly to Dr. J. Harris, June 15, 1908. London Psychiatric Hospital patients' clinical case files, Robert Donnelly, File Number 295. Archives of Ontario.

23 Letter of reply to James Michael Donnelly from Medical Superintendent William John Robinson, June 18, 1908. London Psychiatric Hospital patients' clinical case files, Robert Donnelly, File Number 295. Archives of Ontario.

24 London Psychiatric Hospital patients' clinical case files, Robert Donnelly, File Number 295. Archives of Ontario.

25 "He struggled and shouted." London Psychiatric Hospital patients' clinical case files, Robert Donnelly, June 28, 1908, File Number 295. Archives of Ontario.

26 "He was given 1/100 gr. of Hyoscine at 3:45." (Note: Hyoscine is a general neurotransmitter which can serve as a sedative). London Psychiatric Hospital patients' clinical case files, Robert Donnelly, File Number 295. Archives of Ontario.

27 London Psychiatric Hospital patients' clinical case files, Robert Donnelly, File Number 295. Archives of Ontario.

28 London Psychiatric Hospital patients' clinical case files, Robert Donnelly, June 28, 1908, File Number 295. Archives of Ontario.

29 London Psychiatric Hospital patients' clinical case files, Robert Donnelly, June 29, 1908, File Number 295. Archives of Ontario.

30 Certificate Under 18th Section of "An Act to make further provision as to the Custody of Insane Persons"; 36th Victoria:

> I, James M. Donnelly being nephew of Robert Donnelly
> an inmate of London Asylum for the Insane, admitted
> by certificates request the Medical Superintendent to
> allow him to return to my home on probation; under-
> taking on my part to keep oversight of the said Robert
> Donnelly while he remains at my home, for the period
> of two months from the date of commencement of such

term of probation. I agree also to send to the Medical
Superintendent, a fortnightly account of his condition,
mental and physical, during such period, and in case of
my neglect to do so, to forfeit the right for his readmis-
sion to the said Asylum for the Insane.

See also, "Probation Bond Re: Robert Donnelly," Reg. No. 5924:
Probation Granted: September 19, 1908; Probation Expires:
November 19, 1908; Result: Ret'd December 4, 1908. London
Psychiatric Hospital patients' clinical case files, Robert Donnelly,
September 19, 1908, File Number 295. Archives of Ontario.

31   *London Free Press*, September 29, 1908.

CHAPTER ONE: THE MORNING AFTER

1   Bill Adams, *The History of the London Fire Department of Heroes,
      Helmets and Hoses* (London: London Fire Department, 2002), p. 13.

2   John Lambert Payne, "The Donnelly Case," *Maclean's*, November
      1, 1931. "I was a cub reporter on the *London Free Press* at that
      time, and was early on the scene. As a matter of fact, I was the
      first outsider to visit it." Payne was a career reporter (working
      both for the *London Free Press* and later the *Toronto Star*) and
      civil serviceman, working as a secretary for Conservative Member
      of Parliament Sir John Carling (London). He died in Ottawa and
      his obituary appeared in the *London Free Press* on June 23, 1939.
      He reported on the happenings immediately after the Donnelly
      murders right through to the conclusion of the second trial. He was
      also called as a witness for the prosecution.

3   A stagecoach travelled at an average speed of five miles per hour.
      "Stagecoach." https://en.wikipedia.org/wiki/Stagecoach (accessed
      January 2, 2020).

4   According to the website Ivey Family London Room Digital
      Collections, "The Proof Line Road which Mahlon Burwell
      surveyed in the early 1800s was the main road connecting the

counties bordering Lake Huron to the London area. Prior to 1849 the route between London and Elginfield was just a blazed trail but after improvements were made by a private company, the Joint Stock Road Company initiated by Freeman Talbot, the graded and graveled London Township Proof Line Road saw an increase in travelers. Tolls were charged to cover costs and eventually make a profit on the privatized road." "Paying the Last Toll on the Proof Line Road, London Township, London, Ontario," http://images .ourontario.ca/london/2369866/data?n=1 (accessed May 4, 2019). See also "In 1849, the Provincial Legislature passed legislation permitting private companies to build toll roads. That same year, a local group formed the 'Proof Line Road Joint Stock Company' to grade, macadamize, and bridge the Proof Line Road. The completed road had three toll gates and followed the Richmond Street route north through Arva, Birr, and Elginfield. Several hotels and taverns opened along the road, an indication of its heavy use." London Public Library, "Toll Gates on the Proof Line Road," https://www.londonpubliclibrary.ca/research/local-history/historic-sites-committee/toll-gates-proof-line-road-plaque-no-37 (accessed March 2, 2021).

5   *London Free Press*, February 12, 1880.

6   *London Free Press*, February 12, 1880.

7   *London Free Press*, February 12, 1880.

8   *London Free Press*, February 12, 1880.

9   *London Free Press*, February 12, 1880.

10   *London Free Press*, February 12, 1880.

11   *London Free Press*, February 12, 1880.

12   *The Globe*, March 11, 1880.

13   William Donnelly to E.F. Johnson, February 18, 1881, cited in William Davison Butt, *The Donnellys: History, Legend, Literature.* (PhD diss., University of Western Ontario, 1977), pp. 213–14.

14   *London Free Press*, February 18, 1880.

15   During the second trial it was reported that "J. Lambert Payne, of the *London Free Press*, was called to identify a pair of spectacles which he had picked up near the remains of Mrs. Donnelly. The glasses

of these spectacles were run into a solid lump." *The Toronto Mail,*
January 31, 1881.

16 "The old man and the girl are lying close together in the northwest
corner of the house. The old man's skull was broken, evidently with a
fire shovel which is lying under him." *New York Times,* February 5,
1880.

17 Testimony from Theresa Whalen taken during the second trial:
"I did not notice the iron of a spade about the bodies at all; if
there had been a spade there I would have seen it . . ." *London
Advertiser,* January 26, 1881.

18 "I saw a knife near the body of what I thought was old Mr.
Donnelly; I saw a watch chain afterwards which was picked up; it
was Catherine Toohey [the wife of Patrick Toohey, a family that
also lived on the Roman Line] who picked up the watch chain . . ."
London Advertiser, January 26, 1881.

19 "During last night the skull of James Donnelly, which was fractured, was stolen from the ruins of the building. The portion of the
skull of Mrs. Donnelly and her niece, which remained intact, was
also stolen from the ruins. . . . Underneath the charred remains of
James Donnelly was a pocket knife which was usually carried by
him. The ruins have been visited by hundreds of people, and many
carried away mementoes of their visit in the shape of teeth or bones
of the deceased. . . . Many of the people attracted to the place
by curiosity picked up portions of the bones of the unfortunate
victims, and carried them off as souvenirs of their visit. Indeed,
I was shown this evening a portion of the jawbone of one of the
family." *London Advertiser,* February 6, 1880.

20 *London Advertiser,* February 6, 1880.

21 *London Free Press,* February 12, 1880.

22 See also Payne's testimony: "Out in the fresh-fallen snow in front of
the house were many footprints and a small pool of blood," *London
Free Press,* January 16, 1926. Also, Payne's quote "The freshly
fallen snow about the log house bore the imprint of many feet, and
pools of blood at the front marked the spot where Tom Donnelly
had been clubbed to death." *Maclean's,* November 1, 1931.

23 *London Free Press*, February 12, 1880.

24 *London Free Press*, February 12, 1880.

25 *London Free Press*, February 12, 1880.

26 *Maclean's*, November 1, 1931.

27 Middlesex County Registry Office, Abstract Book, Biddulph to 1866, p. 64, Instrument 128, June 8, 1861, cited in Butt, *The Donnellys: History, Legend, Literature*, p. 55.

28 *London Free Press*, February 12, 1880.

29 *London Free Press*, February 12, 1880.

30 According to "Candles," https://catholicism.org/candles.html (accessed June 15, 2020), a "blessed candle" is passed out at Holy Mass if the parishioners have not brought their own to the ceremony. On February 2, forty days after Christmas, the Latin Rite celebrates the feast of the Purification. It is also called Candlemas because on this day Christ, the Light of the World, entered the holy temple nestled in the arms of His Immaculate Mother. Therefore, this is the day that candles are blessed and passed out. Blessed candles must be made from at least 51 percent beeswax.

31 Nora Donnelly, from her deposition: ". . . then I got a piece of blessed candle and put into his hand and he died in a few minutes . . ." Public Archives of Ontario, Irving Fonds, F1027, 82 08, MS 6500, Unknown, Deposition of Nora Donnelly, March 31, 1880.

32 *Maclean's*, November 1, 1931.

33 *London Free Press*, January 16, 1926.

34 William Donnelly's testimony about the footprints around his property, taken from the first trial: ". . . there were tracks to all the windows in my house except the one opposite to the door that John was shot at; about the centre of the kitchen at the north end; I observed the tracks in the morning; it appeared as if there were a great many people there; it was trampled down all around my place and around Mr. Blackwell's house, which is about twenty feet south of mine; I called Blackwell before I looked at all these tracks; I looked at the ones around the door before I called him; he was partly dressed with pants, shirt, and socks on, and ran down stairs; when I called he looked at the

tracks with me . . ." Public Archives of Ontario, Irving Fonds,
F1027, 82 08, MS6500, Unknown, Deposition of William
Donnelly, February 31, 1880.

35 J.J. Talman Regional Collection, University of Western Ontario
Archives, Donnelly Family Papers, B4878, File 2, G.W. Clay, Letter
to C. Hutchinson from G.W. Clay, February 12, 1880.

CHAPTER TWO: THE THINGS WE DO FOR LAND

1   *London Free Press*, June 24, 1879.
2   David Wood, *Making Ontario* (Montreal: McGill-Queen's
University Press, 2000), p. 48.
3   John Leverton, *Wilberforce Colony from Lucan*, 125 Souvenir
Booklet, 1871–1996.
4   Butt, *The Donnellys: History, Legend, Literature*, pp. 36–37.
5   Huron County, Clerk of the Peace, Criminal Records, information of Mary Ann Thompson, March 15, 1849, and deposition of
witnesses, March 16, 1849.
6   "Irish Canadians," https://en.wikipedia.org/wiki/Irish_Canadians
(accessed April 23, 2020); see also "Coffin Ships," https://historyplace.
com/worldhistory/famine/coffin.htm (accessed August 11, 2020).
7   "Coffin Ships," http://historyplace.com/worldhistory/famine/coffin.
htm (accessed August 11, 2020).
8   "Irish Canadians," https://en.wikipedia.org/wiki/Irish_Canadians
(accessed April 23, 2020); see also "Ontario," https://irishtocanada
.com/ontario/ (accessed December 18, 2020).
9   "The Journey to Ellis [Island]," https://irish-genealogy-toolkit.com/
journey-to-Ellis-Island.html (accessed March 5, 2020).
10 J.J. Talman Regional Collection, University of Western Ontario
Archives, Reaney Papers, Box 26 (B1312), File 51A, Unknown,
Admittance of James Donnelly to Gaol of the Huron District, May 7,
1858. This interview document gives James Donnelly's time in
Canada as being 16 years. See also Butt, *The Donnellys: History,
Legend, Literature*, p. 42.

11 James C. Reaney, *The Donnelly Documents: An Ontario Vendetta* (Toronto: The Champlain Society, 2004), p. xlv, note 69.

12 Per the information on the family tombstone in the cemetery at St. Patrick's Church, Lucan, Ontario, James Sr. would have been twenty-six years old in 1842.

13 Per the information on the family tombstone in the cemetery at St. Patrick's Church, Lucan, Ontario, Johannah would have been nineteen years old in 1842.

14 *The Globe*, February 28, 1880, claims that Donnelly arrived in London in 1844, then relocated to London Township before moving to Biddulph in 1847.

15 "Canada Company," https://thecanadianencyclopedia.ca/en/article/canada-company (accessed January 7, 2020).

16 It is assumed that James Donnelly had leased the land from Grace: "John Grace would hardly have allowed the Donnelly family to squat on his land, to use it without compensation of some kind, until 1855 when . . . he sold the lot." Butt, *The Donnellys: History, Legend, Literature*, p. 593, note 17.

17 Huron County, Clerk of the Peace, Coroner's Inquests; Inquisition on the body of Edward Kennedy, April 1, 1855.

18 Huron County, Clerk of the Peace, Criminal Justice Accounts, 1842, James Scott to Dr. Hamilton, Coroner, October 17, 1842, and account of Morgan Hamilton, Coroner, October 20, 1842, on the death of James Dagg in 1842.

19 Huron County, Clerk of the Peace, Criminal Justice Accounts, 1847, account of George McLeod, Coroner, April 1, 1847. See also Huron County, Clerk of the Peace, Coroner's Inquests, Inquisition on body of Michael McCormick, April 1, 1847.

20 Huron County, Clerk of the Peace, Coroner's Inquests; Inquisition on body of Thomas Shea, February 28, 1957.

21 Huron County, Clerk of the Peace, Coroner's Inquests; Inquisition on the body of James Atkinson, September 19, 1849.

22 Huron County, Clerk of the Peace, Coroner's Inquests; Statement of Coroner George McLeod, May 6, 1847.

23 Huron County, Clerk of the Peace, Coroner's Inquests, Return of Inquests for 1847 in district of Huron by George McLeod, Coroner.

24 Huron County, Clerk of the Peace, Coroner's Inquests, Inquisition on the body of Richard Courcey, June 10, 1847. See also Huron County, Clerk of the Peace, Coroner's Inquests, Return of Inquests for 1847 in district of Huron by George McLeod, Coroner.

25 J.J. Talman Regional Collection, University of Western Ontario Archives, Donnelly Family Papers, Box 4877, File 5, Unknown, Information of Witnesses, Inquest on Bodies of Catherine Garburth and Sarah Harcourt, May 29, 1861.

26 Clerk of the Peace, Census Returns, Huron District, Return of the Inhabitants of Biddulph, April 19, 1850.

27 According to a census taken in 1871, the Donnellys had three milk cows, two boarded cows, ten sheep, six pigs, one cow and four sheep slaughtered or sold for export. The yield from their fifty-acre lot was even more impressive than it had been in 1850: two hundred bushels of spring wheat, twenty bushels of barley, two hundred bushels of oats, ninety bushels of peas, three hundred bushels of potatoes, fifteen acres of hay crop, fifty bushels of apples, twenty pounds of maple sugar, two hundred pounds of butter, forty pounds of wool, fifty yards of homemade cloth and flannel, and two hundred cords of firewood — all from two acres of gardens and orchards and four acres of pastures. J.J. Talman Regional Collection, University of Western Ontario Archives, Reaney Papers, Government of Canada, Donnelly Information, 1871 Census (Various Returns/Schedules), 1871.

28 Huron County, Clerk of the Peace, Criminal Rexcords, April 4, 1856.

29 Assizes were periodic courts that heard major cases, mostly criminal, that were committed to it by Quarter Sessions (local county courts that were held four times per year to deal with civil and criminal cases). Assize Courts were the upper courts and Quarter Sessions the intermediate courts, while minor offences were dealt with summarily by justices of the peace in magistrate's courts.

30 Huron County, Clerk of the Peace, Criminal Records, March Sessions, 1858, Indictment, with notations.

31   *London Times*, January 2, 1846.

32   Huron County, Clerk of the Peace, Criminal Justice Accounts,
      November Sessions, 1846, account of coroner George Fraser, and
      account of sheriff Huron District. See also *London Times*, October 2,
      1846.

33   "The *St. Marys Argus* says: On Friday night, the body of Richard
      Brumbecombe [sic], a farmer residing in Usborne, was found
      murdered on the 7th Concession of Biddulph, about two miles
      from the Proof Line road." *London Free Press*, February 13, 1857.

34   Huron County, Clerk of the Peace, Criminal Records, Indictment,
      November 1862. See also *Huron Signal*, November 14, 1862,
      which carries a report of the trial.

35   William Carleton, *Traits and Stories of the Irish Peasantry, vol. II*,
      7th ed. (London, Wm. Tegg, 1867), p. 362.

36   Reaney, *The Donnelly Documents: An Ontario Vendetta*, p. xxxvi.

37   J.J. Talman Regional Collection, University of Western Ontario
      Archives, Donnelly Family Papers, B4877, File 78, Robert Cooper,
      Letter to J.A. Macdonald, Attorney General, March 28, 1859.

38   "On September 12, 1865, the body of Pat Ryder, the elder, was
      found on the tracks of the Grand Trunk Railway near Lucan, muti-
      lated and decapitated. . . . Local legend says it was murder and that
      the old man's sons were in some way involved." Orlo Miller, *The
      Donnellys Must Die* (Toronto: Prospero Books, 1962), p. 58. See
      also, "Three years later, in September of 1865, Patrick Ryder was
      beheaded by a train on the Grand Trunk Railway track in Biddulph"
      (Middlesex County, Coroner's Inquests, Inquisition on the body of
      Patrick Ryder, September 13, 1865). See also Butt, *The Donnellys:
      History, Legend, Literature*, p. 31 (note 101 appears on p. 588).

39   Huron County, Clerk of the Peace, Criminal Records, information of
      Patrick Hogan, August 23, 1858; see also *St. Marys Argus*, July 29,
      1858.

40   Butt, *The Donnellys: History, Legend, Literature*, p. 45, citing
      Ausable Valley Conservation Report. Toronto: Department of
      Planning and Development, 1949, Part 1, p. 41.

41 At this point in history, Canada's currency was British: "For almost a century, British pounds, shillings and pence were official money in Canada; and, the standard value for the various kinds of money in circulation. . . . In 1858, a law required that accounts of the government of the Province of Canada (now Ontario and Quebec) be kept in dollars instead of pounds. At the same time, the government began to issue its own money to circulate alongside the bills issued by the Bank of Montreal and other banks." "Money in Canada," https://thecanadianencyclopedia.ca/en/article/money (accessed October 14, 2019).

42 Middlesex Registry Office, London, Abstract Book, Biddulph, to 1866, p. 64, Instrument 376, December 10, 1855.

43 Butt, *The Donnellys: History, Legend, Literature*, p. 45.

44 *London Advertiser*, February 16, 1880: "A resident of Lucan, who, for the past thirty years has watched the feud which has culminated in this terrible tragedy, was interviewed by an ADVERTISER reporter this morning. He summed up the whole thing in very few words. The man Farrell, who was killed, and the old man Donnelly, some thirty years ago, quarrelled about the location of lots. This quarrel was never forgotten up to Farrell's death." According to James Reaney (*The Donnelly Documents*, p. 8), ". . . Donnelly's hostility to Farrell was based on a quarrel about location tickets: Farrell thought he should have had VI-18, and Donnelly should have settled on VII-20!"

45 "In any event, on 19 December 1855, Farrell laid a complaint with Magistrate Daniel Shoff against Donnelly for aiming a shot at him in an altercation at Andrew Keefe's tavern on the London Road across from St. Patrick's Church." Reaney, *The Donnelly Documents: An Ontario Vendetta*, p. lii.

46 Butt, *The Donnellys: History, Legend, Literature*, p. 46. Butt cites as his source for the sentence an M.A. thesis by Michael Helm, entitled *Civil Disorders in Biddulph Township 1850–1880, A Case Study of the Donnelly Murders*, Sir George Williams University, 1970.

47 J.J. Talman Regional Collection, University of Western Ontario Archives, Reaney Papers, Box 23 (B1309), File 7B, Unknown,

Court of Common Pleas, Ejectment Notice for James Donnelly from John Grace, May 26, 1856.

48 J.J. Talman Regional Collection, University of Western Ontario Archives, Reaney Papers, Box 23 (B1309), File 7B, Unknown, Court of Common Pleas, Ejectment Notice for James Donnelly from Michael Maher, August 20, 1856.

49 Middlesex County Registry Office, London. Abstract Book, Biddulph to 1886, f. 64, Instrument 414, September 2, 1856.

50 Reaney, *The Donnelly Documents: An Ontario Vendetta*, p. lii: "It was public knowledge that there was no love lost between Donnelly and Farrell. William Porte called Farrell a 'disturbing personage,' said to have been 'noted for irritable disposition since childhood.' (Reaney's source: *London Free Press*, February 12, 1880).

51 "They're all from Tip [Tipperary, Ireland] . . . and when they take a spite against a man, no matter where they may be years afterwards, they'll have revenge. I heard shortly after old Donnelly and Farrell had a row, in which Farrell was killed, that the same men fought in Ireland before coming out to Canada, and when they both got a sup of whiskey into them, the old grudge came up to the top and they went in for revenge." *London Free Press*, February 12, 1880.

52 Butt, *The Donnellys: History, Legend, Literature*, pp. 45 and 594, note 32. See also "Middlesex Court of Chancery, Patrick Ryder v. Michael Feeheley, July 30, 1870, to February 23, 1871: a suit over Lot 16 on the Seventh Concession. The history of the transactions concerning this lot is contained in the plaintiff's Bill of Complaint (August 30, 1870), defendant's Answer (October 16, 1870), and defendant's chancery deposition (November 5, 1870). Farrell had to mortgage the property on January 17, 1857."

53 Butt, *The Donnellys: History, Legend, Literature*, p. 45.

54 "There had been no quarrelling in the forenoon that I could see." Testimony of Patrick Ryan, National Archives of Canada, Provincial Secretary's Correspondence, RG 5, C1, Vol. 539, No. 1653, Huron County.

55 "I considered that Donnelly tried most to keep the quarrel going . . ." Testimony of Michael Carroll. See also, ". . . of

the two, prisoner [Donnelly] seemed the most eager for the quarrel." Testimony of Michael Carroll, Archives of Ontario, RG 22-390-2, Box 31, Env. 1, pp. 400–08, Justice Sir John Robinson's Bench Books, March–May 1858. Courthouse Vault, Goderich, Criminal Proceedings, Assizes, Huron and Bruce Spring Assizes, 1858, Queen v. James Donnelly, Murder of Patrick Farrell, 25 June 1857. And: ". . . thinks it was Donnelly's intention to pick a quarrel with someone when he came to the bee more than to help to do anything." Testimony of William Maloney, National Archives of Canada, Provincial Secretary's Correspondence, RG 5, C1, Vol. 539, No. 1653, Huron County.

56 Testimony of Martin Mackey; Archives of Ontario, RG 22-390-2, Box 31, Env. 1, pp. 400–08, Justice Sir John Robinson's Bench Books, March–May 1858.

57 "I think it might be between two and three o'clock that day when the fight took place." Testimony of Patrick Ryan. See also: "I am acquainted with the deceased Patrick Farrell, in the afternoon he was drunk, himself and Donnelly was quarrelling, began about an hour or two in the afternoon." Testimony of Michael Carroll. National Archives of Canada, Provincial Secretary's Correspondence, RG 5, C1, Vol. 539, No. 1653, Huron County.

58 "There was hard feelings before . . . about land." Testimony of Michael Carroll, Archives of Ontario, RG 22-390-2, Box 31, Env. 1, pp. 400–08, Justice Sir John Robinson's Bench Books, March–May 1858.

59 ". . . a quarrel took place between James Donnelly and Patrick Farrell who was drunk and accused Donnelly for shooting him once before." Testimony of Patrick Ryan, National Archives of Canada, Provincial Secretary's Correspondence, RG 5, C1, Vol. 539, No. 1653, Huron Co.

60 "[I] was at the bee . . . heard prisoner [Donnelly] asked Farrell to spar with him. Farrell said he would not . . ." Testimony of Michael Carroll, Archives of Ontario, RG 22-390-2, Box 31, Env. 1, pp. 400–408, Justice Sir John Robinson's Bench Books, March–May 1858.

61 "I considered that Donnelly tried most to keep the quarrel going, did not see anyone else but Donnelly, that had any dispute with Farrell on that day." Testimony of Michael Carroll, National Archives of Canada, Provincial Secretary's Correspondence, RG 5, C1, Vol. 539, No. 1653, Huron Co. Carroll further testified that, "of the two prisoners [Donnelly] seemed the most eager for the quarrel." Archives of Ontario, RG 22-390-2, Box 31, Env. 1, pp. 400–408, Justice Sir John Robinson's Bench Books, March–May 1858.

62 "Farrell when drunk was fond of wrestling." Testimony of Michael Carroll, Archives of Ontario, RG 22-390-2, Box 31, Env. 1, pp. 400–08, Justice Sir John Robinson's Bench Books, March–May 1858.

63 "Soon after . . . Donnelly came into the field . . . heard that Farrell & Donnelly were fighting and saw they were wrestling and striking, no weapons." Testimony of Cornelius Lanigan, Archives of Ontario, RG 22-390-2, Box 31, Env. 1, pp. 400–08, Justice Sir John Robinson's Bench Books, March–May 1858.

64 "There was no ceasing from the work on account of the words the men did not gather." Testimony of Patrick Ryan; Ryan further adds that "in the first place they were separate about twenty rods from the rest of the men in the field that was the first I had seen of them." And that he himself was 20 to 25 rods away from the fighters (note: a "rod" is a surveyor's tool and unit of length exactly 16½ feet, so he would have been 330 to 412.5 feet away); Cornelius Maloney claimed to be "10 or 12 rods" away (165 to 198 feet away); William Maloney claimed he was "five rods" away (82.5 feet away); Michael Carroll said he was "about four or five rods" (66 to 82.5 feet away). National Archives of Canada, Provincial Secretary's Correspondence, RG 5, C1, Vol. 539, No. 1653, Huron County.

65 National Archives of Canada, Provincial Secretary's Correspondence, RG 5, C1, Vol. 539: ". . . they fought for about 20 minutes or half an hour as near as I could say." Testimony of Patrick Ryan.

66 ". . . heard that Farrell and Donnelly were fighting and saw they were wrestling and striking, no weapons. We parted them." Testimony of Cornelius Lanigan. See also Martin Mackey's

testimony: "they were parted by Lanigan." Archives of Ontario, RG 22-390-2, Box 31, Env. 1, pp. 400–08, Justice Sir John Robinson's Bench Books, March–May 1858. And Cornelius Maloney's testimony: "I saw Cornelius Lanigan separating them." National Archives of Canada, Provincial Secretary's Correspondence, RG 5, C1, Vol. 539, No. 1653, Huron County.

67 "Cornelius Lanigan and Thomas McLaughlin tried to separate Patrick Farrell and James several times . . ." Testimony of Patrick Ryan. National Archives of Canada, Provincial Secretary's Correspondence, RG 5, C1, Vol. 539, No. 1653, Huron County.

68 "The grog boss gave them no more liquor; he gave up the bottle to William Maloney." Butt, *The Donnellys: History, Legend, Literature*, p. 48.

69 "These two men James Donnelly and Farrell were very drunk, the latter was falling about. I heard some say that Farrell was sitting down and some that he was lying down . . ." Testimony of Patrick Ryan. National Archives of Canada, Provincial Secretary's Correspondence, RG 5, C1, Vol. 539, No. 1653, Huron County.

70 "[I] saw both parties about nine or ten minutes before the blow was struck they were in the act of fighting and were put apart, heard Farrell say before he got the blow, that he "had enough and would fight no more." Testimony of William Maloney. National Archives of Canada, Provincial Secretary's Correspondence, RG 5, C1, Vol. 539.

71 "Donnelly asked a chew of Tobacco from me about three or four minutes before the blow was struck." Testimony of Michael Carroll. National Archives of Canada, Provincial Secretary's Correspondence, RG 5, C1, Vol. 539.

72 "A wooden handspike or pry is about seven feet long by three inches thick at the prying end. In the north it is usually made from a hickory or an ironwood or dogwood sapling. The bark is removed and the handle is worked round and smooth. . . ." Herbert A. Shearer, *The Farm Workshop — With Information on Tools and Buildings*, Jepson Press, 2016.

73 "Farrell was quite drunk — Farrell had handspike in his hand." Testimony of Cornelius Lanigan. Archives of Ontario,

RG 22-390-2, Box 31, Env. 1, pp. 400–408, Justice Sir John Robinson's Bench Books, March–May 1858. See also testimony of Patrick Ryan: ". . . there were some handspikes lying about where they were logging." National Archives of Canada, Provincial Secretary's Correspondence, RG 5, C1, Vol. 539, No. 1653, Huron County.

74 "I told Farrell to go home." Testimony of Cornelius Lanigan. Archives of Ontario, RG 22-390-2, Box 31, Env. 1, pp. 400–08, Justice Sir John Robinson's Bench Books, March–May 1858.

75 "He told Witness [Cornelius Lanigan] to keep away or he would hit him with a handspike, which he held in his hand . . ." Testimony from Cornelius Lanigan. Archives of Ontario, RG 22-390-2, Box 31, Env. 1, pp. 400–08, Justice Sir John Robinson's Bench Books, March–May 1858.

76 "I think Martin Mackey told me that he tried to ward off the blow from Farrell . . ." Testimony of Michael Carroll. National Archives of Canada, Provincial Secretary's Correspondence, RG 5, C1, Vol. 539, No. 1653, Huron County.

77 "[I] tried to take it from him . . . Farrell was knocked down." Testimony of Cornelius Lanigan. Archives of Ontario, RG 22-390-2, Box 31, Env. 1, pp. 400–08, Justice Sir John Robinson's Bench Books, March–May 1858. See also testimony of Michael Carroll: "I heard that Martin Mackey and Lanigan had something to do in trying to take a handspike from the deceased when he got the blow that killed him." National Archives of Canada, Provincial Secretary's Correspondence, RG 5, C1, Vol. 539, No. 1653, Huron County.

78 "I saw the deceased Patrick Farrell struck by James Donnelly with a handspike. Deceased was lying down at the time that Donnelly struck him with the handspike. Only saw him strike him once to my knowledge. I consider I was three or four rods from them when the blow was struck. I did not see Farrell fall but saw him on the ground before he was struck. I did not see anyone try to prevent Donnelly from striking him. Donnelly was well able to walk about when he gave the blow after they were separated. Donnelly wheeled away and then turned again; I saw him raise the handspike with both hands

and strike him (Farrell) across the head." Testimony of Cornelius Maloney. National Archives of Canada, Provincial Secretary's Correspondence, RG 5, C1, Vol. 539, No. 1653, Huron County.

79 National Archives of Canada, Provincial Secretary's Correspondence, RG 5, C1, Vol. 539. ". . . on examination of the skull a fracture without any appreciable depression extended directly across the head . . ." Testimony of physician who conducted the autopsy, Charles G. Moore.

80 "[I] heard them say that the man was killed . . ." Testimony of Michael Carroll. Archives of Ontario, RG 22-390-2, Box 31, Env. 1, pp. 400–08, Justice Sir John Robinson's Bench Books, March–May 1858.

81 "I went to him when he was struck and raised up his head, and asked who struck him. I asked a second time . . ." Testimony of Michael Carroll. National Archives of Canada, Provincial Secretary's Correspondence, RG 5, C1, Vol. 539, No. 1653, Huron County.

82 "John [Toohey] made answer that it was Donnelly that struck him." Testimony of Michael Carroll. National Archives of Canada, Provincial Secretary's Correspondence, RG 5, C1, Vol. 539.

83 The testimony here is a little ambiguous. According to Martin Mackey, Donnelly was heard to have said, "He said to us, 'There's your friend for you now and it's five years ago he had a wish to do the deed.'" However, Michael Carroll recollected that he had "heard Donnelly say then that it was either '3 years or 5 years before that he wished to get back — and that his children would have satisfaction when he the prisoner [Donnelly] was in the grave.'" Both quotes appear in Archives of Ontario, RG 22-390-2, Box 31, Env. 1, pp. 400–08, Justice Sir John Robinson's Bench Books, March–May 1858.

84 "Did not see Donnelly strike Farrell but heard someone cry out, 'Donnelly you have murdered the man!'" Testimony of William Maloney. National Archives of Canada, Provincial Secretary's Correspondence, RG 5, C1, Vol. 539, No. 1653, Huron County.

85 National Archives of Canada, Provincial Secretary's Correspondence, RG 5, C1, Vol. 539. ". . . we all went home after the body was taken up to Maloney's . . ." Testimony of Patrick Ryan.

86 ". . . the breath was in him, that was all . . ." Patrick Ryan, National Archives of Canada, Provincial Secretary's Correspondence, RG 5, C1, Vol. 539, No. 1653, Huron County.

87 Reaney, *The Donnelly Documents: An Ontario Vendetta*, p. 21.

88 Testimony of Sarah Farrell. National Archives of Canada, Provincial Secretary's Correspondence, RG 5, C1, Vol. 539, No. 1653, Huron County.

89 "James Donnelly was at his own home on the day after the killing." Butt, *The Donnellys: History, Legend, Literature*, p. 49.

90 "Farrell died on Friday — the day after the bee . . ." Testimony of Michael Carroll, Archives of Ontario, RG 22-390-2, Box 31, Env. 1, pp. 400–08, Justice Sir John Robinson's Bench Books, March–May 1858.

91 ". . . at the residence of the deceased found the body in a very advanced state of decomposition, so much so that it would have been impossible to identify deceased." Testimony of Dr. Charles G. Moore. National Archives of Canada, Provincial Secretary's Correspondence, RG 5, C1, Vol. 539, No. 1653, Huron County.

92 Testimony of Dr. Charles G. Moore. National Archives of Canada, Provincial Secretary's Correspondence, RG 5, C1, Vol. 539, No. 1653, Huron County.

93 "Donnelly was at my house on Sunday night, was there also on Saturday Morning between seven and eight o'clock and said he was sorry for what he had done . . ." Testimony of Michael Carroll. National Archives of Canada, Provincial Secretary's Correspondence, RG 5, C1, Vol. 539, No. 1653, Huron County.

94 Testimony of Michael Carroll. National Archives of Canada, Provincial Secretary's Correspondence, RG 5, C1, Vol. 539, No. 1653, Huron County.

95 Donnelly's flight from the law and information on the various manhunts that followed are taken from Huron County, Clerk of the Peace, Criminal Justice Accounts, December Sessions, 1857 (testimony of John Hodgins); March Sessions, 1858 (testimony of Barber Regan, Jeffrey Harbourn, William Howard and Henry Sutton); June Sessions, 1858 (testimony from Barber Regan, Jeffrey

Harbourn, William Howard, Henry Sutton, Jeremiah Lewis and Adam Hodgins).

96 J.J. Talman Regional Collection, University of Western Ontario Archives, Reaney Papers, Box 26 (B1312), File 51B, Warden, Huron and Bruce Counties, Letter to Administrator of the Government of Canada from the Warden, Huron and Bruce Counties, October 10, 1857. The reward posting read as follows:

REWARDS!! $400 AND $100

The Municipal County Council of the United Counties of Huron and Bruce, offer a reward of $400 for the apprehension and delivery in the County Gaol, Goderich of JAMES DONNELLY of the Township of Biddulph in the County of Huron, accused of murdering Patrick Farrell of the same place, on Thursday the 25th day of June 1857. A further reward of $100 is also offered to any person giving such information as will lead to the conviction of the person or persons harbouring the said James Donnelly.

97 Reaney Papers, Box 26 (B1312), File 51B, Warden, Huron and Bruce Counties.

98 "During the time he was hidden in the neighbourhood, and at times he ventured home. It is even said that he worked on his farm disguised in female garments." *The Globe*, February 6, 1880.

99 *London Free Press*, January 15, 1913.

100 "Haskett applied for the $400 reward, supported by an affidavit from Mrs. Donnelly; quite rightly, collusion was suspected." Reaney, *The Donnelly Documents: An Ontario Vendetta*, p. liii.

101 ". . . Jury returned back with verdict of Guilty Sentenced to be taken to the gaol from [whence?] he came then on M. the 14th September next to the place of execution there to be hanged by the neck until dead." J.J. Talman Regional Collection, University of Western Ontario Archives, Donnelly Family Papers, Box 4877, File 3, Unknown, Sentence for James Donnelly for Murder of Patrick Farrell, May 14, 1858.

102 Reaney, *The Donnelly Documents: An Ontario Vendetta*, p. liv.

103 Butt, *The Donnellys: History, Legend, Literature*, p. 52.

104 J.J. Talman Regional Collection, University of Western Ontario Archives, Reaney Papers, Box 26 (B1312), File 51B, Government of Canada, Order in Council Commuting the Sentence of James Donnelly, July 26, 1858.

105 Reaney, *The Donnelly Documents: An Ontario Vendetta*, p. liv.

106 *London Free Press*, January 15, 1913.

CHAPTER THREE: GROWING UP DONNELLY

1   *London Advertiser*, February 5, 1880.

2   Letter written by Mabel Armstrong to Spencer Armitage-Stanley, University of Western Ontario, Spencer-Stanley Papers, January 10, 1963.

3   *London Advertiser*, February 5, 1880.

4   *London Advertiser*, February 6, 1880.

5   *London Advertiser*, February 5, 1880.

6   Middlesex Clerk of the Peace, Quarter Sessions Minute Book, September 15 and 17, 1864. See also Middlesex Crown County Crown Attorney Docket, 1863–1876. Quarter Sessions, September 1864, and Fall Assizes, 1864.

7   *London Advertiser*, October 22, 1878. "An old lady named Donnelly was charged before Squire Peters yesterday with using abusive and insulting language towards James Carroll, in the township of Biddulph. The complainant, Carroll, swore that Mrs. Donnelly called him a blackguard, thief and rogue [in the court case Carroll alleged that she'd called him a "son of a bitch"], while the defendant's two sons swore positively that the term blackguard was only used. They also swore that Carroll pointed a revolver at Mrs. Donnelly, saying at the same time that he would just as soon shoot her as he would one of her sons. Judgement was reserved until to-day."

8   J.J. Talman Regional Collection, University of Western Ontario
     Archives, Donnelly Family Papers, B4877, File 34, Unknown,
     Ryder v. Donnelly, Arson of Ryder's Barn, January 27, 1880.

9   ". . . a tall powerful woman." *London Advertiser*, February 5, 1880.

10   "She looked like and should have been a man, her sex undoubtedly
     robbing the bare-knuckle prize ring of a prospective champion. In
     later years she sprouted a miniature Vandyke, wore red flannels and
     told of never having been 'much of a beauty.' Her picture proves
     the words to be a gross understatement." Thomas P. Kelley, *The
     Black Donnellys: The True Story of Canada's Most Barbaric Feud*
     (Toronto: Darling Terrace Publishing, 2018). Kindle edition, pp.
     117–23.

11   *London Free Press*, February 12, 1880.

12   *Toronto Mail*, February 13, 1880.

13   "A Close Observer's Opinion," *London Free Press*, February 12,
     1880. It is believed that the "close observer" in this instance was
     the Lucan postmaster, William Porte.

14   Toronto *Globe*, February 6, 1880.

15   *Ottawa Free Press*, February 6, 1880.

16   Toronto *Globe*, February 6, 1880.

17   Reaney, *The Donnelly Documents: An Ontario Vendetta*, p. xxix.

18   *The Globe*, February 7, 1880.

19   "A splitting maul, also known as a *block buster, block splitter,
     sledge axe, go-devil* or *hamaxe* is a heavy, long-handled axe used for
     splitting a piece of wood along its grain. One side of its head is like a
     sledgehammer, and the other side is like an axe. . . . A typical wood
     splitting maul has a head weight of 6 to 8 lb." "Splitting maul,"
     https://en.wikipedia.org/wiki/Splitting_maul.

20   *The Globe*, September 10, 1880.

21   *The Globe*, September 10, 1880.

22   *The Globe*, September 10, 1880. William Donnelly relates that
     the fire broke out in July 1857, however the newspaper report (*St.
     Marys Argus*, July 29, 1858) reveals that it was in July 1858.

23   *The Globe*, September 10, 1880.

24   *The Globe*, September 10, 1880.

25   J.J. Talman Regional Collection, University of Western Ontario Archives, Donnelly Family Papers, Box 4877, File 5, Unknown, Information of Witnesses, Inquest on Bodies of Catherine Garburth and Sarah Harcourt, May 29, 1861.

26   "Atkinson being a very common Biddulph name, precise identification of this one is difficult. Of the six James Atkinsons listed on the 1861 Census of Canada for Biddulph, the three most likely possibilities are aged 18, 17 and 13 in 1857." Butt, *The Donnellys: History, Legend, Literature*, p. 599.

27   Huron County, Clerk of the Peace, Criminal Records, 1857.

28   Terry Culbert, *Lucan: Home of the Donnellys: Linger Longer in Lovely Lucan* (Renfrew, Ontario: General Store Publishing House, 2006), p. 25.

29   Culbert, *Lucan: Home of the Donnellys: Linger Longer in Lovely Lucan*, p. 25.

30   Culbert, *Lucan: Home of the Donnellys: Linger Longer in Lovely Lucan*, p. 25.

31   Reaney, *The Donnelly Documents: An Ontario Vendetta*, pp. lv–lvi.

32   Butt, *The Donnellys: History, Legend, Literature*, p. 55.

33   J.J. Talman Regional Collection, University of Western Ontario Archives, Reaney Papers, Box 26 (B1312), File 51A, Unknown, Prison Record Book, Kingston Penitentiary, January 4, 1861.

34   Reaney Papers, Box 26 (B1312), File 51B, Unknown, Petition to Commute the Sentence of James Donnelly, June 5, 1862. Although she was referred to as Johannah throughout her life, Mrs. Donnelly's actual name was Judith. Her friends usually referred to her as 'Judy' or 'Julie.'

35   Reaney, *The Donnelly Documents: An Ontario Vendetta*, p. xxviii.

36   Reaney, *The Donnelly Documents: An Ontario Vendetta*, pp. lv–lvi.

37   Kingston Penitentiary Punishment Register cited in Culbert, *Lucan: Home of the Donnellys: Linger Longer in Lovely Lucan*, p. 25.

38   Culbert, *Lucan: Home of the Donnellys: Linger Longer in Lovely Lucan*, p. 25.

39   J.J. Talman Regional Collection, University of Western Ontario
     Archives, Donnelly Family Papers, B4877, File 6, Unknown,
     William Ryan v. John Carroll, Assault, February 27, 1863.
40   Middlesex Clerk of the Peace, Quarter Sessions Minute Book,
     September 15 and 17, 1864. See also Middlesex Crown County
     Crown Attorney Docket, 1863–1876 — Quarter Sessions,
     September 1864, and Fall Assizes, 1864.
41   Reaney, *The Donnelly Documents: An Ontario Vendetta*, p. 9,
     note 12.
42   Michael Maher would die in Bay City, Michigan, the following
     year. Reaney, *The Donnelly Documents: An Ontario Vendetta*, p. 8,
     note 4.
43   *London Free Press*, February 12, 1880.
44   Kingston Penitentiary Punishment Register cited in Culbert, *Lucan:
     Home of the Donnellys: Linger Longer in Lovely Lucan*, p. 25.
45   National Archives of Canada, Kingston Penitentiary, RG73, Vol.
     357, Prisoner 4615, Unknown, Kingston Penitentiary Liberation
     Interview, James Donnelly, July 26, 1865. Note: The ques-
     tions listed were not recorded in the liberation book. They are
     included to place James Donnelly's answers in context. Source:
     Canada's Penitentiary Museum, Correctional Services Canada,
     "The Inspector's Minute Book," February 3, 1848–October 1,
     1864, p. 480.

CHAPTER FOUR: LOVE AND WAR

1   Albeit not from any North American institution, but rather from
    the University of Leuven, in Belgium.
2   "Wild Bill Hickok–Davis Tutt Shootout," https://en.wikipedia.org/
    wiki/Wild_Bill_Hickok_-_Davis_Tutt_shootout (accessed January
    22, 2019).
3   In June 1870, the Congress of the United States requested a report
    on trade between Canada and the United States. J.N. Larned, the

editor for the *Buffalo Morning Express*, was tasked with drawing up the report. He spoke with members of the Canadian government and civil service and combed through the Bureau of Statistics in Washington. Within his report he stated that ". . . while for every $100 of wages the average workman received in Ontario, he was paid $165 in currency in New York. . . . While for every $100 of wages that the average workman received in Quebec, he was paid $238 currency . . . in New York"; 41st Congress, 3rd Session, *House Executive Documents*, No. 94, "State of Trade with British North American Provinces," p. 25.

4   Reaney, *The Donnelly Documents: An Ontario Vendetta: Documents*, pp. 30–32.

5   Reaney, *The Donnelly Documents: An Ontario Vendetta: Documents*, pp. 30–32.

6   *London Free Press*, November 3, 1865.

7   ". . . my father was very badly hurt; his collar bone was broken; he was confined to the house for more than a week." Testimony of Sarah Kennedy. *London Free Press*, November 3, 1865.

8   "Patrick Hogan (b. 1831), oldest son of James Hogan, VII-24; rated second class service on 1865 Militia Roll. Found guilty of common assault and sentenced to 3 months in jail at hard labour." Reaney, *The Donnelly Documents: An Ontario Vendetta: Documents*, pp. 30–32.

9   Reaney, *The Donnelly Documents: An Ontario Vendetta: Documents*, p. lviii.

10 Butt, *The Donnellys: History, Legend, Literature*, p. 57.

11 *The Globe*; February 7, 1880. See also Butt, *The Donnellys: History, Legend, Literature*, p. 57.

12 Miller, *The Donnellys Must Die*, p. 53: "With her fugitive husband to care for as well, Johannah now had ten mouths to feed, for the family circle had been swelled by the unofficial adoption of still another boy — William Farrell, son of the man Jim Donnelly had killed. From the day Pat Farrell died, Jim and Johannah assumed the care of his son, bringing him up as one of their own."

13 Reaney, *The Donnelly Documents: An Ontario Vendetta*: pp. lvi–lvii: "In passing, oral tradition has it that the Donnellys

fostered Sarah Farrell's oldest boy, William. There seem to be some grounds for truth to this since, in February 1876, he is seen as a very active member of the Donnelly gang during the Ryder Wedding Riot."

14 Butt, *The Donnellys: History, Legend, Literature*, p. 57.

15 "Graham and one of his witnesses, a woman who had lived with him eleven years, and whom he described as a poor orphan, were habitual tipplers, and encouraged at their house a number of persons of similar habits." *London Free Press*, November 1, 1869.

16 Municipal Council Proceedings for Biddulph Township, September 7, 1862–1891 (specifically for September 7, 1868). University of Western Ontario, Regional Collection, D.B. Weldon Library.

17 Middlesex, Clerk of the Peace, Quarter Sessions Minute Book, June 11, 1869. Donnelly is described as a "student at school."

18 Reaney, *The Donnelly Documents: An Ontario Vendetta*, p. lviii.

19 *London Free Press*, November 1, 1869.

20 *London Free Press*, April 23, 1869.

21 Years later, when he was a constable in Glencoe, William Donnelly would make reference to his club foot thusly: "There is one thing in particular I wish to impress on the minds of the public, and that is — that I am a little tender in the front feet, and to prevent any chance of giving an exhibition of speed across the country in pursuit of a prisoner, I will in most cases use handcuffs." *Glencoe Transcript*, July 9, 1885.

22 See *London Advertiser*, February 10, 1880 for "lawyer" and "plotter of the family" sobriquets.

23 University of Western Ontario, Middlesex County Quarterly Return of Convictions, Court of Quarter Sessions for the Quarter ending September 14, 1869, indicates that there were not three, but four defendants: "Jas Donely, [sic] W. Donely, [sic] Rod'y Kennedy, J. Kennedy."

24 *St. Marys Argus*, July 29, 1869.

25 Reaney, *The Donnelly Documents: An Ontario Vendetta*, p. lix.

26 *The Globe*, February 11, 1880.

27 Biddulph Township Assessment Roll, 1870, 1871 and 1872.

28   According to the Canada Census, 1870, Biddulph Township, Agricultural Return, thirty of the farm's fifty acres had been improved, with two acres in orchards and gardens, ten acres of spring wheat (yielding two hundred bushels), four acres in pasture, two acres of potatoes (yielding three hundred bushels), fifteen acres of hay (yielding twelve tons), twenty bushels of barley, ninety bushels of peas, two hundred bushels of oats, twenty pounds of maple sugar and fifty bushels of apples. They now had four horses that were over three years of age, ten sheep, three milking cows, two "horned cattle," six pigs and two hundred cords of firewood. The farm further produced forty pounds of wool, two hundred pounds of butter, four sheep and one cattle-beast that were either sold for export or killed. In addition to their house, they had constructed two stables and barns, and purchased two each of cars, wagons and sleds, and had three cultivators and ploughs, two fanning mills and one horse rake.

29   Miller, *The Donnellys Must Die*, pp. 38–39.

30   University of Western Ontario Archives, J.J. Talman Regional Collection, Donnelly Family Papers. Spencer Seeley Armitage-Stanley, quoted in Reaney, *The Donnelly Documents: An Ontario Vendetta*, p. 1.

31   The Biddulph Township Council remitted taxes of $8.11 for the Donnelly farm. The reason given was "on account of barn and contents being burnt. Thought to be incendiary." *London Free Press*, December 5, 1870.

32   The Biddulph Township Council remitted taxes because of "barns burnt by incendiarists" and also reported that "Owens is leaving the Township." "Biddulph Municipal Proceedings," *London Free Press*, January 25, 1867.

33   *St. Marys Argus and Review*, February 10, 1871.

34   Reaney, *The Donnelly Documents: An Ontario Vendetta*, p. lxii.

35   *St. Marys Argus and Review*, April 21, 1871.

36   Reaney, *The Donnelly Documents: An Ontario Vendetta*, p. lxiii.

37   Willem Bart de Lint, "Shaping the Subject of Policing: Autonomy, Regulation, and the Constable," (PhD diss., University of Toronto), pp. 13–14. He cites from Greg Marquis, *Policing Canada's*

Century: A History of the Canadian Association of Chiefs of Police (Toronto: University of Toronto Press, 1993).

38 Reaney, *The Donnelly Documents: An Ontario Vendetta*, p. xxxvii.

39 *London Daily Advertiser*, September 2, 1871.

40 *London Free Press*, September 2, 1871 and September 16, 1871. The latter edition of the newspaper contained an intriguing statement of (possibly) Jennie Donnelly's involvement in defending Gray, who was a friend of the family: "The accused had a large number of witnesses supported, whose evidence would doubtless have thrown some light on the suspicion freely expressed by Gray's friends that the charge was a trumped up one. Among them was a little girl named Donnelly [Jennie would have been fifteen at the time], who had come prepared to testify that the prosecutor had tried to induce her by offers of money to connect Gray with the crime."

41 Notes from Enid McIlhargey, dated June 27, 1960. Enid's father-in-law, John McIlhargey, worked for Bob Donnelly in Lucan and his father, Zacharia, was a long-time friend of the Donnelly family. Notes courtesy of Enid's daughter, Ely Errey, from an email to the author on January 15, 2021.

42 Reaney, *The Donnelly Documents: An Ontario Vendetta*, p. lxiii.

43 Miller, *The Donnellys Must Die*, p. 70.

44 Miller, *The Donnellys Must Die*, letter reproduced on p. 72.

45 Miller, *The Donnellys Must Die*, p. 70: ". . . Will had an easy way with people, and that was a good thing for a stage driver to have."

46 Butt, *The Donnellys: History, Legend, Literature*, p. 60.

47 Advertisements for the various stagecoach lines were prevalent in both the *London Advertiser* and the *London Free Press* throughout the 1870s.

48 Butt, *The Donnellys: History, Legend, Literature*, pp. 72–73.

49 *St. Marys Argus*, March 29, 1872.

50 "It was a common thing for stage drivers of opposing lines to meet at stage stations and fight like wild cats, and a man of pugilistic fame often drew double the pay of an ordinary peaceful driver, and fighting qualifications were recognized as a mark of efficiency. . . . "

W.B. Hobson, *Old Stage Days in Oxford County*. Ontario Historical Society, Papers and Records, Vol. XVII (1919), pp. 33–36.

51   Butt, *The Donnellys: History, Legend, Literature*, p. 74.

52   Butt, *The Donnellys: History, Legend, Literature*, p. 373, quoting Heywood, Earl, *Tales of the Donnelly Feud*, Toronto, Waterless Melon Music, Pg. 2, 1971. See also *London Free Press*, August 30, 1973: ". . . one lady who was alive when the Donnellys were competing for the stage coach trade told me they were a pretty respectable bunch, except they sometimes would grab some of the competition's customers if the Donnellys arrived in town first."

53   Miller, *The Donnellys Must Die*, Letter reproduced on p. 73.

54   National Archives of Canada, William Donnelly Fonds, MG29 C72, Margaret Thompson, Letter to William Donnelly, December 24, 1873: "My friends heard all about me writing letters to you, which caused an awful storm . . ."

55   *London Free Press*, February 10, 1874.

56   Reaney, *The Donnelly Documents: An Ontario Vendetta*, p. lxiv.

57   Margaret Thompson, Letter to William Donnelly, December 24, 1873. National Archives of Canada, William Donnelly Fonds, MG29 C72.

58   Middlesex County is an area of land that presently covers the better part of 1,281 square miles and in the Donnellys' day contained no fewer than fifteen townships, of which Biddulph was one, and twenty-four towns and villages. For examples of William Donnelly serving subpoenas on behalf of the Sheriff of Middlesex, see Middlesex Sheriff's Day-Book, February 27, September 22 and October 29, 1873.

59   For the ages and marital status of those mentioned, see Census of Canada 1871; for addresses, see Assessment Rolls for Lucan and for Biddulph, 1873.

60   See note 66.

61   All information regarding the sequence of events and the dialogue that follows for this incident are taken from the newspaper article entitled "The Biddulph Ku-Klux," *London Free Press*, February 10, 1874.

62 Michael Thompson said under oath, "I recognized Michael Donnelly as one of the parties. He was not disguised; I could see his features plainly." *London Free Press*, February 10, 1874.

63 "They had hidden [Margaret] at the farm of their son-in-law, James Toohey, on Concession VII Lot 28." [Biddulph]. Reaney, *The Donnelly Documents: An Ontario Vendetta*, p. lxiii.

64 Under oath, William Thompson Sr. testified that "I recognized Thomas Donnelly, Michael Donnelly, William Donnelly, and Daniel Keefe, as four of the persons who were there, and the third named was the one who drove the team." *London Free Press*, February 10, 1874.

65 *London Free Press*, February 10, 1874. Testimony of Michael Thompson: "After they searched the house they went out."

66 According to testimony given by Ellen Fogarty that was quoted in the *London Free Press*, February 10, 1874, William Thompson Sr., followed in hot pursuit by the conspirators, arrived at her front door at 9 p.m.

67 Testimony of William Thompson Jr. *London Free Press*, February 10, 1874.

68 Reaney, *The Donnelly Documents: An Ontario Vendetta*, pp. 37–41. "Daniel Keefe (b. 1830), son of Matthew Keefe, VI-2g, RC, alcoholic, rioter in the Donnelly gang; six months for stabbing Martin O'Meara in 1872."

69 William Donnelly's letter is published in different forms, with certain omissions in certain presentations. See for example Reaney, *The Donnelly Documents: An Ontario Vendetta*, pp. 36–37; Miller, *The Donnellys Must Die*, pp. 81–82. The letter itself is preserved in the National Archives of Canada, William Donnelly Fonds, MG29 C72, William Donnelly, Letter to William Thompson, January 12, 1874, from which the author's version has been fully transcribed.

70 Butt, *The Donnellys: History, Legend, Literature*, p. 601, note 134: "The handwriting appears to be William Porte's (cf. any passage in his diary); apparently Porte is intervening pseudonymously in an effort to make peace."

71 This statement was not mere hyperbole; a few years later one of the men in William Donnelly's gang of rescuers, William Atkinson, would be hanged by the neck by an anti-Donnelly faction in the hopes that doing so would prompt him to provide them with information that would implicate the Donnelly family. Despite almost dying, he refused to say anything against the Donnellys.

72 National Archives of Canada, William Donnelly Fonds, MG29 C72, P. Mc., Letter to William Thompson, January 12, 1874.

73 Miller, *The Donnellys Must Die*, p. 81.

74 Michael Carroll's statements at the trial, such as, "[I] was at the bee . . . heard prisoner [James Donnelly Sr.] asked Farrell to spar with him. Farrell said he would not. . . . never saw him [Farrell] quarrelling," did not help James Donnelly Sr.'s case. According to author James Reaney, "While other accounts show Farrell to have been quarrelsome and rambunctious, Carroll represents him as a peacelover. His testimony could easily have sealed Donnelly's fate and it certainly justified the first sentence of hanging. Clearly, his evidence fired the Donnelly hostility to him." Reaney, *The Donnelly Documents: An Ontario Vendetta*, p. 26.

75 "Charivari, as it was known in England and Canada, was a way for communities to break up any relationships they didn't approve of. Adulterers, wife beaters and couples seen as having illegitimate marriages were all at risk to have their doors knocked down by an angry mob in the middle of the night. Some communities disapproved of a large age-gap between spouses, or if a widow re-married too soon after her husband died. The intervention involved noisemaking, shaming activities (being paraded around town on a donkey) and sometimes even killing. While they sometimes resulted in the permanent dissolution of the couple, they often were just a way for the community to loudly voice their disapproval of the event — many times life resumed as normal afterwards." "Shivaree: The traditional hazing of our newlywed ancestors," https://findmypast.com/blog/history/shivaree-when-the-whole-community-interrupted-your-wedding-night (accessed December 20, 2020). See also Loretta T. Johnson, Charivari/

Shivaree: "A European Folk Ritual on the American Plains" in *The Journal of Interdisciplinary History* Vo. 20, No. 3 (Winter, 1990), pp. 371–387.

76 Miller, *The Donnellys Must Die*, p. 82.

77 Butt, *The Donnellys: History, Legend, Literature*, p. 64.

78 Miller, *The Donnellys Must Die*, p. 82.

79 Miller, *The Donnellys Must Die*, p. 82.

80 *London Free Press*, February 3, 1874.

81 As cited in letter to William Thompson Sr. from William Donnelly: ". . . if you should succeed, as you say you will, in sending that crowd to Kingston . . ." National Archives of Canada, William Donnelly Fonds, MG29 C72, William Donnelly, Letter to William Thompson, January 12, 1874.

82 Reaney, *The Donnelly Documents: An Ontario Vendetta*, p. lxiv.

83 "Two of the of the prisoners, viz.: Patrick Quigley and James Keefe, did not put in an appearance from some unexplained cause, and will be dealt with as the law directs in all probability for their dilatoriness." *London Free Press*, February 10, 1874.

84 "The witness became very much confused in his evidence, and got mixed as to the dress, features or disguise." *London Free Press*, February 10, 1874.

85 Middlesex County, Clerk of the Peace Criminal Records, June Sessions, 1874, Indictment, Queen v. William Donnelly et al.

86 Middlesex County Court of General Quarter Sessions Minute Book, June 11, June 16 and June 17, 1874.

87 The Toohey clan, as evidenced by James Toohey's willingness to hide Margaret Thompson in his home as a favour to her father, were always willing to help the Thompsons out. That James Toohey had put out word that he would be willing to fight William Donnelly or any member of his gang is inferred from the fact that William Donnelly draws specific attention to Toohey in his letter to William Thompson Sr.: "As far as your sons are concerned there is one of them I would for ever wish to be in friends with; but any time you feel inclined to have them or Mr. Toohey try their muscle, you will please drop a line to me or some of your humble servants

and we will try and accommodate you." National Archives of Canada, William Donnelly Fonds, MG29 C72, William Donnelly, Letter to William Thompson, January 12, 1874.

88 "I saw Daniel Keefe after the affray was over. The day after he was in bed in his own house he told me James Toohey beat him. His eyes were swelled and black." Testimony of William Donnelly. Middlesex County, Clerk of the Peace, Criminal Records, 1874, Keefe v. Toohey, Assault, testimony before Henry Ferguson, February 23, 1874.

89 "Toohey was on top of Keefe. Then either James Keefe or Patrick Quigley took Toohey off Keefe." Testimony of Joseph Fitzpatrick. Middlesex County, Clerk of the Peace, Criminal Records, 1874, Keefe v. Toohey, Assault, testimony before Henry Ferguson, February 23, 1874.

90 Both Keefe and Toohey would end up being tried in the township of Birr, and Magistrate Henry Ferguson ruled that Toohey was the guilty party (Middlesex County, Clerk of the Peace, Criminal Records, 1874, Keefe v. Toohey, Assault). Toohey's conviction would be overturned on appeal (Middlesex General Sessions, Minute Book, 1866–1876, pp. 436 and 438).

91 *London Advertiser*, February 10, 1880.

92 *London Advertiser*, February 21, 1874.

93 *London Advertiser*, February 23, 1874.

94 Reaney, *The Donnelly Documents: An Ontario Vendetta*, p. lxiv.

95 *London Advertiser*, February 10, 1880.

96 William Donnelly: "Kennedy and I were not on good terms at all; we were on good terms before I was married; as soon as I got married we got on bad terms." When asked why this was, Donnelly answered, "Probably some of my brothers beat his brother [referring to Bob and Jim Donnelly's beating of Rhody Kennedy on Lucan's Main Street]. It was after I was married and I had fallen out with him; before this he had never attacked me in any way; he knew better than to strike me; he would never do it again if he did it in daylight. He never gave me any chance; I never tried to get any chance. I have often avoided him for peace sake and kept away

from his father on that account." Testimony of William Donnelly, Archives of Ontario, Aemilius Irving Papers, February 28, 1880.

97 ". . . it appears that Father Gerard thought very highly of the Donnellys, refused to believe the stories told about their outrages, and found them to be 'aristocratic, handsome, and well-dressed,'" Reaney, *The Donnelly Documents: An Ontario Vendetta*, p. lxvi.

98 Registry Office, Abstract Book, Biddulph Book A, Instrument 2709, March 31, 1874, p. 274.

99 ". . . at one time, Clark was supposed to be in line to inherit 50 acres from his uncles, the Maloney brothers, William and Cornelius, in return for supporting them in their old age. When he was given William Maloney's 25 acres, Clark did not honor his commitment to his uncle and drank up the income from the property. It was clear he anticipated to eventually do the same for his other uncle, Cornelius', share." Reaney, *The Donnelly Documents: An Ontario Vendetta*, pp. lxvi–lxvii.

100 University of Western Ontario Middlesex Court Records, Middlesex Coroner's Inquest, March 18, 1875.

101 Testimony from the bartender, Alexander Levitt, who said, "When I put deceased out of my barroom there was Thomas and James Donnelly, Richard Tapp, Mike Sutton and another man that was living with Berryhill in the bar. . . . I did not see the deceased quarrelling with anybody, and I heard no threats. The deceased had nothing to drink in my place yesterday." Middlesex Court Records, Middlesex Coroner's Inquest, March 18, 1875.

102 James Sutton, M.D., a physician from McGillivray, testified: "After viewing the body of the deceased carefully, I could easily understand how the external injuries were caused. They were of such a trifling nature as to be of no use as to accounting for the cause of death, the slight bruise on the forehead could be easily caused by the fall. I am quite satisfied the deceased came to his death from natural causes." Middlesex Court Records, Middlesex Coroner's Inquest, March 18, 1875.

103 "The subsequent inquest concurred with Dr. Sutton's findings. Nevertheless, yet again, the Donnellys had been implicated in an

unsavory incident and Clark's death would be called yet another 'Donnelly murder.'" Reaney, *The Donnelly Documents: An Ontario Vendetta*, p. lxvii.

104 A lis pendens is "a notice filed in the public records to indicate that a legal proceeding is pending that asserts a claim against title to or some other interest in real property." "Lis Pendens," https://ca.practicallaw.thomsonreuters.com/6-556-9885?transition-Type=Default&contextData=(sc.Default)&firstPage=true&bhcp=1 (accessed June 8, 2019).

105 Reaney, *The Donnelly Documents: An Ontario Vendetta*, p. lxvii.

106 Public Archives of Ontario, Canada Company Papers, Series B3, Vol. 2, Register of Lands, Huron Tract, No. 3, 1828–1852, p. 431; see also B3, Vol. 29, Register of Leases, Huron Tract, 1842–1868, no. 927 and B3, Vol. 32, Register of Leases for Ten Years, Huron/Tract, 1852–1867, no 7059.

107 *Ottawa Free Press*, February 6, 1880, indicates that James Donnelly Jr. had assumed the previous tenant's lease of the property.

108 Middlesex County Queen Bench and Common Pleas, Docket Book, 1869–1881.

109 University of Western Ontario, Queen's Bench Pleading Book: 1874–75, p. 19.

110 "Donnelly couldn't pay subsequent instalments on the sale price of his lease, fell in arrears of rent to the Canada Company, and ran down the property. The Canada Company evicted him . . . and sold the property to newcomer Joseph Carswell, who offered to pay Donnelly for his improvements. But Donnelly demanded the full sum of his leasehold interest (which no longer legally existed since his lease had ended with his eviction), demanding a price near the freehold value. When Carswell refused to pay that amount, several misfortunes followed." Wilson, Catharine Anne, *Tenants in Time: Family Strategies, Land, and Liberalism in Upper Canada*, Montreal: McGill-Queen's University Press, 2009; pg. 160.

111 Butt, *The Donnellys: History, Legend, Literature*, p. 68.

112 As related by Carswell in the Toronto *Globe*, February 11, 1880, and the *London Free Press*, February 12, 1880.

113 Carswell quoted in the Toronto *Telegram*, February 11, 1880.

114 *London Advertiser*, August 2, 1875.

115 For all Carswell's suspicions of the Donnellys, see *Globe* and *Telegram*, February 11, 1880, and *London Free Press*, February 12, 1880.

116 *London Free Press*, July 27, 1875.

117 A reporter from the *London Free Press* commented, "Do his statements bear sifting?" and seeks to condense Carswell's stories (". . . here followed a lengthy story about a supposed attempt on the part of Bob Donnelly to take his life in broad daylight . . ."), *London Free Press*, February 12, 1880; while another reporter indicated that "The grounds for fear could not be clearly learned." *Telegram*, February 11, 1880.

118 All information regarding this incident is drawn from Middlesex County, Clerk of the Peace, Criminal Records, 1876, Queen v. James Donnelly Jr., Larceny.

CHAPTER FIVE: HELL ON WHEELS

1 "The highest ambition of the young man in early days was to be a stage driver, not that the remuneration could have been any inducement as they received ten or twelve dollars per month, but the exciting life seemed to overcome the many hardships." W.B. Hobson, "Old Stage Coach Days in Oxford County," Papers and Records of the Ontario Historical Society XVII (1919): pp. 33–36. J.J. Talman Regional Collection, University of Western Ontario Archives, Reaney Papers, Box 27 (B1313), File 13.

2 Auston Steward, *Twenty-Two Years a Slave, and Forty Years a Freeman; Embracing a Correspondence of Several Years, While President of Wilberforce Colony, London, Canada West* (Electronic Edition). Originally published by William Alling, Rochester, 1856. Published online at https://docsouth.unc.edu/fpn/steward/steward .html#steward190 (accessed August 25, 2019).

3 https://docsouth.unc.edu/fpn/steward/steward.html#steward190 (accessed August 26, 2019).

4   "Austin Steward (1793–1869), https://blackpast.org/african-american-history/steward-austin-1793-1869/ (accessed September 1, 2019).

5   *Exeter Times*, April 30, 1874.

6   Clerk of the Peace Correspondence, Ferguson to Hutchinson, May 13, 1876.

7   A newspaper ad for the Donnelly stage read: "Crediton and London stage — Leaves Crediton every morning at 4 and Lucan at 6, arriving at London at 9 o'clock. Returning, leaves the City Hotel at 2 p.m. and Lucan at 5 p.m., arriving at Crediton at 7 p.m." *London Daily Advertiser*, June 2, 1875.

8   *London Advertiser*, January 8, 1875; see also *London Advertiser*, February 16, 1880.

9   There exists some confusion as to the way this matter was settled. According to the *London Advertiser*, January 8, 1875, William Donnelly, as the owner of the rival stage line, was fined ten dollars; while Mike and John Donnelly were fined five dollars each. However, the same *London Advertiser* newspaper indicated in its February 16, 1880, edition, that the case was withdrawn before going into court with "each party paying its own costs."

10   *Exeter Times*, January 20, 1875.

11   "Flannigan, the person to whom it was addressed, threw it on the floor and trampled it to pieces." *London Advertiser*, February 16, 1880.

12   Once again, the case was "withdrawn before going into court," with "each party paying its own costs." *London Advertiser*, February 16, 1880.

13   *London Advertiser*, February 4, 1875.

14   Middlesex County, Coroner's Inquests, Inquisition on the body of William Brooks, July 1, 1875; see also *London Free Press*, July 3, 1875, and *Exeter Times*, July 8, 1875.

15   "When the wheel came off, the horses ran away. Donnelly stopped his stage. Horses ran about 80 rods. I got out before they were stopped and followed them down thinking the driver was still with the stage. Mr. Cobbledick of McGillivray came along with

waggon and picked up driver and called to me that driver was Killed." Testimony of David Johns. University of Western Ontario, Middlesex Court Records, Middlesex Coroner's Inquest, Death of William Brooks, July 1, 1875.

16 "I assisted Donnelly to put deceased in the wagon." Testimony of Robert Dempsey: Middlesex Court Records, Middlesex Coroner's Inquest, Death of William Brooks, July 1, 1875.

17 Butt, *The Donnellys: History, Legend, Literature*, p. 79.

18 Reaney, *The Donnelly Documents: An Ontario Vendetta*, p. 25.

19 Testimony of David Johns, University of Western Ontario, Middlesex Court Records, Middlesex Coroner's Inquest, Death of William Brooks, July 1, 1875.

20 Middlesex Court Records, Middlesex Coroner's Inquest, Death of William Brooks, July 1, 1875. Verdict read by Foreman John Lewis.

21 Reaney, *The Donnelly Documents: An Ontario Vendetta*, p. 45, note 420.

22 "Flanagan stage passed me at the 11 concession of London Township." Testimony of Thomas Donnelly. University of Western Ontario, Middlesex Court Records, Appeal, McLeod v. Donnellys, February 22, 1876.

23 *Exeter Times*, July 8, 1875.

24 "I had ten passengers; three in the driver's seat, besides myself, seven on the stage." Testimony of Thomas Donnelly. University of Western Ontario, Middlesex Court Records, Appeal, McLeod v. Donnellys, February 22, 1876.

25 "The Ladies wanted a drink of water at the Swartz Hotel." Testimony of Thomas Donnelly. Middlesex Court Records, Appeal, McLeod v. Donnellys, February 22, 1876.

26 "When between Mr. Young's store and the pump I turned in and he did not turn in. He McLeod turned and opposite the barn — I was going for the nearest post. When I got opposite the heap of stones at the pump he run into me when he got opposite the stones. There was about seven to eight feet between us. We were then side by side. He then turned into me he made a quick turn, as quick a turn

as ever I seen. He made a short-turn to the right crowding me right into the stones. He pulled me right up on top. The stones broke one of my wheels. His wheel caught in my harness, and pulled off the horse, and caught my horse's hind leg, and broke the tung and upset the stages to the left." Testimony of Thomas Donnelly. Middlesex Court Records, Appeal, McLeod v. Donnellys, February 22, 1876.

27 "I asked him what he done that for? [He said] he would do it again if he got the chance." Testimony of Thomas Donnelly. University of Western Ontario, Middlesex Court Records, Appeal, McLeod v. Donnellys, February 22, 1876.

28 Testimony of John B. Cade. Middlesex Court Records, Appeal, McLeod v. Donnellys, February 22, 1876.

29 Middlesex County, Clerk of the Peace, Criminal Records, Robert McLeod appellant vs. William and Michael Donnelly, respondents, testimony of witnesses before Henry Ferguson, JP, September 1, 1875; see also Ferguson's Notice of Conviction, September 9, 1875; Letterbooks from the Office of the Clerk of the Peace, Middlesex County, to Ferguson, September 7, 1865. See also Reaney, *The Donnelly Documents: An Ontario Vendetta*, p. 48, note 425.

30 *London Daily Advertiser*, September 8, 1875.

31 Middlesex County, Clerk of the Peace, Criminal Records, Notice of Appeal, September 11, 1875.

32 University of Western Ontario, Summons to William and Michael Donnelly to appear in ten days in Middlesex County Court, regarding the suit of Louisa Lindsay; judgement roll, September 25, 1875, Louisa Lindsay v. William and Michael Donnelly; identical judgement roll, same date, Martha Lindsay v. the same two defendants.

33 *Exeter Times*, September 23, 1875.

34 *Exeter Times*, September 23, 1875.

35 Miller, *The Donnellys Must Die*, p. 85.

36 Butt, *The Donnellys: History, Legend, Literature*, p. 83.

37 Reaney, *The Donnelly Documents: An Ontario Vendetta*, p. lxix.

38 Years later when Patrick Donnelly happened to be in London, the following conversation was overheard between two villagers (*London Daily Advertiser*, May 23, 1881):

"That's him."

"Who? The little fellow?"

"Yes, the small man."

"My eye! I thought those Donnellys were giants."

39 The account of the dialogue exchanged and of the brawl that followed is from the Middlesex County, Clerk of the Peace, Criminal Records, 1876; also Middlesex County, Court of General Quarter Sessions, Minute Book, 1866–1876, pp. 473, 508–09.

40 "I remember the trial of Keefe; I gave evidence in that trial; Keefe was charged with maiming Joseph Berryhill of London Township; I gave evidence of words I heard in the evening; the fight was at ten o'clock at night." William Donnelly, quoted from A.D. Aemilius Irving Papers, March 1, 1880, reproduced in Reaney, *The Donnelly Documents: An Ontario Vendetta*, p. 78.

41 "He [James Keefe] pulled out part of my beard." Testimony of Joseph Berryhill. J.J. Talman Regional Collection, University of Western Ontario Archives, Donnelly Family Papers, B4877, File 9, Unknown, Queen v. James Donnelly et. al., Assault and Wounding Joseph Berryhill, September 20, 1875.

42 "The wounds in my head were dressed by Dr. Hassock — afterwards." Testimony of Joseph Berryhill. J.J. Talman Regional Collection, University of Western Ontario Archives, Donnelly Family Papers, B4877, File 9, Unknown, Queen v. James Donnelly et al., Assault and Wounding Joseph Berryhill, September 20, 1875.

43 Testimony of James Curry, J.J. Talman Regional Collection, University of Western Ontario Archives, Donnelly Family Papers, B4877, File 11, Unknown, Queen v. Thomas Donnelly et al., Assault and Robbery Against James Curry, December 14, 1875.

44 Rhody Kennedy's version of events is taken from J.J. Talman Regional Collection, University of Western Ontario Archives, Donnelly Family Papers, B4877, File 14, Unknown, Queen v. Thomas Donnelly et al., Arson, Patrick Flanagan's Stables, March 11, 1876.

45 "I reside in Sarnia. I am a Veterinary Surgeon. I was living in Lucan on September last. I remember the night Joseph Berryhill

was beaten in September last. I took a walk with John McConnel to the Railway Station. We came back and we went in Walker's Hotel. We there met Thomas Donnelly, James Donnelly, Michael Donnelly and Robert Donnelly and James Keefe, and William Atkinson. . . . Either Thomas or James Donnelly asked us in at Isaac White's Tavern where we had several drinks." Testimony of James Churchill. University of Western Ontario, Middlesex Court Records, Queen v. Thomas Donnelly et al., Arson and Attempt at Arson, September 17 and October 4, 1875.

46 Testimony of James Churchill, Middlesex Court Records, Queen v. Thomas Donnelly et al., Arson and Attempt at Arson, September 17 and October 4, 1875.

47 "Lucan, Oct. 4 — The stables of P. Flannigan [sic], stage proprietor in Lucan, was totally consumed at one o'clock last night. Incendiary. It was a very narrow escape from a larger conflagration." *London Free Press,* October 5, 1875.

CHAPTER SIX: TRIALS AND TRIBULATIONS

1 "I slept in the same room as Flannigan [sic] at the Queens hotel, . . . Flannigan [sic] told me that night he had heard something and was going to watch and would let me know if anything turned up, he would not take off his clothes." Testimony of Malcolm McIsaac. University of Western Ontario, Middlesex Court Records, Queen v. Thomas Donnelly et al., Arson and Attempt at Arson, September 17 and October 4, 1875.

2 "I observed the fire between 12 and 1 o'clock." Testimony of Malcolm McIsaac. Middlesex Court Records, Queen v. Thomas Donnelly et al., Arson and Attempt at Arson, September 17 and October 4, 1875.

3 Middlesex Court Records, Queen v. Thomas Donnelly et al., Arson and Attempt at Arson, September 17 and October 4, 1875. Testimony of Patrick Flanagan. Patrick Flanagan had been suspicious that something untoward had been in the works for some time. ("I had been

suspecting something.") The Lucan veterinarian, James Churchill, had previously shared with him what Tom Donnelly had threatened to do back on September 17 and Flanagan had been on tenterhooks ever since. Granted, Donnelly's threat had been vague ("I'll have my revenge yet"), but the fact that Donnelly had been attempting to set fire to Flanagan's stable at the time that he said it (at least according to Churchill) convinced the stagecoach line proprietor that someone was soon going to make a move on his stables.

4   "I was at the fire and saw James, John and Thomas at the fire." Testimony of Henry Quarry. Middlesex Court Records, Queen v. Thomas Donnelly et al., Arson and Attempt at Arson, September 17 and October 4, 1875.

5   "I know nothing about the fire. It was half over when I went out. Jack Donnelly was on the pump . . ." Testimony of Robert Mason. Middlesex Court Records, Queen v. Thomas Donnelly et al., Arson and Attempt at Arson, September 17 and October 4, 1875.

6   "I reside in Lucan. I was at the fire and don't remember seeing any of the Donnellys there except Thomas, who was carrying water . . ." Testimony of Peter Anderson. Middlesex Court Records, Queen v. Thomas Donnelly et al., Arson and Attempt at Arson, September 17 and October 4, 1875.

7   "They were getting out the horses. The stables were totally destroyed all the horses got out — eight were there." Testimony of Patrick Flanagan. Middlesex Court Records, Queen v. Thomas Donnelly et al., Arson and Attempt at Arson, September 17 and October 4, 1875.

8   Kelley, *The Black Donnellys*, pp. 57–61.

9   Max Haines, "The Donnelly Massacre," *Truro Daily News*. August 9, 2008. https://pressreader.com/canada/truro-news/20080809/281865819255578 (accessed May 12, 2020) and "The Black Donnellys and the Biddulph Horror," http://black-donnellys.com/the-story/ (accessed on May 13, 2020).

10   Here we are presented with our first problem with the story, as the Donnelly stage always left Lucan for London at 6 a.m. — not 6:45 a.m. (This is a minor point, admittedly, as Kelley may not have

had access to the newspaper advertisements for the times of the
Donnelly stage runs when he wrote his book.) See advertisement in
the *London Free Press* on October 6, 1875:

DONNELLY'S EXETER & LONDON STAGE —
Leaves Exeter every morning at 4, and Lucan at 6,
arriving in London at 9 o'clock.

11 The description of the battle and of the dialogue that preceded and
followed it are taken from Kelley, *The Black Donnellys: The True
Story of Canada's Most Barbaric Feud*, pp. 966–1109.

12 "At nine o'clock on the evening of October 1, the barns and stables
of John Flanagan, telegraph agent at the village of Ireland, a few
miles from Lucan, were set on fire and totally destroyed with all
contents. Flanagan was a relative of Pat Flanagan, the Donnellys'
competitor. Pat's turn came three days later, at one o'clock on the
morning of October 4." Miller, *The Donnellys Must Die*, p. 85.

13 "John [Flanagan] discovered the atrocities that had occurred in
his barn on the night of August 23, 1875, around six a.m. on the
following morning when he went there to harness up for the first trip
to London." Kelley, *The Black Donnellys*, Kindle edition, p. 966.

14 Witness, for example, the newspaper articles entitled "Riot
in Biddulph" in the *London Free Press*, January 9, 1858, and
"Old-Fashioned Faction Fight in Lucan," in the *London Advertiser*,
March 8, 1877. Perhaps if the alleged brawl took place far enough
outside of London, then it is possible that the London papers did
not receive word about it in time to report on it, and that it would
have been reported in a newspaper from one of the outlying towns
or villages. To this end, an interesting report appears in the *Exeter
Times* on January 22, 1874: "A riot between some of our villagers
and a number of people from Biddulph who had spent the day
in laying in a stock of whiskey took place on the Main street last
Saturday evening. The result was a few cracked heads." This report
is intriguing and holds out some possibility that Kelley's story might
be true, as it indicates that "a number of people from Biddulph,"

which, of course, is where the Donnellys hailed from, fought with "some of our villagers." As John Flanagan's stables were not that far away from Exeter (approximately ten and a half miles south), and as Flanagan had started his stage line on November 1, 1874, and the Donnellys in 1873, perhaps this might be the story about the brawl in question and Kelley merely got his dates wrong.

15 "Inside the coach and ready to be off, were three passengers, a farm implements salesman and two women. One of the latter was destined to live to an unusual age. In later life she settled in British Columbia and before her death related the story of that wild morning to some scribe, who eventually wrote an article on it." Kelley, *The Black Donnellys*, Kindle edition, p. 1010.

16 *London Free Press*, November 24, 1875.

17 *London Free Press*, December 1, 1875.

18 *London Free Press*, December 4, 1875.

19 Registrar of the Gaol at London, December 4, 1875; Letterbooks from Office of the Clerk of the Peace, Middlesex County, to Henry Ferguson, December 29, 1875.

20 See *London Free Press*, December 15, 1875, and testimony in Middlesex County Clerk of the Peace, Criminal Records, 1876, Queen v. James and Thomas Donnelly, Robbery, testimony before Lawrence Lawrason, December 14, 1875, and Clerk of the Peace Correspondence, Hutchinson, Charles Letters and Papers, Lawrason to Hutchinson, March 25, 1876.

21 *London Free Press*, December 18, 1875.

22 *Exeter Times*, December 30, 1875.

23 Letterbooks from Office of the Clerk of the Peace, Middlesex County, to Lawrason, December 29, 1875; see also Middlesex County Clerk of the Peace, Criminal Records, Warrant to Apprehend Thomas and Robert Donnelly, December 29, 1875. On the back of the warrant is a notation that the defendant is bailed until January 13, 1876.

24 Reaney, *The Donnelly Documents: An Ontario Vendetta*, p. lxxiv.

25 *Exeter Times*, February 3, 1876.

26 *London Free Press*, January 24, 1876.

27 Donnelly Family Papers, University of Western Ontario, Lindsay v. Donnelly record; also, Statement of Costs, January 26, 1876.

28 Middlesex County, Clerk of the Peace, Criminal Records, 1875, McLeod v. Donnellys, Affidavits of Disbursements, February 22, 1876.

29 Middlesex County, Clerk of the Peace, Criminal Records, 1876, Queen v. Rhody Kennedy, Perjury, January 13, 1876.

30 When Kennedy was brought in to testify in the trial held on February 12, 1876, he mentioned he was employed as a guard on the Bryant/Crawley stage.

31 Both the *Exeter Times*, January 20, 1876, and the *London Free Press*, January 24, 1876, indicate that it was the Flanagan Stage that had been destroyed. However, the *London Advertiser* on April 20, 1876, noted that it had been Bryant's stage, which would indicate that Bryant had taken possession of the stage line from Flanagan by this point in time.

32 The dialogue and actions described are based on or taken from J.J. Talman Regional Collection, University of Western Ontario Archives, Donnelly Family Papers, B4877, File 12, Unknown, Queen v. John and Robert Donnelly, Assault Against Peter McKellar, March 18, 1876.

33 "Bowey's" was said in reference to the Queen's Hotel, as its proprietor was William Bowey. Similarly, "McLean's" was said in reference to the Central House Hotel that was owned by Bob McLean and was located just a few yards from the Queen's Hotel.

34 "LUCAN UNPLEASANTNESS. — Michael Donnelly, stage driver, Lucan, was arrested yesterday [Tuesday, January 25, 1876], on a warrant threatening to take the life of Peter McKellar, on the road between London and Lucan on Monday [January 24, 1876]. He was bailed to keep the peace in the afternoon. Donnelly is also charged by Henry Brien with using insulting and abusive language on the public highway." *London Free Press*, January 26, 1876.

35 The incidents and dialogue that transpired are taken from Middlesex County Clerk of the Peace Criminal Records, 1876, Queen v. William Donnelly, Perjury, February 12, 1876.

36 Butt, *The Donnellys: History, Legend, Literature*, p. 92.

37 *London Advertiser*, January 26 and 27, 1876.

38 Both charges are outlined in *London Advertiser*, January 26 and 27, 1876.

39 Clerk of the Peace Correspondence, Hutchinson, Charles, Letters and Papers, Henry Ferguson to Charles Hutchinson, January 28, 1876.

40 London Police Court Returns of Convictions, January 26, 1876.

41 Rhody Kennedy being appointed a special constable is reported in the *London Free Press*, January 31, 1876, and he describes himself thusly in his testimony: "On the 28th day of January I had a Warrant placed in my hands to arrest Robert Donnelly and John Donnelly for an Assault upon Peter McKellar and I was sworn as a Special Constable for the Execution of that Warrant," University of Western Ontario, Middlesex Criminal Records, Queen v. James Donnelly, Assault, 28 January 1876.

42 Middlesex Criminal Records, Queen v. James Donnelly, Assault, January 28, 1876. Testimony from Rhody Kennedy: "He [Robert Donnelly] pulled out a revolver and told me to let go of him — I had told him when I arrested him that he was my prisoner in the name of the Queen."

43 "I then started to go to Kennedy's Assistance and was met by John Donnelly and several others. John threatened to shoot me if I went to assist Kennedy." Testimony of Peter McKellar. Middlesex Criminal Records, Queen v. James Donnelly, Assault, January 28, 1876.

44 "James Donnelly then caught me by the arm and told me to let him go and kicked me severely in the body and brought me down on my knees. Then Robert bit me with his teeth and took a piece out of my lip, the scar of which now shows." Testimony of Rhody Kennedy. See also testimony of Peter McKellar: "I saw James Donnelly kicking Kennedy, and had hold of Kennedy by the arm. Kennedy was severely beaten and wounded. . . ." University of Western Ontario, Middlesex Criminal Records, Queen v. James Donnelly, Assault, January 28, 1876.

45 "I was severely beaten by James and he was the means of rescuing Robert from my Custody and forcing him away from me. The other

Donnellys were standing by urging them on." Testimony of Rhody
Kennedy. Middlesex Criminal Records, Queen v. James Donnelly,
Assault, 28 January 1876. See also testimony of Constable John
Bawden: "When I came up Kennedy had hold of Robert Donnelly
— and Robert Donnelly at the same time [was] beating Kennedy
with a revolver on the head. Kennedy was beaten severely and
wounded about the head and face. I pulled off James Donnelly and I
saw John Donnelly pull Robert who escaped away from Kennedy."
J.J. Talman Regional Collection, University of Western Ontario
Archives, Donnelly Family Papers, B4877, File 15, Unknown, Queen
v. John Donnelly and Robert Donnelly, Assault & Wounding Rhody
Kennedy, March 18, 1876.

46 "Robert's escape was of long duration. There are no records of
subsequent action against him concerning the January 24 assault on
McKellar. A warrant is issued February 17, 1876 for his arrest (and
James Donnelly Jr.'s) on the charge of beating Kennedy, January 28,
1876; but he appears to have left Biddulph and Canada at this time,
not appearing in any of the sources until June 1877." Reaney, *The
Donnelly Documents: An Ontario Vendetta*, p. 56.

47 Letterbooks from the Office of the Clerk of the Peace, Middlesex
County, Hutchinson to Ferguson, January 31, 1876.

48 Middlesex County Clerk of the Peace Criminal Records, 1876,
Queen v. William Donnelly, Perjury.

49 *London Advertiser*, February 12 and 17, 1876.

50 Letterbooks from the Office of the Clerk of the Peace, Middlesex
County, to Ferguson, February 14, 1876.

51 Letterbooks from the Office of the Clerk of the Peace, Middlesex
County, to Ferguson, February 18 and 22, 1876, and to Rhody
Kennedy, February 22, 1876. See also Hutchinson, Charles, Letters
and Papers, Ferguson to Hutchinson, February 24, 1876.

52 *London Advertiser*, February 17, 1876.

53 Letterbooks from the Office of the Clerk of the Peace, Middlesex
County, to Henry Ferguson, February 18 and 22, 1876, and to
Rhody Kennedy, February 22, 1876. See also Hutchinson, Charles,
Letters and Papers, Ferguson to Hutchinson, February 24, 1876.

54 Middlesex County Clerk of the Peace, Criminal Records, Queen v. James Donnelly, Assault, testimony of Rhody Kennedy February 17, 1876.

55 "The Northern Ku Klux," *The London Free Press*, January 1876 — precise date not indicated, but presented in its entirety in Miller, *The Donnellys Must Die*, pp. 91–92.

56 Flanagan is named by McKinnon in letters that the detective wrote to Charles Hutchinson. See, as examples, Hutchinson, Charles, Letters and Papers, McKinnon to Hutchinson, February 22, 1876, and February 26, 1876. While he indicates that his employers are "authorities and citizens of Lucan" (February 26), which suggests the involvement of power brokers such as the Stanley brothers, it is evident that McKinnon's primary contact is Patrick Flanagan.

CHAPTER SEVEN: HUGH MCKINNON, P.I.

1 *Hamilton Spectator*, November 28, 1865; see also *Toronto Mail*, February 9, 1880.

2 "Hugh McKinnon." http://biographi.ca/en/bio/mckinnon_ hugh_13E.html (accessed November 27, 2019).

3 "Hugh McKinnon." https://electricscotland.com/history/canada/ mckinnon_hugh.htm (accessed November 29, 2019).

4 "McKinnon, Hugh." http://biographi.ca/en/bio/mckinnon_ hugh_13E.html (accessed November 27, 2019).

5 McKinnon lost his job, left his post and, despite being married, checked into a Toronto hotel for five days under an assumed name with the wife and sister of Hamilton impresario T.H. Gould. http:// biographi.ca/en/bio/mckinnon_hugh_13E.html (accessed November 27, 2019). This same online article reveals that while serving as Liberal candidate James Hamilton Ross's campaign chairman, he assaulted his vice-chairman over non-payment of a bill for whiskey and cigars. He also lost his job on the police force in Hamilton for the brutal beating of a reporter (*Hamilton Spectator*, November 28,

1865, see also *Hamilton Times*, November 28, 29, 30, December 6, 7, 9, 21 and 22, 1865.

6   *Toronto Mail*, February 9, 1880.

7   *Toronto Mail*, February 9, 1880.

8   Toronto *Globe*, March 4, 1880, see also the *Hamilton Spectator*, February 9, 1880.

9   Toronto *Globe*, April 17, 1880. See also: "[The] Donnellys were on guard at once and on the first day after the hopeful sleuth's arrival, Michael Donnelly told a policeman friend in London that a new detective was in Lucan to watch them." Butt, *The Donnellys: History, Legend, Literature*, p. 97.

10   Toronto *Globe*, April 17, 1880. The fact that the Donnellys were aware of his every move seems to have been known to McKinnon, who wrote to Charles Hutchinson that "I don't know if this is true, or if so, how they know." Hutchinson, Charles, Letters and Papers, McKinnon to Hutchinson, February 26, 1876.

11   McKinnon's jottings on these potential leads consist of five pages, and can be found within the Middlesex County Clerk of the Peace Criminal Records, 1876, Queen v. Thomas, James, and John Donnelly, Arson, March 11, 1876.

12   Hutchinson, Charles, Letters and Papers, McKinnon to Hutchinson, February 22 and 26, 1876.

13   On January 26, 1876, John Hodgins had written to the Chairman of Quarter Sessions seeking the appointment of John Bawden and John Courcey as constables. On February 9, 1876, Bernard Stanley had written to the chairman requesting the appointment of John Reid.

14   University of Western Ontario, Clerk of the Peace Correspondence, Hugh McKinnon to Charles Hutchinson, February 22, 1876.

15   *London Free Press*, February 10, 1874.

16   Toronto *Globe*, September 10, 1880.

17   Toronto *Globe*, April 17, 1880.

18   All dialogue and actions unless otherwise noted are drawn from the Middlesex County Clerk of the Peace Criminal Records, 1876, Queen v. William Donnelly, Shooting with intent, testimonies before Lawrason, March 10 and March 18, 1876.

19 John Courcey testimony cited in J.J. Talman Regional Collection, University of Western Ontario Archives, Donnelly Family Papers, B4877, File 16, Unknown, Queen v. John, James Jr. and William Donnelly, Assault and Wounding Constable Bowden, Reid and Courcey, March 14, 1876.

20 "Richard Tapp (b. 1859), CE, hostler at Revere House, always witnessed against the Donnellys." Reaney, *The Donnelly Documents: An Ontario Vendetta*, p. 43, note 415.

21 "The greatest excitement prevailed amongst the villagers, and threats of lynching were freely indulged in by the exasperated populace," *London Free Press*, February 26, 1876.

22 "Telegrams were at once despatched to Stratford, London, Sarnia, St. Marys and other points to the police, informing them of the circumstances, and asking their detention. The telegram mentioned the names of William, James and John Donnelly and William Farrell as the aggressors, and as they are well known to the officers of the surrounding towns, the probability is that their capture will be effected in a very short time." *London Free Press*, February 25, 1876.

23 Thomas Johnston, quoted in the Toronto *Globe*, April 17, 1880.

24 "The telegram mentioned the names of William, James and John Donnelly and William Farrell as the aggressors, and as they are well known to the officers of the surrounding towns, the probability is that their capture will be effected in a very short time." *London Free Press*, February 25, 1876. See also *London Free Press*, February 26, 1876: "The search for Farrell and William Donnelly is being vigorously prosecuted." It would be the better part of two years before James Keefe would be arrested. See also Middlesex County Clerk of the Peace Criminal Records, 1877, Queen v. James Keefe, Assault on constable, indictment, December Sessions, 1877; Middlesex Court of Quarter Sessions Minute Book, 1876–1885, pp. 109–10.

25 ". . . they found James Donnelly in the house of Dan Keefe, in the Township of Biddulph, and secured him. He was discovered lying between two bed ticks." *London Free Press*, February 26, 1876.

Note: the phraseology "bed ticks" is suggestive of some strain of bed bug; however, it refers to feather "ticks" or feather mattresses.

26 ". . . this forenoon the prisoners, John and James Donnelly, were brought to London Jail by Constables Bawden and Courcey." *London Free Press*, February 26, 1876.

27 *London Free Press*, February 26, 1876.

28 Butt, *The Donnellys: History, Legend, Literature*, p. 102.

29 *London Free Press*, February 28, 1876: "Michael Donnelly, a Lucanite, has been fined $3 and costs by the Police Magistrate, for committing an assault on Rhody Kennedy." For the report that Donnelly had used abusive language on Kennedy, see the *London Advertiser*, March 2, 1876.

30 London Police Court Return of Convictions, February 26, 1876.

31 Middlesex County Clerk of the Peace Criminal Records, 1876, Queen v. James and John Donnelly, Arson, statement of Patrick Flanagan, February 26, 1876.

32 Michael Donnelly is speaking in reference to an article that was, in fact, entitled "The Donnelly Tribe," that was published in the *London Free Press* on February 18, 1876.

33 Michael Donnelly's letter, published in the *London Advertiser*, March 2, 1876.

34 Butt, *The Donnellys: History, Legend, Literature*, p. 102.

35 Middlesex County Clerk of the Peace Criminal Records, 1876; Information of John Bawden, March 2, 1876.

36 For Esdale's history of drunkenness, see Middlesex Quarterly Returns of Convictions, October 12, 1872, and September 24, 1873.

37 *London Free Press*, March 11, 1876.

38 Middlesex County Clerk of the Peace Criminal Records, 1876, Queen v. Alex Levitt, Robbery, statement of John Barry, February 29, and testimony before William and Bernard Stanley and William Ryan, JPs, March 1.

39 *London Advertiser*, March 2, 1876, and *London Free Press*, March 3, 1876.

40 *London Advertiser*, March 2, 1876.

41 The London newspaper that printed this story is unnamed, but Orlo Miller, in whose book the article was reprinted, indicates that it ran in an edition "at the beginning of March." Miller, *The Donnellys Must Die*, pp. 95–96.

42 All the dialogue and actions presented of this incident are drawn from the testimonies presented within the University of Western Ontario, Middlesex Court Records, Queen v. Hugh McKinnon et al., Assault, Lucan, March 2, 1876. Testimony before James Owrey, J.P.

43 Butt, *The Donnellys: History, Legend, Literature*, p. 105.

44 *London Advertiser*, March 8, 1876.

45 *London Free Press*, March 8, 1876.

46 Ely Errey, quoted from an email to the author on January 15, 2021.

47 *London Advertiser*, March 15, 1876.

48 *London Free Press*, March 26, 1876.

49 David Glass was the brother of the Middlesex County Sheriff William Glass, as well as a Queen's Council, and former mayor and alderman of London. See Chester Glass, Compiler, *Hon. David Glass — Some of His Writings and Speeches* (New York: Trow Press, 1909), pp. 1–5.

50 *London Free Press*, March 31, 1876.

51 *London Free Press*, March 31, 1876.

52 Letterbooks from the Office of the Clerk of the Peace, Middlesex County, Hutchinson to Scott, April 20, 1876.

CHAPTER EIGHT: THE WINDS OF CHANGE

1 "Toronto Central Prison," https://en.wikipedia.org/wiki/Toronto_Central_Prison (accessed March 2, 2019).

2 "Toronto Central Prison," https://en.wikipedia.org/wiki/Toronto_Central_Prison (accessed March 2, 2019).

3 Chris Bateman, "A Short and Violent History of Toronto's Central Prison," https://blogto.com/city/2012/10/a_short_and_violent_history_of_torontos_central_prison/ (accessed March 3, 2019).

4   Chris Bateman, "A Short and Violent History of Toronto's Central Prison," https://blogto.com/city/2012/10/a_short_and_violent_history_of_torontos_central_prison/ (accessed March 3, 2019). Bateman quotes from Peter Oliver's book, *Terror to Evil-Doers': Prisons and Punishment in Nineteenth-Century Ontario* (Toronto: University of Toronto Press, 1998), although he does not provide the page number for his excerpt.

5   Butt, *The Donnellys: History, Legend, Literature*, p. 112.

6   *London Advertiser*, May 1, 1876.

7   Letterbooks from the Office of the Clerk of the Peace, Middlesex County, Hutchinson to Mowat, May 15, 1876, in which the Crown attorney included McKinnon's letter.

8   Letterbooks from the Office of the Clerk of the Peace, Middlesex County, Hutchinson to Mowat, May 15, 1876.

9   Butt, *The Donnellys: History, Legend, Literature*, p. 116.

10   William Porte's diary, July 10, 1876.

11   ". . . in the Spring Walker's partner Ted Crawley had quit in disgust, retreating to his smaller Exeter-to-Crediton line which he co-owned with Patrick Flanagan . . ."; Butt, *The Donnellys: History, Legend, Literature*, p. 118.

12   The hotels in Lucan during the 1870s were the Royal, Walker House, Dublin House, Central Hotel, Fitzhenry Hotel, Revere House and Queen's Hotel per information drawn from "Map of Downtown Lucan Showing Landmarks," https://canadianmysteries.ca/sites/donnellys/archives/map/indexen.html# (accessed December 21, 2020).

13   "Lucan," https://canadianmysteries.ca/sites/donnellys/characters/buildingsandsites/2942en.html (accessed December 21, 2020).

14   *London Advertiser*, December 10, 1876.

15   William Donnelly is on the Eighth Concession by December 1876; see Charles Hutchinson, Letters and Papers, Atkinson to Hutchinson, December 7, 1876.

16   J.J. Talman Regional Collection, University of Western Ontario Archives, Donnelly Family Papers, B4878, File 7, Charles Hutchinson Letter Book, 1875–78, p. 435:

Oct 21, 1876

P McIlhargey Esq, JP Biddulph

Dear Sir,

I beg to inform you that the application of Wm McBride
& Michael Donnelly for appointment as county constables
was submitted to the court at the recently held adjourned
sessions of the peace, & that it was not considered
advisable by said court to make the appointments.

Yours truly,

Charles Hutchinson, Clerk of the Peace

17 *London Advertiser*, December 14, 1876.
18 *London Advertiser*, December 21, 1876.
19 William Donnelly would, in fact, become highly respected for his
    breeding of horses and would have two full stables. As evidence of
    this see the *Stratford Weekly Herald*, February 11, 1880.
20 A letter written from William Atkinson to William Donnelly, dated
    May 11, 1876, is included in Hutchinson, Charles, Letters and
    Papers, Clerk of the Peace Correspondence, Glass to Hutchinson,
    June 14, 1876.
21 "William Atkinson had lived with relatives in Michigan until
    mid-May when he wrote to his wife to send him money for his fare
    back home. By the time funds were sent to him at the end of May,
    William Atkinson was on his way home to Biddulph. By the time of
    the Middlesex June Sessions he was still somewhere in Michigan."
    Butt, *The Donnellys: History, Legend, Literature*, pp. 114–15.
22 London *Advertiser*, November 10, 1876.
23 Reaney, *The Donnelly Documents: An Ontario Vendetta*,
    p. lxxix: ". . . Constable Bawden had interfered with William
    Atkinson's attempt to sue Hugh McKinnon and his cronies for
    'hanging' him in March of 1876. Bawden arrested him in the
    noon break of the trial before his supporting witnesses could
    testify."
24 *London Free Press*, December 16, 1876.

25 "James Donnelly was released on December 30, 1876, and brought to Middlesex Gaol, where, despite other charges of misdemeanors, he was released on bail of $800 which his father and another Biddulph farmer raised." Reaney, *The Donnelly Documents: An Ontario Vendetta*, p. lxxviii.

26 See note 25.

27 "He [Crown attorney Charles Hutchinson] never proceeded with either charge." Butt, *The Donnellys: History, Legend, Literature*, pp. 117–18.

28 "Albert MacLean, son of Robert MacLean, owner of the Central Hotel, was possibly one of those of the Volunteer Militia pursuing Donnellys on February 4, 1876." Reaney, *The Donnelly Documents: An Ontario Vendetta*, p. 64, note 466. And "Since most of these men belonged to the local militia regiment that had pursued the Donnellys after the 'Wedding Riot,' this was another reason for a local, destructive rampage." Reaney, *The Donnelly Documents: An Ontario Vendetta*, p. lxxix.

29 *Exeter Times*, January 17, 1877.

30 *Exeter Times*, January 18, 1877.

31 William Porte's diary, entries for Friday, March 9, 1877, Tuesday, March 13, 1877 and Saturday, March 17, 1877.

32 *London Free Press*, April 11, 1877.

33 *London Free Press*, April 16, 1877.

34 *London Free Press*, April 16, 1877.

35 *London Advertiser*, May 3, 1877.

36 Although the attack on Joseph Watson occurred on April 28, 1877, it was reported in the *London Advertiser* on May 2, 1877, the *London Free Press* on May 5, 1877, and the *Exeter Times* on May 10, 1877.

37 For accounts of the arson of McLean's stable see William Porte's diary entry, Friday, May 11, 1877. See also Reaney, *The Donnelly Documents: An Ontario Vendetta*, p. lxxx. See also Butt, *The Donnellys: History, Legend, Literature*, p. 121.

38 For an account of the arson of Bernard Stanley's outbuildings see William Porte's diary entry, Saturday, May 12, 1877. See also

Reaney, *The Donnelly Documents: An Ontario Vendetta*, pp. lxxx and xxix.

39 *London Free Press*, May 18 and 19, 1877; see also *London Advertiser*, May 24, 1877.

40 *London Free Press*, March 26, 1877.

41 "It seems that Greir, a watchman appointed with another to watch the property the night after the Stanley fire, was fired at and shot in the leg." *London Free Press*, May 18, 1877. Regarding the name of the person who was shot (and who would later claim that he saw Bob Donnelly with a rifle under his coat), the spelling of his last name is anything but exact. The *London Free Press* spells it "Greir"; Charles Hutchinson spells it "Grear" in a letter dated April 29, 1879; Hutchinson then spells it "Greer" in a letter dated May 9, 1879; while authors Reaney and Miller give his name as "George Gear." Given that most of the authors have gone with "George Gear," the author is siding with the majority on this one.

42 "Boys have been amusing themselves lately by throwing stones at the door and shutters of a certain barber shop situated on the front street. This is a gentle reminder to the inmates that there is more going on inside than the mere shaving of beards and other tonsorial trimmings." *London Daily Advertiser*, June 17, 1874. The suspicion was that the barber, William Berry, was running a bootleg operation out of his shop.

43 Entry in Postmaster William Porte's diary: "Tuesday, May 15, 1877. James Donnelly died today." William Porte Diaries.

44 *St. Marys Argus*, February 5, 1880.

45 Butt, *The Donnellys: History, Legend, Literature*, p. 121: "James Donnelly Jr. the oldest son of the Donnelly family died of appendicitis; he was thirty-five years old." Butt cites the following newspapers in support of the cause of death being appendicitis: *London Free Press*, February 12, 1880, the statement of Dr. Sutton of Clandeboye; *London Advertiser* May 12, 1877; and *London Free Press*, March 1, 1880 — unfortunately, one of the three newspaper accounts Butt cites was apparently published three days before James Donnelly Jr. died, which would give it a degree

of prescience that borders on the supernatural, and Dr. Sutton's handwritten death certification statement on the matter did not support appendicitis but rather "inflammation of the lungs" as the cause of death. Reaney supports Butt's conclusion of appendicitis in *The Donnelly Documents: An Ontario Vendetta*, p. xxix: "While it was claimed by his doctor that he had died of natural causes (appendicitis) . . ." — again, this was not claimed by Dr. Sutton in his registration of the death for the provincial government. As does Miller, *The Donnellys Must Die*, p. 109: "A Dr. Sutton states that he was a friend of the family and on the death-certificate listed the cause of death as 'acute appendicitis.'" Again, it would appear that the poor doctor is misquoted here.

46   "History of Tuberculosis," https://cpha.ca/history-tuberculosis (accessed March 1, 2019).

47   In January 2000, Johns Hopkins School of Medicine reported that an embalmer became infected by the disease from working on a corpse: "Man Catches TB From Corpse," http://news.bbc.co.uk/2/hi/health/619259.stm (accessed June 24, 2019).

48   Scans of the relevant pages of the book of interments at St. Patrick's can be found here: http://ancestorsatrest.com/cemetery_records/stpats-int.shtml (accessed June 25, 2019). The deaths and burials of the other Donnelly family members, including William in 1897, are indicated, but not James or Michael Donnelly.

49   Miller, *The Donnellys Must Die*, pp. 108–09.

50   Ontario Death Registration for James Donnelly Jr., Archives of Ontario.

51   Doug McGuff, M.D., email correspondence with the author, October 28, 2019.

52   Anthony Drohomyrecky, M.D., email correspondence with the author, October 28, 2019.

53   O. Ruuskanen, E. Lahti, L.C. Jennings, D.R. Murdoch (April 2011). "Viral Pneumonia." *Lancet* 377 (9773): 1264–75.

54   William Osler, *The Principles and Practice of Medicine*, 3rd ed. (New York, 1898), 108–37; Smart, Charles, ed., *The Medical and Surgical*

History of the War of the Rebellion (Washington, D.C., 1888), pt. 3, vol. 1, 751–810.

55　"Pneumonia History," https://news-medical.net/health/Pneumonia-History.aspx (accessed October 18, 2019).

56　Dr. Mathew Lively, "'The Most Fatal of All Acute Diseases': Pneumonia and the Death of Stonewall Jackson," https://civilwarmonitor.com/blog/the-most-fatal-of-all-acute-diseases-pneumonia-and-the-death-of-stonewall-jackson (accessed October 18, 2019).

57　Excerpts from the interview:

> How many brothers and sisters of the patient are living?
> Answer: 2
> Ages of each:
> Answer: Brother — 59 years; Sister — 51 years
> How many brothers and sisters are dead?
> Answer: 5 brothers
> Age in each instance at time of death, and cause of death:
> James Donnelly — [age] about 35, pneumonia;
> William — [age] 52, due to some form of lung trouble;
> Michael — killed, [age] 29; John [age] 25 and Thomas
> [age] 24, murdered — 4th Feb. 1880. Interview with
> Robert Donnelly, May 26, 1908, in Lucan, Ontario,
> report of James Sutton M.D. London Psychiatric
> Patient File for Robert Donnelly, Archives of Ontario.

58　"An update on the 'old man's friend,'" https://health.harvard.edu/newsletter_article/An_update_on_the_old_mans_friend (accessed on October 20, 2019).

59　"Plundering and stealing is more than usually in the ascendant in this village. A Vigilance Committee is now being talked of for the suppression of open violence and midnight thievery." *London Advertiser*, February 1, 1877. See also *London Free Press*, May 18, 1877: "A Vigilance Committee is talked of."

1   William Porte Diaries for 1877. The diary excerpts cited also appear in Miller, *The Donnellys Must Die*, p. 110.

2   William Porte Diaries, Fires in Lucan, September 11, 1864 to September 5, 1898.

3   *London Free Press*, May 23, 1877.

4   *London Advertiser*, February 5, 1880.

5   Toronto *Globe*, February 20, 1880.

6   *London Free Press*, February 16, 1880.

7   *Toronto Mail*, February 13, and April 9, 1880; Toronto *Globe*, February 5; *Sarnia Observer*, February 6, 1880.

8   "Donnelly's legend lives on in Thorold," https://thoroldnews.com/local-news/donnellys-legend-lives-on-in-thorold-1226182 (accessed February 2, 2020).

9   Toronto *Globe*, November 20, 1946. See also Reaney, *The Donnelly Documents: An Ontario Vendetta*, pp. xxiv-xxv.

10 James Reaney. "Whisky in a Tin Cup!" *Simcoe's Choice: Celebrating London's Bicentennial, 1793–1993* (Toronto: Dundurn, 1992), p. 172. See also: http://contentdm.ucalgary.ca/digital/collection/p22007coll8/id/308402 (accessed April 6, 2020).

11 *London Advertiser*, June 23, 1877. See also Toronto *Globe*, June 21, 1877. As William Butt points out, "In the Quarterly Returns entry [Middlesex Quarterly Returns of Convictions, June 21, 1877] they [Walker and Donnelly] are listed as co-defendants, the plaintiff being Frederick Allen. It seems likely that they were not fighting each other: in the Quarterly Returns such cases are presented as two separate entries, the plaintiff in the first entry being the defendant in the second, and vice versa. Thus, the Donnelly-Walker-Watson Stage alliance seems to be still intact." Butt, *The Donnellys: History, Legend, Literature*, p. 62, Note 251.

12 *London Advertiser*, June 23, 1877: "At Lucan, Thomas Donnelly has been fined five dollars and costs . . . and William Walker was fined one dollar and costs . . ."

13 "The Fitzhenry Hotel with its stables and Mr. Gleeson's stable burned down this morning. Donnelly stage and horses in same." William Porte's diary entry, July 5, 1877.

14 Toronto *Globe*, September 10, 1880.

15 *London Advertiser*, July 12, 1877: "During the late Maloney fire a fight took place . . . between Donnelly and Hocher, a Dutchman."

16 *London Advertiser*, July 12, 1877.

17 Middlesex County, Clerk of the Peace Coroner's Inquests, Inquisition into the fire at the Queen's Hotel, June 14 and June 28, 1877.

18 *London Advertiser*, June 21, 1877.

19 William Porte's diary entry, June 6, 1877.

20 William Porte's diary entry, August 31, 1877.

21 Applications, Correspondence, and Oaths re Officer of Country Constable, Middlesex, Hutchins to Elliot, August 29, 1877.

22 *Exeter Times*, October 23, 1878.

23 *Exeter Times*, February 20, 1879.

24 Letterbooks from the Office of the Clerk of the Peace, Middlesex County, 1877, to Everett, May 9, 1879.

25 William Porte's diary, undated entry; see also *Exeter Times*, March 13, 1879.

26 Letterbooks from the Office of the Clerk of the Peace, Middlesex County, to Peters, February 17, 1878.

27 The final print advertisement for the Donnelly stagecoach appeared in the *London Advertiser* on February 22, 1878.

28 "One of the first notices of a route travelled by a stagecoach in Upper Canada appeared in an advertisement in the *Upper Canada Gazette* on May 26, 1798. The owners of this line, J. Fairbanks and Thomas Hind, advertised a route between Newark and Chippawa that was served three times a week. The cost was $1 per passenger." "The Stagecoach," https://historymuseum.ca/cmc/exhibitions/cpm/chrono/ch1798ae.html (accessed April 15, 2019).

29 The second phase of railway building in Canada came with Confederation in 1867. As historian George Stanley wrote in *The Canadians*, "Bonds of steel as well as of sentiment were needed

to hold the new Confederation together. Without railways there would be and could be no Canada."

30 "Due to the delay and the uncertainty of ever receiving any bonuses at all, Great Western became impatient and had their surveyors move the stakes 2 miles to the west. By this maneuver, Great Western completely bypassed both township and town, much to their everlasting annoyance." Huron Historical Notes, Huron Historical Society, 1993, Volume XXIX, ISSN 0822-9503, p. 25.

31 For Michael Donnelly accepting a job with the Grand Trunk Railway see *London Advertiser*, February 9, 1880. For his move to St. Thomas see *London Advertiser*, December 10, 1879.

32 Returns of Convictions, August 31, 1877.

33 Returns of Convictions, December 6, 1877. See also *London Advertiser*, December 13, 1877.

34 The Elginfield Hotel was Matthew Glass's tavern in Elginfield, which sat roughly two and three-quarter miles southeast from Lucan.

35 *London Advertiser*, January 24, 1878.

36 *London Advertiser*, January 24, 1878. See also the *London Free Press*, January 24, 1878.

37 *London Advertiser*, September 19, 1877.

38 *London Advertiser*, September 19, 1877.

39 The various outrages that Michael Feeheley committed upon his wife and sons are drawn from University of Western Ontario, Middlesex Court of Chancery, 1873, Feeheley v. Feeheley.

40 For an account of how in debt the Feeheley farm would be, see University of Western Ontario, Middlesex Court of Chancery, 1881, Donnelly v. Feeheley.

41 James Feeheley confided to Patrick Donnelly, ". . . there is not any person in the world that I would sooner see or liked [better] than your brother Tom." J.J. Talman Regional Collection, University of Western Ontario Archives, Donnelly Family Papers, B4877, File 61, Unknown, Statements Regarding the Feeheleys, July 10, 1881.

42 Details of this incident are taken from Middlesex County Clerk of the Peace, Criminal Records, 1879, Queen v. Thomas Donnelly,

Larceny, testimony before Atkinson, McCosh and McIlhargey, April 7, 1879.

43   William Porte's diary entry, January 1, 1878.

44   William Porte's diary entry, January 2, 1878.

45   *London Free Press*, February 12, 1880.

46   Miller, *The Donnellys Must Die*, pp. 126–27.

47   *London Free Press*, March 6, 1878.

48   *London Advertiser*, March 15, 1878.

49   Returns of Convictions, March 9, 1878.

50   *London Free Press*, March 20, 1978.

51   William Porte's diary entry, November 12, 1887.

52   The James Carroll in this instance was the son of Michael Carroll (a neighbour of the Donnellys and a witness for the prosecution at James Donnelly Sr.'s trial for murder). He was born in 1857 and was the younger brother of Mary Thompson (nee Carroll), the woman who later claimed that her cow was stolen by the Donnellys and who, along with her husband, William Thompson Jr., was chivareed by the Donnelly brothers. The James Carroll of later infamy in the story was born in 1850, and was the son of Roger Carroll. While the Carroll clan was quite large (and included the Mahers), Roger Carroll and his sons were not related to Michael Carroll's family.

53   According to James Reaney, "Tom Ryan was bailed for $800, a sum which his father and James Donnelly Sr. divided between them" (Reaney, *The Donnelly Documents: An Ontario Vendetta*, p. lxxix), while according to Butt, "On July 17 Thomas Ryan was released when his father and James Donnelly Sr. each provided five hundred dollars in bond" (Butt, *The Donnellys: History, Legend, Literature*, p. 133).

54   Butt, *The Donnellys: History, Legend, Literature*, p. 133.

55   *London Advertiser*, January 5, 1878.

56   *London Advertiser*, January 10, 1878.

57   *London Advertiser*, September 19, 1877.

58   *London Free Press*, March 20, 1878.

59   *London Free Press*, March 20, 1878.

60   *London Advertiser*, March 27, 1878.

61 Testimony of James Donnelly Sr.: ". . . prisoner [Robert Donnelly] was living at Glencoe up to four or five weeks ago . . ." *London Free Press*, April 1, 1878.

62 Tampering (definition): "Everyone who wilfully attempts in any manner to obstruct, pervert or defeat the course of justice in a judicial proceeding . . ." https://laws-lois.justice.gc.ca/eng/acts/c-46/section-139.html (accessed January 5, 2020).

63 *London Advertiser*, March 28, 1878.

64 *London Advertiser*, March 28, 1878.

65 The following are the accounts of the fight. William Porte: "Row between Jack Donnelly and Constable William Hodgins this afternoon; had a fight down near the foundry and Jack Bawden showing fair play with his revolver." (William Porte's diary entry, March 28, 1878); "On Thursday [March 28] afternoon one of the Donnelly boys and Constable Hodgins met upon the street and entered into conversation about an item in the 'Tizer [*London Advertiser* newspaper], to the effect that a rescue of the prisoner Donnelly would be attempted whilst he was lying in the lock-up here. Words grew pretty warm between them, the result of which was that they challenged each other to out and fight. They then withdrew to one of the back streets and went at it in true pugilistic style. They were surrounded by some 100 or more spectators and allowed to pummel each other for a length of time, to the disgrace of the onlookers. One of the spectators displayed his revolver and intimated that he would shoot the first man who interfered until either party cried 'Hold, enough.'" (*London Free Press*, March 30, 1878); "On Friday Constable Hodgins and one of the Donnellys deliberately retired to Kenny's blacksmith shop and for the space of thirty minutes pounded each other in a brutal manner. Probably the most disgraceful part of the proceeding was the fact that nearly one hundred of the villagers attended the fight, and looked in without any effort being made to part the combatants, the fight coming to an end by one of the pugilists crying enough. The Lucanites can hardly expect anything better than rowdy-ism when citizens of all grades

hasten to feast their eyes on scenes of brutality and lawlessness."
London Advertiser, April 1, 1878.

66 Returns of Convictions, April 5, 1878, and April 8, 1878.

67 Miller, *The Donnellys Must Die*, p. 125.

68 *London Advertiser*, June 13, 1878; see also *Toronto Morning News*, January 1, 1884, in which William Donnelly refers to the help provided to Samuel Everett by influential Lucan men.

69 "Everett sought help in his prosecution from William Stanley, a merchant magistrate and councillor." Butt, *The Donnellys: History, Legend, Literature*, p. 145.

70 *London Free Press*, April 1, 1878.

71 *London Free Press*, 30 March 1878.

72 *London Free Press*, 30 March 1878.

73 As quoted in Miller, *The Donnellys Must Die*, p. 126.

74 Legal Papers: Robert Donnelly vs. Calder et al., Sale of Goods, 1874–1875. University of Western Ontario, Donnelly Papers, Box 1-7.

75 James Donnelly Sr.'s testimony: "Mr. McBride, a carpenter engaged in building a granary for me, and with whom prisoner [Robert] was working, came in; prisoner was living at Glencoe up to four or five weeks ago; John Hodgins and Jim Keefe came in that night about eight o'clock, and stayed till ten minutes to 12, when McBride and they left; it couldn't be possible for Bob to be at Lucan that night, as he only went to bed a short time before these people left." *London Free Press*, April 1, 1878.

76 "The facts seem to be that the constable was on his way home about midnight, Monday, and as he reached his front door, he stopped a moment to fondle his dog, when a heavy charge of buckshot was driven into the door of his dwelling." *London Advertiser*, March 20, 1878.

77 *London Free Press*, April 1, 1878.

78 *London Advertiser*, April 1, 1878.

79 *London Advertiser*, April 1, 1878.

80 *London Free Press*, April 1, 1878.

1   "A canal town such as Thorold had its share of blacksmith shops,
    competition must have been fierce. Franklin H. Becker was one,
    his shop located on Front Street South near the Canal. He must
    have come to the Thorold area, earlier the first date I found on
    him is 1877. That is the year or possibly the next that he and
    Patrick formed a partnership, 'Becker and Donnelly.' Patrick may
    at one time worked for Becker also boarded at his home." William
    Chajkowsky, "Patrick Donnelly: Last Brother from Lucan."
    https://patrick-donnelly.webs.com/patrickdonnelly.htm (accessed
    December 29, 2020).

2   The infant mortality rate in Ontario in the 1800s was 115 deaths
    out of every 1,000 children born (11.5 percent), https://opentextbc.
    ca/postconfederation/chapter/1-2-historical-demography-of-canada-
    1608-1921/#return-footnote-1350-14 (accessed August 11, 2019).
    As of 2012, this number had improved to 4.9 deaths out of every
    1,000 children born (0.49 percent). "Rate of Infant Mortality in
    Canada in 2012, by province or territory." https://statista.com/
    statistics/568800/infant-mortality-rate-by-province-or-territory-
    canada/ (accessed December 30, 2020).

3   *Exeter Times*, May 30, 1878.

4   *Exeter Times*, May 30, 1878; see also *Exeter Times*, August 15,
    1878, and *London Free Press*, August 5 and August 17, 1878.

5   Public Archives of Ontario, Irving Fonds, F1027, 82 80, MS6500,
    Deposition of William Hodgins, February 31, 1880.

6   Toronto *Globe*, March 12, 1880.

7   Butt, *The Donnellys: History, Legend, Literature*, p. 154.

8   "Carroll was a sales agent for the Thomson and Williams
    Manufacturing Co., makers of agricultural implements. The factory
    was at Erie and Gore Streets in Stratford. "Carroll had returned
    from working in Michigan as foreman on the railway in 1877. His
    intention was to assert his claim to his father's farm." Reaney, *The
    Donnelly Documents: An Ontario Vendetta*, p. 73, note 485.

9   Reaney, *The Donnelly Documents: An Ontario Vendetta*, p. 34, note 395.

10   Huron County Registry Office, Last Will and Testament of Rodger Carroll, February 16, 1873.

11   Huron County Registry Office, Last Will and Testament of Rodger Carroll, February 16, 1873. See also Middlesex Court of Chancery, 1882, Carroll et al. v. Delahay et al., and the Middlesex County Surrogate Court, Non-Contentious Business Book, 1859–1886, entry no. 1059.

12   John Donnelly's testimony repeating James Maher's accusation against the family for cutting off the tails of his horses is found in Middlesex County Clerk of the Peace, Criminal Records; 1879, Queen v. Michael Blake et al., Trespass, testimony before Magistrate Peters, September 20, 1879.

13   Returns of Convictions, August 2, 1878.

14   *London Advertiser*, August 16, 1878.

15   Returns of Convictions, August 2, 1878.

16   James Carroll's statement is taken from the Middlesex County Clerk of the Peace, Criminal Records, 1878, Donnelly v. Carroll, Pointing a pistol, testimony October 19, 1878. See also Carroll v. Donnelly, Assault, testimony, October 16, 1878, and Queen v. Carroll, Assault, testimony October 26, 1878.

17   *London Advertiser*, April 8, 1879.

18   "Template: Population of Michigan cities and counties (1870 Census," https://en.wikipedia.org/wiki/Template:Population_of_Michigan_cities_and_counties_(1870_Census), accessed January 3, 2020.

19   Land Registry Office, Bad Axe, Michigan, August 20, 1874.

20   Undated statement of Edward Ryan in with the Middlesex County Clerk of the Peace, Criminal Records, 1879, Queen v. Thomas Donnelly, Larceny, testimony before Atkinson, McCosh and McIlhargey, April 7, 1879.

21   William Porte's diary entry, September 26, 1878, and *London Free Press*, October 3, 1878.

22 For information on the Pacific Scandal and its impact on Canadian politics, please see https://thecanadianencyclopedia.ca/en/article/pacific-scandal (accessed November 8, 2019); see also https://thecanadianencyclopedia.ca/en/article/pacific-scandal, and "Pacific Scandal," https://en.wikipedia.org/wiki/Pacific_Scandal (accessed November 8, 2019) and "1878 Canadian federal election," https://en.wikipedia.org/wiki/1878_Canadian_federal_election (accessed November 9, 2019).

23 Statement of William Henry Seward quoted in Pierre Berton, *The National Dream: The Great Railway, 1871–1881*, Toronto: Anchor Canada,1970, p. 10.

24 "Pacific Scandal," http://biographi.ca/en/theme_macdonald.html?project_id=98&p=26 (accessed January 5, 2020).

25 *London Free Press*, September 15, 1875; *London Free Press*, September 24; *London Free Press*, November 19, 1878, *London Free Press*, May 7, 1879; *London Free Press*, May 28, 1879; *London Free Press*, November 20, 1880.

26 *London Free Press*, September 15, 1875.

27 "Middlesex North," https://en.wikipedia.org/wiki/Middlesex_North (accessed November 10, 2019).

28 "Section NO. 3 still gave the Liberals a big majority: 79 for the Grits, 40 for the Tories." Reaney, *The Donnelly Documents: An Ontario Vendetta*, p. xxxii.

29 *Exeter Times*, May 30, 1878.

30 "I heard he spoke of Bob last summer. He also spoke of Bob at the sale on Saturday last." Testimony of John Donnelly. J.J. Talman Regional Collection, University of Western Ontario Archives, Donnelly Family Papers, B4877, File 25, Unknown, John Donnelly vs. James Carroll, Threats to Shoot, October 14, 1878.

31 "Tom told me that Carroll said he could lick all the Donnellys . . ." Testimony of John Donnelly. J.J. Talman Regional Collection, University of Western Ontario Archives, Donnelly Family Papers, B4877, File 25, Unknown, John Donnelly vs. James Carroll, Threats to Shoot, October 14, 1878. See also: "I told him I did not want to fight but if he would meet me at Whalen's Corners, I

would fight him and lick all the Donnellys." Testimony of James Carroll. University of Western Ontario, Middlesex County Clerk of the Peace, Criminal Records, London, October 26, 1878, Queen v. John & William Donnelly, Assault, testimony before John Peters.

32 "I heard of the row at Dawe's [barn] raising and of the row at the sale." Patrick Keefe's testimony drawn from J.J. Talman Regional Collection, University of Western Ontario Archives, Donnelly Family Papers, B4877, File 25, Unknown, John Donnelly vs. James Carroll, Threats to Shoot, October 14, 1878.

33 University of Western Ontario, Middlesex Court Records, Lucan, October 21, 1878, Queen v. Carroll, Assault, Testimony of John Donnelly before McCosh and Crunican.

34 "I would ask Carroll why he used my name the first time I saw him. I intended to speak to him if I met him on the road." Testimony of John Donnelly. J.J. Talman Regional Collection, University of Western Ontario Archives, Donnelly Family Papers, B4877, File 25, Unknown, John Donnelly vs. James Carroll, Threats to Shoot, October 14, 1878.

35 "I remember the Sunday before the row I saw John Donnelly down the road on that day. Bobby Keefe and Jimmy Maher was with me." Testimony of Patrick Keefe. J.J. Talman Regional Collection, University of Western Ontario Archives, Donnelly Family Papers, B4877, File 25, Unknown, John Donnelly vs. James Carroll, Threats to Shoot, October 14, 1878. See also: "Pat Keefe & Jimmy Keefe were present when I spoke to Maher on Sunday." Testimony of John Donnelly. J.J. Talman Regional Collection, University of Western Ontario Archives, Donnelly Family Papers, B4877, File 25, Unknown, John Donnelly vs. James Carroll, Threats to Shoot, October 14, 1878.

36 "I said on Sunday, 'Where is that Carroll, big fighting man?'" Testimony of John Donnelly. J.J. Talman Regional Collection, University of Western Ontario Archives, Donnelly Family Papers, B4877, File 25, Unknown, John Donnelly vs. James Carroll, Threats to Shoot, October 14, 1878.

37 "He [Maher] said, 'He is at McDonell's.'" Testimony of John
   Donnelly. J.J. Talman Regional Collection, University of Western
   Ontario Archives, Donnelly Family Papers, B4877, File 25,
   Unknown, John Donnelly vs. James Carroll, Threats to Shoot,
   October 14, 1878. See also, Reaney, *The Donnelly Documents: An
   Ontario Vendetta*, p. 75, note: 490: "Dan McDonell (1838–1896),
   b. New Brunswick, RC, Irish, farmer VII-31 Biddulph, brother
   Jeremiah (b. 1836) lived there. His wife, Eleanor, was James
   Carroll's aunt."

38 "I asked John Donnelly on Sunday if he wants to whip Carroll and
   he said, 'No.'" Testimony of Patrick Keefe. J.J. Talman Regional
   Collection, University of Western Ontario Archives, Donnelly
   Family Papers, B4877, File 25, Unknown, John Donnelly vs. James
   Carroll, Threats to Shoot, October 14, 1878.

39 Testimony of John Donnelly. J.J. Talman Regional Collection,
   University of Western Ontario Archives, Donnelly Family Papers,
   B4877, File 25, Unknown, John Donnelly vs. James Carroll,
   Threats to Shoot, October 14, 1878.

40 Testimony of John Donnelly. Middlesex Court Records, Lucan,
   October 21, 1878, Queen v. Carroll, Assault on October 5.

41 "I was going to get some notes from a man I had sold a fanning
   mill." Testimony of James Carroll. University of Western Ontario,
   Middlesex Court Records, Queen v. John & William Donnelly,
   Assault, October 16, 1878. Testimony before John Peters, J.P. A
   fanning mill was a large hand-cranked device that "removed straw,
   chaff, stones, dirt and dust, weed seeds, and light immature seeds
   from wheat, oats, rye, barley, and other grains. It was important to
   remove contaminants for better preservation during storage, to have
   mold- and grit-free flour, and for securing viable seed free of weed
   seeds that would compete with a growing cereal crop. Fanning mills
   were a great technical advance over winnowing, the hand-process
   of pouring grain from one container to another in a breeze to blow
   away the lighter matter." "Remember the Old Fanning Mill?"
   https://crookedlakereview.com/articles/101_135/
   126winter2003/126palmer3.html (accessed November 15, 2019).

42 While there is plenty of evidence of James Carroll acting and talking tough, there is no account of him ever having emerged victorious in any one-on-one fistfights he entered into while in Biddulph.

43 "I got home on the morning in question about 8 o'clock. John was ploughing in the field by the house near the road. Thomas was in the act of coming from the other place." Testimony of William Donnelly. University of Western Ontario, Middlesex Court Records, Lucan, October 21, 1878, Queen v. Carroll, Assault on October 5, 1878. Testimony before McCosh and Crunican.

44 "He [Tom] went to the pump and got a drink of water. John came from the plough got a drink of water asked me some questions about our brother Mike, and then went to plough again." Testimony of William Donnelly. Middlesex Court Records, Lucan, October 21, 1878, Queen v. Carroll, Assault on October 5, 1878.

45 "Tom began to tell me about a row Carroll was trying to raise with him on the Saturday night before." Testimony of William Donnelly. Middlesex Court Records, Lucan, October 21, 1878, Queen v. Carroll, Assault on October 5, 1878.

46 "I feared he [Tom] and Carroll would fight again on account of having the row on the previous Saturday." Also, "Tom was at the house talking to me when Carroll came up. I told Tom not to mind Carroll if he challenged him out to fight every day of the week. Carroll wanted law not fight." Testimony of William Donnelly, J.J. Talman Regional Collection, University of Western Ontario Archives, Donnelly Family Papers, B4877, File 25, John Donnelly vs. James Carroll, Threats to Shoot, October 14, 1878. William Donnelly had been suspicious of James Carroll's motives ever since the incident at the barn raising several months previously when Carroll had been loudly proclaiming that Bob Donnelly had gotten a light sentence. After all, Carroll was a relative newcomer to Biddulph and had little to no interactions with the Donnelly family up until that point. So suspicious was William of Carroll's motives that he approached Ned Maher, another uncle of James Carroll's: "I told Ned Maher what Carroll said. I said Carroll was a queer

fellow and asked Maher what it was of Carroll's business how long a sentence Bob got." Testimony of William Donnelly, J.J. Talman Regional Collection, University of Western Ontario Archives, Donnelly Family Papers, B4877, File 25, John Donnelly vs. James Carroll, Threats to Shoot, October 14, 1878.

47 "I told him not to fight every day in the week. Carroll wanted law not fight. . . . I told Tom to go into the house and he went in before the row began." Testimony of William Donnelly. J.J. Talman Regional Collection, University of Western Ontario Archives, Donnelly Family Papers, B4877, File 25, Unknown, John Donnelly vs. James Carroll, Threats to Shoot, October 14, 1878.

48 "I figured he [Tom] and Carroll would fight again on account of having the row on the previous Saturday." Testimony of William Donnelly. J.J. Talman Regional Collection, University of Western Ontario Archives, Donnelly Family Papers, B4877, File 25, Unknown, John Donnelly vs. James Carroll, Threats to Shoot, October 14, 1878.

49 "Tom went in the house and I sat down on the steps of the front door." Testimony of William Donnelly. Middlesex Court Records, Lucan, October 21, 1878, Queen v. Carroll, Assault on October 5, 1878.

50 "I was ploughing in the field about one rod from the road." Testimony of John Donnelly. University of Western Ontario, Middlesex Court Records, Lucan, October 21, 1878, Queen v. Carroll, Assault on October 5, 1878. Testimony before McCosh and Crunican.

51 "On passing the Donnellys' place I saw John Donnelly come out of the house, and commenced ploughing in the field. He saw me, and called saying he wanted to talk to me. I paid no attention to him. He kept calling after me. I told him I did not want to talk to him." Testimony of James Carroll. University of Western Ontario, Middlesex Court Records, Queen v. John & William Donnelly, Assault, October 16, 1878. Testimony before John Peters, J.P.

52 The remainder of the dialogue from this incident, unless otherwise indicated, is taken directly from John and William Donnelly's

testimony from the University of Western Ontario, Middlesex Court Records, Lucan, October 21, 1878, Queen v. Carroll, Assault on October 5, 1878. Testimony before Messrs McCosh and Crunican, J.P.s. John Donnelly v. James Carroll. Trial before Messrs McCosh and Crunican, J.P.s. The dialogue also includes passages from James Carroll's testimony, taken from the University of Western Ontario, Middlesex Court Records, Queen v. John & William Donnelly, Assault, October 16, 1878. Testimony before John Peters, J.P.

53　"The complainant, Carroll, swore that Mrs. Donnelly called him a blackguard, thief and rogue, while the defendant's two sons swore positively that the term blackguard was only used. They also swore that Carroll pointed a revolver at Mrs. Donnelly, saying at the same time that he would just as soon shoot her as he would one of her sons." *London Advertiser*, October 22, 1878.

54　"John and William Donnelly were charged with assaulting James Carroll by throwing stones at him. They were each fined $3 and costs, which they paid, and in addition required to find bail for their good behaviour." *London Advertiser*, October 16, 1878.

55　Notation on the testimony document in Carroll v. Donnelly, Assault, testimony, October 16, 1878.

56　Returns of Convictions, October 15, 1878.

57　University of Western Ontario, Donnelly Family Papers, Notice of Appeal, October 23, 1878; Middlesex General Sessions Minute Book, 1876–1885, pp. 193 and 209, and Sessions Minute Book, pp. 194, 202 and 225; see also Charles Hutchinson, Letters and Papers, Clerk of the Peace Correspondence, Bill of appellant's costs in Donnelly v. Carroll, Appeal, December Sessions, 1878.

58　*London Advertiser*, December 23, 1878.

CHAPTER ELEVEN: THE PRIEST AND THE CLUB-FOOTED DEVIL

1　*London Free Press*, February 7, 1879.

2　The Monthly Packet of Evening Readings for Members of the English Church, Volume 3, John and Charles Mozley (1852), p. 215.

3   Butt, *The Donnellys: History, Legend, Literature*, p. 161.

4   *London Advertiser*, February 26, 1880.

5   *Catholic Record*, October 24, 1879.

6   Toronto *Globe*, March 2, 1880.

7   "Connolly's rapport was instant and solid with respectable
     Protestant merchants in Lucan, men such as Bernard and William
     Stanley who had travelled in Europe as he, John Connolly, had."
     Butt, *The Donnellys: History, Legend, Literature*, p. 161; see also
     London Free Press, April 15, 1879.

8   "Our barns were burnt, our horses' tongues cut out, our cattle
     disembowelled, and no one was safe who ever said a word
     against the Donnellys." The person quoted in this statement is
     described by the reporter as "a gentleman well known in Lucan
     and Biddulph, who occupies a high position, and who is univer-
     sally respected." It is believed that this person is William Stanley
     (Reaney, *The Donnelly Documents: An Ontario Vendetta*, p. 126).
     If so, then these were most likely some of the charges that Father
     Connolly heard when speaking with the Stanleys. See also *London
     Advertiser*, February 5, 1880.

9   Toronto *Globe*, February 7, 1880.

10   "I was speaking to Stephen McCormack, the father of the boy
     who drove the priest around, and he told me he fancied the priest's
     mind had been poisoned against our family during his visit on the
     Roman Line. He also said his son told him that the priest was kept
     over two hours in conversation in one house." William Donnelly
     quoted in the Toronto *Globe*, March 2, 1880.

11   "Mr. Wm. Stanley, Reeve of the village, was fearless in stating that
     two years ago the Donnellys were the terror of the township."
     Toronto *Globe*, February 7, 1880.

12   Toronto *Globe*, March 2, 1880.

13   Toronto *Globe*, March 2, 1880.

14   Toronto *Globe*, March 2, 1880.

15   Toronto *Globe*, March 2, 1880.

16   "Cornelius Maloney, in return for food, raiment, and shelter, sells
     twenty-five acres of Concession VI Lot 17 to James Donnelly Sr. for

one dollar. . . . in return for their care, it would be they who would have his 25 acres of good land. . . . Cornelius Maloney had already moved to the Donnelly home [1875], where he would subsequently die on 29 December 1879." Reaney, *The Donnelly Documents: An Ontario Vendetta*, pp. lxvi–lxvii. See also Chapter Four: "Love and War."

17 Per the family tombstone.

18 "[John Connolly] . . . emigrating in 1864 to Quebec . . ." Butt, *The Donnellys: History, Legend, Literature*, p. 161.

19 William Donnelly: "'He [Father Connolly] also spoke to my cousin Bridget, the murdered girl; enquired about her late arrival from Ireland, and was quite friendly with her.'" Toronto *Globe*, March 2, 1880.

20 Per the family tombstone.

21 Toronto *Globe*, March 2, 1880.

22 "Lawlessness in Usborne," *London Free Press*, March 4, 1879. See also William Donnelly's statement about the event: "'In the latter end of February [February 28] my house was broken into by three masked men, who bound my hands to the bedstead and told me I had $400 in the house and they wanted it. One of them fired two shots over me, with an intention of frightening me, while the other searched an adjoining room where my wife and a hired girl were sleeping. They abstracted $132 from a trunk, but overlooked $38 belonging to the girl that lay on a stand.'" Toronto *Globe*, March 2, 1880.

23 ". . . [the robbers] proceeded to another bedroom, occupied by Mrs. Donnelly and a servant-girl, who by this time were screaming loudly, having been alarmed by the shots. They threatened to shoot the women unless they covered their heads . . . Mrs. Donnelly was in a delicate state of health, having recently been confined, and the shock received has resulted in a very serious prostration . . ." *Exeter Times*, quoted from Miller, *The Donnellys Must Die*, p. 139.

24 Toronto *Globe*, March 2, 1880.

25 "A Mrs. Fogarty was also robbed of $240, a short time since by men of a similar description. There is work for a detective in that vicinity." *Exeter Times*, as quoted in Miller, *The Donnellys Must Die*, p. 139.

26 James Maher Jr. was the young man (now seventeen years of age) that John Donnelly had inquired of regarding James Carroll's whereabouts. The son of James Maher Sr., James Jr. would later be one of the men taken prisoner for the murder of the Donnelly family.

27 Toronto *Globe*, March 2, 1880.

28 *London Advertiser*, April 8, 1879.

29 *London Free Press*, February 12, 1880.

30 All dialogue from the encounter between Constable Everett and Constable Hodgins in the Queen's Hotel is quoted from Middlesex County Clerk of the Peace, Criminal Records, 1879, Queen v. Hodgins, Assault, testimony before Peter, April 28, 1879, and from Queen v. Everett, Assault, testimony before Atkinson, McCosh and McIlhargey, April 15, 1879.

31 *London Advertiser*, February 6, 1880.

32 *London Advertiser*, February 6, 1880.

33 John Donnelly quoted by William Donnelly in the Toronto *Globe*, March 2, 1880.

34 Middlesex County Clerk of the Peace Criminal Records Queen v. Thomas Donnelly, Larceny, April 8, 1879.

35 Middlesex County Clerk of the Peace, Criminal Records, 1879, Queen v. Donnelly, Larceny, certificate of dismissal, April 8, 1879.

36 *Exeter Times*, April 10, 1879; *London Advertiser*, April 11, 1879; *Catholic Record*, April 11, 1879; and the *London Free Press*, April 11 and 14, 1879.

37 *London Free Press*, April 11 and 15, 1879.

38 J.J. Talman Regional Collection, University of Western Ontario Archives, Donnelly Family Papers, B4878, File 11, Charles Hutchinson, Charles Hutchinson Letter Book, April 29, 1879.

39 *London Advertiser*, February 7, 1880; see also the *London Free Press*, February 12, 1880.

40 Letterbooks from the Office of the Clerk of the Peace, Middlesex County, to McCosh, May 9; to Everett, May 9; and to Matthewson, May 14, 1879.

41 J.J. Talman Regional Collection, University of Western Ontario

Archives, Donnelly Family Papers, B4878, File 11, Charles Hutchinson, Charles Hutchinson Letter Book, May 9, 1879.

42 "In the middle of March, I moved to Whalen's Corners . . ." Statement from William Donnelly published in the Toronto *Globe*, March 2, 1880.

43 *Exeter Times*, October 3, 1878.

44 *Catholic Record*, October 17, 1879; see also the *London Advertiser*, February 7, 1880.

45 Toronto *Globe*, March 2, 1880.

46 *London Free Press*, May 13, 1879.

47 Toronto *Globe*, March 2, 1880.

48 Toronto *Globe*, March 2, 1880.

49 Toronto *Globe*, March 2, 1880.

50 Toronto *Globe*, March 2, 1880.

51 Toronto *Globe*, March 2, 1880.

52 Toronto *Globe*, March 2, 1880.

53 Toronto *Globe*, March 2, 1880.

54 Toronto *Globe*, March 2, 1880.

55 Toronto *Globe*, March 2, 1880.

56 *Toronto Mail*, February 13, 1880.

57 *London Advertiser*, February 6, 1880.

58 *Toronto Mail*, February 13, 1880.

59 *Toronto Mail*, February 13, 1880.

60 *London Advertiser*, February 6, 1880.

61 Toronto *Globe*, March 2, 1880.

62 Toronto *Globe*, March 2, 1880.

63 Toronto *Globe*, March 2, 1880.

64 *London Advertiser*, February 6, 1880.

65 "[Father Connolly] continually spoke about the letter I had sent him, and telling his congregation not to have anything to do with me. I suppose he formed the opinion from the stories he had heard that I was bad company for anybody." William Donnelly quoted in the Toronto *Globe*, March 2, 1880.

66 Toronto *Globe*, March 2, 1880.

67 "On her [Johannah Donnelly's] last visit she informed me they [the Donnelly sons] were going to London for confession." Father Connolly quoted in the *Toronto Mail*, February 13, 1880.

68 Toronto *Globe*, March 2, 1880.

69 "It is too bad that people should be pulled about by such characters as those Donnellys; they would swear any decent man's life away. There will have to be something to stop it — to form a Vigilant Committee and get them out of the township." James Maher, quoted by Constable Charles Pope during the time of James Carroll's re-arrest on April 10, 1879 on the charge of pointing a revolver at Johannah Donnelly. Library of the Law Society of Upper Canada, Judge's Note Books, Common Pleas, Book IV, 1881, Middlesex Special Commission, Biddulph Murders: Osler (trial notes of Justice Featherston Osler), pp. 43 and 67.

70 *London Advertiser*, February 12, 1880.

71 A photocopy of the oath and the appended signatures is in J.J. Talman Regional Collection, University of Western Ontario Archives, Donnelly Family Papers, B4877, File 52, Unknown, Queen v. James Carroll, et. al., Charge of Murder, March 13, 1880.

72 Father Connolly's testimony as found in the Middlesex County Clerk of the Peace Criminal Records, 1879, Donnelly v. Maher et al., Trespass, September 27, 1879.

73 "He [Father Connolly] then proposed to form this society, and said that he would consider all those who declined to join it as backsliders and sympathisers of this gang, meaning, I suppose, our family. Also, that if any of these sympathisers or backsliders took sick they were to send for William Donnelly to visit them instead of him." William Donnelly, quoted in the Toronto *Globe*, March 2, 1880.

74 "The book remained at the church for two or more Sundays. A total of ninety-four men appended their names to the oath, for it was regarded as such. The first was James Gleeson. The name of Patrick Breen, acknowledged to be the chairman of the Vigilance Committee, was there, and that of James Carroll and that of James Feeheley. Not a single member of the Donnelly family signed the document, nor was any asked to do so." Miller, *The Donnellys Must Die*, p. 142.

75   Toronto *Globe*, March 2, 1880.

76   Toronto *Globe*, February 28, 1880.

77   *London Free Press*, August 27, 1879; see also Catholic Record, July 11, 1879.

CHAPTER TWELVE: THE COW AND THE FIDDLE

1   *Glencoe Transcript*, September 17, 1885.

2   Toronto *Globe*, March 2, 1880.

3   Toronto *Globe*, March 2, 1880.

4   William Donnelly quoted in the Toronto *Globe*, March 2, 1880. "Ned Ryan was the man who accused my brother Tom of the robbery already mentioned. Last fall, when the farmers were getting their grain threshed, Tom told Martin Curtin, who owned a threshing machine, not to have anything to do with the threshing of Ryan's grain . . . The result was that Curtin refused to thresh for Ryan . . ."; See also "During last fall, Ryan engaged a man named Curtin to come and thresh for him. Thomas Donnelly heard of it and gave Curtin warning that his machine would be destroyed if he attempted to thresh for Ryan. Upon this threat Curtain refused to do any threshing for Ryan." Father Connolly, quoted in the *London Advertiser*, February 6, 1880.

5   Father Connolly, quoted in the *London Advertiser*, February 6, 1880.

6   In a letter that Patrick Donnelly wrote to Crown attorney Charles Hutchinson, he claims that Father Connolly had told him that "there was a society existing in Biddulph previous to his coming there. He obtained his information through the confessional. He also said they drifted away from the one he had formed back to the old one." J.J. Talman Regional Collection, University of Western Ontario Archives, Donnelly Family Papers, B4878, File 2, Patrick Donnelly, Letter to Charles Hutchinson from Patrick Donnelly, March 12, 1880.

7   "William Feeheley told me in presence of James Hogin [sic] that . . . Pat Breen made all the bylaws and Dan Keenan kept the

books . . ." Testimony of Patrick Donnelly, J.J. Talman Regional Collection, University of Western Ontario Archives, Donnelly Family Papers, B4877, File 63, Unknown, Statements About the Feeheleys, ca. April 31, 1881–July 31, 1881. However, according to Father Connolly, this was not the case: "This committee, so far as I can learn, had no officers, and met only at the call of the member who had been victimized . . ." *London Advertiser*, February 6, 1880. Father Connolly's belief is backed up by the testimony of William Thompson in this regard: ". . . as far as I know I don't know whether there was any head of the committee; I don't know whether there was a president or chairman; we never elected a chairman that I know of at the meetings; there never was a vote at any meeting that I attended; I have attended perhaps four of the meetings . . ." Testimony of William Thompson. Evidence at the Coroner's Inquest and Preliminary Examination, Aemilius Irving Papers, F 1027-3, File 82-8, Transcript of the Donnelly Murder Case, 1880 (MS 6500) Public Archives of Ontario, Toronto.

8   "A respectable farmer, living next door to the priest, signed his name to the declaration in church, but after the meetings started at the schoolhouse he was continually tormented by men who attended the same to come and join them, which he refused to do, as he understood it was a sworn society. No one was allowed to attend their meetings who had not taken the oath . . ." William Donnelly quoted in the Toronto *Globe*, March 2, 1880; see also "There was something said to me about an oath; I think a man asked me if I would take my oath; it was said in connection with my joining the society." Martin Hogan Jr. quoted from Evidence at the Coroner's Inquest and Preliminary Examination, Aemilius Irving Papers, F 1027-3, File 82-8, Transcript of the Donnelly Murder Case, 1880 (MS 6500) Public Archives of Ontario, Toronto.

9   ". . . the members, although not taking an oath in a theological sense, making a solemn declaration, and, without using the form 'So help me God,' kissed the book." Father Connolly quoted in the *London Advertiser*, 6 February 1880.

10   "The society was for the purpose of discovering anything that
     might be stolen in the neighbourhood, and placing the guilt on
     the proper parties. But it soon fell through, and a sworn society
     was formed, with headquarters at the Cedar Swamp Schoolhouse.
     It was composed of men in direct opposition to our family and
     I believe their sole object was to drive us out of the township."
     William Donnelly quoted in the Toronto *Globe*, March 2, 1880.

11   Toronto *Globe*, March 2, 1880.

12   *London Advertiser*, March 7, 1881.

13   Toronto *Globe*, March 2, 1880.

14   William Donnelly quoted in the *London Free Press*, February 23,
     1880.

15   "The Vigilance Committee had met, and, upon Mr. Ryan's applica-
     tion, guaranteed to Curtin the value of his machine and any loss of
     time he might have." Father John Connolly quoted in the *London
     Advertiser*, February 6, 1880.

16   *London Advertiser*, February 6, 1880: "Curtin then threshed for
     Ryan, but they found that the sheaves had been filled with iron . . ."

17   "Curtin . . . threshed Ryan's grain. Pieces of iron were found
     hidden in some of the sheaves, and Tom was accused of having
     put them there." William Donnelly quoted in the Toronto *Globe*,
     March 2, 1880.

18   "From Ryan's, Curtin went to Dan Ryder's, for whom he was to
     thresh. In the morning the machine was found broken. Everyone
     had it that the Donnellys did the damage." William Donnelly
     quoted in the Toronto *Globe*, March 2, 1880.

19   William Donnelly maintained that it was the priest who financially
     guaranteed the safety of Curtin's threshing machines, whereas
     Father Connolly (see Note 15 above) said it was the Vigilance
     Committee that did so.

20   William Donnelly quoted in the Toronto *Globe*, March 2, 1880.

21   Testimony of Mary Thompson. Middlesex County Clerk of the
     Peace, Criminal Records, 1879, Donnelly v. Maher et al., Trespass,
     September 27, 1879.

22   Toronto *Globe*, March 2, 1880.

23 According to an 1871 Census for Biddulph, the Donnellys owned three milking cows. J.J. Talman Regional Collection, University of Western Ontario Archives, Reaney Papers, Box 26 (B1312), File 51A, Government of Canada, Donnelly Information, 1871 Census (Various Returns/Schedules), 1871.

24 Butt, *The Donnellys: History, Legend, Literature*, p. 176, citing Hutchinson, Charles Letters and Papers, Donnelly to Hutchinson, February 28, 1880 and the Toronto *Globe* March 2–3, 1880.

25 William Thompson testimony cited from Evidence at the Coroner's Inquest and Preliminary Examination, Aemilius Irving Papers, F 1027-3, File 82-8, Transcript of the Donnelly Murder Case, 1880 (MS 6500) Public Archives of Ontario, Toronto.

26 Testimony of Thomas Marshall quoted in *London Free Press*, October 7, 1880.

27 Testimony of William Thompson. Evidence at the Coroner's Inquest and Preliminary Examination, Aemilius Irving Papers, F 1027-3, File 82-8, Transcript of the Donnelly Murder Case, 1880 (MS 6500) Public Archives of Ontario, Toronto.

28 "[The Vigilance Committee] came to Michael Powe's, where young Ryan was working, and arrested him on a charge of using abusive language towards Pat Dewan, a committeeman. They also accused Ryan of stealing the cow, and said the next thing to be done was to find her." William Donnelly quoted in the Toronto *Globe*, March 2, 1880.

29 J.J. Talman Regional Collection, University of Western Ontario Archives, Donnelly Family Papers, B4878, Charles Hutchinson, Charles Hutchinson Letter Book, Donnelly to Hutchinson, September 18, 1880.

30 "At the break of day about forty [Vigilance] committeemen and Hodgins . . . came to Michael Powe's . . ." William Donnelly quoted in the Toronto *Globe*, March 2, 1880.

31 "The crowd [of] thirty-five did go to Donnellys place. There was three or four I noticed that had sticks. I did not see any revolvers." Testimony of James Carrigan. J.J. Talman Regional Collection, University of Western Ontario Archives, Donnelly Family Papers,

B4877, File 33, Unknown, Queen v. John Donnelly, Perjury Charge of Michael Blake, October 30, 1879. See also testimony of William Thompson Jr.: "We went on Donnelly's place to look for my cow, perhaps twenty or thirty of us: we had no search warrant. Mr. Donnelly took us up on that. Kennedy, McGlaughlin, James Ryder, James Carroll and about thirty others went on to old Donnelly's." Evidence at the Coroner's Inquest and Preliminary Examination, Aemilius Irving Papers, F 1027-3, File 82-8, Transcript of the Donnelly Murder Case, 1880 (MS 6500) Public Archives of Ontario, Toronto.

32 "At the break of day about forty committeemen and Hodgins armed with all kinds of clubs, and one carrying a rifle, came to Michael Powe's. . ." William Donnelly quoted in the Toronto *Globe*, March 2, 1880.

33 Testimony of James Keefe. Library of the Law Society of Upper Canada, Judge's Note Books, Common Pleas, Book IV, 1881, Middlesex Special Commission, Biddulph Murders: Osler (Trial Notes Of Justice Featherston Osler), p. 60.

34 Toronto *Globe*, March 2, 1880, and *Toronto Mail*, October 7, 1880.

35 "The cow was found that same morning by an old man named Quigley, who drove it to Thompson's before the gang got back." William Donnelly quoted in the Toronto *Globe*, March 2, 1880. See also testimony from William Thompson Jr.: "We found the cow in William McLaughlin's woods." Evidence at the Coroner's Inquest and Preliminary Examination, Aemilius Irving Papers, F 1027-3, File 82-8, Transcript of the Donnelly Murder Case, 1880 (MS 6500) Public Archives of Ontario, Toronto.

36 All dialogue from this incident unless otherwise indicated is taken from testimony of John Donnelly, James Donnelly Sr. and Thomas Hines. J.J. Talman Regional Collection, University of Western Ontario Archives, Donnelly Family Papers, B4877, File 29, Unknown, "John Donnelly Complaint, Trespass on His Land," September 10, 1879; Middlesex County, Clerk of the Peace, Criminal Records, 1879, Queen v. James Maher et al., Trespass, testimony before Peters, September 20 and 27, 1879;

University of Western Ontario, archives, Donnelly Papers, Articles: Contemporary Newspaper Reports, 1880, Box 2-15, unsourced newspaper article #8, and from Blake v. Donnelly, Perjury, testimony before Stanley, October 30, and before Grant, November 25, 1879; also Library of the Law Society of Upper Canada, Judge's Note Books, Common Pleas, Book IV, 1881, Middlesex Special Commission, Biddulph Murders: Osler (Trial Notes Of Justice Featherston Osler), p. 61.

37 "Carroll told him to hold his tongue . . . Carroll told him . . . that they could break his bones at his door and he could not help himself." William Donnelly quoted in the Toronto *Globe*, March 2, 1880.

38 William Donnelly quoted in the Toronto *Globe*, March 2, 1880.

39 Toronto *Globe*, March 2, 1880.

40 "We'll go to brother-in-law's now." William Donnelly quoting John Kennedy Jr. in Toronto *Globe*, March 2, 1880.

41 Testimony of Thomas Marshall quoted in the *Toronto Mail*, October 7, 1880.

42 *Toronto Mail*, October 7, 1880. See also testimony of Thomas Marshall, Library of the Law Society of Upper Canada, Judge's Note Books, Common Pleas, Book IV, 1881, Middlesex Special Commission, Biddulph Murders: Osler (Trial Notes of Justice Featherston Osler), p. 60.

43 Testimony of James Keefe quoted in *London Advertiser*, October 6, 1880.

44 Toronto *Globe*, March 2, 1880.

45 The incident and dialogue with Edward Sutherby are taken from Library of the Law Society of Upper Canada, Judge's Note Books, Common Pleas, Book IV, 1881, Middlesex Special Commission, Biddulph Murders: Osler (Trial Notes of Justice Featherston Osler), p. 61, testimony of Edward Sutherby; William Donnelly quoted in the newspaper article "Six Hours with William Donnelly" published in the Toronto *Globe*, March 2, 1880; and the *London Advertiser*, October 6, 1880.

46 Butt, *The Donnellys: History, Legend, Literature*, p. 478.

47　"When I saw that Sitting Bull (Kennedy) and the Black Militia, as they were called . . ." Toronto *Globe*, March 2, 1880.

48　Toronto *Globe*, March 2, 1880.

49　Toronto *Globe*, March 2, 1880.

50　Toronto *Globe*, March 2, 1880.

51　Middlesex County Clerk of the Peace, Criminal Records, 1880, Queen v. James and Johannah Donnelly, Arson, testimony of Mary Carroll, January 27, 1880; see also Toronto Globe, February 9, 1880.

CHAPTER THIRTEEN: DIVINE OUTLAWS

1　J.J. Talman Regional Collection, University of Western Ontario Archives, Donnelly Family Papers, B4878, File 11, Charles Hutchinson, Charles Hutchinson Letter Book, September 10, 1879.

2　J. J. Talman Regional Collection, University of Western Ontario Archives, Donnelly Family Papers, B4877, File 29, Unknown, "John Donnelly Complaint, Trespass on His Land," September 10, 1879.

3　*Exeter Times*, March 20, 1879.

4　*London Free Press*, September 2, 1879. See also the *Exeter Times*, September 4, 1879.

5　Toronto *Globe*, March 2, 1880.

6　William Donnelly, who was present at the trial, recalled that "Ryan acknowledged calling Dewan names, but denied having threatened to cut his heart out." Toronto *Globe*, March 2, 1880.

7　William Donnelly: "Father Connolly jumped up, and addressing Mr. McDiarmid, Ryan's lawyer, accused him of trying to make his client perjure himself." Toronto *Globe*, March 2, 1880.

8　William Donnelly: "He [Ryan] was fined a small sum." Toronto *Globe*, March 2, 1880.

9　Toronto *Globe*, March 2, 1880.

10　All dialogue between Father Connolly and Michael Powe is taken from William Donnelly's interview in the Toronto *Globe*, March 2, 1880.

11 Toronto *Globe*, March 2, 1880. It's interesting to observe that Powe, despite claiming that Ryan would be owed thirty dollars in wages (and receiving that amount from the priest), only gave Ryan twenty dollars, evidently pocketing ten dollars for himself.

12 Toronto *Globe*, March 3, 1880.

13 John Kennedy Sr. is referring here to his youngest son, Michael Kennedy, who, apart from his father, had remained a friend of the Donnellys. Reaney, *The Donnelly Documents: An Ontario Vendetta*, p. 90, note 509.

14 All dialogue quoted between the priest and John Kennedy Sr. is from "Six Hours with William Donnelly," Toronto *Globe*, March 2, 1880.

15 William Donnelly's recounting of the content of Father Connolly's sermon is from Toronto *Globe*, March 3, 1880.

16 *London Advertiser*, October 6, 1879. The testimony of John Cain speaks to the meeting the Society held to appoint a constable.

17 Toronto *Globe*, October 9, 1880. The testimony of Michael Blake speaks to John Blake's work in preparing the petition for James Carroll's appointment.

18 J.J. Talman Regional Collection, University of Western Ontario Archives, Donnelly Family Papers, B4877, File 84, Unknown, Petition Requesting the Appointment of James Carroll as Constable, October 6, 1880.

19 *London Advertiser*, September 20, 1879.

20 Testimony of Charles Pope. Library of the Law Society of Upper Canada, Judge's Note Books, Common Pleas, Book IV, 1881, Middlesex Special Commission, Biddulph Murders: Osler (Trial Notes of Justice Featherston Osler), p. 44.

21 Testimony of Father John Connolly. Middlesex County, Clerk of the Peace, Criminal Records, 1879, Donnelly v. Maher et al., Trespass, September 27, 1879.

22 Testimony of Father John Connolly. Middlesex County, Clerk of the Peace, Criminal Records, 1879, Donnelly v. Maher et al., Trespass, September 27, 1879.

23 Toronto *Globe*, March 2, 1880.

24 Middlesex County, Clerk of the Peace, Criminal Records, 1879,
Queen v. Thomas Donnelly, Larceny, statement of Edward Ryan,
September 27, 1879.

25 Testimony of William Hodgins. Library of the Law Society of
Upper Canada, Judge's Note Books, Common Pleas, Book IV,
1881, Middlesex Special Commission, Biddulph Murders: Osler
(Trial Notes of Justice Featherston Osler), pp. 44–45.

26 Testimony of James Feeheley. Middlesex Special Commission,
Biddulph Murders: Osler (Trial Notes of Justice Featherston Osler),
pp. 15–17. See also the *London Advertiser*, April 8, 1879.

27 Toronto *Globe*, March 2, 1880.

28 Toronto *Globe*, March 2, 1880.

29 Toronto *Globe*, March 2, 1880.

30 Toronto *Globe*, March 2, 1880.

31 Toronto *Globe*, March 2, 1880.

32 Toronto *Globe*, March 2, 1880.

33 The incident and dialogue of Tom Donnelly's arrest by James
Carroll are taken from the *London Advertiser*, January 29, 1881,
and testimony of William Simpson and of John Kent. Library of the
Law Society of Upper Canada, Judge's Note Books, Common Pleas,
Book IV, 1881, Middlesex Special Commission, Biddulph Murders:
Osler (Trial Notes of Justice Featherston Osler), pp. 58–59.

34 *London Free Press*, September 26, 1879.

35 Middlesex County, Clerk of the Peace, Criminal Records, 1879,
Queen v. James Maher et al., Trespass, September 27, 1879.

36 *London Advertiser*, September 29, 1879.

37 Middlesex County, Clerk of the Peace, Criminal Records, 1879,
Queen v. Thomas Donnelly, Larceny, September 27, 1879.

38 James Carroll quote cited by William McDiarmid in the Toronto
Globe, January 29, 1881.

39 Clerk of the Peace Correspondence, Cameron to Hutchinson,
October 20, 1879.

40 "On the morning of the 9th went in company with Constable to
the House of William Donnelly in Biddulph. Got there about 8 a.m."
Testimony of James Carroll. University of Western Ontario,

Middlesex County, Clerk of the Peace, Criminal Records, Queen v. John Donnelly, Aiding Escape from Arrest, October 14, 1879, in Granton, before J.P. James Grant.

41 The timeline and incidents of Constable Hodgins and Carroll's attempt to arrest Tom Donnelly, unless otherwise noted, are taken from Middlesex County, Clerk of the Peace, Criminal Records, 1879, Queen v. Thomas Donnelly, Larceny, September 27, 1879, and Middlesex County Clerk of the Peace, Criminal Records, 1879, Queen v. John Donnelly, Aiding a felon to escape, testimony before Grant, October 17, 1879.

42 Testimony of Mary Thompson: "I saw William Donnelly that morning — he was coming from the direction of his own house. I saw Thomas Donnelly in his father's field, also saw John Donnelly sometime in the same field as Thomas was. Saw William Donnelly drive into his father's place and saw William Donnelly go out into the field where John and Thomas were. He was close enough to them; that is, John and Thomas, to have conversation with them. The time was then about 11 a.m. by our clock, but that is nearly an hour fast by the school time. I saw William Donnelly leave the other two, that is John and Thomas." University of Western Ontario, Middlesex County, Clerk of the Peace, Criminal Records, Queen v. John Donnelly, Aiding Escape from Arrest, October 14, 1879, in Granton, before J.P. James Grant.

43 Testimony of William Hodgins. Middlesex County, Clerk of the Peace, Criminal Records, Queen v. John Donnelly, Aiding Escape from Arrest, October 14, 1879.

44 Testimony of James Carroll. Middlesex County, Clerk of the Peace, Criminal Records, Queen v. John Donnelly, Aiding Escape from Arrest, October 14, 1879.

45 Testimony of James Carroll. Middlesex County, Clerk of the Peace, Criminal Records, Queen v. John Donnelly, Aiding Escape from Arrest, October 14, 1879.

46 Testimony of James Carroll. Middlesex County, Clerk of the Peace, Criminal Records, Queen v. John Donnelly, Aiding Escape from Arrest, October 14, 1879.

47 James Ryder's statement reported in the *London Advertiser*, October 8, 1880.

48 Library of the Law Society of Upper Canada, Judge's Note Books, Common Pleas, Book IV, 1881, Middlesex Special Commission, Biddulph Murders: Osler (Trial Notes of Justice Featherston Osler), p. 19, testimony of Thomas Keefe.

49 Middlesex Special Commission, Biddulph Murders: Osler (Trial Notes of Justice Featherston Osler), p. 61, testimony of Edward Sutherby.

50 Middlesex County, Clerk of the Peace, Criminal Records, 1879, Queen v. John Donnelly, Aiding a felon to escape from arrest, testimony before James Grant, October 17, 1879.:

51 University of Western Ontario, Middlesex County, Clerk of the Peace, Criminal Records, Queen v. John Donnelly, Aiding Escape from Arrest, October 14, 1879 in Granton, before J.P. James Grant. Testimony of James Carroll.

52 Letterbooks from the Office of the Clerk of the Peace, Middlesex County, Hutchinson to Grant, October 14, 1879:

> Dear Sir,
> To assist a felon to escape is an indictable offence at common law. It cannot be disposed of summarily. The following facts must be proved:
>   1st That the part assisted is guilty of the felony charged.
>   2nd That the accused assisted him to escape.
>   3rd That the accused at the time he assisted the felon to escape, knew that he had committed a felony.

53 James Donnelly posted $400 and Mitchell Haskett $200. Notice to Defendant and Sureties, dated October 20, 1879, signed by Magistrate John Peters. University of Western Ontario, Legal Papers: Thomas Donnelly, Robbery, 1879, Donnelly Papers, Box 31.

54 "I have issued subpoenas for the witnesses examined before the magistrates when the case was dismissed. I see a number of other

names on the indictment but as they were not examined before the Grand Jury, & as I don't know whether their evidence would be of any use, I do not propose issuing subpoenas for them, unless satisfied as to the value of their testimony." Letterbooks from the Office of the Clerk of the Peace, Middlesex County, Hutchinson to Blake, October 18, 1879.

55 Middlesex, Criminal Courts, Case Registers, Vol. 3, p. 137.

56 Malcolm C. Cameron, the Crown prosecutor, would later write a letter explaining why the case against Tom Donnelly was not pursued. Letter reproduced in Miller, *The Donnellys Must Die*, p. 156:

> [Ned] Ryan and a young lawyer in London came to me and represented that Ryan had been robbed by Donnelly — that the J.P.s were afraid to act and would not send Donnelly up for trial and that justice could not be obtained otherwise than by going directly before the grand jury. With a good deal of hesitation, I sent the bill before the grand jury. I afterwards discovered that the case had been investigated once, if not twice by the J.P.s and dismissed. Under these circumstances I did not feel inclined to proceed. I think the lawyer's name was Blake but am not sure.

57 Middlesex County, Clerk of the Peace, Criminal Records, 1879, Queen v. John Donnelly, Perjury, testimony before Stanley, October 30, 1879.

58 J.J. Talman Regional Collection, University of Western Ontario Archives, Donnelly Family Papers, B4878, File 11, Hutchinson to Stanley, Charles Hutchinson Letter Book, November 6, 1879.

59 Toronto *Globe*, March 2, 1880.

60 William Hall charged with assault, *London Free Press*, April 15, 1879; see also James Lalley charged with assaulting Mr. L. Meredith, *London Free Press*, June 28, 1879.

61 Garibaldi Epperson was charged with larceny, *London Free Press*, April 18, 1879.

62 James Young was charged with being drunk and incapable of taking care of himself, *London Free Press*, August 5, 1879.

63 University of Western Ontario, Donnelly Family Papers, information of Carroll before Grant, November 20, 1879.

64 Middlesex County, Clerk of the Peace, Criminal Records, 1879; Queen v. Donnelly, Perjury, testimony before Grant, November 25, 1879; see also Recognizances of prosecutors to testify, Notice of committal of John Donnelly, and bail recognizance of John Donnelly — all November 26, 1879 — in the same file. Middlesex County, Clerk of the Peace, Criminal Records, 1879; Queen v. Donnelly, Perjury, testimony before Grant, November 25, 1879; see also Recognizances of prosecutors to testify, Notice of committal of John Donnelly, and bail recognizance of John Donnelly — all November 26, 1879 — in the same file.

65 J.J. Talman Regional Collection, University of Western Ontario Archives, Donnelly Family Papers, B4878, File 11, Charles Hutchinson Letter Book, December 31, 1879.

66 Toronto *Globe*, March 2, 1880.

67 Testimony of James Feeheley. *London Advertiser*, October 15, 1880.

68 *London Advertiser*, February 10, 1880.

69 Butt, *The Donnellys: History, Legend, Literature*, p. 189.

70 *London Free Press*, March 3, 1880.

71 *London Advertiser*, February 14, 1880.

72 For information on the Michigan property owned by the Donnellys, see Porte's diary entries: July 2, 1877; August 28, 1877; April 8, 1878; June 24, 1879; and October 4, 1879.

73 "When Patrick was home a few months ago he discussed the question of removal, but the old man could not be persuaded to go. He did not like the idea of leaving the homestead at his time of life, and his wife agreed with him. Patrick was disappointed, and says that on his return home he wrote back that something would happen if they did not leave." Toronto *Globe*, February 7, 1880.

74 *Toronto Mail*, March 10, 1880.

75 Father William Flannery, the forty-nine-year-old pastor of Holy Angels Parish, St. Thomas. He had been its parish priest since

1870. Michael Donnelly and his wife and children attended his parish, as did William and Nora when they were in St. Thomas.

76 Toronto *Globe*, March 2, 1880.

CHAPTER FOURTEEN: DEATH AND LIBERATION

1 "The Tragical Death of the Great Jumbo," *Maclean's*, November 12, 1955. https://archive.macleans.ca/article/1955/11/12/the-tragical-death-of-the-great-jumbo-a-macleans-flashback (accessed November 29, 2019).

2 "Jumbo the Elephant Monument," https://ontariossouthwest.com/listing/jumbo-the-elephant-monument/1646/ (accessed November 28, 2019).

3 "Railway City Tourism," https://railwaycitytourism.com/about.html (accessed November 29, 2019).

4 "St. Thomas, Ontario," https://en.wikipedia.org/wiki/St._Thomas,_Ontario (accessed November 28, 2019).

5 During St. Thomas's growth as the railway epicentre of the province, its population grew apace, rising from 1,700 people in 1860 to 10,000 in 1880. See "The Railway City: The Past," https://railwaycitytourism.com/blog/the-railway-city-the-past (accessed December 1, 2020) for the former statistic, and "St. Thomas Timeline," https://stthomaspubliclibrary.ca/wp-content/uploads/2018/04/St.-Thomas-Timeline.pdf (accessed December 1, 2020) for the latter.

6 "Canada Southern Railway Station," https://en.wikipedia.org/wiki/Canada_Southern_Railway_Station (accessed December 2, 2020).

7 The following testimony from the men Mike Donnelly worked with attest to his popularity. James Muir: "I knew Donnelly well. He was a good-hearted fellow"; James Marrs: "Donnelly always behaved himself with me"; Robert Brooks: "I never saw Donnelly in a row. I heard he was a good man . . ."; Joel Pritchard: "They all said Donnelly was a pretty good man"; Francis Perry: "I never heard of anything about [Mike Donnelly] except that he was a good man."

J.J. Talman Regional Collection, University of Western Ontario Archives, Reaney Papers, Box 25, (B1311), File 43, Matthew Crooks Cameron, Bench book of Justice Matthew Crooks Cameron, Spring Assizes, 1880.

8   Reaney Papers, Box 25, (B1311), File 43. The following testimony from the men that Mike Donnelly worked with attest to his having a reputation as a capable fighter. James Muir: "I knew he would fight if anyone interfered"; James Marrs: "He had the name of being a good fighter. I heard of his being in other rows and being the best man."

9   James Muir: "I had on one occasion backed up my train and knocked some of the train and I heard that William Lewis had said if he had been on the train he would have knocked me into the pit"; Robert Brooks: "Tremellon and Donnelly had some words. That one said the other backed the cars off the track — that was all the words they had"; Freeman Slaght: "About a week before this I heard [William Lewis] and a man named Greenwood talking. I heard [Lewis] say to Greenwood that, 'if Donnelly ever slapped you in the face, don't take it. If you can't get away with him I will.'" Testimony taken from Queen v. William Lewis, J.J. Talman Regional Collection, University of Western Ontario Archives, Reaney Papers, Box 25, (B1311), File 43, Matthew Crooks Cameron, Benchbook of Justice Matthew Crooks Cameron, Spring Assizes, 1880.

10   "Canadian Southern Railway," https://canada-rail.com/ontario/railways/CASO.html (accessed December 3, 2020).

11   Unless otherwise noted, all activity and dialogue are drawn from testimony in Queen v. William Lewis, J.J. Talman Regional Collection, University of Western Ontario Archives, Reaney Papers, Box 25, (B1311), File 43, Matthew Crooks Cameron, Benchbook of Justice Matthew Crooks Cameron, Spring Assizes, 1880; see also the Toronto *Globe*, May 15, 1879, *Toronto Mail*, May 15, 1880 and *Norfolk Reformer*, May 21, 1880.

12   "I made a postmortem with Dr. Bowlby on Michael Donnelly. The cause of death was a wound in the right iliac region — the region of the groin. It was with a sharp instrument; it went into

the femoral vein — it opened it an inch and bled profusely and passed upwards into the abdomen and did not injure the peritoneum. The knife produced would inflict such a wound. He lived fifteen or twenty minutes afterwards. The cause of death was the loss of blood. There was no other wound." Testimony of Alex C. Duncombe, physician. Queen v. William Lewis, Reaney Papers, Box 25, (B1311), File 43, Matthew Crooks Cameron, Benchbook of Justice Matthew Crooks Cameron, Spring Assizes, 1880.

13 *London Free Press*, December 10, 1879.

14 Testimony of Constable Thomas Henry. Queen v. William Lewis, J.J. Talman Regional Collection, University of Western Ontario Archives, Reaney Papers, Box 25, (B1311), File 43, Matthew Crooks Cameron, Benchbook of Justice Matthew Crooks Cameron, Spring Assizes, 1880.

15 Reaney, *The Donnelly Documents: An Ontario Vendetta*, p. lxv.

16 Testimony of William Thompson Jr.: "James Carroll called in when he was going up and down; he built a pig pen for me before Christmas; he used to stop nights now and again; when he was working for me he might have been away some nights; between the time he left me and the time of the murder he slept at my place three or four times in the same room with his brother." Testimony of William Thompson Jr. Aemelius Irving Papers, F 1027-3, File 82-8, Transcript of the Donnelly Murder Case, 1880 (MS 6500) Public Archives of Ontario, Toronto, Testimony of William Thompson Jr., February 27, 1880.

17 "Mike Donnelly buried at 11 o'clock and 30 minutes today. A large funeral, the majority Protestants." William Porte's diary entry, December 12, 1879.

18 See Reaney, *The Donnelly Documents: An Ontario Vendetta*, pp. lxv–lxvi, for additional details about Flora McKinnon and her son, Thomas Donnelly Jr. The information, such as it exists, is based largely upon a letter that was written to Donnelly author Orlo Miller on April 8, 1954, by C.M. Macfie, of Appin, who was at one time a member of the Ontario Legislature. Evidently Tom Donnelly's son lived for a time in a farmhouse north of Glencoe and

died at the age of eighteen as a result of being kicked in the stomach by a horse. Prior to this, his mother had married another man after Tom Donnelly's death, but her new husband had mistreated the boy. William Donnelly had tried to look out for his nephew, giving him a stallion worth eighty dollars and a gold watch. The stepfather took possession of the stallion and sold it while at a bar in Glencoe for five dollars. William Donnelly sued and was able to get the horse back for his nephew. (University of Western Ontario Sheriff's Process Book #12 for January 24, 1891.) The boy ultimately changed his surname to that of his adopted parent, Thomson, and, after his death, was buried in an unmarked pauper's grave within the Eddie Cemetery, which sits between Glencoe and Appin.

19   Toronto *Globe*, February 13, 1880.

20   "About this time my brother Mike was buried in December, Tom took the pledge from the priest, which he kept till his untimely removal . . ." Toronto *Globe*, March 2, 1880.

21   "As far as the old people were concerned, I esteemed them as much as any people in the parish. Since the death of Mike Donnelly, they have been to communion." Father John Connolly quoted in the *London Advertiser*, February 6, 1880. See also *London Advertiser*, February 7, 1880.

22   *London Advertiser*, February 7, 1880.

23   A letter from Jennie Donnelly to her surviving brothers, written after the death of their parents, states, "If my father's little pet dog that he got from Harry Phair is alive, I trust you will send him to me, and I will keep him till he dies of old age." *London Free Press*, February 12, 1880. The only other reference to the Donnelly family dog is from Thomas Keefe, who states that he owns the dog, a bulldog, that belonged to "old Mr. Donnelly." From him we learn that the dog's name is "Jack." *London Advertiser*, May 15, 1882.

24   "On 29 December, the Donnellys' old friend and boarder, Cornelius Moloney, was waked at the Donnelly house . . . ," Reaney, *The Donnelly Documents: An Ontario Vendetta*, p. ci.

25   *London Advertiser*, January 29, 1881, containing the testimony of Vigilance Committee members William Casey and Martin Darcy.

26 Letterbooks from the Office of the Clerk of the Peace, Middlesex County, Johnson to Casey, December 30, 1879, records the issue of Statutes; see also List of Officers and Justices of the Peace, etc., 1858–1891, for date of Casey's appointment.

27 Cameron Willis, Operations Supervisor for Canada's Penitentiary museum, email correspondence with the author, November 22, 2019.

28 Information regarding daily prison life in Kingston Penitentiary in the nineteenth century from Cameron Willis, Supervisor for Canada's Penitentiary museum, email correspondence with the author, November 22, 2019.

29 According to Cameron Willis, operations supervisor at Canada's penitentiary museum, "There was a Robert Stewart at the time who was blacksmith instructor at the Penitentiary. Robert was apparently working in that industry at the penitentiary." Email to the author, September 9, 2019.

30 "The cats" is in reference to the "cat o' nine tails," commonly shortened to "the cats," a type of multi-tailed whip that originated as an implement for severe physical punishment, "notably in the Royal Navy and British Army, and also as a judicial punishment in Britain and some other countries." "Cat o' nine tails," https://en.wikipedia.org/wiki/Cat_o%27_nine_tails (accessed October 15, 2019). For information on its use in Kingston Penitentiary: "The cat-o'-nine-tails is a rawhide whip used to lash prisoners no more than 36 times, or 50 for assaulting an officer. A surgeon remains nearby to treat the open wounds that most recipients of the punishment develop." *Globe and Mail*, "Kingston Penitentiary: Canada's Most Famous Prison Closes Its Doors," Steve Cameron, September 29, 2013.

31 Robert Donnelly Exit Interview at Kingston Penitentiary. Interview conducted by John Creighton, Esquire, January 7, 1880. Courtesy of the Correctional Service of Canada.

32 "Discharged: January 10, 1880," Robert Donnelly Exit Interview at Kingston Penitentiary. Interview conducted by John Creighton, Esquire, January 7, 1880. Courtesy of the Correctional Service of Canada.

33 "Bob Donnelly came home from Kingston at 4 o'clock a.m. Sunday morning (Jan. 11). Looked well." William Porte's diary entry, January 11, 1880.

CHAPTER FIFTEEN: THE NIGHT PAT RYDER'S BARN
WENT UP IN FLAMES

1 "Robert Keefe's daughter Martha, who was a credit to Biddulph, as is also all her family. She was married to Michael Quigley, a well-to-do young farmer in the township." William Donnelly quoted from the Toronto *Globe*, March 2, 1880.

2 "The Donnelly boys were not anxious to go to the wedding on account of the death of a brother. I don't recollect if Mr. Donnelly said to the boys to go to the wedding." Bridget Donnelly quoted from her testimony in J.J. Talman Regional Collection, University of Western Ontario Archives, Donnelly Family Papers, B4877, File 34, Unknown, Ryder v. Donnelly, Arson of Ryder's Barn, January 27, 1880.

3 Reaney, *The Donnelly Documents: An Ontario Vendetta*, p. 109, note 547.

4 "I was dressmaking. I was working for the Donnellys before the wedding. I went with Miss Donnelly's petticoats. I arrived at the Donnellys' house on the day of the wedding about one o'clock in the afternoon . . . and remained overnight." Testimony of Bridget O'Connor. J.J. Talman Regional Collection, University of Western Ontario Archives, Donnelly Family Papers, B4877, File 34, Unknown, Ryder v. Donnelly, Arson of Ryder's Barn, January 27, 1880.

5 "I did not go to the wedding; I was not invited. I was not asked to go to the schoolhouse on that night." Testimony of Bridget O'Connor. J.J. Talman Regional Collection, University of Western Ontario Archives, Donnelly Family Papers, B4877, File 34, Unknown, Ryder v. Donnelly, Arson of Ryder's Barn, January 27, 1880. Bridget Donnelly's reason for not attending was "because I was a stranger. Mr. and Mrs. Donnelly, myself, and Miss O'Connor

remained at home." Testimony of Bridget Donnelly. J.J. Talman
Regional Collection, University of Western Ontario Archives,
Donnelly Family Papers, B4877, File 34, Unknown, Ryder v.
Donnelly, Arson of Ryder's Barn, January 27, 1880.

6   "I was very much disturbed by Mr. Donnelly coughing [the past] two
weeks but on this particular night I was awake all night." Testimony
of Bridget Donnelly. J.J. Talman Regional Collection, University
of Western Ontario Archives, Donnelly Family Papers, B4877, File
34, Unknown, Ryder v. Donnelly, Arson of Ryder's Barn, January
27, 1880. See also: "Mr. Donnelly on the evening of the wedding
had a bad cold and was coughing much. Mr. Donnelly slept in the
room next to the one we slept in. . . . A board partition separates
the rooms in which we slept the night of the fire. The partition
does not reach up to the ceiling. I did not sleep well on this night;
was disturbed by Mr. Donnelly coughing." Testimony of Bridget
O'Connor. Donnelly Family Papers, B4877, File 34, Unknown,
Ryder v. Donnelly, Arson of Ryder's Barn, January 27, 1880).

7   "Mrs. Donnelly was knitting a stocking." Testimony of Bridget
O'Connor. Donnelly Family Papers, B4877, File 34, Unknown,
Ryder v. Donnelly, Arson of Ryder's Barn, January 27, 1880.

8   "I said they were having a good time at the Wedding. Miss Donnelly
replied they were having a good time." Testimony of Bridget
O'Connor. Donnelly Family Papers, B4877, File 34, Unknown,
Ryder v. Donnelly, Arson of Ryder's Barn, January 27, 1880.

9   "Bridget made cakes and we all had tea together." Testimony
of Bridget O'Connor. Donnelly Family Papers, B4877, File 34,
Unknown, Ryder v. Donnelly, Arson of Ryder's Barn, January 27,
1880.

10   "Went to bed about eleven o'clock. All parties went to bed at
eleven o'clock." Testimony of Bridget O'Connor. Donnelly Family
Papers, B4877, File 34, Unknown, Ryder v. Donnelly, Arson of
Ryder's Barn, January 27, 1880.

11   "On the night of the fire a wedding took place nearby, about
two hundred rods distance from me — one son James and Mary
returned about the beginning of the fire. I think Patrick came

home earlier." Testimony of Patrick "Grouchy" Ryder. J.J. Talman Regional Collection, University of Western Ontario Archives, Donnelly Family Papers, B4877, File 34, Unknown, Ryder v. Donnelly, Arson of Ryder's Barn, January 27, 1880.

12 Testimony of Thomas Keefe. Aemilius Irving Papers, F 1027-3, File 82-8, Transcript of the Donnelly Murder Case, 1880 (MS 6500) Public Archives of Ontario, Toronto.

13 Testimony of Patrick "Grouchy" Ryder. Donnelly Family Papers, B4877, File 34, Unknown, Ryder v. Donnelly, Arson of Ryder's Barn, January 27, 1880.

14 Testimony of Bridget O'Connor. Donnelly Family Papers, B4877, File 34, Unknown, Ryder v. Donnelly, Arson of Ryder's Barn, January 27, 1880.

15 "Uncle and I said it was the schoolhouse. Miss O'Conner said it was not the schoolhouse; she saw the smoke coming over the schoolhouse." Testimony of Bridget Donnelly. Donnelly Family Papers, B4877, File 34, Unknown, Ryder v. Donnelly, Arson of Ryder's Barn, January 27, 1880.

16 Testimony of Bridget O'Connor, citing a statement from James Donnelly Sr. Donnelly Family Papers, B4877, File 34, Unknown, Ryder v. Donnelly, Arson of Ryder's Barn, January 27, 1880.

17 Butt, *The Donnellys: History, Legend, Literature*, p. 197.

18 "I met the Donnellys the next day and I cannot say how many were there but Thomas Donnelly was one of the number. I said 'they burnt my barn' and then passed on. John Carroll [not related to the other Carrolls] was in the wagon with me and Michael Carroll, Patrick Ryder [Jr.], James Ryan [a former landlord of William Donnelly]." Testimony of Patrick "Grouchy" Ryder. J.J. Talman Regional Collection, University of Western Ontario Archives, Donnelly Family Papers, B4877, File 34, Unknown, Ryder v. Donnelly, Arson of Ryder's Barn, January 27, 1880. See also the *London Advertiser*, January 20, 1880.

19 Regional collection, D.B. Weldon Library, University of Western Ontario, Donnelly Family Papers, Information of Ryder, before Casey, January 15, 1880.

20   Toronto *Globe*, March 2, 1880.

21   Toronto *Globe*, March 2, 1880. William Donnelly recollected that "Ryder went before Mr. Casey, J.P., who is married to his cousin, and took out warrants for John, Tom, Robert and myself, charging us with the incendiary act. When he found out we were at a wedding that night, he quietly laid our warrants aside and took out two more, one for my father and one for my mother."

22   Testimony of Patrick "Grouchy" Ryder. J.J. Talman Regional Collection, University of Western Ontario Archives, Donnelly Family Papers, B4877, File 34, Unknown, Ryder v. Donnelly, Arson of Ryder's Barn, January 27, 1880.

23   Toronto *Globe*, March 2, 1880.

24   ". . . on the same Sunday he [Father Connolly] hoped that a ball of fire would fall from Heaven on the house owned by those who burned Ryder's buildings . . ." William Donnelly quoted in the Toronto *Globe*, March 2, 1880.

25   *London Advertiser*, February 6, 1880.

26   Toronto *Globe*, March 2, 1880.

27   The arrest of Johannah Donnelly and the involvement of James Fewings as reported in the *Toronto Mail*, October 7, 1880 and the *London Advertiser*, October 7, 1880.

28   Johannah was typically called Judy or Julie by close friends; she was baptized as Judith [Magee], and was more formally referred to as Johannah.

29   University of Western Ontario, Middlesex County Middlesex Court Records, Queen v. James and [Johannah] Donnelly, Arson (January 15, 1880), Lucan, January 22, 1880.

30   *London Free Press*, October 7, 1880, testimony of William Casey.

31   *London Free Press*, February 12, 1880; see also *London Free Press*, October 6, 1880.

32   Testimony of Patrick "Grouchy" Ryder. J.J. Talman Regional Collection, University of Western Ontario Archives, Donnelly Family Papers, B4877, File 34, Unknown, Ryder v. Donnelly, Arson of Ryder's Barn, January 27, 1880.

33 Donnelly Family Papers, B4877, File 34, Unknown, Ryder v. Donnelly, Arson of Ryder's Barn, January 27, 1880.

34 "Prisoners James Donnelly and Julia Donnelly are bailed on their own recognizance to appear here on Thursday at ten o'clock forenoon bail to the amount of $500 to appear as above at Granton. — Wm. Casey J.P.; James Grant J.P.; Phillip Mowbray J.P. Granton, 29th January 1880." Donnelly Family Papers, B4877, File 34, Unknown, Ryder v. Donnelly, Arson of Ryder's Barn, January 27, 1880.

35 Testimony of Mary Carroll. Donnelly Family Papers, B4877, File 34, Unknown, Ryder v. Donnelly, Arson of Ryder's Barn, January 27, 1880.

36 See Note 6.

37 Toronto *Globe*, March 2, 1880.

38 J.J. Talman Regional Collection, University of Western Ontario Archives, Donnelly Family Papers, B4877, File 34, Unknown, Ryder v. Donnelly, Arson of Ryder's Barn, January 29, 1880. See also James Donnelly's letter to Edmund Meredith indicating the trial being put off until February 4, 1880, as reported in the *London Advertiser*, February 4, 1880.

39 Toronto *Globe*, March 2, 1880. The "inner ring" William is referring to is the inner circle of the Vigilance Committee, the group within the group that made the decisions as to what action the group was to take. It consisted of people of like mind toward the Donnellys: men who had an axe to grind with the family, such as James Carroll, William Thompson Jr., John Kennedy Jr. and James Maher.

CHAPTER SIXTEEN: FINAL DAYS

1 Carroll is mistaken in this as there had only been three adjournments up to this point.

2 The only farmer in the district who matches this description would be Joseph Carswell, who had blamed the Donnellys for all his

misfortunes to the point where most people no longer believed him. However, to dust off this chestnut, Carroll had to go back not two years but almost six years to 1874, when the arson had occurred. For some bizarre reason this was Carroll's kind of case — old, with insufficient evidence to prosecute successfully, with an oblique link to the Donnelly family.

3 *London Advertiser*, February 3, 1881.

4 "During the last weekend in September a severe electrical storm swept through the township and caused a good deal of damage. Lightning struck William Kent's house, burned down Thomas Courcey's barn and stables and smashed Jim Donnelly's 'double buggy.' In the midst of the storm the home of a Mrs. Hogan caught fire from the explosion of a lamp and was destroyed. The *London Free Press* correspondent reported she was ill and expected to die, but did not further identify her. The storm must have caused some of the older and more superstitious residents of Biddulph to recall, uneasily, the prophecy made twenty-two years before by a priest of St. Patrick's that the "hand of God" would smite this lawless community. It must also have given the Vigilance Committee some satisfaction in that most of the sufferers were Protestants and/or friends of the Donnelly family." Miller, *The Donnellys Must Die*, p. 156.

5 "On the following Sunday he offered $500 reward for private information that would lead to the detection of the guilty parties. . . . On the same Sunday he hoped that a ball of fire would fall from Heaven on the house owned by those who burned Ryder's buildings. . . ." William Donnelly quoted in the Toronto *Globe*, March 2, 1880.

6 William Porte's diary entries from 1878 indicated a fire on September 25, 1878 (Ned Ryan's barn, arson), while his diary entries from 1879 reveal three fires: March 17, 1879 (Gully house); August 1, 1879 (Dominion Hotel); and October 8, 1879 (Jackson's stables). William Porte's diary entries, Fires in Lucan, September 25, 1878; March 17, 1879; August 1, 1879; October 5, 1898.

7 Toronto *Globe*, March 2, 1880.

8   Evidence at the Coroner's Inquest and Preliminary Examination,
    Aemilius Irving Papers, F 1027-3, File 82-8, Transcript of the
    Donnelly Murder Case, 1880 (MS 6500), Testimony of William
    Casey, March 9, 1880. Public Archives of Ontario, Toronto.

9   "I don't know for certain whether my brother William belonged to
    the Vigilance Committee or not, they say he does." Testimony of
    James Feeheley. Evidence at the Coroner's Inquest and Preliminary
    Examination, Aemilius Irving Papers, F 1027-3, File 82-8, Transcript
    of the Donnelly Murder Case, 1880 (MS 6500), March 9, 1880.
    Public Archives of Ontario, Toronto.

10 Testimony of James Feeheley. *London Advertiser*, January 26, 1881.

11 Testimony of Frank West. University of Western Ontario Archives,
    J.J. Talman Regional Collection, Middlesex Court Records, Queen
    v. Wm. & Robert Donnelly, Arson, March 18, 1881.

12 "I then said to him [James Feeheley], 'you must have known there
    was going to be murder.' He said they told him they were going
    to pull the Donnellys out, and hang them, till they told who burnt
    Ryder's barn. He said he knew nothing about their intention
    to kill any one . . . he told me not to open my mouth to a soul
    about that, until he got out of the country, that all he wanted was
    protection and he would tell the whole of it." Testimony of John
    H. McConnell, clerk of the municipality of the village of Lucan.
    J.J. Talman Regional Collection, University of Western Ontario
    Archives, Donnelly Family Papers, B4877, File 54, Various
    Authors, Information on Murders, 1881, ca. 1881.

13 University of Western Ontario, Papers Relating to Queen v. James
    Carroll et al., unsigned memo in the handwriting of Charles
    Hutchinson, recording a statement made by Keefe on September 23,
    1881.

14 Letterbooks from the Office of the Clerk of the Peace, Middlesex
    County, Hutchinson to Irving, undated, p. 501 of the 1880–1881
    volume.

15 Letterbooks from the Office of the Clerk of the Peace, Middlesex
    County, Hutchinson to Irving, undated, p. 501 of the 1880–1881
    volume.

16   Reaney, *The Donnelly Documents: An Ontario Vendetta*, p. 1,
      note 79, and p. cxliii, note 327: "Interview with Spencer Armitage-
      Stanley (1899–1976) in the seventies at his house in Toronto.
      Blessed with a great interest in Biddulph genealogy, he was related to
      the Armitages and told me that Mr. and Mrs. Donnelly had dinner
      at his grandfather's house the Sunday before they were murdered."

17   Apart from the local orphans and outcasts that Johannah had
      fed and sheltered over the years, there exist other stories of the
      Donnelly family's benevolence to strangers that have endured:
      "'Donnellys were friends unless bothered,' an ex-Biddulpher
      states; they always offered their water trough to passing riders
      and were the first to help a neighbour who became sick." (Butt,
      The Donnellys: History, Legend, Literature, p. 375, citing an
      interview conducted by James Reaney with G. Trevethick of St.
      Thomas, March 9, 1972); "On another occasion their son George
      [of Hibbert Township] made a horseback trip to Lucan for reaper
      repairs; when overtaken by night he dropped in at a farm home
      where he and his horse were fed and sheltered, and, as an added
      service, his horse in the morning was brought to the door ready
      for his journey. His host — the Black Donnellys of Biddulph."
      (University of Western Ontario, Donnelly Family Papers, Stafford
      Johnson to Miller, July 4, 1966); "A former Biddulph resident
      insists that 'although the Donnellys might have had some bad
      habits, a kinder lot of boys you wouldn't want to meet.'" (Donnelly
      Family Papers, A.S. Garrett to Miller, December 10, 1955,
      enclosing partial transcript of an undated *St. Marys Journal-Argus*
      interview with Leonard D. Stanley of Biddulph.)

18   "I am told that it numbers about 110 members . . ." William
      Donnelly quoted in the *Toronto Mail*, February 13, 1880.

19   *Toronto Mail*, February 20, 1880.

20   *London Advertiser*, January 31, 1881.

21   *Toronto Mail*, February 20, 1880.

22   *Toronto Mail*, February 20, 1880.

23   *Toronto Mail*, February 20, 1880.

24   Toronto *Globe*, March 2, 1880.

25   Toronto *Globe*, March 2, 1880.

26   *Toronto Mail*, February 20, 1880.

27   *London Advertiser*, February 6, 1880.

28   *London Advertiser*, February 4, 1880; see also *London Free Press*,
     February 12, 1880.

29   *London Free Press*, February 13, 1880.

BIBLIOGRAPHY

ARCHIVE SOURCES

Aemilius Irving Papers, Public Archives of Ontario, Toronto.

Archives of Ontario. Robert Donnelly, Casebook 1162: London
    Psychiatric Hospital patients' clinical case files, Robert Donnelly,
    File Number 295.

Assessment Rolls for Lucan and for Biddulph, 1873.

Bench Books, Justice Sir John Robinson, March–May 1858. Courthouse
    Vault, Goderich, Ontario, Criminal Proceedings.

Biddulph Township Assessment Roll, 1870, 1871 and 1872.

Canada Census, Biddulph Township, 1870, 1871.

Canada's Penitentiary Museum, Kingston, Ontario.

Correctional Service of Canada.

Huron County, Clerk of the Peace, Coroner's Inquests.

Huron County, Clerk of the Peace, Criminal Justice Accounts.

Huron County, Clerk of the Peace, Criminal Records.

Huron County Records, 1857–58.

Huron County Registry Records.

Huron District, Clerk of the Peace, Census Returns.

Huron Historical Notes, Huron Historical Society, 1993, Volume XXIX.

Library of the Law Society of Upper Canada, Judge's Note Books,
Common Pleas, Book IV, 1881.

Middlesex County Court of General Quarter Sessions Minute Book,
June 11, June 16 and June 17, 1874.

Middlesex Court Records.

Middlesex County Registry Office.

Middlesex County Sheriff's Day-Book, December 27, 1873.

Middlesex County Queen Bench and Common Pleas, Docket Book,
1869–81.

Middlesex Special Commission, Biddulph Murders: Osler (Trial Notes of
Justice Featherston Osler).

National Archives of Canada, Provincial Secretary's Correspondence.

Ontario Historical Society XVII (1919), Papers and Records.

Public Archives of Ontario.

University of Western Ontario Archives, J.J. Talman Regional
Collection, Donnelly Family Papers.

University of Western Ontario Archives, J.J. Talman Regional
Collection, Reaney Papers.

University of Western Ontario, Spencer-Stanley Papers.

University of Western Ontario, Orlo Miller Papers.

41st Congress, 3rd Session, *House Executive Documents*. No. 94, "State
of Trade with British North American Provinces."

BOOKS

Adams, Bill. *The History of the London Fire Department of Heroes,
Helmets and Hoses*. London Fire Department, 2002, first edition.

Berton, Pierre. *The National Dream: The Great Railway, 1871–1881*.
Toronto: Anchor, 1970.

The Biddulph Tragedy. London, 1880.

Biggar, C.R.W. *Sir Oliver Mowat — A Biographical Sketch*. Toronto:
Warwick Bros. and Rutter Ltd., 1905.

Carleton, William. *Traits and Stories of the Irish Peasantry, vol. II.* London, Wm. Tegg, 1867, seventh edition.

Culbert, Terry. *Lucan: Home of the Donnellys: Linger Longer in Lovely Lucan.* Renfrew: General Store Publishing House, 2006.

Doty, Christopher. *The Donnelly Trial: A new play based on the court transcripts of the only man brought to trial for the murders of the Donnelly family in 1880.* London: Christopher Doty, 2005.

Fazakas, Ray. *In Search of the Donnellys*, second rev. ed. Trafford: Kindle Edition, 2012.

Fazakas, Ray. *The Donnelly Album: The Complete & Authentic Account of Canada's Famous Feuding Family.* Trafford, Kindle Edition, 2013.

Glass, Chester, Compiler. *Hon. David Glass — Some of His Writings and Speeches.* New York: Trow Press, 1909.

History of the County of Middlesex, Canada. Toronto and London: W.A. & C.L. Goodspeed, Publishers, 1889.

Hobson, W.B. *Old Stage Days in Oxford County.* Ontario Historical Society, Papers and Records, Vol. XVII (1919).

Kelley, Thomas P. *The Black Donnellys: The True Story of Canada's Most Barbaric Feud.* Darling Terrace Publishing. Kindle Edition, 2016.

Leverton, John. *Wilberforce Colony from Lucan.* 125 Souvenir Booklet, 18711996.

Marquis, Greg. *Policing Canada's Century: A History of the Canadian Association of Chiefs of Police.* Toronto: University of Toronto Press, 1993.

McEvoy, M. (Editor and Compiler). *The Province of Ontario Gazetteer and Directory, Containing Precise Descriptions of the Cities, Towns and Villages in the Province with the Names of Professional and Business Men and Principal Inhabitants Together with a Full List of Members of the Executive Governments, Senators, Members of the Commons and Local Legislatures, and Officials of the Dominion, And a Large Amount of Other General, Varied and Useful Information, Carefully Compiled from the Most Recent and Authentic Data.* C.E. Anderson

& Co., Proprietors. Toronto: Robertson & Cook Publishers, Daily
Telegraph Printing House, 1869.

McKeown, Peter. *A Donnelly Treatise: After the Massacre*. Kindle
Edition. Self-Published, 2004.

Miller, Orlo. *The Donnellys Must Die*: Toronto: Prospero Books, 2001.

Morgan, Henry J. (Editor). *The Dominion Annual Register and Review
for the Fourteenth and Fifteenth Years of the Canadian Union,
1880–1881*. Montreal: John Lovell & Son, 1882.

Mozley, John and Charles. *The Monthly Packet of Evening Readings for
Members of the English Church*, Volume 3, 1852.

Oliver, Peter. *Terror to Evil-Doers: Prisons and Punishment in Nineteenth-
Century Ontario*. Toronto: University of Toronto Press, 1998.

Osler, William. *The Principles and Practice of Medicine*. 3rd ed. D.
Appleton and Co., New York, 1898.

Reaney, James, C. *The Donnelly Documents: An Ontario Vendetta*.
Toronto: The Champlain Society, 2004.

Salts, J. Robert, *You Are Never Alone: Our Life on the Donnelly
Homestead*, J. Robert Salts, Publisher, London, 1996.

Shearer, Herbert, A. *The Farm Workshop — With Information on Tools
and Buildings*. Read Books Ltd. Redditch, England, 2016.

Simcoe's Choice: Celebrating London's Bicentennial, 1793–1993.
Toronto, Dundurn, 1992.

Smart, Charles, ed. *The Medical and Surgical History of the War of the
Rebellion*. Washington, D.C., 1888, pt. 3, vol. 1.

Steward, Austin. *Twenty-Two Years a Slave, and Forty Years a Freeman;
Embracing a Correspondence of Several Years, While President of
Wilberforce Colony, London, Canada West* (electronic edition).
Originally published by William Alling, Rochester, 1856.

Wilson, Catharine Anne, *Tenants in Time: Family Strategies, Land, and
Liberalism in Upper Canada*, Montreal: McGill-Queen's University
Press, 2009; p. 160.

Wood, David. *Making Ontario*. Montreal: McGill-Queen's University
Press, 2000.

PH.D. THESES

Butt, William Davison, *The Donnellys: History, Legend, Literature,*
Ph.D. thesis. Faculty of Graduate Studies, The University of
Western Ontario, February 1977.
De Lint, Willem, Bart. *Shaping the Subject of Policing: Autonomy,*
Regulation, and the Constable. A thesis submitted in conformity
with the requirements for the degree Doctor of Philosophy, Centre
of Criminology, University of Toronto, 1997.

NEWSPAPERS

Catholic Record
Daily Journal, Evansville, Indiana
Exeter Times
Glencoe Transcript
Guelph Daily Mercury
Hamilton Spectator
Hamilton Times
Huron Signal-Star
Listowel Banner
London Advertiser
London Free Press
London Times
Lucan Sun
Montreal Star
Morning News
New York Times
Norfolk Reformer
Oakland Daily Evening Tribune
Ottawa Free Press
Sarnia Observer
St. Marys Argus and Review
Stratford Weekly Herald

Toronto *Globe*
Toronto *Mail*
Toronto *Telegram*
Truro Daily News
Upper Canada Gazette

PERIODICALS

Maclean's magazine
Lancet (April 2001)

CORRESPONDENCE

Anthony Drohomyrecky, MD, email correspondence with the author,
    October 28, 2019.
Cameron Willis, Operations Supervisor for Canada's Penitentiary Museum,
    email correspondence with the author, November 22, 2019.
Doug McGuff, MD, email correspondence with the author, October 28,
    2019.
Enid McIlhargey, email correspondence with the author, January–
    February 2021.
Notes from Enid McIlhargey, dated June 27, 1960, courtesy of Enid's
    daughter, Ely Errey.
Notes from John Joseph McIlhargey; courtesy of Ely Errey.

ONLINE SOURCES

http://ancestorsatrest.com/cemetery_records/stpats-int.shtml
http://biographi.ca/en/bio/mckinnon_hugh_13E.html
http://black-donnellys.com/the-story/
http://businessdictionary.com/definition/tampering.html
http://canadahistory.com/sections/eras/nation%20building/Scandal.html

http://contentdm.ucalgary.ca/digital/collection/p22007coll8/id/308402

http://historyplace.com/worldhistory/famine/coffin.htm

http://images.ourontario.ca/london/2369866/data?n=1

http://lostrivers.ca/points/porkpacking.htm

http://news.bbc.co.uk/2/hi/health/619259.stm

http://oldandinteresting.com/history-feather-beds.aspx

https://andersonfuneralservices.com/blogs/blog-entries/1/Articles/35/
The-History-of-a-Traditional-Irish-Wake.html

https://archive.macleans.ca/article/1955/11/12/the-tragical-death-of-the-
great-jumbo-a-macleans-flashback

https://blackpast.org/african-american-history/steward-austin-1793-1869/

https://blogto.com/city/2012/10/a_short_and_violent_history_of_
torontos_central_prison/

https://ca.practicallaw.thomsonreuters.com/6-556-9885?transitionType=
Default&contextData=(sc.Default)&firstPage=true&bhcp=1

https://canada-rail.com/ontario/railways/CASO.html

https://canadianmysteries.ca/sites/donnellys/home/indexen.html

https://catholicism.org/candles.html

https://celticlife.com/the-irish-wake/

https://civilwarmonitor.com/blog/the-most-fatal-of-all-acute-diseases-
pneumonia-and-the-death-of-stonewall-jackson

https://ckphysiciantribute.ca/doctors/christopher-william-flock/

https://collectionscanada.gc.ca/confederation/023001-3010.40-e.html

https://connollycove.com/insight-irish-wake-superstitions-associated/

https://cpha.ca/history-tuberculosis

https://crookedlakereview.com/articles/101_135/126winter2003/
126palmer3.html]

https://culbertfamilyhistory.blogspot.com/2018/11/the-donnellys-lucan-
biddulphs-most.html

https://dotydocs.theatreinlondon.ca/Archives/donnelly/auditions.htm#irving

https://electricscotland.com/history/canada/mckinnon_hugh.htm

https://en.wikipedia.org/wiki/1878_Canadian_federal_election

https://en.wikipedia.org/wiki/Canada_Southern_Railway_Station

https://en.wikipedia.org/wiki/Cat_0%27_nine_tails

https://en.wikipedia.org/wiki/Irish_Canadians

https://en.wikipedia.org/wiki/Middlesex_North
https://en.wikipedia.org/wiki/Oliver_Mowat
https://en.wikipedia.org/wiki/Pacific_Scandal
https://en.wikipedia.org/wiki/Splitting_maul
https://en.wikipedia.org/wiki/St._Thomas,_Ontario
https://en.wikipedia.org/wiki/Stagecoach
https://en.wikipedia.org/wiki/Template:Population_of_Michigan_cities_
    and_counties_(1870_Census)
https://en.wikipedia.org/wiki/Toronto_Central_Prison
https://en.wikipedia.org/wiki/Wild_Bill_Hickok_-_Davis_Tutt_shootout
https://health.harvard.edu/newsletter_article/An_update_on_the_old_
    mans_friend
https://historymuseum.ca/cmc/exhibitions/cpm/chrono/ch1798ae.html
https://in2013dollars.com/us/inflation/1880?amount=4000
https://irish-genealogy-toolkit.com/journey-to-Ellis-Island.html
https://lib.uwo.ca/archives/virtualexhibits/londonasylum/index.html
https://news-medical.net/health/Pneumonia-History.aspx
https://ontariossouthwest.com/listing/jumbo-the-elephant-monument/1646/
https://opentextbc.ca/postconfederation/chapter/1-2-historical-demography-
    of-canada-1608-1921/#return-footnote-1350-14
https://ourworldindata.org/human-height
https://patrick-donnelly.webs.com/patrickdonnelly.htm
https://pressreader.com
https://railwaycitytourism.com/about.html
https://railwaycitytourism.com/blog/the-railway-city-the-past
https://statista.com/statistics/568800/infant-mortality-rate-by-province-or-
    territory-canada/
https://stthomaspubliclibrary.ca/wp-content/uploads/2018/04/
    St.-Thomas-Timeline.pdf
https://thecanadianencyclopedia.ca/en/article/canada-company
https://thecanadianencyclopedia.ca/en/article/pacific-scandal
https://thecanadianencyclopedia.ca/en/article/toronto
https://theglobeandmail.com/news/national/kingston-penitentiary-
    closes-its-doors-as-canadas-most-famous-prison/article14598900/?
    page=all

https://theglobeandmail.com/report-on-business/economy/a-brief-history-
of-the-canadian-dollar/article1366590/

https://thegoldenstar.net/community/caroll-was-respected-in-golden-
despite-being-a-mass-murderer/

https://thoroldnews.com/local-news/donnellys-legend-lives-on-in-
thorold-1226182

https://worthpoint.com/worthopedia/antique-1800s-large-heavy-solid-
brass-427211127

https://xe.com/currencyconverter/convert/?Amount=101%2C165.10&
From=USD&To=CAD

ACKNOWLEDGEMENTS

T he author is beholden to all the Donnelly authors and researchers who came before him, each of whom has broadened our understanding of the Donnelly story. There exists a mountain of data — court transcripts; letters and diaries; newspaper articles from many different newspapers in many different towns, villages and cities; magazine articles; town histories; genealogical records and photographs — but these authors were the first to sift through these materials until a timeline of sorts was formed. The writers whose work was particularly thorough were Ray Fazakas, William Butt, James Reaney and Orlo Miller. Fazakas is worthy of particular praise, as he has engaged in decades of exhaustive research (including tracking down descendants of the Donnellys, which required him to travel over two continents) that has continued on long after his two books on the Donnellys were published. He also was the first to bring to light most of the photographs that may presently be seen in museum displays and online articles (and books such as the one you are reading presently).

Without his tireless efforts we may never have known what many of the characters in the drama looked like. I am particularly beholden to him for graciously allowing me to utilize photographs from his collection for my books and for sharing his insights with me during the creation of the maps that appear in both volumes. He remains the preeminent Donnelly authority in the world. I am also grateful to William Butt, PhD, who was the first to bring a great deal of the above indicated primary sources of information to print. His research was staggering, and his doctorate very well deserved. He was also very supportive to me during the writing and research of this book, encouraging me to develop ideas that came originally from his thesis. He further allowed me to use certain quotes and sources that appeared in his thesis for which I am grateful.

I also extend my deep appreciation to Anne Quirk and the wonderful staff at the University of Western Ontario's Archives and Research Collections Centre for sending me copies of all of the legal papers, correspondence, Letterbooks of Charles Hutchinson, researchers' notes, arts and entertainment and miscellaneous items relating to the Donnelly family, their murders and court cases, ranging from 1856–1973. As the Covid pandemic prevented me from going in person to the university for certain research, they were kind enough to bring the University archives to me. This material was hugely helpful in deciphering the behind-the-scenes activity that went on during the Coroner's Inquest, the Preliminary Hearings and the two trials. A special thank you is also due to the efforts of the good people and staff of the London Room within the London Public Library, who were inordinately patient with me and helpful in the extreme. Thomas Levesque, the museum supervisor of the Lucan Area Heritage & Donnelly Museum, went above and beyond in answering my questions and in providing access to specific materials I requested to further my research on the Donnellys. Tremendous assistance was also provided by the staff at the Ontario Archives, who allowed me to access rare documents that shed further light on the Donnelly story. I was also fortunate to make the acquaintance of Ely Errey, who provided notes from her mother and father (John and Enid McIlhargey) on their family's memories of the Donnellys, as well as the wonderful photograph of Bob and Tom Donnelly, which was given to her grandfather by no less a figure than Bob Donnelly himself.

Appreciation is also due to literary agent extraordinaire Beverley Slopen whom I was fortunate enough to hoodwink into taking on this project and who convinced me that I would need to write more than an overview to interest a Canadian publishing house (and she was correct, of course). Also owed a huge debt of gratitude is Jen Hale, without question the best and most entertaining copyeditor I've ever had the pleasure to work with. Her suggestions and amendments resulted in a far superior manuscript than the one I first submitted. I am further indebted to Jack David and the great staff of ECW Press, who insisted on my telling the full story of the Donnellys, rather than creating an abridged version, for which I am grateful, as I am for the great personal interest the publishing house has shown in my rendering of the Donnelly story.

A big thank-you is owed to professionals in law enforcement, such as Detective Vicki Hornick, who was willing to analyze the data (particularly with regard to matters of law and the courts and to advise on matters of procedure). I'm beholden as well to medical doctors such as Anthony Drohomyrecky and Doug McGuff, who offered me the benefit of their insights into pathology, particularly pneumonia and anti-anxiety medications used in asylums during the turn of the last century.

And then there are family and friends with whom I would speak about the manuscript at various stages of its progression, and who offered their input as to whether or not the story was as fascinating as I thought it was — people like my family members Terri, Riley, Taylor, Brandon and Ben Little (who also created the artwork used in the Preface of Volume II), and friends such as Kerri Stewart, Marcela Avendano, Tom Walking, Sue Morrison, John Vellinga, Jeremy Hymers , and Anne and Rod Mundy. A special nod of appreciation is reserved for Ravel von Rose, better known as Jonathan Ross, whose constructive (and well warranted) literary criticism helped to shape the manuscript. All these people, and more, went into the creation of this book and to each is owed an enormous debt of gratitude.

ABOUT THE AUTHOR

J ohn Little is the bestselling author of *Who Killed Tom Thomson?* (Skyhorse Publishing, New York). Little has authored over 40 books on subjects ranging from philosophy and history to exercise and martial arts, in addition to being an award-winning filmmaker. He is a contributor to Salon.com, the *Toronto Star* (Canada's largest daily newspaper) and has been interviewed by CNN, Canada AM, NPR, A&E, *People Magazine*, *Entertainment Weekly* and the Family Channel. He resides in Bracebridge, Ontario, with his wife, Terri, and children Riley, Taylor, Brandon and Ben.

INDEX

Page numbers in bold indicate photographs or maps.

Carroll, James (Donnelly nemesis), 227; altercation with Donnelly clan, 243–48, 446n38, 446n41, 447n42, 447n46, 448n51, 448nn47–48, 449nn53–54; anti-Donnelly prejudice, 234–35, 236; arrests James Sr. and Johannah Donnelly, 354; arrests John Donnelly, 322; attempted arrest and arrest of Tom Donnelly, 316–17, 319–23, 463n40; auction incident, 241–43, 444nn30–31, 445n34, 445n36; background, 215, 230–33, 439n52, 442n8; Carswell case, 477n2; charges and countercharges, 248, 249–50; as constable, 309–10, 361; fights Thomas Keefe, 265; inheritance dispute, 231, 232–33; and James Feeheley, 365–67; Mike Donnelly's funeral, 339; Ned Ryan incident, 264, 311, 318–19; obsession, 322, 360–61; on ostracism, 327; politics, 241; residence and employment, 233–34, 235–36; Ryder barn burning, 354–57, 358, 359; as suspect, 16; wandering heifer incident, 287, 289, 291, 292, 293, 294, 297, 460n37

Carroll, John, attack on, 58

Carroll, Mary (neighbour), 299, 356, 357

Carroll, Michael: and Donnelly-Farrell fight, 37, 38, 41, 95–96, 390n55, 391nn57–58, 391n60, 392nn61–62, 392n64, 393n71, 394nn76–77, 395nn80–83, 396n90, 396n93

Carroll, Michael (brother to James), 231, 232, 233–34, 296

Carroll, Roger, 231–32, 233, 439n52

Carroll, William, 231, 232, 233–34

Carswell, Joseph, 104–5, 152–53, 412n110, 477n2

Casey, John, 205

Casey, William, 27, 343, 352, 354, 355, 358, 364

Catholic-Protestant tensions, 18, 26–27, 159, 162. See also community, rural; Roman Catholic faction

Cavanagh, John, 229, 235

Cayley, William, 26, 44

Cedar Swamp Schoolhouse, 279, 284, 288, 362

Central Prison, conditions and brutality, 178, 178–79, 180

the chain (prison punishment), 60

chivaree, 96–97, 408n75

Churchill, James, observations and testimony, 125–27, 129, 133–34, 417n45

Clark, Dan, 102–3, 162, 411n99, 411nn101–3

Clay, George Walter, 15

"clever detective," call for, 148. See also McKinnon, Hugh

Cobbledick, Samuel, 114–15, 414n15

coffin ships, 20

Cohalan, William, 53

Colin, Robert, 239

Collins, Henry, 142, 174, 185, 186, 210

Collisson, Martin, 285

colonization, 22

Donnelly, Bob (Robert), 128,
201; after Berryhill brawl,
125, 417n45; altercation with
Peter McKellar, 139–41; arson
charges, 167; assault charges,
137, 147; attempted arrest by
Rhody Kennedy, 143–46, 147,
155, 423nn41–45, 424n46;
Everett shooting trial and
conviction, 218–19, 220–27,
228, 234, 236, 242, 266–68,
441nn75–76, 444n30; and
James Carroll, 361; and Joseph
Carswell dispute, 104, 105;
loses child, 228; marries Annie
Currie, 84; prison and release,
226, 249, 339, 343–47, 473n33;
Ryder barn burning, 352;
vandalism, coincidental, 202;
vigilante mob anecdote, 131;
violent tendencies, 105, 201;
whereabouts unknown, 183,
201, 219, 440n61. See also
Donnellys; London Asylum for
the Insane
Donnelly, Bridget (cousin), 257,
290–91, 349, 350, 356, 357–58,
371, 451n19, 473n2
Donnelly, Ellen (née Hines) (Mike
Donnelly's wife), 100, 207, 339,
354
Donnelly, James (Bob's nephew),
xix, xx, xxi, xxvii, xxix, 137,
380n30
Donnelly, James Sr., 360;
altercation at O'Keefe farm,
72–73; attempt to evict, 33–34;
attempts to shoot Patrick Farrell,
32–33, 35, 36, 389n45, 391n59;
buys Grace's land, 34–35;

children of, 34; conflicts with
Roman Catholic faction, 72,
73; corpse, 6, 7, 9, 11, 383n16;
Donnelly-Farrell-Grace land
deal, 31–32, 389n44; early
farming efforts, 24–25, 387n27;
emigrates to Canada, 20, 21,
385n10, 386n14; evades law,
41–43, 78, 397n98, 397n100;
Everett shooting trial, 223,
441n75; fights and fatally
injures Patrick Farrell, 35,
36–39, 41, 43, 390nn50–51,
390nn54–55, 391–93nn57–71,
393–96nn73–86, 396nn89–90;
firearms kept ready, 329–30;
gifts land for school, 56; lease
of Grace's land, 22, 31, 386n16;
on leaving Biddulph, 372; and
Michael Feeheley, 211–12; pays
bail for Thomas Hines, 219;
pays bail for Thomas Ryan,
215; philosophy of life, 73–74;
prison life and aftermath, 54–55,
57–58, 59–61, 62–63; prospers,
103; Ryder barn burning,
350, 351, 353, 354, 355, 356,
357–58, 372–73, 473–74nn5–6,
477n34; shoots at Patrick
Farrell, 32–33, 35, 36, 389n45,
391n59; state of mind, 330, 360,
372, 374; trial and conviction,
43–44, 397n101; vigilante mob
anecdote, 131, 132; wandering
heifer incident, 290, 292–95,
296, 317–18, 458n31. See also
Donnellys
Donnelly, Jennie (Jane), 43, 47,
63, 97, 227, 342, 354, 405n40,
471n23

Donnelly, Jim (James) (son), **194**;
assault of Ann Robinson, 54;
assault of James Curry, 123,
136, 162, 165; assaults Thomas
Gibbs, 105–6; attack on Rhody
Kennedy, 145, 147, 156,
423n44–45, 424n46; Berryhill
brawl, 121, 122, 126, 136, 177,
417n45; death and controversy,
193–200, 433n45; eviction suit
against, 103–4, 412n110; hunt
for, 164, 427nn24–25; land
agreement, 65, 103; land dispute
with Joseph Carswell, 104–5,
413n117; post office break-in,
70–71; released from prison,
188–89, 432n25, 432n27; Ryder
wedding riot, 156, 157–58,
162, 427n24; stable burning,
129, 134, 165, 419n4; threat to
burn stable, 123–25, 138–39;
threat to take Patrick Flanagan's
life, 125; time in the U.S., 71;
vandalism, coincidental, 189–90;
vigilante mob anecdote, 130–31;
violent tendencies, 105. *See also*
Donnellys
Donnelly, Johannah, **45**;
altercation with James Carroll,
244, 246, 247–48, 249, 449n53;
and Bill Farrell, 66, 402n12;
children of, 34; contradictory
testimony about, 45–47; corpse,
7; early farming efforts, 24–25,
48, 387n27; emigrates, 20,
21, 48; and Father Connolly,
312–13, 340–41; historical
record, lack of, 45; legal charges
against, 47–48, 58, 398n7;
manages farm, 48, 59, 63; name,

57, 400n34, 476n28; petitions
on behalf of James Sr., 44,
55–57, 78; physical appearance,
49, 399n9–10; raises children
alone, 44, 48, 50–51, 57, 63;
Ryder barn burning, 346, 350,
353, 354, 355–56, 357–58, 361,
473n5, 474n7, 477n34; on sons'
behaviour, 48, 258, 341; state
of mind, 368–71; visits husband
in prison, 56; wandering heifer
incident, 290–91, 296–97, 299,
301. *See also* Donnellys
Donnelly, John: abstinence,
268–69; altercation with James
Carroll, 244–48, 446nn37–38,
447nn43–44, 448nn50–51,
449n54; altercation with Peter
McKellar, 139–41, 155–56;
assault of Ann Robinson, 54;
assault conviction, 177; and
attack on Rhody Kennedy,
145–46; attempted arrest by
Rhody Kennedy, 143–44,
423n41, 423n43, 423n45;
auction incident, 242–43,
444nn30–31, 445nn35–36;
death, 12–14; and Father
Connolly, 311, 312; fights
William Hodgins, 219–20, 243,
246, 440n65; helps brother
escape, 321, 322, 323; hunt
for and arrest of, 164, 167,
427n22, 427n24; land-for-care
arrangement, 103; marriage/
failure of marriage, 74; perjury
charges, 323–27; petitions for
brother's release, 249, 251,
267–68, 344; released from
prison, 182; Ryder wedding

riot, 156, 157, 158–60, 161–62; stable burning, 129, 165, 419n4; threatens Peter McKellar, 145, 423n43; trespass charges against mob, 302–3, 311, 317–18; vigilante mob anecdote, 131; wandering heifer incident, 291–94, 296. *See also* Donnellys

Donnelly, Mike, 331; altercation with Peter Keller, 141–43, 422n34; applies to be constable, 183, 430n16; assault charges, 111, 414n9; assaults Patrick Flanagan, 111; assaults Rhody Kennedy, 164–65, 428n29; Berryhill brawl, 121, 125, 133, 417n45; death and funeral, 335–40, 342, 469n12, 470n17; fights Hocher, 206–7, 437n15; house burned, 202, 207; illegal imprisonment of, 169–70, 175; letter regarding Ryder wedding riot, 165–67, 168, 428n32; life in St. Thomas, 333–35, 468–69nn7–9; marriage and children, 100, 183, 207, 333, 339; partner in stagecoach business, 107–8, 167, 183–84; as railway brakeman, 209–10, 333–34, 335; as stagecoach driver, 81, 82, 112–15, 118, 414n15, 415n16; sued for negligence, 118–19, 138; and Thompson affair, 86, 88, 89, 97, 98; vigilante mob anecdote, 131. *See also* Donnellys

Donnelly, Nora (née Kennedy) (wife of William), 14, 100–101, 180, 181, 228, 255–56, 258–59, 320, 384n31, 451nn22–23

Donnelly, Pat (Patrick) (James Sr.'s son): appearance, 120, 416n38; apprenticeship, 65; Berryhill brawl, 119, 120, 121; carriage manufacture, 227, 442n1; compared to brothers, 181, 228; James Curry assault, 136; in London, 108; marriage and children, 78, 228; McKinnon attempts to charge, 168; robbery charges, 99–100; urges parents to move, 329, 467n73; vigilante mob anecdote, 131. *See also* Donnellys

Donnelly, Patrick (James Sr.'s brother), 43, 44

Donnelly, Tom (Thomas), 128; abstinence, 340, 471n20; accused of barn burning, 236; altercation with James Carroll, 244–48, 249, 447nn44–46, 448nn47–49; animosity toward Patrick Flanagan, 125–26; arrest and attempted arrest by Hodgins, 229–30, 260, 262; arrested by James Carroll, 316–17; arson charges, 167; assaults and robs James Curry, 123, 124, 136; attempted arrest by James Carroll, 319–23; auction incident, 241–43, 444nn30–31, 445n34, 445n36; beats Frederick Allen, 205–6, 436nn11–12; Berryhill brawl, 121, 122–23, 133, 136, 417n45; Biddulph and Lucan lambs, 210, 216, 217; character and outlook, 228–29, 280, 281; charged with assault, 137; death, xiv, 7, 383n22; Elginfield Hotel

Committee (second), 283–84, 284–85, 358, 456n8, 457n10; vigilante mob anecdote, 131, 132; wandering heifer incident, 287, 289, 295, 296, 297–99, 458n28, 458n30, 459n35, 460n37; as a young man, 68–70. *See also* Donnellys; stagecoach lines and wars; Thompson affair

Donnelly schoolhouse, xiv, 11–12, 56, 348, 349, 352

Donnellys: after Jim Donnelly's death, 200, 207; alcohol use, 268–69, 340, 471n20; allegations of horse butchery, 204–6, 234, 241, 293; altercation with James Carroll, 243–48; and anti-crime charter, 277; attitude to law, 77; barn burned, 73–74, 404n31; benevolence of, 66, 480n17; blamed for Dan Clark's death, 102–3, 411nn101–3; boycott St. Patrick's, 275, 277, 454n67; charges against, 176–77, 181, 248, 249; children as young adults, 65–66; collective character, 50–51, 92, 124, 185, 201; and community, 53–54, 56, 57; deaths of, 435n57; family farm, 71, 300, 404n28; family headstone, xi, xv; and Feeheley family, 211–12; following Mike Donnelly's death, 342, 348; friendships, 66, 101–2, 235, 316, 316, 339, 349, 368, 462n13; hunt for, 162–65, 176, 189, 427n22, 427nn24–25, 428n26; and justice, 188; and Ku Klux Klan, 154; land-for-care

arrangement with Cornelius Maloney, 102–3, 257, 300, 342, 450n16, 471n24; in later years, 227–29; marriages and churches, 101; ostracized, 327–29; philosophy, 73–74; physical appearance, 49–50; politics, 239, 240–41, 300; public opinion, 15, 77, 164, 165, 166–67, 168, 200, 253–54, 328–29, 416n38, 428n32, 480n17; reconciliation with Father Connolly, 340–41, 471n21; and Roman Catholic faction, 73, 75, 78–79, 97, 99–100, 200, 234, 251, 253, 254, 274; rumours about, 152; Ryder barn burning, 351–54; and Ryder family, 299–300, 302; secret committee against, 47; suspicions of Hugh McKinnon, 151–52, 426nn9–10; take in Bill Farrell, 66, 402nn12–13; at time of James Sr.'s release, 62–63; vigilante mob anecdote, 129–33, 420n14, 421n15. *See also* individual family members' names

Donohue, John, 137

Duncombe, Alexander, 337–38, 469n12

Dunigan incident, 51–52

elephant and train collision, 331–32

Elginfield Hotel brawl, 210–11

Esdale, William, 167

Everett, Samuel: altercation with Hodgins, 260–62; background, 207–8; bails out Tom Donnelly, 317; Donnelly-Hodgins fight,

220; enemies, 213–14; fired, 304; interrupts Carroll-Keefe fight, 265; John Flynn's assault, 229; lamp-lighting conflict, 303–4; Ned Ryan incident, 213; plot against, 214–17; recants shooting incident, 266–68; shooting incident and trial, 217–19, 220–27, 228, 441n69

Farrell, Bill (William): arson charges, 167; hunt for, 163, 163–64, 173, 427n22, 427n24; Ryder wedding riot, 160–62, 166, 167; taken in by Donnelly family, 66, 402nn12–13
Farrell, Kurb, 77–78
Farrell, Patrick: death of, 15, 16, 40, 56–57, 396nn89–90; Donnelly-Grace-Farrell land deal, 31–32, 389n44; fights James Donnelly Sr., 35, 36–39, 41, 43, 390nn50–51, 390nn54–55, 391–93nn57–71, 393–96nn73–86; shot at by James Donnelly, 32–33, 35, 36, 389n45, 391n59; son of, 66, 402nn12–13. *See also* Farrell, Bill
Farrell, Sarah, 39, 41, 66
Fazakas, Ray, xv
Feeheley, Bridget, 212
Feeheley, James: background, 211–12, 217; barn burning, 236; and James Carroll, 311, 365; Ned Ryan incident, 212–13; role in massacre, 364–67, 375, 479n12
Feeheley, Michael, 58, 211–12, 217
Feeheley, William, 211, 287, 292, 365, 375, 455n7, 479n9
Ferguson, Charles, 146–47

Ferguson, Henry, 118, 135, 137, 138–39, 143, 146–47
Fewings, James, 354, 361
First Nations peoples, 2
Fitzhenry Hotel, fire, 202, 206, 437n13
Flanagan, John: and parcel delivery incident, 112, 414n11; stables burned, 132, 420nn12–14; vigilante mob anecdote, 129–33, 420nn12–14
Flanagan, Patrick: assaulted by Mike Donnelly, 111; assaulted by unknown assailant, 135; background, 109–10; buys stagecoach line, 110; death of William Brooks, 115; hires detective, 148, 425n56; Joseph Berryhill, 120; legal action against Donnellys, 118, 126, 134–35, 138; life threatened, 125; sells stagecoach line, 139; stables burned, 124–25, 127, 128–29, 132, 137, 153, 165, 169, 418n47, 418nn1–3, 419nn4–7, 420n12; vigilante mob anecdote, 129–33, 420n12. *See also* McKinnon, Hugh; stagecoach lines and wars
Flannery, William (Father), 330, 467n75
Flynn, John, 229, 235
Fogarty, Ellen, 89–90, 98, 259, 407n66, 451n25
Fogarty, Michael, testimony, 98, 409n84

Gear, George, 196, 221, 222, 266, 267–68, 433n41
Gerard (Father), 101, 411n97

Gibbs, Thomas, 105–6
Gibson, Sylvanus, 189
Gibson factory, fire, 189
Glass, David, 67, 177, 181, 221, 222, 223, 224, 249, 429n49
Glass, Michael, 211
Glavin, Catherine, 231–32
Grace, John: Donnelly-Farrell-Grace land deal, 31–32, 389n44; leases land to James Donnelly, 22, 386n16; seeks to evict James Sr., 33–34; sells land to James Sr., 34; sells land to Michael Maher, 30–31
Graham, John, 66–68, 403n15
grain prices, 30, 33
Grand Trunk Railway (GTR), 52–53, 210, 331
Grant, James, 322, 323, 326, 342, 465n52
Gray, Arthur, 172, 174, 186, 189
Gray, Tom, 76–77, 405n40
Great Western Railway, 209, 438n30
gunmen, hired, 192–93, 433n41
gun-theft incident, 66–68

Harcourt, Sarah, murdered, 53
Harlton, Thomas, 26–27
Harrigan, James, 293
Harvard Medical School, 199
Haskett, Mitchell, 43, 316, 317, 323, 465n53
Hawkshaw, John, 81–82
Head, Edmund, 44
Heenan, James, 293, 294
Heenan, John, 283
heifer. See wandering heifer incident
Henry, Thomas, 338

Hines, Thomas, 219, 290–91, 294, 311
Hobson, W.B., 107
Hocher-Donnelly fight, 206–7, 437n15
Hodgins, James (butcher), 186, 189–90
Hodgins, James (magistrate), 26, 29
Hodgins, Jim, 174
Hodgins, John, 223–24, 441n75
Hodgins, William: altercation with Everett, 260–62; arrest and attempt to arrest Tom Donnelly, 229–30, 260, 262, 319–23; arrests Thomas Hines, 219; assaults Everett, 265; fights John Donnelly, 219–20, 243, 246–47, 440n65; promoted, 304; wandering heifer incident, 289, 290
Hogan, Patrick, 64–65, 402n7–8
Holmes, John, 26, 42
horse mutilation and butchery, 202, 203–6, 234, 241, 293
horse thievery incident, 269–74
Hossack, Thomas, xx–xxi
"Huron Tract," 21–22
Hutchinson, Charles: on arrest of John Donnelly, 322, 465n52; and Donnelly-Kennedy charges and countercharges, 146, 147; and Donnelly-McKellar altercation, 143; Everett shooting trial, 220–21; and Hugh McKinnon, 153–54, 426n10; investigates Everett shooting allegations, 266, 267–68; and Malcolm Cameron, 319; and perjury trial, 324,

326–27; trespass case, 302; and
William Donnelly's release, 180
Hyndman, John, 41

immigrants: attitude to law, 27–30,
33–34, 75; death rate, 20;
hardships, 23; hostility toward,
17–18; mindset, 20–21
infant mortality, 228, 442n2
Intercolonial Railway, 208
Inter-Oceanic Railway Company,
238, 239

Jackson, Thomas J. "Stonewall,"
198
Johns, David, 115, 414n15
Johnston, Thomas, 163
Jumbo the elephant, 331–32

Keefe, Daniel: assaults James
Toohey, 99, 410n88–90; hides
Jim Donnelly, 164, 427n25; and
Thompson affair, 86, 87, 90,
91, 97; violent tendencies, 92,
407n68
Keefe, James: assault of John Flynn,
229; auction incident, 242,
243, 445n35; Berryhill brawl,
119, 120–22, 136, 417n45,
417nn40–41; Elginfield Hotel
brawl, 210–11; hunt for, 163,
427n24; James Curry assault,
123; and James Toohey, 99,
410n89; John Flynn assault, 235;
Ryder wedding riot, 160, 162;
Thompson affair, 86, 97, 98, 119;
warns John Donnelly, 367
Keefe, James Sr., 296, 312, 354
Keefe, Patrick, 242, 243, 445n35
Keefe, Thomas, 265, 349, 350

Keefe/Quigley wedding, 348–50
Kelley, Thomas P., xiii, 129–30,
132, 133, 419n10, 420n14,
421n15
Kelly, James, 269–70
Kennedy, John (Jr.): post-office
break-in, 70–71; sister's marriage
to William Donnelly, 100–101,
410n96; Vigilance Committee
(second), 285, 288, 304,
325, 327, 460n40, 477n39;
wandering heifer incident, 291,
295, 296, 298
Kennedy, John (Sr.): assaulted
by Patrick Hogan, 64–65,
402nn7–8; bails out Thomas
Ryan, 304, 307; daughter's
marriage to William Donnelly,
100–101
Kennedy, Rhody (Rhodace):
appointed special constable,
143, 423n41; assault charge and
conviction, 134, 135; assaulted
by Mike Donnelly, 164–65,
428n29; attempts to arrest Bob
Donnelly, 144–46, 155, 183,
188, 423nn41–45, 424n46;
charges and countercharges, 137,
146–47, 156; charges Donnelly
brothers with assault, 136–37;
Donnelly threat to Flanagan
stables, 123–25; as guard on
stage line, 139–41, 143, 144,
422n30; perjury trial, 138–39;
post office break-in, 70–71; sent
to jail, 147; sister's marriage
to William Donnelly, 101;
testimony, 134, 137; threshing-
machine accident, 64
Kent, John, 316, 317

Thompson, William Jr.: confronted by William Donnelly, 91–92; domestic arrangements, 79; house search by Donnelly gang, 91, 92; marriage to Mary Carroll, 95–97; Mike Donnelly's funeral, 339; wandering heifer incident, 287, 288, 289, 290, 291, 292; wedding and chivaree, 95–97

Thompson, William Sr.: and attempt to rescue Margaret Thompson, 88–90, 407n64, 407n66; files complaint against William Donnelly, 97; opposes daughter's marriage, 79–80, 84; testimony, 98

Thompson affair: chivaree on wedding night, 96–97; courtship and proposal, 79–80, 82–83; Ellen Fogarty's involvement, 89–90, 407n66; hearing and acquittal, 98, 99; immediate aftermath and confrontations, 91–92, 95; letters to William Thompson Sr., 92–95; Margaret requests rescue, 84–85, 98; Margaret's letters, 62, 80, 83, 84, 85, 91, 98, 99, 406n54; rescue attempt, 85–90, 154; tavern fight and end of affair, 99; William Donnelly acquitted, 98

threshing machine incident, 53, 280–83, 285–86, 285–87, 455n4, 457nn15–19

Toohey, Dennis, 52–53

Toohey, Hugh, 211

Toohey, James, 88, 98–99, 407n63, 409n87, 410nn88–90

Toohey, John, 38, 52–53, 395n82

Traits and Stories of the Irish Peasantry (Carleton), 28

trespass case against mob, 301–3, 310–11, 317–18

tuberculosis, 194–95, 434n47

Upper Canada, 1, 2, 3, 20, 25

vandalism, random acts, 189–93, 199, 202–4, 206–7, 222, 259–60

Vigilance Committee (first): talk of, 200, 435n59; torture of William Atkinson, 174; and William Denby, 169. *See also* anti-crime society (Father Connolly); Vigilance Committee (second)

Vigilance Committee (second): appointment of constable, 308–10; bring perjury charges, 323–27; formed, 283–85, 455–56nn7–8, 456–57nn9–10; hunt for Tom Donnelly, 321–22, 323; inner ring, 359, 477n39; James Feeheley as spy, 364–67; Keefe-Quigley wedding, 349–50; legal firepower, 342–43, 354, 355; in local press, 318; massacre plans, 359, 362–64, 367–68; name, 318; ostracism campaign, 313–16; ostracism of Donnellys, 327, 329; plan massacre, 368–71; Ryder barn burning, 351–52, 353; size, 480n18; Thomas Ryan's banishment, 306–7; threshing incident, 285–87; and Tom Donnelly, 285; trespass charges, 301–3, 310–11, 317–18; wandering heifer incident, 287–90, 295, 304, 458n28, 458n30. *See also* anti-crime

society (Father Connolly);
Vigilance Committee (first)
vigilante mob anecdote, 129–33,
420n14, 421n15
Volunteer Militia, 162–63, 164,
176, 188–89, 432n28

Walker, William: beats Frederick
Allen, 205–6, 436nn11–12;
Berryhill brawl, 121; businesses,
208; buys stagecoach line, 182;
fire in stables, 190, 192; horses
butchered, 202, 203, 204;
stagecoach merger, 184
Walsh, John (Bishop), 252, 313–15
wandering heifer incident:
aftermath, 299–300, 301–2,
304; Donnellys accused of theft,
287; heifer spotted and returned,
289, 290, 459n35; James Sr.,
Johannah, and John Donnelly
face mob, 290–95, 296, 458n31;
mob forms and marches,
289–90; Peace Society involved,
287–90, 295, 458n28, 458n30;
Thomas Ryan accused, 289, 290,
292; William Donnelly faces
mob, 289, 295, 296, 297–99

Watson, Joseph, 183, 184, 190–91,
192
West, Francis, 366
Whalen, Ann, 11, 356
Whalen, John, 10–11, 18
Whalen, Patrick, 11, 18, 82, 223,
356
Wilberforce, Ontario, 18–19, 108,
154–55
Wilberforce, William, 108
Willis, Cameron, 344, 472n29
Wilson, Adam, 221, 225, 266
Wilson, John, 44

You're Never Alone (Salts), xiii